MEDIEVAL JEWS AND THE CHRISTIAN PAST

THE LITTMAN LIBRARY OF
JEWISH CIVILIZATION

Dedicated to the memory of
LOUIS THOMAS SIDNEY LITTMAN
*who founded the Littman Library for the love of God
and as an act of charity in memory of his father*
JOSEPH AARON LITTMAN
and to the memory of
ROBERT JOSEPH LITTMAN
who continued what his father Louis had begun

יהא זכרם ברוך

*'Get wisdom, get understanding:
Forsake her not and she shall preserve thee'*

PROV. 4:5

*The Littman Library of Jewish Civilization is a registered UK charity
Registered charity no. 1000784*

MEDIEVAL JEWS
AND
THE CHRISTIAN PAST

◆

*Jewish Historical Consciousness in
Spain and Southern France*

◆

RAM BEN-SHALOM

TRANSLATED BY CHAYA NAOR

London
The Littman Library of Jewish Civilization
in association with Liverpool University Press

The Littman Library of Jewish Civilization
Registered office: 4th floor, 7–10 Chandos Street, London WIG 9DQ

in association with Liverpool University Press
4 Cambridge Street, Liverpool L69 7ZU, UK
www.liverpooluniversitypress.co.uk/littman

Managing Editor: Connie Webber

Distributed in North America by
Oxford University Press Inc., 198 Madison Avenue,
New York, NY 10016, USA

First published in Hebrew by the Ben-Zvi Institute as
Mul tarbut notsrit: toda'ah historit vedimuyei avar bekerev
yehudei sefarad veprovans biyemei habeinayim
© Ram Ben-Shalom 2006

English edition © The Littman Library of Jewish Civilization 2015
First published in paperback 2023

Catalogue records for this book are available from the
British Library and the Library of Congress
ISBN 978-1-802070-32-3

Publishing co-ordinator: Janet Moth
Copy-editing: Mark Newby
Proof-reading: Philippa Claiden
Index: Meg Davies
Designed by Pete Russell, Faringdon, Oxon.
Typeset by Hope Services (Abingdon) Ltd.

Printed and bound in Great Britain by
CPI Group (UK) Ltd., Croydon, CR0 4YY

Acknowledgements

THIS BOOK summarizes the path of study and research I embarked on when I was an undergraduate and pursued during my graduate studies at Tel Aviv University. I am profoundly grateful to the teachers who directed my interest to the fields I engage in and introduced me to the discipline of history and to research methodology. The Middle Ages were for me a remote, neglected era in my undergraduate studies until my last year. Then, in the classes given by Professor Zvi Ankori on Byzantine Jewry, I first realized how fascinating this period is. My interest and curiosity were aroused by a diversity of topics and people that merited primary historical research or rethinking and examination. As a result, for my MA I decided to abandon the field of Holocaust studies, which until then had been my main interest, and to focus on the medieval period. Assisted by Professor Eleazar Gutwirth, I acquired an 'admission ticket' to the social, mental, and cultural world of Spanish Jewry. His guidance, while I was working on my MA thesis, greatly broadened my horizons, and I became cognizant of the close intellectual and social links between the Jews of Spain and southern France. Professor Joshua Efron was a devoted teacher of the doctrine of early Christianity and apocalyptic thought and made me aware of how important it is to read primary historical sources critically. In the fascinating seminars given by the late Professor Amos Funkenstein and Professor Morris Kriegel, I was exposed to new topics, such as messianism and historiography. In my doctoral studies, I gained experience with new methodological tools, became familiar with additional research approaches, and absorbed much knowledge about the Jewish–Christian discourse from my teacher and adviser Professor Jeremy Cohen, who masterfully supervised my research and managed to overcome all the thorny problems that arose during its various stages. His unwavering support and astute, prolific ideas helped me greatly in my further research after I completed my Ph.D. While completing my doctorate I was already teaching at the Open University of Israel, where I was privileged to make the acquaintance of Professor Ora Limor and to learn much from her. Throughout, from the beginning of my work on my dissertation until now, she has been generous with her good advice, her knowledgeable and close reading, her challenging ideas, and her encouragement.

I am greatly indebted to my parents, my late father Shmuel Ben-Shalom and my mother Rivka Ben-Shalom, née Zilberstein, who did not give in to my caprices and pushed me, almost against my will, to begin my university studies during the period of my post-adolescent rebelliousness. A family friend, Professor Shalom Perleman of Tel Aviv University, also joined in their effort to persuade me to enrol in the university. Since then, I have been a grateful recipient of his counsel and affection.

My love goes to my wife, Yael Katz Ben-Shalom, whom I met in the lecture hall of the Gilman Building of Tel Aviv University and who has steadfastly supported me even during the long hours when I was not at her side, working on my research in the libraries or at home. Thank you, Yael, for your inspiration, support, sensitivity, and love, and for everything I have learned from you. My love also goes out to my son Nur, who was born when I was writing the research proposal for my doctorate and now has grown into a creative classical musician and talented clarinettist.

I am grateful to the Ben-Zvi Institute, the academic committee, and the past and present heads of the institute, and in particular to Professors Haggai Ben-Shammai, Avraham Grossman, and Menahem Ben-Sasson, who supported me and were involved in the various stages of the writing of the Hebrew edition; to the scientific secretary Michael Glatzer, who spent much time and effort on its publication, for his skills, patience, and good will; and in particular to the editor Varda Lehnhardt, who, with her vast knowledge and capabilities, saved me from making embarrassing errors. I also thank my learned colleagues Dr Javier Castaño, who was always glad to give me valuable advice and to find important bibliographical items for me in Spanish libraries, and Dr Avriel Bar-Levav, the breadth of whose knowledge was extremely helpful to me.

The Open University greatly supported me in the writing of the Hebrew book—both with a generous grant by the research authority to the Ben-Zvi Institute and with the necessary administrative assistance, from my early days at the university until the present. I thank the members of the departments of history, philosophy, and Judaic studies and the staff of the Open University, who on a daily basis are engaged in creating an intellectual, social, and human environment.

This English edition is an abridged version of the original Hebrew.

Contents

Note on Transliteration

THE transliteration of Hebrew in this book reflects consideration of the type of book it is, in terms of its content, purpose, and readership. The system adopted therefore reflects a broad approach to transcription, rather than the narrower approaches found in the *Encyclopaedia Judaica* or other systems developed for text-based or linguistic studies. The aim has been to reflect the pronunciation prescribed for modern Hebrew, rather than the spelling or Hebrew word structure, and to do so using conventions that are generally familiar to the English-speaking reader.

In accordance with this approach, no attempt is made to indicate the distinctions between *alef* and *ayin*, *tet* and *taf*, *kaf* and *kuf*, *sin* and *samekh*, since these are not relevant to pronunciation; likewise, the *dagesh* is not indicated except where it affects pronunciation. Following the principle of using conventions familiar to the majority of readers, however, transcriptions that are well established have been retained even when they are not fully consistent with the transliteration system adopted. On similar grounds, the *tsadi* is rendered by 'tz' in such familiar words as barmitzvah. Likewise, the distinction between *ḥet* and *khaf* has been retained, using *ḥ* for the former and *kh* for the latter; the associated forms are generally familiar to readers, even if the distinction is not actually borne out in pronunciation, and for the same reason the final *heh* is indicated too. As in Hebrew, no capital letters are used, except that an initial capital has been retained in transliterating titles of published works (for example, *Shulḥan arukh*).

Since no distinction is made between *alef* and *ayin*, they are indicated by an apostrophe only in intervocalic positions where a failure to do so could lead an English-speaking reader to pronounce the vowel-cluster as a diphthong—as, for example, in *ha'ir*—or otherwise mispronounce the word.

The *sheva na* is indicated by an *e*—*perikat ol*, *reshut*—except, again, when established convention dictates otherwise.

The *yod* is represented by *i* when it occurs as a vowel (*bereshit*), by *y* when it occurs as a consonant (*yesodot*), and by *yi* when it occurs as both (*yisra'el*).

Names have generally been left in their familiar forms, even when this is inconsistent with the overall system.

Introduction

Remember the days of old,
Consider the years of ages past;
Ask your father, he will inform you,
Your elders, they will tell you.

DEUTERONOMY 32:7

TO WHAT EXTENT were the Jews of the Middle Ages conscious of the history of the peoples around them? That is, were they at all interested in the historical traditions of the Christians of western Europe? Were they familiar with Christian historiography or oral traditions? Did they incorporate historical stories, anecdotes, or ideas drawn from Christian history or traditions into their writings? These questions have up till now been only cursorily discussed in the literature, but, to my mind, they are key to understanding not only the world outlook and spiritual concerns of medieval Jews but also the process of their integration into European society. My contribution to this important discussion focuses on the Jews of the Iberian peninsula and 'Provincia' (southern France) between the twelfth and the fifteenth centuries.

The theory proposed by Yosef Hayim Yerushalmi—a seminal authority on Jewish historiography—was that Jews saw the essence of their relationship to the non-Jewish world as having been set out in the legends and homilies of rabbinic aggadah and that there was therefore little need to be concerned with the history of non-Jewish society. There was somewhat more interest in world events when they were such as to encourage messianic fervour, but even then it was tempered by biblical models such as the four kingdoms of the book of Daniel and the final battle of Gog and Magog. Thus, in Yerushalmi's view, the interest that sixteenth-century figures such as Elijah Capsali and Joseph Hakohen took in the history of non-Jews was a completely new phenomenon.[1]

My understanding of the subject when I embarked on this research was rather different. I intuited that Jews of a scholarly bent would have been familiar with the sources through which historical knowledge was transmitted in the Middle Ages, both written and oral—for example, Christian chronicles, tales of kings

---

[1] Yerushalmi, *Zakhor*, 36; see also 60–3.

and lives of saints, translations of classical works, and popular dramas such as mystery plays and pageants—and that through these sources they would have obtained a clear image of Christian culture and a fundamentally positive one.

In order to demonstrate this, I tried to find every piece of Jewish writing, of whatever type, and examine it for evidence of an awareness of the traditions, ideas, or values of the surrounding Christian society. Some caution was necessary, of course: for example, I needed to be aware that medieval concepts of historical truth—whether acceptance by the general public, the Augustinian test based on the standing and moral authority of the speaker or writer, the degree of harmony between events in the secular world and divine providence, or the continuity between past and present events—were different from modern ones. A further problem was that, since popular beliefs were given considerable credence in medieval historiography, history was not always distinct from collective memory: historical facts were mixed with events that never happened, and the boundary between history and fiction was very blurred.[2] But whatever the sources of historical information in Jewish writings—whether it derived from Christian chronicles, hagiography, or exempla, which cannot always be determined unequivocally—the important point is that historical information about the Christian world is in fact found in Jewish writings.

Amos Funkenstein has observed that the corpus of writings on Jewish law (halakhah) itself incorporates a historical consciousness: distinctions are drawn between the customs of different periods, and there is an awareness of when the various rabbis and commentators lived, the changing value of money, and the changing significance of institutions. Funkenstein compared this historical consciousness with that of medieval commentators on Roman law and found a similar historical awareness.[3] I find his analysis very useful and propose expanding it to cover all the information in the Jewish collective memory, not only accurate knowledge of times and places but also the vast and diverse non-factual historiographical knowledge that had apparently crept in from a variety sources. I agree with Funkenstein when he says:

Western historical consciousness does not contradict collective memory, but rather is a developed and organized form of it. Nor does it contradict historiographical creation, for both lie at its base and are nurtured by it. All three express the same 'collective mentality' and the expression is always manifest in the individual who recalls and expresses it.[4]

---

[2] See Shopkow, *History and Community*, 122–6.

[3] Funkenstein, *Perceptions of Jewish History*, 17.

[4] Funkenstein, 'Collective Memory and Historical Consciousness' (Heb.), 27; see id., *Perceptions of Jewish History*, 18–19.

My study demonstrates that the Jews of Spain and southern France in the late Middle Ages had some knowledge of Christian history and were not indifferent to it. Certain circles of learned Jews regarded the history of other peoples as part of a general culture in which they too shared; hence, there were historical events that they related to and used for didactic and intellectual purposes. An interesting question is whether this consciousness of a shared history extended to shared values. On what was there consensus, and on what did they disagree? What historical concepts did Jewish society absorb as a result of contact with Christians? What images of the past were shared by the two societies?

My analysis rests on consideration of four key issues covered in medieval Jewish historiography: the image of Rome, Jesus and early Christianity, the history of the Christian Church, and the history of the Iberian kingdoms. An introductory chapter discusses the genres of Jewish historical writing between the twelfth and early sixteenth centuries and the reasons for Jewish interest at that time in the history of other peoples. Some of the authors had access to Christian historiographical literature; others were familiar with the history only through oral traditions. The discussion of their different motives for historical writing—polemical, moral or didactic historiographical, scientific—provides the background for a detailed examination of the four topics covered in the chapters that follow through which I attempt to arrive at an understanding of the role of Christian culture in the historical consciousness of the Jews of Spain and southern France.

A fundamental issue is the attitude of Jews to their own history. Medieval Jewish society is often described by scholars as intellectually and spiritually oriented towards a glorious future at the End of Days, which served as a counterbalance to the dismal present. According to this approach, a large part of Jewish creative energy outside the halakhic sphere was directed towards envisioning a messianic period in which Jewish society would recover its ancient glory and tower above the surrounding peoples because of its moral and social justice.[5] Accordingly, the End of Days was the subject of systematic study and speculation by medieval Jews, while the past, both recent and distant, was considered uninteresting. Worse, it was regarded as so replete with suffering and persecution as to actually support Christian arguments that God had abandoned the Jewish people. On this view, if there was any advantage to be gained from the systematic study and knowledge of history, it was to be gained mainly from studying the biblical period. Knowledge of the history of the patriarchs, the forty years wandering in the wilderness after the Exodus, and the kings of the First Temple

[5] See e.g. G. D. Cohen, 'Esau as Symbol in Early Medieval Thought'; id., 'Messianic Postures of Ashkenazim and Sephardim'; see also Schwartz, *The Messiah in Medieval Jewish Thought* (Heb.).

period inspired medieval Jews to construct images of an ancient 'golden age' that would be revived in the days of the messiah and could be used as the basis for creating eschatological utopias of a reconstructed and reformed world.[6] The perception of the Bible as an all-encompassing and divine source of knowledge, along with a profound interest in the messianic period, largely succeeded in suppressing any Jewish interest in the history of the Middle Ages—that long period between the golden days of antiquity and the future messianic era. Jews were no more interested in their own history than they were in the history of the various peoples among whom they had lived since the destruction of the First Temple: put simply, the past was devoid of any significance.

The only exception to this was the attitude to the Second Temple period. It was seen as a time that produced key figures, leaders, and sages who influenced political events and the development of the Jewish religion. Events such as the Maccabean and Bar Kokhba revolts and the destruction of the Temple provided political, moral, and religious lessons. Information on this period reached medieval Jews primarily through the *Book of Josippon* (*Sefer yosipon*), the medieval Hebrew adaptation of Josephus, which was regarded as an authoritative source and in some circles even had a quasi-sacred aura. No attempt was made to learn anything else about the period: any lacunae were filled by aggadic material from the talmudic and midrashic literature. The occasional contradictions between the *Book of Josippon* and the talmudic and midrashic legends were not critically discussed but reconciled by exegesis or allegory.

According to this approach, the major element in the consciousness of medieval Jewry was collective memory, a memory nurtured by ritual and liturgy rather than historical writing. To put that another way, only those historical events that had passed through the filter of ritual had any chance of surviving in memory. The traumatic events of Jewish history—for example, the destruction of the Temple or the burning of the Talmud—were commemorated in lamentations (*kinot*), penitential prayers (*seliḥot*), and fasts. Historical memory was preserved through prayer and ritual not through chronicles, whose objective was to preserve the chain of tradition of the Oral Torah—that is, to present an unbroken line of authoritative figures from the biblical period to the chronicler's own time—rather than to present 'history' in the wider sense. History per se was of little importance: even the great medieval thinker Maimonides regarded historiography as 'time wasted on trivial matters'.[7]

---

[6] See Scholem, *Explications and Implications* (Heb.), i. 155–90.

[7] Yerushalmi, *Zakhor*, 31–52; see Maimonides on Mishnah *San.* 10: 1; see also Myers, 'Of Marranos and Memory', esp. 9–10.

Critical examination, however, reveals a more complex picture. Many medieval Jewish sources reveal an interest not only in Jewish history but in Christian history too. There was an awareness that the Middle Ages was a period in which historical events of significance to Jews took place and important Jewish figures lived. Calamities such as the massacres during the First Crusade in 1096, blood libels, and the burning of the Talmud were certainly regarded as worthy of memory, but so were less traumatic events including general cultural phenomena such as the destruction of Troy, the exploits of Hercules, and the coronation of Alfonso X the Wise of Castile. Transmitting the chain of tradition was certainly a major concern of medieval Jewish chronicles, but it was not the only one, and such sources contained much information concerning the history and culture of other peoples.

This is not to minimize the significance of Jewish collective memory in the Middle Ages.[8] Prayer and rituals were of supreme importance in education, socialization, and shaping Jewish consciousness.[9] Lamentations, for example, were important in recollecting the past and passing it on to the next generation—particularly those written in Spain, which, unlike those written in Ashkenazi lands, not only bewailed the massacres but also described the course of events and commemorated the communities that were destroyed.[10] It is also questionable whether Maimonides' attitude to historiography was shared by all or even a majority of Jews. Did only a few Jewish scholars follow Moses ibn Ezra in regarding ignorance of historiography as a cultural flaw, or was there another school that called for the adoption of the Christian approach to historiography and viewed historical discourse as a worthwhile pursuit? In fact, Maimonides' own position on history was complex. Despite the comment cited earlier, he certainly had vast

---

[8] See Bonfil, 'How Golden was the Age of the Renaissance in Jewish Historiography?', esp. 80–3. Gutwirth claimed that 'obviously, not a Jewish distaste for history but the mediaeval notions of history are behind this apparent lack of concern for the past *wie es eigentlich gewesen* [as it actually, or essentially, was]' ('The Expulsion from Spain and Jewish Historiography', 141). Chazan noted the distinctions drawn by Yerushalmi and Funkenstein and suggested a broader framework for Funkenstein's concept of historical consciousness, which also included narrative material ('The Timebound and the Timeless', 8). Ron Barkai also adopted Funkenstein's position. In his view, the flourishing Christian historiography of Europe was an outcome of the writers' political and geographical identities. He claimed that most Jewish historiography of the Middle Ages was written in Spain or for Jews of Spanish origin because of the patriotic feelings of Spanish Jews and their sense of superiority over Jews from other countries (see Barkai, Introduction to Moreno Koch (ed.), *Dos crónicas hispanohebreas del siglo XV*, 14–16).

[9] See e.g. Marcus, *Rituals of Childhood*; Goldin, *Uniqueness and Togetherness* (Heb.), 42–66.

[10] See Pagis, 'Lamentations over the Persecutions of 1391 in Spain' (Heb.); Einbinder, *No Place of Rest*, esp. 61–83.

historical knowledge that he did not hesitate to use for didactic and other purposes.[11]

Yerushalmi's view was that there was no Jewish historiography between the twelfth century, when Moses ibn Ezra proposed that Jews should learn from the Islamic science of history and take up historical writing, and the early sixteenth, when Solomon ibn Verga repeated the call. For Yerushalmi, Ibn Verga's *Shevet yehudah*, a key part of the revival of Jewish historiography that followed the Expulsion from Spain, was a seminal work.[12] But, since supposedly no Jewish writer had engaged in historiography for 350 years, how did Ibn Verga learn of the historical events that he included in his book? Were his sources only prayer and ritual or also historical chronicles? My view is that Ibn Verga unquestionably referred to historical chronicles. These works, many of which were anonymous, have subsequently been lost and are now known only from his book.[13] They were characterized by Yitzhak Baer as 'short didactic writings' that briefly testified, from a profoundly religious viewpoint, to acts that took place so that they might remain for posterity.[14] Some of Solomon ibn Verga's information may also have originated from books by his relative Judah ibn Verga, as he himself notes at the beginning of *Shevet yehudah*.[15]

Some of the historical works known to medieval Jews such as Solomon and Judah ibn Verga are worth mentioning. Profayt Duran's *Ma'amar zikhron hashemadot*, now lost, served as a historical source for Isaac Abravanel, Solomon ibn Verga, Samuel Usque, and probably Solomon Alami ibn Lahmish.[16] Hayim Galipapa's, *Emek refa'im*, also now lost, was the source of an extract that was quoted (and possibly adapted) by Joseph Hakohen.[17] Other works worthy of mention include Samuel Çarça's brief chronicle of the civil war in Castile, written in the 1360s;[18] a Provençal chronicle copied in the fifteenth century and published

[11] See Baron, 'The Historical Outlook of Maimonides'; Y. Ben-Sasson, *Jewish Thought* (Heb.), 33–129; Funkenstein, *Perceptions of Jewish History*, 131–58; id., *Nature, History and Messianism in Maimonides* (Heb.). Special emphasis should be placed on the description of the messianic movements by Maimonides (*Epistle to Yemen*, 162).

[12] Yerushalmi, *Zakhor*, 33–4. On *Shevet yehudah*, see J. Cohen, 'The Blood Libel in Solomon ibn Verga's *Shevet Yehudah*'; id., 'Polemic and Pluralism'.

[13] For examples, see Ibn Verga, *Shevet yehudah*, 52–5, 70–1; see also Baer, 'New Comments on *Shevet yehudah*' (Heb.); Shohat, notes (Heb.) to Ibn Verga, *Shevet yehudah*, 180.

[14] Baer, Introduction (Heb.) to Ibn Verga, *Shevet yehudah*, 12.

[15] Although this may be pseudepigraphical (see Ibn Verga, *Shevet yehudah*, 19; Baer, Introduction (Heb.), ibid. 8).

[16] See Graetz, *The History of the Jews* (Heb.), vi, app. 1; Talmage, Introduction (Heb.) to Profayt Duran, *Polemical Writings*, 11; Kozodoy, 'A Study of the Life and Works of Profiat Duran'.

[17] See Joseph Hakohen, *Emek habakha*, 80–1.

[18] Çarça, *Mekor hayim*; see Gutwirth, 'History and Intertextuality in Late Medieval Spain'.

by Abraham David;[19] and a list from Provence and Languedoc, which recorded events up to 1300 contained in 'A Pamphlet Recounting the Events of the Kings of Edom', which belonged to Shem Tov Shanzolo.[20]

Only a part, and perhaps only a small part, of the historical writings of Spanish Jewry is extant. Robert Bonfil has attributed this to the persecutions of the Middle Ages. Thus, for example, he argues that the preservation of the chronicle *Megilat aḥima'ats* in a single manuscript in the archives of Toledo Cathedral suggests that such works were found in the libraries of Spanish Jews before the Expulsion, but that in times of distress their owners were forced to part with them. He states that the few vestiges of the lost works reinforces the impression that the considerable historical writing of the sixteenth century was an organic continuation of a long historiographical tradition.[21] Bonfil's position is supported by comments made in a number of medieval sources. Abraham ben Samuel Zacut mentions the books (plural) that he used in surveying Jewish history from the period of the *ge'onim* (the heads of the Babylonian academies from the seventh to the twelfth century) until his own time at the end of the fifteenth century. Immanuel Aboab, writing in the seventeenth century, mentions that sometime between 1615 and 1625 he saw a Hebrew manuscript that described at length the causes and events of the Expulsion.[22] Elijah Capsali, who in 1523 described the Expulsion from Spain primarily on the basis of first-hand accounts from refugees, mentions finding a report that contained the wording of the Edict of Expulsion, its date, and the names of the reigning monarchs, Ferdinand and Isabella.[23] A family chronicle, *Minḥat zikhron mazkeret avon*, written immediately after the Expulsion from Spain, provides information about the tradition of family chronology in Spain.[24] One can add to this list Isaac ben Samuel of Acre's *Sefer divrei*

---

[19] David, 'A Fragment of a Hebrew Chronicle' (Heb.).

[20] See Shatzmiller, 'Provençal Chronography in the Lost Work of Shem Tov Shanzolo' (Heb.). This important chronographical list was added to Solomon ibn Verga's *Shevet yehudah* by his son Joseph ibn Verga. It contains many events of Jewish and general history, such as the persecution of Jewish communities in Béziers (1168), Montpellier (1198), and Toulouse (1217) and the blood libel in Valréas (1247); the conquest of the Land of Israel by Saladin (1187); the Third Lateran Council (1179); the massacre in Béziers during the Albigensian Crusade (1209); and the final domination by Prince Charles I of Anjou of the rebellious cities in Provence (1262). Shatzmiller assumed that an early copier of the chronicle resided in Languedoc, while the end of it was copied in Provence (see ibid. 59; see also Benayahu, 'A Source on the Expellees in Portugal and Their Departure for Thessalonica' (Heb.); C. Roth, 'Historiography', col. 556).

[21] Bonfil, 'The Legacy of Spanish Jewry in Historical Writings' (Heb.), 758.

[22] Aboab, *Nomología*, 2: 26 (ed. Orfali, 260).

[23] Capsali, *Seder eliyahu zuta*, Introduction (ed. Shmuelevitz, Simonsohn, and Benayahu, i. 11).

[24] See Hacker, 'New Chronicles on the Expulsion of the Jews from Spain' (Heb.), 219–23; see also the chronicle of Isaac ben Jacob ibn Faraj in Marx, 'The Expulsion of the Jews from Spain', esp. 100–1; Benayahu, 'Rabbi David Benveniste and His Letter to Rabbi Abraham ibn Yaish' (Heb.).

hayamim, which apparently contained hagiographical material relating to Jewish mysticism,[25] and genealogical family chronicles such as *Sefer hayahas*, which was in the possession of the Ibn Yahya family but lost 'in the numerous exiles and calamities of Spain'.[26]

Another issue I take up is the notion that chronicles of the chain of tradition are of little historiographical importance. On this matter, Funkenstein commented that up to the eleventh century, the historical conceptions of Jewish scholars did not differ substantially from those of Christians.[27] He argued that secular history written by Christians was primarily political, focused on rulers and their actions. In contrast, the chain of tradition was similar to ecclesiastical history. Jews did not see themselves as political agents, so the precise course of political events did not seem to them 'worthy of memory'.[28] But the virtual absence of Jewish historiography did not mean a total absence of Jewish historical consciousness, since the latter was to be found in biblical commentaries and halakhic writings as well as in myths and historical traditions.[29]

My view is that the Jews who wrote chronicles of the chain of tradition used a similar historiographical approach to that of Christian chroniclers. They consulted the available sources and tried as far as possible to propose reasonable dates and to present events in chronological order. They also proposed their own interpretations of events and were selective in their choice of material in order to omit embarrassing historical facts and give more prominence to flattering ones.

It is interesting in this context to see how historical consciousness and interest in the past functioned among Jewish converts to Christianity. A famous example from the fifteenth century is the work of the Halevi family from Burgos— Pablo de Santa María, archbishop of Burgos; his nephew, Álvar García de Santa María; and his son, Alonso de Cartagena, who succeeded him as archbishop of Burgos, all three of whom wrote political chronicles about the monarchies in Spain.[30] Recently the emergence of historiographical writing in fifteenth-century

---

[25] See Tishby, *Wisdom of the Zohar* (Heb.), 28–33; Idel, *Kabbalah*, 286 n. 5. More information on the subjects in *Sefer divrei hayamim* can be found in Isaac of Acre, *Otsar hayim* (MS Guenzburg 774 (Russian State Library, Moscow—Institute of Microfilmed Hebrew Manuscripts, no. 47921)); see also Idel, 'Kabbalah and Ancient Philosophy in the Works of R. Isaac and Judah Abravanel' (Heb.), 102 n. 30.

[26] Ibn Yahya, *Shalshelet hakabalah*, 39: 1; see David, 'The Historiographical Work of Gedaliah ibn Yahya' (Heb.), 4, 15–17, 253 n. 4.

[27] Funkenstein, *Perceptions of Jewish History*, 15.   [28] Ibid. 16.   [29] Ibid. 16–17.

[30] See e.g. Cirot, *Les Histoires générales d'Espagne*, 4–6, 10, 12, 18; Morreale, 'Vernacular Scriptures in Spain', 488–90. Pablo de Santa María also wrote an educational historiographical poem in Castilian, entitled 'Las siete edades del mundo' (probably between 1416 and 1418), for his student, who later became King Juan II of Castile. He probably also wrote a prose history known as *Suma de las crónicas de España* (see Peri, 'A Historical Poem in Old Castilian' (Heb.); Deyermond, 'Written by the Victors', esp. 71–6; Szpiech, 'Scrutinizing History'). Álvar García de Santa María wrote the

Castile and Pablo de Santa María's historiographical poem *Siete edades del mundo* (Seven Ages of the World) have been analysed in the light of the phenomenon of conversion and exegetical polemic with Judaism.[31] The Conversos' historical interests were not entirely a new phenomenon and its Jewish roots are discussed in Chapter 5.

Contrary to Yerushalmi's claim, Jews expressed very favourable views of historical writing and its necessity long before Solomon ibn Verga's time. For example, the fourteenth-century scholar Shem Tov ben Abraham ibn Gaon, one of Maimonides' disciples, wrote about the sources at Maimonides' disposal: 'They were accepted things taken from the verses of the prophets, sermons, and legends . . . and also in non-Jewish sources that recount the events of past times and the history of events in the days of the sages.'[32] In his view, Maimonides did not find sufficient material in biblical and talmudic sources to support his messianic views and therefore needed to make use of history books. Thus history books were necessary, even if only for clarification.

In contrast, although Isaac ben Solomon ibn Sahula did not express any personal support for the study of history, his *Meshal hakadmoni*, written in 1281, provides evidence that it existed in Spain because it accuses Jews of responding to the tribulations they were suffering by neglecting the Torah and preferring instead to find consolation in the 'books of the enemies [Christians] and books of history'.[33] In 1391 Don Judah ibn Yahya lamented the massacre of the Spanish Jews and enumerated their many virtues, which were now sorely missed, including the knowledge of history—'my knowledge of past events is lacking'.[34] Thus, from his point of view, historical knowledge was a key characteristic of Spanish Jewry before the Expulsion.

Similarly, Gersonides (Levi ben Gershom of Provence, 1288–1344; known in Jewish sources as Ralbag) acknowledged the value of historical sources. In his discussion of Ahasuerus (Xerxes), he noted three benefits to be gained from history books: pleasure, help in falling asleep, and lessons for the future.[35] Isaac Abravanel also considered historiography important. In the introduction to his commentary on the Former Prophets, he cited the three major reasons for them

Crónica de Juan II de Castilla (see Gómez Redondo, 'Don Álvar García de Santa María'). Alonso de Cartagena also wrote a 'universal history' (see Cantera Burgos, *Álvar García de Santa María y su familia de conversos*).

[31] See Szpiech, 'Scrutinizing History'.

[32] Ibn Gaon, *Migdal oz*, on Maimonides, *Mishneh torah*, 'Laws of Kings', II: 207–8.

[33] Ibn Sahula, *Meshal hakadmoni*, 5.

[34] Judah ibn Yahya, 'Yehudah veyisra'el de'u mar li meod', in Bernstein, *By the Rivers of Spain* (Heb.), 206.

[35] Gersonides on Esther 6: 1; see Yassif, '*Penai* and *ruah rehavah*' (Heb.), esp. 902–3.

having been written as theological, moral, and historiographical—'to know the history of the world, in each and every generation'.[36] He further demonstrated the necessity of historiography by pointing out that it was a common practice among other peoples:

And if each and every state in its writing, and each and every people in its language, has attempted to encompass and know the earliest years of their history, generation after generation, to have knowledge of all the past years, then the children of Israel . . . ought also to know and understand the branching out of the generations, from the beginning of Creation until the exile from Jerusalem, and until the coming of Shiloh [the end of the world (see Gen. 49: 10)].[37]

Isaac Abravanel, whose biblical commentaries made much use of the historical knowledge available to him, stressed that it was not sufficient to record only the distant (biblical) past; rather, historiographical work must continue until the End of Days. He also devoted an entire book (*Yemot olam*) to Jewish history from the time of Adam to his own time. The book is now lost, but it seems that it described the ordeals suffered by Jews in Christian and Muslim lands and clarified controversial chronological points.[38] Many later writers learned about historical events from Abravanel's work,[39] and his books came to be regarded as reliable sources for more explicitly historiographical works. Yerushalmi was aware of the wealth of historical information in Abravanel's commentaries, but he argued that they did not constitute historiographical writing, since such information was of secondary importance, and claimed that the existence of *Yemot olam* demonstrated that Abravanel was cognizant of the difference between his commentaries and true historiography. The question of whether a book that contains historical information but is devoted to other subjects can be defined as historiography is perhaps a valid one, though it seems to me that Abravanel's commentaries are consistent with Yerushalmi's definition of historiography as the simple recording of events from the human past:

The minimal condition to be satisfied emanates from the very word 'historiography' in its literal and etymological meaning—and that is simply, the 'writing of history'—in the sense of recording events out of the human past. Whatever its other aims, qualities and contents, a 'historiographical' work must be anchored in a recital of concrete events that

[36] Abravanel, *Perush linevi'im rishonim*, Introduction, 6.   [37] Ibid.

[38] See Abravanel, *Ma'ayenei hayeshuah*, 2: 3 (Jerusalem edn., 288); Abravanel on Kings, Introduction (*Perush linevi'im rishonim*, 427) .

[39] See Benayahu, Introduction (Heb.) to Capsali, *Seder eliyahu zuta*, iii. 22; Breuer, Introduction (Heb.) to Gans, *Sefer tsemaḥ david*, 23, 25; David, 'The Historiographical Work of Gedaliah ibn Yahya' (Heb.), 194; Rossi, *Meor einayim*, 'Imrei binah', 1: 12 (Vilna edn., 180–9; trans. Weinberg 239–51); Shohat, notes (Heb.) to Ibn Verga, *Shevet yehudah*, 172, 'Index of Names', s.v. Isaac Abravanel; Shtober, Introduction (Heb.) to Sambari, *Sefer divrei yosef,* 50, 81.

possess a temporal specificity. Those events need not be political. They may be biographical, social, literary. But they must be there.[40]

These examples show that Maimonides' denunciation of historiography was not shared by all Jews, and that during the late Middle Ages many Jews from Spain and southern France took an interest in past events, held historiography in esteem, and took part in a lively historical discourse. It is the central role of historical discourse in the consciousness of Spanish and Provençal Jewry that I intend to demonstrate.

[40] Yerushalmi, 'Clio and the Jews', 611.

CHAPTER ONE

Genres and Motives

IN THE MIDDLE ages historical consciousness played an important role in shaping society and culture for Christians and Jews alike. However, it is difficult to isolate historical consciousness from religion during this period, as the teleological tradition of the Bible had influenced both Christians and Jews. The Graeco-Roman historiographical approach, which attempted to record the events of the past for posterity (those that merited being remembered and preserved) and to explain them by means of natural and human circumstances and concepts, was relegated to the sidelines or merged into a new system bound by a transcendent paradigm and directed towards an eschatological end.[1]

The religious importance of Jewish chronology was demonstrated some time before 1140 by Judah Halevi in the *Book of the Kuzari*. He held that the Jews' acceptance of one chronological span from the Creation onwards was proof of the accuracy of Moses' prophecies.[2] In the early fifteenth century Shimon ben Tsemah Duran (known in Jewish sources by the acronym Rashbats) argued that the agreement of 'all the generations' on a common chronology was one of the key proofs of the creation of the world *ex nihilo*.[3] This view was shared by the overwhelming majority of Jews and Christians in the Middle Ages: the world was created by God, and divine providence would control history until its end. Disagreements between Christians and Jews concerned the precise timing of events, the intentions of divine providence, and the correct interpretation of its manifestations.

Jewish historiography focused on correlating Jewish chronology, general chronology, and Christian chronology. This was a similar approach to Christian writers, who developed methods of correlating biblical history and general history to further the Church's mission to disseminate Christianity in the pagan Hellenist-Roman world. To persuade pagans to convert, the Church Fathers had first to introduce them to the history contained in the Old Testament: a history that was unfamiliar and that began with a couple (Adam and Eve) of whom they

---

[1] See Arieli, 'New Horizons in Eighteenth- and Nineteenth-Century Historiography' (Heb.), 151–4.   [2] Judah Halevi, *The Book of the Kuzari*, i: 44–52 (trans. Hirschfeld, 15–17).
[3] Shimon b. Tsemah Duran, *Sefer magen avot*, 3.4.96a.

had never heard. In addition, they had to prove that this 'new' history was more accurate, reliable, and significant than classical history.[4] In his *Chronicle*, Eusebius presented the history of all the kingdoms and nations of the classical and eastern worlds in parallel columns correlated with the genealogies of the Bible.[5] This method and the new historiographical schema he introduced in his *Church History* served as models for most of the important historiographical works written in the Middle Ages, including many of the universal chronicles composed in the Iberian peninsula, particularly in Castile and Catalonia.[6]

The correlation of Jewish chronology with Christian and general chronology was one of the many components of medieval Jewish–Christian discourse. On the one hand, this suggests that Jews had a unified approach to history, in which they saw themselves as full participants. On the other, the timing and meaning of historical events (such as the Exodus from Egypt, the rise of the Roman empire, the birth of Jesus, and the spread of Christianity) were part of the religious polemic with Christianity. A Jewish writer who linked an event from Jewish history (especially one from the biblical or Second Temple periods) to an event or figure from general history would be aware (regardless of whether it was original or traditional) of its religious implications, be they messianic, apocalyptic, interpretative, or ideological. Like the Bible—the shared sacred text that was the foundation and motivation for the ongoing religious debate—important post-biblical events could provoke lively polemic.

Jews and Christians also shared an apocalyptic outlook based on the book of Daniel. They tried to find a correlation between the 'evil empires' and their struggles with each other and calculations of the End of Days and the redemption of the 'chosen people'. According to apocalyptic thought, historical events follow one unbroken line of development, directed by divine decree, and destined to end in a number of eschatological events.[7] The debate about the nature of redemption (collective or personal), its timing, its content, and its objects was linked in apocalyptic thought to a historical polemic about the meaning of the past, the precise time of different events, and their interpretation. Hence broad historical knowledge was required: Jerome stated that 'in order to understand the last parts of Daniel, one needs to know the history of the Greeks . . . in addition, Josephus and

---

[4] See Momigliano, 'Pagan and Christian Historiography', 84.

[5] On Eusebius's *Chronicle*, see Barnes, *Constantine and Eusebius*, 111–21; Mosshammer, *The Chronicle of Eusebius*; Mortley, *The Idea of Universal History*, 151–204.

[6] See Chesnut, 'Eusebius, Augustine, Orosius, and the Later Patristic and Medieval Christian Historians'; Mortley, *The Idea of Universal History*; Cirot, *Les Histoires générales d'Espagne*, esp. 12–31; Peri, 'A Historical Poem in Old Castilian' (Heb.), 57; Brezzi, 'Chroniques universelles du Moyen Âge et histoire du salut'; Milikowski, '*Seder olam* and Jewish Chronology' (Heb.), 66–7.

[7] See e.g. Funkenstein, *Perceptions of Jewish History*, 70–87; McGinn, *Visions of the End*, esp. 1–36.

those who cite Josephus, in particular of our Livy and of Pompeius Trogus and Justin. All of them write and teach the history of the last vision."[8] During the Middle Ages, Jews similarly realized that in order to debate with Christians about the prophecies in the book of Daniel they needed to acquire general historical knowledge.

Religious polemic and apocalypticism were important reasons why Jewish scholars in Spain and southern France engaged in historiography. Other motives included the moral lessons that could be found in history and intellectual curiosity. Often these motives were intertwined, and it is difficult to identify a single or even an overriding one. For example, in the writings of Abraham bar Hiyya and Isaac Abravanel, apocalyptic-messianic views of universal history are woven into religious polemic. Their messianic views were influenced by the debate with Christianity about the coming of the messiah (in the past or the future), and they put forward their commentaries on historical events as counter-history to the Christian narrative.

POLEMIC

Apocalypticism

The scientist and philosopher Abraham bar Hiyya, author of *Megilat hamegaleh*, who lived in the first half of the twelfth century, was the first Jew in Christian Spain to attempt to correlate Jewish and Christian chronologies. He proposed a Jewish world history to counter the Christian one and provided an astrological interpretation of this history in order to determine the End of Days.[9] He probably learned the method of correlating chronologies from Christian historiography, since the works of Justus of Tiberias, who had also used it, were lost. However, it was also to be found in the *Book of Josippon*, so, although much in *Megilat hamegaleh* was innovative, correlating chronologies was not totally new to the Jewish world.[10]

---

[8] Jerome on Dan., Introduction, cited in Rokeah, *Judaism and Christianity in the Light of Pagan Polemic* (Heb.), 148.

[9] Ibid. Abraham bar Hiyya learned astrological interpretation from the works of the Muslim writers Masa Allah (eighth century) and Abu Maaser (ninth century). Events of the past were analysed and forecasts for the future made on the basis of the positions of the planets in the constellations (see Barkai, *Science, Magic, and Mythology in the Middle Ages* (Heb.), 28). According to Abraham bar Hiyya, each of the nations had a ruling planet and all important historical events were the result of the conjunctions and separations of Saturn and Jupiter (see *Megilat hamegaleh*, 5: 116; Barkai, *Science, Magic, and Mythology in the Middle Ages* (Heb.), 31; see also Abraham ibn Ezra, 'Visions of Rabbi Abraham ibn Ezra' (Heb.)).

[10] See e.g. *Sefer yosipon*, 1: 2 (ed. Flusser, 18–19); see also Bowman, 'Sefer Yosippon', 286–9; Y. Dan, 'Josephus and Justus of Tiberias' (Heb.).

Not all the historical 'facts' in *Megilat hamegaleh* are accurate, as Abraham bar Hiyya made no attempt to verify them, but simply used them to support his polemical arguments. However, despite this and its apocalyptic and astrological nature, *Megilat hamegaleh* became a historiographical source in every sense. It was used by later Jewish historiographers to determine the chronology of the Crusades, for example;[11] Manichaeism (a dualist religion founded by Mani and prevalent in Persia from the third to the seventh centuries) became known to later writers through *Megilat hamegaleh*; and traces of Abraham bar Hiyya's influence can be found in the writings of Abraham ibn Daud, Isaac Arama, and Abraham Zacut.[12] His polemical use of history also served as a model for other commentators, who similarly tried to link verses from Daniel and other prophets with events in world history. This type of commentary required detailed information about events of the past, especially from the Second Temple period, and general knowledge about events of the writers' own time. The more detailed knowledge the commentator demonstrated, the more reliable and persuasive he was thought to be.

Abraham bar Hiyya explicitly stated that his intention in *Megilat hamegaleh* was 'to show to all the nations of the world, from the words of their scholars, that all the religions that emerged in the world after the Torah was given to the Jews were religions of wickedness, oppression, false prophecy, and delusion'.[13] In his opinion, history corresponded with the visions in the book of Daniel, which, when interpreted astrologically, proved that Judaism was the true religion. He also found precise correlations between the eras of world history and the seven days of Creation, a view influenced by Christian theology and the historical thought of the Church Fathers Irenaeus and Augustine, as well as of Isidore of Seville (560–635).[14] However, his interpretation of historical events has a distinctly anti-Christian slant.[15] Although he believed that there were numerous ways to refute Christian claims about the coming of the messiah, he preferred to

[11] See e.g. Abravanel, *Ma'ayenei hayeshuah*, 11: 5 (Jerusalem edn., 390); Zacut, *Sefer yuḥasin* (ed. Filipowski, 204*b*, 250*b*).   [12] See Zacut, *Sefer yuḥasin* (ed. Filipowski, 202*b*–203*a*).

[13] Abraham bar Hiyya, *Megilat hamegaleh*, 5: 145.

[14] See Guttmann, *Philosophie des Judentums*, 128–31; Guttmann, Introduction (Heb.) to Abraham bar Hiyya, *Megilat hamegaleh*, p. xiii. Guttmann thought Abraham bar Hiyya took his methodology from Isidore of Seville. Funkenstein assumed that he took it from Augustine, because Abraham bar Hiyya's concept of time is entirely Augustinian and he alludes to Augustine's *rationes seminales* theory (*Perceptions of Jewish History*, 115–16). On Augustine's concept of history, see Luneau, *L'Histoire de salut chez les pères de l'église*, 256–85, 411–12; on Irenaeus, see ibid. 93–6; see also Stitskin, *Judaism as a Philosophy*; Vajda, 'Les Idées théologiques et philosophiques d'Abraham bar Hiyya'; Wigoder, Introduction (Heb.) to Abraham bar Hiyya, *Hegyon hanefesh ha'atsuvah*.

[15] Abraham bar Hiyya, *Megilat hamegaleh*, 2: 35–6; see Baer, 'Eine jüdische Messiasprophetie auf das Jahr 1186', 120–1 n. 1; Funkenstein, *Perceptions of Jewish History*, 103–5, 199–200.

advance his own interpretation of the theory of eras, perhaps because he knew that the theory was accepted by Christian historiographers and would be difficult to contradict.

The apocalyptic approach used by Abraham bar Hiyya had existed from ancient times; however, the growth of Christianity, with its messianic apocalypticism, in the second century drove the early rabbis to suppress apocalyptic speculation within Judaism, and it fell out of favour.[16] Apocalypticism also declined among Christians after Christianity became the official religion of the Roman empire in the fourth century and especially after the publication of Jerome's commentaries (in particular the one on the book of Daniel).[17] It revived in western Europe at the end of the first Christian millennium and during the Crusades, and Abraham bar Hiyya's commentary on Daniel can be seen as part of this phenomenon.[18] Sa'adiah Gaon (d. 942) and the non-rabbinic Karaite commentators on Daniel preceded this revival, and Sa'adiah was an extremely important source for Abraham bar Hiyya.[19] Moreover, as far back as the ninth century, a group of persecuted Christians in Muslim Spain had developed what could be called a 'topical apocalypticism', according to which the true meaning of Daniel's visions could be found in recent historical events. Their major innovation was the inclusion of the prophet Muhammad in the cosmic scheme, seeing him as the 'little horn' that arose from the ten horns of the fourth beast (Dan. 7: 7–8).[20] However, there is no evidence that this group had any influence on Abraham bar Hiyya: for example, in his work, Muhammad is the 'contemptible man' (Dan. 11: 21).[21] Among Christians, the revival of apocalypticism was manifested in the middle of the twelfth century in the writings of Anselm von Havelberg, and later, from 1180, it gained an immense impetus from the work of Joachim da Fiore.[22]

[16] See Even Shmuel (ed.), *Midrashim of Salvation* (Heb.); Funkenstein, *Perceptions of Jewish History*, 78–9.

[17] See Cohn, 'Medieval Millenarism'; Luneau, *L'Histoire de salut chez les pères de l'église*; Southern, 'Aspects of the European Tradition of Historical Writing, 3', 162–3.

[18] See Baer, 'Eine jüdische Messiasprophetie auf das Jahr 1186'; Funkenstein, *Perceptions of Jewish History*, 80; Landes, 'The Massacres of 1010', esp. 103; Prawer, 'Christian Perceptions of Jerusalem in the Early Middle Ages' (Heb.), 273–5.

[19] See e.g. Abraham bar Hiyya, *Megilat hamegaleh*, 4: 98–9; Guttmann, Introduction (Heb.), ibid., pp. x–xii.

[20] See Southern, 'Aspects of the European Tradition of Historical Writing, 3', 163–4. The ten horns symbolize the ten barbarian peoples who destroyed the Roman empire. The main source is Paul Álvaro's *Indiculus luminosus*. On the Christian group, see Colbert, *The Martyrs of Córdoba*. The tiny horn was regarded as an allusion to the Islamic world in a number of texts from the Judaeo-Muslim world (see e.g. Mann, 'An Early Theologico-Polemical Work', 443 n. 113).

[21] Abraham bar Hiyya, *Megilat hamegaleh*, 4: 95–6.

[22] See Southern, 'Aspects of the European Tradition of Historical Writing, 3', 165–7; Reeves, *Joachim of Fiore*, 1–28.

Isaac Abravanel (1437–1508) reacted to Christian interpretations of the book of Daniel and, continuing the trend set by Abraham bar Hiyya, presented his own. Knowledge of the ancient world that he had acquired from Christian literature helped him to undercut Christian hermeneutics, in particular the interpretation of the fifth kingdom as a prophecy of the Church's dominion from the time of Jesus. Abravanel showed that the fifth kingdom is actually the kingdom of Israel, headed by the future messiah-king. His main argument was based on the nature of the four previous kingdoms. Each of them consisted of one people who had not ruled any of the other empires and who came from a different land. The Babylonians and the Persians differed both ethnically and geographically, as did the Persians and the Greeks, and the Greeks and the Romans. Hence the fifth kingdom would also belong to a different people, who inhabited its own land. However, according to the Christian interpretation, the fifth kingdom (the Church) was a union of the two previous kingdoms (Greece and Rome) and resided in exactly the same geographical region.[23]

Another of Abravanel's arguments concerned the division of the fourth kingdom. In the book of Daniel, Nebuchadnezzar dreams of a statue with two different feet: one of iron and the other of clay. Daniel interpreted the dream as representing the division of the fourth kingdom into two: one as strong as iron, the other as weak as clay. During this kingdom, the eternal fifth kingdom would be established (Dan. 2: 33, 41–4). Some Christian commentators maintained that this referred to the division of powers between the Roman emperors and their aides. Abravanel rejected this, claiming that the rule of Roman emperors was usually absolute, and they rarely chose to share their powers. According to Abravanel, Daniel would never have interpreted the dream on the basis of an unusual aspect of the fourth kingdom, and the meaning should be found in a more prominent feature of it.[24] He pointed out that Christianity had spread throughout the inhabited world—Asia, Africa, and Europe—but all the Christian countries in Africa and most of those in Asia had abandoned Christianity and accepted Islam. Thus Christianity was dominant in Europe, but in the large areas under Islamic control it was a minority religion, and the greater part of the world did not believe in Jesus or his teachings.[25] This was the true meaning of the division of the fourth king-

---

[23] Abravanel, *Ma'ayenei hayeshuah*, 6: 2 (Jerusalem edn., 309).   [24] Ibid.

[25] The argument about the success of Islam compared with Christianity was a common one in anti-Christian polemics (see e.g. Ibn Musa, *Magen varomaḥ*, 71, 103, 121; Limor, *Die Disputationen zu Ceuta (1179) und Mallorca (1286)*, 22; Nahmanides, *Vikuaḥ haramban*, 49 (ed. Chavel, 311); *Nizzahon vetus*, §242 (ed. Berger, 162)).

dom—the pagan Roman empire was divided into two powers: strong, iron Islam and weak, clay Christianity.[26]

Abravanel's polemical apocalypticism required knowledge of general history, especially of the First and Second Temple periods (the time of the three first kingdoms and the beginning of the fourth) and after (the period of the fourth kingdom according to the Jewish interpretation, the fifth according to Christians). The idea that the fourth kingdom was a joint kingdom of Christianity and Islam was not original to Abravanel. It also occurs in Gersonides' interpretation of Daniel.[27] However, Gersonides only occasionally used external historiographical information and did not develop his apocalyptic commentary into an all-embracing historical method, while Abravanel improved on the interpretative methods of his predecessors and supported them with a broad, persuasive historiographical infrastructure.

Christian biblical commentaries of the fourteenth and fifteenth centuries, such as Nicholas of Lyra's *Postillae* (1322–9) and Pablo de Santa María's *Scrutinium scripturarum* (1434), developed a historical orientation based on the literal meaning of the text. Older Jewish apocalyptic commentaries, such as those of Nahmanides and Gersonides, became obsolete and could no longer be used to refute Christian historical interpretations. In response, Abravanel adopted the Christian approach and used it to counter Christian arguments and create an alternative apocalyptic and historical world-view.[28]

The Crusades

While messianism and apocalyptism were important elements of Christian– Jewish polemic, a third feature was the use made in Jewish writings of the struggle

---

[26] Abravanel, *Ma'ayenei hayeshuah*, 6: 2 (Jerusalem edn., 310); see Lawee, 'On the Threshold of the Renaissance', 310. In his commentary on Daniel, Nicholas of Lyra asserted that the two feet represented the division of the Roman empire between Constantinople and Rome (see Zier, 'Nicholas of Lyra on the Book of Daniel', 188 n. 37).

[27] Gersonides on Dan. 2: 45.

[28] 'Since Nahmanides wrote and also Nissim Gerondi, as well as Rabbi David Kimhi, that the Romans are the sons of Edom . . . but gave no argument or evidence for their words, I [Abravanel] have come to reply to the words of this bitter enemy [Pablo de Santa María] according to the prevailing explanation and what I have seen in the words of the narrators' (Abravanel on Isa. 35: 10 (*Perush al nevi'im aharonim*, 171)). On the commentary of Nicholas of Lyra, see J. Cohen, *The Friars and the Jews*, 170–91; Krey, 'The Apocalypse Commentary of 1329'; Zier, 'Nicholas of Lyra on the Book of Daniel'; on Pablo de Santa María, see Baer, *A History of the Jews in Christian Spain*, ii. 139–58, 472–3 n. 38; Cantera Burgos, *Álvar García de Santa María y su familia de conversos*; Serrano, *Los conversos Don Pablo de Santa María y Don Alfonso de Cartagena*. Ibn Musa replied to Nicholas of Lyra in *Magen varomah*, and there too he makes extensive use of historical knowledge (*Magen varomah*, 69–71, 79–81; see J. Cohen, *The Friars and the Jews*, 192–5). Abravanel contended in several places with the

between Christianity and Islam over the Land of Israel. Abraham bar Hiyya was the first in a long line of Jewish writers in Spain and Provence to discuss the Crusades. He described the Islamic conquest of the Land of Israel, the transfer of power between the Umayyad and Abbasid dynasties, and the First Crusade, all of which he saw as the fulfilment of Daniel's prophecies. In his view, the nations of the world were merely pawns in God's hands, which directed the course of history according to the plan revealed in the book of Daniel. Empires rose and fell, but the most important thing about them was their attitude to Jews. Islam treated the Jews of the Arabian peninsula harshly at first but tempered its attitude when the Umayyad caliphate was established in Damascus. The Abbasid caliphate, on the other hand, reintroduced a hostile policy. However, the Crusaders were the worst, because they desecrated the Temple.[29]

The religious view of history as directed by God has its roots in the Bible, and Abraham bar Hiyya learned it from Sa'adiah Gaon's commentary on Daniel. The difference between Abraham bar Hiyya and Sa'adiah lies in their interpretation of events, not in the method they employed. Sa'adiah identified the desecration of the Temple described in Daniel with the destruction of the Temple by Titus, while Abraham bar Hiyya applied it to his own time and identified it with the conquest of Jerusalem by the Crusaders.[30] According to him, biblical verses must be interpreted in the light of current and past events and should only be interpreted as prophecies of the future when no correspondence can be found with known events. Sa'adiah Gaon could, therefore, not be criticized for failing to foretell the future: the destruction of the Temple by Titus did indeed correspond to the event in the book of Daniel, and Sa'adiah had to interpret it as he did. However, because of his greater historical perspective, Abraham bar Hiyya was able to understand the chronological problem with Sa'adiah's interpretation[31] and reinterpret the book of Daniel, bringing the end of the 'wicked kingdom of Edom' (Christianity) closer to his own time.

Abraham bar Hiyya's interpretation was a reaction to the Christian understanding of the First Crusade. Christians saw it as a second Exodus, the fulfil-

commentaries of Nicholas of Lyra and Santa María (see e.g. Abravanel on Isa. 35: 10 (_Perush al nevi'im aḥaronim_, 170–2)).

[29] Abraham bar Hiyya, _Megilat hamegaleh_, 4: 97–8; see Dinburg, 'The House of Study and Prayer for Jews on the Temple Mount' (Heb.), esp. 54–6.

[30] Abraham bar Hiyya, _Megilat hamegaleh_, 4: 98–9; see Guttmann, Introduction (Heb.), ibid., p. xi.

[31] See Abraham bar Hiyya, _Megilat hamegaleh_, 4: 98–9. To a certain extent, Abraham bar Hiyya's method is similar to Augustine's. According to Augustine, any historical interpretation of the Bible should be given preference and only in the absence of such an interpretation should a figurative interpretation be sought (_On the Literal Interpretation of Genesis_, 8: 1).

ment of a divine command to leave the countries where they were sojourning and settle in a promised land. The mission that had been given to the Jews was taken from them by Jesus 'and assigned to those who believe in him, the new Israelites'.[32] The sanctity of Jerusalem became a major element in Christian claims to the Land of Israel and justifications of the conquest,[33] and Christians exploited their victory in the missionary propaganda they spread among the Jews. The Christian beliefs that Jesus would appear again for the Last Judgement in Jerusalem, the heavenly Jerusalem would spread throughout the world, and the Jews would acknowledge Jesus as the messiah was disseminated from the beginning of the eleventh century. Many Christians viewed the crusade as the start of the End of Days and expected a mass conversion of Jews.[34] Echoes of this can be found in the poem 'Yode'i hefitsuni' by Judah Halevi, Abraham bar Hiyya's younger contemporary,[35] which describes how Christians used their possession of the Temple Mount to try to convert Jews. For at least fifty years after the conquest of Jerusalem, a sense of spiritual renewal prevailed in western Christianity, and there was a widespread sense that current events reflected a divine plan.[36] There was messianic ferment in several Jewish communities as well.[37] In the light of this, Abraham bar Hiyya felt he could play down the significance of the destruction of the Temple by Titus and emphasize the conquest of Jerusalem by the Crusaders. He interpreted 'they will desecrate the temple, the fortress' (Dan. 11: 31) as a reference to the removal of all the Jews from Jerusalem by the Christians, while he understood 'capture a fortress city' (Dan. 11: 15) as a reference to Titus's destruction of the Temple.[38] His use of the same prophecies from the book of Daniel as the Christians countered their claims that the crusade heralded the beginning of the End of Days and their demands that the Jews immediately convert to Christianity.

According to the Christians, the fact that there were now no Jews in Jerusalem and that churches were established on the Temple Mount was proof of the victory

---

[32] Guibert of Nogent, *Deeds of God through the Franks*, 123–5, 137–40; see also Baldric of Dol, *History of Jerusalem*, 14; Prawer, 'Christian Perceptions of Jerusalem in the Early Middle Ages' (Heb.), 278–81, n. 108; Riley-Smith, *The First Crusade and the Idea of Crusading*, 50–136.

[33] See Shine, 'Jerusalem in Christian Spirituality' (Heb.), 216–17.

[34] See Prawer, *Histoire du Royaume Latin de Jérusalem*, i. 181–4; id., *The History of the Crusader Kingdom in the Land of Israel* (Heb.), i. 96–7.

[35] Judah Halevi, 'Yode'i hefitsuni', in Shirman, *Hebrew Poetry of Spain and Provence* (Heb.), i. 482; see also Baer, 'The Political Situation of Spanish Jewry in the Time of R. Judah Halevi' (Heb.), 266.

[36] See e.g. Fulcher of Chartres, *A History of the Expedition to Jerusalem*, 360.

[37] See Aescoly, *Jewish Messianic Movements* (Heb.), 171–2; Cohn, 'Medieval Millenarism', 33–4; Prawer, *The History of the Crusader Kingdom in the Land of Israel* (Heb.), i. 93–6, 421–5; id., *The Crusaders* (Heb.), 258–61, 286–9; Shine, 'Jerusalem in Christian Spirituality' (Heb.), 255–8.

[38] Abraham bar Hiyya, *Megilat hamegaleh*, 4: 99–100.

of Christianity and its status as the true religion. However, Abraham bar Hiyya viewed this as sacrilege, evidence that the end was drawing near, and that Christianity would soon fall: 'This wrath will be immense [enough] to destroy only the Gentile nations, and Israel will have from it, with God's help, only gain profit and a great salvation.'[39] He adopted and developed the Christian idea of the spread of the heavenly Jerusalem: at the End of Days the Land of Israel would spread and 'expand . . . to a huge breadth until it fills the entire world'.[40] This expansion would not, however, mean the victory of the Church and the conversion of the Jews but the victory of the Jews and their seizure of all non-Jewish lands.

The Crusades and Christian control of the Holy Land were, from the twelfth century onwards, an integral part of the religious polemic between Christians and Jews. For example, the monk who debated with Jacob ben Reuben, author of *Milḥamot hashem* (written in 1170, apparently in Gascony), pointed to two new historical phenomena of the twelfth century—the Crusades to the Land of Israel, which fulfilled Moses' prophecy: '[He will] cleanse the land of his people' (Deut. 32: 43); and knights who stopped living by the sword and devoted themselves to the worship of God in churches and monasteries.[41] The claim that the Christians were successful in the Crusades seems to have been quite effective in the religious debates, and, as I have noted, Abraham bar Hiyya countered it with his own historical and messianic interpretations.

In the thirteenth century, as Christian setbacks in the Land of Israel became known in Europe, they were exploited by Jewish thinkers. The poet Judah Alharizi, who visited Jerusalem in 1216 or 1217, described the Jewish resettlement of the city since 1187, when it had fallen to Saladin, who had invited the Jews to return (as had Cyrus (Ezra 1: 2–4)). In Alharizi's eyes, Saladin was an emissary of God called upon to take the Temple out of the hands of the Christians.[42] Meir ben Shimon Hame'ili of Narbonne also exploited the Muslim victories in polemic with Christians, pointing out the great discrepancy between the biblical prophecies, which the Christians applied to the Crusaders in the Holy Land, and the victories of the Muslims. He placed special emphasis on the surrender of

---

[39] Abraham bar Hiyya, *Megilat hamegaleh*, 4: 102.

[40] Ibid. 110; see Idel, 'On the Land of Israel in Medieval Jewish Mystic Thought' (Heb.), 200–3; Shine, 'Jerusalem in Christian Spirituality' (Heb.), 246–9; Vajda, 'Les Idées théologiques et philosophiques d'Abraham bar Hiyya', 216.

[41] See Berger, 'Gilbert Crispin, Alan of Lille, and Jacob ben Reuben'; Rosenthal, Introduction to Jacob b. Reuben, *Milḥamot hashem*, pp. x–xi.

[42] See Alharizi, *Taḥkemoni*, 16 (ed. Yahalom and Katsumata, 264); Prawer, *Histoire du Royaume Latin de Jérusalem*, ii. 85 n. 16; id., *The History of the Crusader Kingdom in the Land of Israel* (Heb.), ii. 79; id., *The History of the Jews in the Latin Kingdom of Jerusalem*, 66–70; Grossman, 'Saladin's Victory and the Aliyah of the Jews of Europe to the Land of Israel' (Heb.).

the kingdom of Tyre,[43] the sinking of Crusader ships,[44] and the fall of Antioch—the symbol of Crusader control of Syria—in 1268.[45] He argued that the Crusades and the wars in the Land of Israel, which led to the devastation of the land while the Jews were in exile, proved that the End of Days had not yet begun, contrary to Christian claims.[46] He also drew attention to the number of Christians killed in the wars and the large sums of money required to ransom prisoners from the Muslims.[47]

In the fourteenth century the philosopher Nissim ben Moses of Marseilles used the Crusades for polemical purposes in *Ma'aseh nisim*. He followed Nahmanides in interpreting 'I will make the land desolate, so that your enemies who settle in it shall be appalled by it' (Lev. 26: 32), as proof that the wars and devastation in the Land of Israel were evidence that the land rejected the enemies of the Jews.[48] Nahmanides did not deem it necessary to specify particular historical events, but Nissim ben Moses expanded upon the idea in a brief historical survey. First Rome ruled over the Land of Israel and the emperor Hadrian banished the Jews from Jerusalem. Afterwards, the Muslims overcame the Romans, conquered the land, and ruled over it until Nissim ben Moses' time. Although during this period the Christians took control of the region twice (probably referring to the First Crusade in 1099 and Frederick II's reconquest of Jerusalem in 1229), the Muslims took it back each time. The situation in the country during this period was marked by unrest: the Christian inhabitants suffered under Muslim rule, the Muslim inhabitants suffered under Christian rule, and people were unable to live

[43] Meir b. Shimon Hame'ili, *Milḥemet mitsvah* (ed. Blau, 339, 354). The reference is probably to the request by Philip de Montfort, Lord of Tyre, for a truce with the Mamluk sultan, Baybars (see Prawer, *Histoire du Royaume Latin de Jérusalem*, ii. 479–80; id., *The History of the Crusader Kingdom in the Land of Israel* (Heb.), ii. 467–8;). On Meir ben Shimon Hame'ili, see Chazan, 'Polemical Themes in the Milhemet Mizvah'; id., 'Anti-Usury Efforts in Thirteenth Century Narbonne'; Stein, *Jewish–Christian Disputations in Thirteenth-Century Narbonne*.

[44] Meir b. Shimon Hame'ili, *Milḥemet mitsvah* (ed. Blau, 354). In my opinion, the reference here is to the crusade organized by James I of Aragon in 1269. The fleet sailed from Barcelona, but a storm drove it off course, and it landed at Aigues-Morte in southern France, close to where Meir ben Shimon Hame'ili lived (see Prawer, *Histoire du Royaume Latin de Jérusalem*, ii. 494; id., *The History of the Crusader Kingdom in the Land of Israel* (Heb.), ii. 481).

[45] Meir b. Shimon Hame'ili, *Milḥemet mitsvah* (ed. Blau, 354); see Prawer, *Histoire du Royaume Latin de Jérusalem*, ii. 483; id., *History of the Crusader Kingdom in the Land of Israel* (Heb.), ii. 471).

[46] Meir b. Shimon Hame'ili, *Milḥemet mitsvah* (ed. Blau, 328–9).

[47] Ibid. 352, 353. In his view, the Crusades led to moral flaws in Christian society, for example, because the Crusaders delayed repaying their loans, they took false oaths, which was one of the reasons for their defeat. See Meir b. Shimon Hame'ili, *Milḥemet mitzvah* (ed. Herskowitz, 101). On the Crusades in Jewish–Christian disputations, see R. Ben-Shalom, 'Between Official and Private Dispute', 64. See the interesting note about the feudal system in Cyprus where the king allocated estates to 300 knights (Moses ibn Tibbon, *Sefer pe'ah*, 70 (ed. Kreisel, Sirat, and Israel, 193)).

[48] Nahmanides on Lev. 26: 32 (ed. Chavel, 190).

their lives properly. Moreover, the Mongols tried repeatedly to conquer Jerusalem, but—according to a rumour Nissim ben Moses reported—were unable to stay in the Land of Israel for very long, because the rivers and springs could not provide sufficient water for their huge armies.[49] Nevertheless, when the threat of a Mongol invasion arose people abandoned the cities until the danger had passed.[50] For Nissim ben Moses, all this demonstrated divine providence: Christian failure to conquer and bring peace to the Land of Israel reflected the non-fulfilment of their messianic hopes and confirmed the Jews' expectations that the prophecies would be fulfilled in the future.

The Land of Israel under Muslim rule was also an important topic in Jewish–Christian polemic in the fifteenth and the early sixteenth centuries. For example, in 1456 the Spanish Jew Hayim ibn Musa attacked Christianity by pointing out that the Muslims controlled the Church of the Holy Sepulchre and other sites sacred to Christians. In a disputation with a priest, he accused the Christians of abandoning the church and other sites to the rule of Islam.[51] To this, a knight who was present retorted that it was divine punishment for Christians and Jews alike, because they were neglecting their houses of prayer in the lands where they lived.[52]

Aaron of Lunel (b. 1452) wrote a brief chronicle of the life of Jesus, in which he stated that Christian claims about the link between Jesus's Crucifixion and the destruction of the Temple led him also to discuss the struggle between Christians and Muslims for control of the Land of Israel. He viewed the events with the benefit of several centuries' hindsight and surveyed the Crusader conquest in 1099, the liquidation of the first Crusader kingdom after eighty-eight years, Saladin's conquests, and later crusades by French and English kings. His report is marred by some errors, but it does contain quite comprehensive information. He gave the dates of the Crusades and Crusader rule, and his chronicle contains many details that are not generally mentioned in polemical works. He ended by emphasizing the final and complete Muslim victory in the Land of Israel.[53]

[49] Nissim b. Moses, *Ma'aseh nisim* (ed. Kreisel), 396–7; see Halkin, 'Rabbi Nissim of Marseilles' (Heb.); Sirat, 'The Political Ideas of Nissim ben Moses of Marseilles' (Heb.), 54.

[50] See e.g. Matthew Paris, *Chronica majora*, iv. 308–9. In the biblical interpretations of the philosopher Joseph ibn Caspi, a contemporary of Nissim ben Moses in Provence, there are also some brief comparisons of Mongolian tactics in the Land of Israel and Mamluk tactics in Egypt. Ibn Caspi also emphasized the quick, intensive Mongol raids (see R. Ben-Shalom, 'The Unwritten Travel Journal to the East of Joseph ibn Caspi' (Heb.), esp. 30).

[51] Ibn Musa, *Magen varomaḥ*, 103. This argument had already appeared in a disputation in the thirteenth century (Rosenthal, 'A Religious Disputation' (Heb.), 65; see Chazan, 'A Medieval Hebrew Polemical Mélange').

[52] Ibn Musa, *Magen varomaḥ*, 103; see also R. Ben-Shalom, 'Between Official and Private Dispute', 58.

[53] MS Hebrew 263 (Bibliothèque nationale, Paris), fo. 68*a*; cf. Neubauer, *The Order of the Sages and Historical Events* (Heb.), i. 191–2.

In *Sefer yuḥasin*, probably written between 1480 and 1513, Abraham ben Samuel Zacut dealt at length with the wars between Christians and Muslims in the Land of Israel. In the third chapter, he included information on the conquests of Jerusalem, associating them with the spread of Islam in the east and with a meeting between Rabbi Isaac, head of the academy in Babylonia, and Caliph Ali ibn Abi Talib.[54] In the fourth chapter, he commented on an erroneous tradition according to which Jerusalem was conquered by the Christians in 1027 and corrected the date to 1099, following Abraham bar Hiyya.[55] However, his main discussion of the Crusades is in the sixth chapter and occurs in the context of the struggle between Christianity and Islam. Zacut does not make explicit polemical use of his historical information about the Crusades, but he does place special emphasis on the destruction of churches. He describes the damage done to the tomb in the Church of the Holy Sepulchre by the Muslims, its desecration in 1012 during the reign of Caliph Al-Hakim, and its restoration by the Byzantine emperor Constantine Monomachus in 1048; the defeat of the Crusader kingdom of Jerusalem by Saladin in 1187 and the destruction of Christian churches and ritual paraphernalia (particularly church bells); the destruction of Jerusalem and Christian sacred structures during the reign of Sultan Al-Malik in 1219 and the enormous efforts of the Christians to protect the Church of the Holy Sepulchre; and the destruction of the sepulchre by the Khorezmians in 1244.[56] Christian defeats in the Crusades were a boon for Jewish polemicists, and the historical information in *Sefer yuḥasin* was an easily accessible source for those engaged in religious disputations.

Isaac Abravanel, like Abraham bar Hiyya, dealt with the Crusades within an apocalyptic framework based on the writings of the prophets and the early rabbis. In his commentary, the nations of Gog and Magog are the Islamic peoples, and, according to *Midrash tehilim* on the book of Psalms, they would attack Jerusalem three times.[57] Abravanel explained that the first two attacks had already

---

[54] Zacut, *Sefer yuḥasin* (ed. Filipowski, 204*b*). The meeting between R. Isaac and Ibn Abi Talib is described in a letter from Sherira Gaon (see Gil, *The Kingdom of Ishmael during the Period of the Geonim* (Heb.), i. 67); on Abraham Zacut, see Cantera Burgos, *Abraham Zacut*; Lacave, 'El "Sefer Yuhasin" de Abraham Zacut'; Neuman, 'Abraham Zacut, Historiographer'; on his work on astronomy, see B. R. Goldstein, 'The Hebrew Astronomical Tradition'; on his last years in the Land of Israel, see David, 'On the History of the Sages in Jerusalem in the Sixteenth Century (Heb.), 238–40; Shohat, 'Rabbi Abraham Zacut in the Yeshivah of Rabbi Isaac Shulal' (Heb.); on the date of composition of *Sefer yuḥasin*, see Freiman, Introduction (Heb.) to Zacut, *Sefer yuḥasin*, p. x.

[55] Zacut, *Sefer yuḥasin* (ed. Filipowski, 212*a*); see Neuman, 'Abraham Zacut, Historiographer', 607.

[56] Zacut, *Sefer yuḥasin* (ed. Freiman, pp. xli–xlii). Freiman included a version of chapter 6 of *Sefer yuḥasin* from MS Hebrew d.16 (Neubauer 2798) (Bodleian Library, Oxford) at the end of his Introduction to Filipowski's edition. See also n. 108 below.

[57] *Midrash tehilim*, 118: 12 (ed. Buber, 484).

occurred—when the Muslims took the Land of Israel from the Byzantine empire and when the Crusaders were driven from the country after having ruled it for eighty-five years—and that the third would come only after another Christian conquest of the Land of Israel, following which the Muslims would take it for the last time.[58] He erred in his assessment of the duration of the first Crusader kingdom: it lasted eighty-eight years, from 1099 to 1187. However, his historical knowledge of the conquest of Jerusalem in 1099 was based not only on general estimates from Jewish sources (he mentions Abraham bar Hiyya) but also on Christian chronicles, and he knew many details about those who participated in the crusade. For example, he mentioned that it took place during the pontificate of Pope Urban II; that soldiers from France and England were involved, as well as from Italy; and that after they conquered the Land of Israel they crowned Gottfried of Bouillon, a French nobleman, king.[59] Abravanel could also have gathered some of this information from Hebrew chronicles, such as an anonymous list from Provence and Languedoc from around 1300, which contained a description of Saladin's conquest of Jerusalem in 1187 and the Crusader siege of Acre in 1189.[60]

Some modern scholars play down the importance of the Crusades in Jewish–Christian polemic;[61] however, in the light of the above, it seems that they had a central role and the theme can be traced from its beginning in Abraham bar Hiyya's *Megilat hamegaleh*, through Nissim ben Moses' *Ma'aseh nisim*, to Isaac Abravanel's *Ma'ayenei hayeshuah*. In my view, all these authors revealed only some of the facts known to them about the historical events, according to their polemical or apocalyptic needs.

The Use of Christian Historiography and Historical Information

Abraham bar Hiyya's successor in historiography in Spain was the philosopher Abraham ibn Daud. In *Sefer hakabalah*, written in 1160–1, Ibn Daud linked the history of the Jews with the annals of the kings of Rome and Persia and located philosophers and scientists, such as Hippocrates, Aristotle, Ptolemy, and Galen, within Jewish chronology.[62] Although biblical historiography is a precedent for this approach, and the same trend is evident in the *Book of Josippon*, it would have been possible for Ibn Daud to ignore these trends and choose a narrower perspec-

---

[58] Abravanel on Zech. 14: 1 (*Perush al nevi'im ukhetuvim*, 283). On Abravanel, see Lawee, *Isaac Abarbanel's Stance towards Tradition*; Netanyahu, *Don Isaac Abravanel*.

[59] Abravanel, *Ma'ayenei hayeshuah*, 2: 3 (Jerusalem edn., 289).

[60] The list is in Ibn Verga, *Shevet yehudah*, 146; see Introduction, n. 20 above.

[61] See Lasker, 'The Impact of the Crusades on the Jewish–Christian Debate'.

[62] Ibn Daud, *Sefer hakabalah*, ch. 3, lines 47, 68–9; ch. 4, line 101 (ed. Cohen: Heb. section, 21, 23, 30; Eng. section, 29, 30–1, 40).

tive that concentrated solely on Jewish history. Ibn Daud added two appendices to his book: *The History of Rome from Its Foundation until the Beginning of the Muslim Empire* (*Zikhron divrei romi miyom hibanutah ad tehilat malkhut yishma'el*) and *The History of the Kings of Israel during the Second Temple Period* (*Divrei malkhei yisra'el bevayit sheni*).[63] The former is almost entirely devoted to Roman history, with only occasional mention of events from Jewish history, apparently making Ibn Daud the first Jew to write an entire work devoted to non-Jewish history. While Baron considered Ibn Daud's history rather primitive by modern standards, he recognized that for his contemporaries it offered new perspectives, in particular because he was adept at using Christian sources, including Paulus Orosius, Hydatius, and Isidore of Seville,[64] and provided historical interpretations of geographical names.[65] Ibn Daud's major source for early Roman history was the *Book of Josippon*, with additional information from Christian books. However, for the period after the destruction of the Second Temple, his only sources are Christian historiography. At the end of the *History of Rome*, Ibn Daud noted that it was an abridged history of the Roman era and should not be regarded as a comprehensive work.[66] This suggests that he had access to more historical information than he included.

Ibn Daud did not explain the purpose of his *History of Rome* in the book itself, but at the end of *Sefer hakabalah* he wrote: 'The *History of Rome* is intended to inform [its readers] when the Gospels were written.'[67] He claimed that the work served a polemical purpose by showing that the Gospels were late compositions (300 years after Christ according to Christian chronology, 420 according to Jewish tradition) and of no great historical value. However, it is possible that this should not be taken at face value, as such declarations often had an apologetic purpose. Baron was aware of this but, nevertheless, accepted what Ibn Daud said and stressed the polemical aspects of the *History of Rome*.[68] Gerson Cohen followed Baron but also stressed its Hispanocentrism, which he regarded as its central theme.[69] I would emphasize its Hispanocentrism even more strongly. Although there is a section on Emperor Constantine, and Ibn Daud assigned

[63] See G. D. Cohen, Introduction and notes to Ibn Daud, *Sefer hakabalah*, pp. xlii–xxxii; Baron, *A Social and Religious History of the Jews*, vi. 209–10.

[64] See Klein and Molner, 'Rabbi Abraham ben David' (Heb.), *Hatsofeh lehokhmat yisra'el*, 8 (1924), 24–5. [65] Baron, *A Social and Religious History of the Jews*, vi. 210.

[66] Ibn Daud, *Zikhron divrei romi* (Mantua edn., 62; see also 61; ed. Vehlow, 132); on Ibn Daud's creative use of the *Book of Jossipon*, see Vehlow, Introduction to Ibn Daud, *Zikhron divrei romi*, 30; on his use of Christian sources, see ibid. 31–7. For a detailed analysis of Ibn Daud's book see Fernández Urbina and Targarona Borrás, 'La historia romana'.

[67] Ibn Daud, *Sefer hakabalah*, ch. 7, lines 438–9 (ed. Cohen: Heb. section, 74; Eng. section, 103).

[68] Baron, *A Social and Religious History of the Jews*, vi. 210.

[69] G. D. Cohen, Introduction and notes to Ibn Daud, *Sefer hakabalah*, pp. xxii–xxiii, 253–62.

him a decisive role in the development of Christianity, this is not the main theme of the book. There is also much on the history of Christianity from the time of Constantine but no direct polemic.[70] In the light of this, it is possible that Ibn Daud's claim that the *History of Rome* was solely a polemical work may have been intended to mollify those Jews who felt the need for an ideological justification for historiography, because it was a new genre in Jewish literature. I discuss this claim at greater length in Chapter 3.

Haim Hillel Ben-Sasson suggested that Ibn Daud's work should be viewed against the background of the cultural awakening known as the twelfth-century renaissance,[71] which had an effect on all the countries of western Europe. The renaissance involved a revitalization of philosophy and science, including historiography.[72] Several aspects of history that would be given greater emphasis in later historiography appeared for the first time in the *History of Rome*. Whereas Abraham bar Hiyya wrote *Megilat hamegaleh* as a polemical work and used historical information solely for that purpose, in the *History of Rome* polemic is a secondary matter (perhaps only a pretext), because Ibn Daud is motivated mainly by historical and scientific interests. In this context, it is interesting to note that at the end of the fifteenth century, after nearly 350 years of Jewish historiographical writing, Abraham Zacut permitted himself to add three more justifications for engaging in historiography alongside polemic.[73]

The apologetic and polemical approach to world history is also evident in *Igeret ya'akov mivenetsiah*, a letter written by Jacob ben Elijah of Venice (a citizen of Montpellier) apparently between 1261 and 1263 to Paul Christiani, a Jew who had converted to Christianity, became a Dominican friar, and attempted to have the Talmud banned.[74] In his letter, Jacob ben Elijah argued that in the final reckoning Christiani's betrayal of his people would not ultimately be to his advantage.[75] To make his point, he related five historical episodes from the far west of

[70] Ibn Daud, *Zikhron divrei romi* (Mantua edn., 23; ed. Vehlow, 120–1).

[71] H. H. Ben-Sasson, 'On Medieval Trends in Jewish Chronography' (Heb.), 380–2; see R. L. Benson and Constable (eds.), *Renaissance and Renewal in the Twelfth Century*; Haskins, *The Renaissance of the Twelfth Century*.

[72] See Barkai, *Science, Magic, and Mythology in the Middle Ages* (Heb.), 79–94; Deyermond, 'El "Auto de los reyes magos" y el renacimiento del siglo XII'; Linehan, *History and the Historians of Medieval Spain*, 204–312; McCluskey, 'Malleable Accounts'.

[73] See Zacut, *Sefer yuḥasin* (ed. Filipowski, 231a–232a).

[74] Much has been written on the author's identity and place of residence. For a survey of the various opinions, see Chazan, 'The Letter of R. Jacob ben Elijah to Friar Paul'; among the numerous studies, see Mann, 'Une source de l'histoire juive au XIIIe siècle'; Stow, 'Jacob of Venice and the Jewish Settlement in Venice'.

[75] See Chazan, *Barcelona and Beyond*, 25–7; id., 'The Letter of R. Jacob ben Elijah to Friar Paul'; J. Cohen, 'The Mentality of the Medieval Jewish Apostate', 35–40; Mann, 'Une source de l'histoire juive au XIIIe siècle'; Shatzmiller, 'Paulus Christiani', 203.

the Jewish world (Spain and Morocco) to the far east (Byzantium and Babylonia) that demonstrated how rulers who oppressed Jews were severely punished by God. He summed up his approach to history in one sentence: 'And now I will remind you of what you knew and you heard, how God rendered their fate upon their heads, and they who devoured his people said: "We shall not be held guilty" [see Jer. 50: 7].'[76] His historiographical method was far simpler than Abraham bar Hiyya's, which was anchored in complex apocalyptic interpretation and precise astrological calculations. For Jacob ben Elijah Jews were at the centre of the historical process, even if the major figures of history appeared to be the non-Jewish rulers.

The first two episodes related by Jacob ben Elijah concern the collapse of the Almohad kingdom and the conquest of Majorca by James I of Aragon, which I will discuss in Chapter 5. The third and fourth involve the Romaniot Jews of Byzantium. The first of these deals with the Jews of Epirus during the Latin empire of Constantinople (1204–61) and describes a series of abuses of Jews by the despot Theodore II Comnenus Ducas, who ruled from 1214 to 1230, including confiscation of possessions and denial of fair trials. There are no references to any anti-Jewish measures by Theodore in Byzantine sources, but Steven Bowman suggests that he may have taken these steps in order to finance a war against the Bulgarian tsar, John II Asen.[77] Jacob ben Elijah depicts Theodore as the biblical Pharaoh, whose heart was hardened by God. Because of his mistreatment of Jews, God made him bold and led him to violate his treaty with John Asen against the dukedoms of Nicaea. Eventually Theodore was defeated in battle in 1230, and John Asen demanded that his eyes be put out by two Jews, because the Jews had been the main victims of his misrule. However, they took pity on him and refused to carry out the punishment. They were sentenced to death and thrown off a mountain. Two others were chosen to carry out the sentence, and Theodore was blinded.[78] Jacob ben Elijah's account casts light on unknown aspects of Jewish life in Epirus and serves as a unique historical source for the history of the Jews of Byzantium.

Jacob ben Elijah's knowledge of Byzantine history, the names of emperors, and their dynasties is also evident in the next story,[79] which depicts the attitude of

[76] Jacob b. Elijah, *Igeret ya'akov mivenetsiah*, 23. On the historiographical principle of divine retribution in the works of Sephardi chroniclers after the Expulsion, see Orfali, 'La retribución divina en la historiografía sefardí'.

[77] Bowman, *The Jews of Byzantium*, 14.

[78] Jacob b. Elijah, *Igeret ya'akov mivenetsiah*, 24–5; see Bowman, *The Jews of Byzantium*, 12–16; Mann, 'Une source de l'histoire juive au XIIIe siècle', 372.

[79] Jacob b. Elijah, *Igeret ya'akov mivenetsiah*, 25–7; see Bowman, *The Jews of Byzantium*, 228–31 and bibliography.

the Byzantine emperor John III Ducas Vatatzes (1222–54)[80] to Jews during the Latin empire:

Let it be told to you what Vatatzes who ruled in Yavan [Greece] did to us. Evil seduced him and aroused his spirit to raise his hand against our faith and to profane the Torah of our Lord. . . . In that year his sleep fled him and his fever increased and a stench arose from him. And Vatatzes was like wine that had been left unopened like a seething pot and his intestines were like a bloated cauldron; he was covered with boils as strong as iron. And the cursed waters gathered within him; his heart trembled and the maggots gathered in his bones. He could not pass water, his mouth passed an excretion, and his tongue was like a burning flame hungry for bread and yearning for water; he was inflicted with severe inflammation of his knees and hips. . . . Is this not the fate of those who plunder us and the destiny of those who rob us? . . . His son Laskaris ruled after him, because he was his firstborn. He ruled for some days, and all of his officials were afraid of him because anger rested in his bosom. Thus he found no peace, for troubles and many bad problems and events surrounded him and hurts, pains, agonies, and many other bad maladies until he became sick of living and all his desires were oriented towards death. . . . In the prime of his life he too died and was cut off from his people. Afterwards there sat upon his throne one of his servants who had poured water on his hands with all his majesty. Cautious in his speech, he summoned a scribe and gathered all the sages of Israel throughout his kingdom. With fear in their hearts they came to greet him. He said to them, 'Well I know that Vatatzes oppressed you, therefore he was not successful. Now go and worship the Lord your God, you and your sons and daughters. Keep my commands and bless me also and ever ask my peace and well being. I will protect you, and you will keep silent.' And it came to pass while this king was sitting on the throne of his kingdom, he annihilated all the servants of Vatatzes and all the elders of his house and destroyed all the advisers of his son as well as his officials together so that none remained. And Laskaris had a son. The king took him and gouged out his eyes and castrated him destroying his ability to reproduce. Thus he caused both his body and his soul to suffer. His ancestors sinned but were no more, so he suffered for their transgressions.[81]

John's seat was in Nicaea, and he prepared the ground for the restoration of Greek control of Constantinople and was later canonized by the Eastern Church. Jacob ben Elijah describes how John forced Jews to convert to Christianity and was punished with illness and a painful death.[82] He gives very precise details of this, which contradict the glorious image of John presented by most Greek histori-

[80] See Lewin, 'Eine Notiz zur Geschichte der Juden im Byzantinischen Reiche'; Mann, 'Une source de l'histoire juive au XIIIe siècle', 372–3 n. 1.

[81] Jacob b. Elijah, *Igeret ya'akov mivenetsiah*, 25–7; see Bowman, *The Jews of Byzantium*, 229–30.

[82] See Ankori, *An Encounter in History* (Heb.), 154–5; Bowman, *The Jews of Byzantium*, 18. According to Bowman, the order against the Jews was issued in 1254, after the emperor fell ill, not as Jacob ben Elijah described it (ibid. 230 n. 12).

ans; however, it has a solid base in fact and is substantiated by the Byzantine historian Nicephoros Gregoras.[83] John's son and heir, Theodore II Laskaris (1254–8), reigned for only four years and died at the age of 36. Jacob ben Elijah mentioned his short reign, the ordeals he experienced—apparently referring to his relations with the Byzantine nobility and the defeats he suffered in the war with Michael, despot of Epirus—and his early death. Theodore's successor— Michael VIII Palaeologos (1258/9–82)—is described as 'one of his servants who had poured water on his hands'. He was a general in the service of the emperors of Nicaea, and after Theodore's death he seized power as the regent of the child-emperor John IV Laskaris (1258–61). John was imprisoned and blinded in 1261 on Michael's orders. Jacob ben Elijah notes that John Laskaris was not guilty himself, but suffered for the sins of his fathers. A description of the castration of the child-emperor marks the end of the Laskaris dynasty and the beginning of the Palaeologos dynasty.[84]

Jacob ben Elijah described the reign of Michael Palaeologos as a new chapter in the history of Byzantine Jews, when religious persecution stopped and they could live as Jews.[85] Michael allowed Jews to live in Byzantium, because he anticipated that it would bring him good fortune. Readers of the letter would probably already know that Michael had recovered Constantinople and were meant to interpret his political success as a direct result of his positive attitude towards Jews.

The fifth episode concerns the end of the Abbasid caliphate.[86] Jacob ben Elijah's description is true to the facts. The Mongols under Hülegü captured Baghdad in 1258 and killed the last Al-Musta'sim caliph, putting an end to the Abbasid dynasty in the east. Jacob ben Elijah describes how, before the conquest of Baghdad, 'certain elements' appealed to the caliph for help against the Mongols who had been hounding them. In my view, the 'certain elements' were the Assassins, the Nizari Ismailis, who had been defeated by the Mongols in Babylonia two years earlier in 1256, after the fall of their mountain fastness, Alamut. According to Jacob ben Elijah, members of the sect pressured the caliph to change his attitude towards the Jews and to levy taxes on the head of the Jewish community, the exilarch Samuel ben David, and the head (*gaon*) of the Baghdad academy to finance the war against the Mongols. According to the chronicler Ismail ibn Khatir, who died in 1373, nearly all the Muslims in Baghdad were massacred

[83] Jacob b. Elijah, *Igeret ya'akov mivenetsiah*, 25–7; see Bowman, *The Jews of Byzantium*, 17; Starr, *Romania*, 23 n. 10.

[84] Bowman notes that only the blinding is mentioned in the Byzantine sources (*The Jews of Byzantium*, 231 n. 26).

[85] See Ankori, *An Encounter in History* (Heb.), 155; Bowman, *The Jews of Byzantium*, 19.

[86] Jacob b. Elijah, *Igeret ya'akov mivenetsiah*, 27–9.

during the conquest, and only Jews and Christians were spared. In the years immediately following, the situation of the Jews was much improved, until the persecutions and massacres were renewed in 1285 and 1291 after the Muslim population was once again established in the city. Jacob ben Elijah's claim that the status of the exilarch was maintained under Mongol rule is unique and, as such, extremely important.[87] In his view, the Mongol victory over the Abbasid caliphate and the final defeat of the Assassins was further proof that the Jews were at the centre of history.

Jacob ben Elijah's description of the sack of Baghdad reveals his attitude to historical events. Some Jews regarded the Mongols as the descendants of one of the ten lost tribes and described their expansion in apocalyptic terms as the war of Gog and Magog.[88] For example, writing at about that time, the Hebrew poet Meshullam da Piera described the collapse of the Abbasid caliphate as the victory of the ten tribes and anticipated the rebuilding of the Temple during his own lifetime.[89] Jacob ben Elijah, however, stuck closer to historical fact: the persecutors of the Jews were punished by being deprived of political power and injured personally. The Abbasid caliphate was conquered and the dynasty's reign in Baghdad came to an end.

The end of the Abbasid caliphate is the last event that Jacob ben Elijah adduces as proof of the centrality of the Jews to history. The rise and fall of empires were the result of their treatment of Jews. The death of Theodore II Comnenus Ducas, the demise of the Laskaris dynasty, and the fall of the Abbasid caliphate all stemmed from the rulers' mistreatment of the Jews in their kingdoms. In contrast, the success of Michael Palaeologos was a result of his good relationship with Jews. It may seem that Jews were excluded from the political arena, but in fact they had participated in every important historical event. The history of non-Jews is therefore also the history of the Jewish people who live among them, and it is impossible to separate general history from the particular history of the Jews. Jacob ben Elijah's Judaeocentric outlook was similar to that of Maimonides, although the latter focused primarily on the biblical and talmudic periods,[90] and the former stressed events from the more recent past. A similar approach was articulated later by Solomon ibn Verga in *Shevet yehudah*.[91]

---

[87] See Boyle, 'The Dynastic and Political History of the Il-Khans'; Gil, *The Kingdom of Ishmael during the Period of the Geonim* (Heb.), i. 430–1, 443–4; Levzion, 'Islamic Sects' (Heb.), 192; Mann, 'Une source de l'histoire juive au XIIIe siècle', 373–4; see also id., 'The Office of the Exilarch in Babylonia' (Heb.), 24–5.

[88] See Aescoly (ed.), *Jewish Messianic Movements* (Heb.), 164–7.   [89] Da Piera, *Shir ge'ulah*.

[90] See Baron, 'The Historical Outlook of Maimonides', esp. 111–13.

[91] Ibn Verga, *Shevet yehudah*, 70.

One could argue that all these examples show is that Jacob ben Elijah acquired just enough knowledge of general history to serve his apologetic purposes. However, he was probably also motivated to search for historical information by an interest in the condition of Jews throughout the world and curiosity about the political actions of kings and rulers, and when necessary he introduced this information into his work. There is evidence of this in another part of *Igeret ya'akov mivenetsiah*, which contains a long list of Christian hagiographical traditions (discussed in Chapter 4). Here too, the reason for dealing with hagiography is the religious disputation with Paul Christiani, but Jacob ben Elijah's analysis of Christian traditions attests to his broad intellectual horizons and his positive attitude towards the historical and literary aspects of hagiography, without any direct connection to Jewish–Christian polemic.

Another writer who made effective polemical use of Christian historiographical sources was Profayt Duran, who lived until around 1414. Duran is known as a scholar in many fields: philosophy, astronomy, grammar, biblical commentary, historiography, and polemics.[92] He developed historical and scientific methods, including a critical approach to texts,[93] and adopted the polemical techniques of the mendicant friars.[94] In his polemical works, Duran used (in addition to the New Testament) the writings of Jerome and Augustine, Peter Lombard's *Sentences*, Vincent de Beauvais' *Mirror of History*, and Nicholas of Lyra's *Postillae*.[95]

One example of Duran's method is his attempt, in *Shame of the Gentiles* (*Kelimat hagoyim*), to use the Gospels to show that Jesus and his disciples did not wish to nullify the Torah and its commandments (a theory accepted today by many scholars of early Christianity). According to this view, the abolition of circumcision and the rejection of other commandments by Paul were solely for non-Jews, in order to facilitate the spread of the new faith.[96] In this context, Duran felt it was important to show that the Gospels were written before the destruction of the Temple, and he cited a Christian tradition, which he found in Vincent de Beauvais' *Mirror of History*, that Peter and Paul were executed in Rome by Emperor Nero, who reigned before Vespasian, who was emperor when the Temple was destroyed.[97] He took this to mean that all of Jesus's disciples had died before the destruction of the Temple, and hence the Gospels must have been

---

[92] See Gutwirth, 'Religion and Social Criticism in Late Medieval Rousillon', esp. 135–6 nn. 1–2; Talmage, Introduction (Heb.) to Profayt Duran, *Polemical Writings*, 9–11; Kozodoy, 'A Study of the Life and Works of Profiat Duran'.

[93] Gutwirth, 'History and Apologetics in XVth Century Hispano-Jewish Thought'.

[94] J. Cohen, 'Profiat Duran's "The Reproach of the Gentiles"'.

[95] See Profayt Duran, *Kelimat hagoyim*, 5, 12 (ed. Talmage, 30, 64–5); Talmage, Introduction (Heb.) to Profayt Duran, *Polemical Writings*, 19.

[96] Profayt Duran, *Kelimat hagoyim*, 4 (ed. Talmage, 24–9).   [97] Ibid. (ed. Talmage, 26).

written earlier. Duran returned to this in another chapter, in which he tried to arrange the events of Christian history from the time of Jesus to the destruction of the Temple chronologically. There, based on the same source, he wrote that Peter and Paul arrived in Rome in the second year of Nero's reign and that in his last year as emperor Nero tried them for being Christians. He added that during his execution Paul turned eastwards, in the direction of the Temple, and prayed in Hebrew—putative proof of his atonement but certainly evidence of a strong attachment to the Temple.[98] The Christian descriptions of Paul's and Peter's executions also enabled Duran to attack an important Christian dogma: the transfer of Jesus's authority to Peter and from him to the papacy. Duran stressed that he found no mention of the transfer of authority from Peter to anyone else: 'for nothing is written that Peter gave his power to another to take his place in that mission when Nero, emperor of Rome, killed him for having preached faith in Jesus'.[99]

Christian chronology was therefore extremely important to Duran's polemic, and the historical proofs he cited against the Christians were based primarily on Christian sources. Another example is the ordination of priests and clerical celibacy. He claimed that ordination to the priesthood dated back to the time of Jesus's disciples, whereas the demand for celibacy did not appear until 700 years later.[100] Here Duran used one of the techniques of the mendicant friars, who distinguished between true and false passages in the Talmud and attempted to find in it—'like pearls in a dunghill'[101]—proof of Jesus's messiahship and divinity. Duran argued that the Christian doctrines of clerical celibacy and poverty were the fulfilment of one of Paul's prophecies, which envisaged Christianity's break with the original true faith.[102] Thus, Paul's writings served—as the talmudic and the midrashic literature did for the mendicant friars—as raw material: susceptible to negative interpretations, on the one hand, and to interpretations that supported Duran's understanding of historical events, on the other. In this fashion, Duran directly attacked the mendicant orders, which adhered, like the priesthood in general, to the idea of celibacy.

Isaac Abravanel's fundamental ideas belonged in one way or another to the old Jewish apocalyptic commentaries, nevertheless he felt that knowledge of general history and historiography, based on Christian sources, was the best means of

---

[98] Profayt Duran, *Kelimat hagoyim*, 11 (ed. Talmage, 60); see also Talmage, ibid., nn. 6, 8; Profayt Duran, *Teshuvot be'anshei aven*, 3: 6 (ed. Niclós Albarracín, 77); Niclós Albarracín, ibid. 21 n. 11; Carlos del Valle Rodríguez, ibid. 53 n. 32.

[99] Profayt Duran, *Kelimat hagoyim*, 8 (ed. Talmage, 45). Further on he raises the possibility that Peter nonetheless appointed someone, but he casts doubt on his authority to do so.

[100] Ibid. 9 (ed. Talmage, 47).

[101] Martini, *Dagger of Faith*, Introduction, 5 (Farnborough edn., 2–3), cited in J. Cohen, *The Friars and the Jews*, 137.   [102] Profayt Duran, *Kelimat hagoyim*, 9 (ed. Talmage, 47).

replying to the Christians. Abravanel also had access to Flavius Josephus's *Jewish Antiquities* and *Jewish War* in Latin translations, both of which were extremely important sources for Christian historiography in the Middle Ages. As mentioned above, Jerome stated that familiarity with Josephus was needed to understand the prophecies in the book of Daniel; and Cassiodorus, in his important book *Institutes of Divine and Secular Learning*, written around 560, counted them among the profane books that were necessary reading. As a result, they enjoyed a wide circulation, and for 1,000 years they were among the most widely read works of history.[103] In Yitzhak Baer's opinion, Abravanel was the first Jew, after the author of the *Book of Josippon*, to read Josephus.[104] Abraham Zacut was also familiar with Josephus's work and made wide use of his books,[105] but Hayim ibn Musa probably preceded both of them. In *Magen varomaḥ*, written in 1456 in response to Nicholas of Lyra's *Quaestio de adventu Christi*,[106] he grappled with several claims based on Josephus, including the 'Flavian testimony' (the section of *Jewish Antiquities* which mentions Jesus), that proof of the divinity of Jesus could be found in Jewish writings. Where Hebrew versions of Latin works were available, Ibn Musa compared the two versions in order to refute Christian arguments based on inaccurate translations. He claimed, for example, that Jerome's Latin translation of the Old Testament ought to be rejected because it differed from the Hebrew. One might have expected him to make a similar claim about the Latin translation of Josephus. The absence of the Flavian testimony from the *Book of Josippon* could have been grounds for an out-and-out refutation of Nicholas of Lyra's argument. However, Ibn Musa voiced no criticism of the differences between the *Book of Josippon* and the Latin *Jewish Antiquities*, which he believed to be written by Joseph ben Gorion (the Hebrew writer to whom the *Book of Josippon* is traditionally ascribed). Instead, he accepted the Flavian testimony as authentic. This does not mean that Ibn Musa accepted Nicholas of Lyra's citations of Josephus uncritically. As he stated, he was not obliged to believe everything written by Joseph ben Gorion, just as the Christians did not believe everything written in their history books. In addition, he stressed that Josephus regarded Jesus as a sage, not a prophet, a messiah, or a god.[107]

[103] See Guenée, *Histoire et culture historique dans l'Occident médiéval*, 302–3.

[104] Baer, 'Don Isaac Abravanel's Attitude to History and the State' (Heb.), 405; see Cirot, *Les Histoires générales d'Espagne*, 65.   [105] Neuman, 'Abraham Zacut, Historiographer', 616.

[106] *Quaestio de adventu Christi* was widely circulated and much used by Christian polemicists (see J. Cohen, *The Friars and the Jews*, 180–95).

[107] Ibn Musa, *Magen varomaḥ*, 109–11; see Cahn, 'Moses ben Abraham's Chroniques de la Bible'; Schreckenberg, *Die Flavius-Josephus-Tradition in Antike und Mittelalter*, id., *Rezeptionsgeschichte und textkritische Untersuchungen zu Flavius Josephus*.

Ibn Musa's, Zacut's, and Abravanel's use of Josephus's works attests to the growing openness to Christian historical sources during the second half of the fifteenth century but probably also reflects the need for broader historical knowledge in order to contend successfully with Christian polemics.

Use of Pagan Myths

At the beginning of chapter 6 of *Sefer yuḥasin*, Abraham Zacut followed one of the standard rules of rhetoric in the Middle Ages and provided an *accessus ad autores* or 'Introduction to the Author', explaining the purpose of his writing:[108] 'the knowledge of what has happened at all times to every nation . . . will be greatly beneficial to the [people of] Israel living within the Christian nation when disputing with them on their religion'.[109] Similar statements were also made in other sixteenth-century Jewish chronicles.[110] Many scholars have taken the 'Introduction to the Author' at face value and assumed that *Sefer yuḥasin* was written simply as an anti-Christian polemic, but they have generally failed to show why.[111] In fact, polemic was only part of the picture. Zacut had several other motives for writing, including an interest in history generally and in its moral and didactic possibilities.

Zacut's polemical method is well illustrated in his discussion of virgin births in Greek and Roman mythology, one of the main subjects of chapter 6 of *Sefer yuḥasin*.[112] In writing about the Pleiades (the seven daughters of Atlas and Pleione), Zacut discussed the third daughter Taygete (whom he called Ishtonifeis) at some length: 'The third [was], Ishtonifeis, mistress of Mars and mother of Apharkon and Zilabon, about whom it was said that she was eternally a virgin. And this is difficult for the Christians in their religion.'[113] Zacut demonstrated

---

[108] See Neuman, 'The Shebet Yehudah and Sixteenth Century Historiography', 86; Quain, 'The Medieval "Accessus ad auctores"'; Sermoneta, 'Engaging in the Liberal Arts in Jewish Society in Fourteenth-Century Italy' (Heb.), 254–5. *Sefer yuḥasin* was divided into six 'chapters' by Filipowski, its editor, not by Zacut. There is, however, some logic to the division, and it is useful (see Lacave, 'El "Sefer Yuhasin" de Abraham Zacut', 27). The sixth 'chapter' is a universal chronicle written later than the rest of *Sefer yuḥasin*. It has its own 'Introduction to the Author'.

[109] Zacut, *Sefer yuḥasin* (ed. Filipowski, 231*a*).

[110] For example, Elijah Capsali and Joseph Hakohen used the Expulsion from Spain to justify their interest in the history of Venice and the Ottomans (see Benayahu, Introduction (Heb.) to Capsali, *Seder eliyahu zuta*, iii. 15–21). However, a critical study of their works suggests they had other motives.

[111] Freiman, Introduction (Heb.) to Zacut, *Sefer yuḥasin*, p. ix; Baer, 'R. Abraham ben Samuel Zacut' (Heb.), col. 320.

[112] See R. Ben-Shalom, 'Graeco-Roman Myth and Mythology in the Historical Consciousness of Medieval Spanish Jewry' (Heb.); id., 'Polemic Historiography in *Sefer yuḥasin*' (Heb.).

[113] Zacut, *Sefer yuḥasin* (ed. Filipowski, 234*a*). Taygete was a nymph who served Artemis (Diana) and hunted with her. Like the other companions of Artemis, she was a virgin. Her son (by Zeus) was Lacedaemon (see Graves, *The Greek Myths*, 152, 473).

the polemical possibilities of the myth: Taygete, just like Mary the mother of Jesus, remained a virgin after giving birth. The story of Taygete is even more impressive than Mary's, since she remained a virgin after giving birth to two children, while Mary gave birth to only one.

The comparison between the birth of Jesus and the pagan myth was not new. It had been raised in religious disputations between pagans and Christians and between Jews and Christians in the second century CE.[114] However, this argument disappeared from Jewish–Christian disputations until the fifteenth century. Zacut apparently learned it from Shimon ben Tsemah Duran, whose *Magen avot* is often quoted in *Sefer yuḥasin* as a source of information on Jesus and Christianity.[115] According to Duran, belief in sexual intercourse between women and gods was common in the Hellenistic world. He cites an example from the *Alexander Romance* in which the magician Nectanebo misled Olympia (Alexander's mother) into believing that she had coupled with the god Ammon and then appeared to King Philip in dream and informed him that his wife had been impregnated by a god.[116] In Duran's view, the Christians combined one of Isaiah's prophecies ('Look, the virgin is with child and shall bear a son, and shall name him Immanuel' (Isa. 7: 14)[117]) with these pagan mythological stories and produced the myth of the Virgin Birth. However, a careful examination of the *Alexander Romance* shows that Duran was able to attack only the story of the birth from the Holy Spirit, not the issue of virgin birth itself.[118] Abraham Zacut's story supplements the picture drawn by Duran. The story of Taygete shows that the myth of virgin birth also existed in pagan mythology, and thus one can say— based on both of these stories—that birth from the Holy Spirit and Mary's virginity are pagan beliefs introduced into Christianity.

A link was made between the pagan myth and Christianity not only in order to challenge the uniqueness of Mary: it was part of a re-evaluation of Christianity in the fifteenth century that attempted to show that Christianity had pagan Hellenistic roots. On the one hand, polemicists placed Jesus within rabbinical Judaism and stressed that he did not challenge the Torah but was merely a pious

---

[114] See Justin Martyr, *Dialogue with Trypho*, 67; Rokeah, *Judaism and Christianity in the Light of Pagan Polemic* (Heb.), 30–1.

[115] See Freiman, Introduction (Heb.) to Zacut, *Sefer yuḥasin*, p. xv; Zacut, *Sefer yuḥasin* (ed. Filipowski, 200a).

[116] See Bonfils, *The Book of the Gests of Alexander of Macedon*, 12; *A Hebrew Alexander Romance*, 3–5, 40–4.

[117] 'Virgin' is the Greek and Latin translation of the Hebrew word *almah*, which was understood by Jews as 'young woman'.

[118] Shimon b. Tsemah Duran, *Keshet umagen*, 26. He felt it was important to cite an example from the *Alexander Romance* rather than from other mythological stories, because it is clear in the former that deceit and magic are involved.

fool;[119] on the other, they stated that his disciples and their followers distorted his teachings and introduced pagan elements. This is how Zacut understood the connection between the ancient pagan festival of the god Mercury and the Christian festival of May Day:

The first Pleiade is called Maia, the mother of Mercury, who was the third mistress of Jupiter, and the month of May was named after her, and then the Maias, [who were thought to be] respectable ladies, and the merchants would offer sacrifices and celebrations to Mercury, and that is the custom even nowadays in the land of Edom on the first day of May.[120]

Zacut believed that the May Day festivities were a direct continuation of the annual festival of the Roman merchants dedicated to Mercury, the god of commerce.[121] During the Middle Ages, May Day celebrations were accompanied by rites and processions in which young men were adorned with branches, leaves, and flowers, and in many cases these festivals were occasions for sexual licentiousness. In many places, it was also customary to light bonfires and emulate ancient rites of sacrifice. Modern anthropological research has noted the connection between May Day rituals and pagan sacrifices,[122] and Zacut drew a similar conclusion for polemical purposes. The polemical aspect here may not be as striking as in the case of Taygete, but the perception of the Christian festival as a pagan custom is consistent with the re-evaluation of Christianity as a religion closely linked to paganism. Knowledge of pagan myths enabled Jews to examine the origins of Christianity and to remove it as far as possible from the biblical world, a popular technique among Spanish Jews and Conversos in the seventeenth century, who were familiar with classical literature and Graeco-Roman mythology.[123]

MORAL LESSONS AND EXEMPLA

Seeking moral lessons from history was a common practice among the sages of the Talmud and Midrash. It is no wonder, then, that Jewish writers in the Middle Ages also adopted this approach and wrote exempla—anecdotes and short stories which exemplify a moral principle or an abstract idea presented as reports of actual events. The assumption that God directed history prevailed in the Middle

---

[119] Profayt Duran, *Kelimat hagoyim*, 4 (ed. Talmage, 24).

[120] Zacut, *Sefer yuḥasin* (ed. Filipowski, 234*a*).

[121] See Shatzman, *History of the Roman Republic* (Heb.), 326–7.

[122] See Frazer, *The Golden Bough*, i. 120–35; ii. 617–22; Ladero Quesada, *Las fiestas en la cultura medieval*, 54–7.

[123] See Kaplan, *From Christianity to Judaism*, 252–62; R. Ben-Shalom, 'The Foundation of Christianity in the Historical Perceptions of Medieval Jews'; id., 'Graeco-Roman Myth and Mythology in the Historical Consciousness of Medieval Spanish Jewry' (Heb.), 488–92.

Ages and was accepted by Jews and Christians alike. This assumption made it possible to interpret historical events as having theological and moral causes as well as natural ones. Natural-historical and moral-theological explanations generally did not contradict one another. For example, victories in battle were explained as the result of superior forces, as well as the result of God assisting one side or punishing the other.[124]

An example from *Megilat hamegaleh*, shows how Abraham bar Hiyya used an exemplum to teach a moral lesson.[125] It related how the wise Shabor, king of Persia, thwarted the schemes of Mani (216–77), the founder of Manichaeism.[126] The purpose of the story was to repudiate Manichaeism and show its dangerous consequences. Abraham bar Hiyya outlined the history of the world according to the prophecies in the book of Daniel and astrology. In his view, Mani was the second of three founders of false religions: the first was Emperor Constantine, who imposed Christianity on Rome, and the third was Muhammad. Constantine died shortly after the Christianization of the Roman empire, Mani was hanged by Shabor, and Muhammad was 'a scoundrel who lacks all majesty' and the 'mad one' (because of his epilepsy).[127] Abraham bar Hiyya intended to show the worthlessness of these religions compared with Judaism:

And I found in the history books of the nations that in the days of that *dybbuk* [conjunction of two stars], the evil Mani conspired in the land of Babylonia, and said there were two gods. One controls the good and the other controls the bad. [He also spoke] other nonsense that he thought would incite [people] to follow his erroneous ways and misled the world. Mani was one of the great ones of his family, and he became well known in the land of the Chaldeans and the Persians and in all of Babylonia and with his vain words incited many people. He collected a large, strong army and had in mind to go to Babylon and to raise a siege against it in the days of Shabor the king. He is known as Bahram son of Bahram, and he is the seventh among the kings called Shabor. And when King Shabor heard of [Mani] and his reputation and the many people collecting around him, he feared him and was frightened to do battle with him and sought in his heart some cunning, wise advice. He sent messengers to Mani by his greatest ministers and slaves to inform him that he believed in his words and his prophecy and wished to join him in his erroneous ways. With words of appeasement, he called upon him to come to Babylon, so that he might learn from him the customs of his religion and

---

[124] See Guenée, *Le Métier d'historien au Moyen Âge*, 209–10; on exempla, see Yassif, *The Hebrew Folk Tale* (Heb.), 137–8, 310–24, and bibliography, 606–7 n. 57, 640–1 n. 38.

[125] See Coleman, *Ancient and Medieval Memories*, 294–302.

[126] See Ort, *Mani*; Puech, *Le Manichéisme*.

[127] Abraham bar Hiyya, *Megilat hamegaleh*, 5: 137–8. Since Abraham bar Hiyya was unable to link Muhammad's death with the foundation of Islam (as he linked the deaths of Constantine and Mani to the foundations of their religions), he chose to attack his madness and humble origins (ibid. 140).

strengthen and assist him, until all the nations complied with his error. When Mani heard the words of Shabor's messengers, he found them pleasing, believed in them, and was seduced by them, and he went to Babylon with the messengers and all the great statesmen who believed in him and his ministers: about 400 in number. The king of Babylonia came out to meet and welcome him and placed him upon the throne before the people. And he ordered that all who came with him be brought into the royal palace to break bread with him. And when they came into his capital, they were all slaughtered upon one stone, and he ordered that they be hung upon the trees of the orchard within the capital. And then he said unto Mani: 'Arise and come into the house, and I will show you there my faith in your prophecy and the rightness of your words.' And he was brought into the orchard, where all of his company were hung. And [Shabor] said to him: 'You have said there are two gods. And one of them, he who controls evil, has ordered me to slaughter all these and hang them, and to inform everyone in the world that he is more powerful than the second god, who controls the good. And it seems to me that a great disagreement has occurred between them, the one who wanted your mission and the one who did not. And the best thing for a man like you is to be hung with those who believed in him, because of the disagreement between the two gods over him.' And he ordered that he be slaughtered and hung with the others. And that wicked man and all those with him died, and their memory was lost from the world, as the constellations of the stars testified. And it seems to me that in relation to that wicked Mani, Daniel said: 'His place will be taken by one who will dispatch an officer to exact tribute for royal glory, but he will be broken in a few days, not by wrath or by war' [Dan. 11: 20].[128]

Shabor's cunning is illustrated in the trick he used to bring Mani to Babylonia. The main message of the story, however, lies in Shabor's words to Mani in the orchard after he has killed his followers. Shabor takes Mani's doctrine to absurdity: if there are two gods in the world, how can one know which the founder of the doctrine is following? The belief that a bad god exists disrupts the order of the world and is likely to lead to the violation of all moral codes. Shabor's actions and his wisdom illustrate for the reader the perils of dualism and the damage anyone coming into contact with it is likely to incur.

Abraham bar Hiyya claimed that he consulted 'the history books of the nations'.[129] Baron suggested that Al-Biruni's *Chronology of Ancient Nations* could have been one of these,[130] especially as Al-Biruni also reported that Mani was

---

[128] Abraham bar Hiyya, *Megilat hamegaleh*, 5: 138–9.

[129] See G. D. Cohen, Introduction and notes to Ibn Daud, *Sefer hakabalah*, 41, notes to lines 147–51. According to Cohen, Abraham bar Hiyya relied on Muslim chronicles, and Ibn Daud received information about Mani from Abraham bar Hiyya or his source.

[130] Baron, 'The Historical Outlook of Maimonides', 72 n. 141; see Al-Biruni, *The Chronology of Ancient Nations*, 189–92. Another possible source is the book by Ahmed ben Avi Yakub Eli-Yacoubi, *Tarih*, in which a religious debate between Mani and the high priest of Persia is mentioned (see Ort, *Mani*, 31, 186–7).

hanged, whereas he actually died in prison after being captured by Bahram I.[131] Abraham bar Hiyya also erred in calling the king of Persia Shabor instead of Bahram I. As Baron remarked, however, among Jewish writers Shabor was the name of every Persian king, and it is also clear that Abraham bar Hiyya regarded Shabor and Bahram as the same person.[132] From the standpoint of people living in the twelfth century, who were familiar with the story from the Muslim chronicles (and perhaps also from oral traditions), it was historical truth in every sense.

The story about Mani also appears in Abraham ibn Daud's *Sefer hakabalah*, although there are fewer historical details, and the Persian king's great wisdom and how he succeeded in killing Mani are omitted.[133] Isaac Arama, an important fifteenth-century Spanish preacher, made homiletic use of the exemplum in his *Akedat yitshak*. Although he took it in full from *Megilat hamegaleh*, he made no mention of Abraham bar Hiyya but did refer to his source: 'the history books of the nations'.[134] Arama, like Abraham bar Hiyya, was interested in extracting a moral lesson from Mani's death. For Abraham bar Hiyya, it served to illustrate his historical view of the development of evil religions, while Arama included the exemplum within a homiletic discussion of 'Hear, O Israel! The Lord is our God, the Lord alone' (Deut. 6: 4) and monotheism. He attempted to show that dualism resulted from a philosophical error and that this error led to Mani's end. A large part of *Akedat yitshak* is devoted to Arama's criticism of the more extreme Jewish philosophers, and this exemplum is also aimed at them.[135] Obviously none of the Jewish philosophers challenged monotheism, but what Arama wanted to show was that philosophical thinking could lead to absurdity. In other parts of his book, he enumerated in detail the errors and misconceptions of philosophers and claimed that there was heresy in radical philosophy. Consequently, the reader could conclude that these philosophers would suffer the same fate as Mani or that radical philosophy leads to immorality. In order to reach this conclusion, Arama changed the story slightly. According to Abraham bar Hiyya, Mani's entourage consisted of 'all the great statesmen who believed in him and his ministers: about 400 in number'. Arama wrote that Mani came to Babylon with '400 of the greatest philosophers who adhered to his faith'.[136] Abraham bar Hiyya's polemical interest was directed outwards, and hence he was mainly interested in Mani as the

---

[131] See Asmussen, 'Manichean Literature'; Ort, *Mani*, 192, 212.

[132] Baron, *A Social and Religious History of the Jews*, vi. 428 n. 70.

[133] Ibn Daud, *Sefer hakabalah*, ch. 4, lines 108–10 (ed. Cohen: Heb. section, 30–1; Eng. section, 41); see G. D. Cohen, Introduction and notes, ibid. 41, notes to lines 150–1.

[134] See Arama, *Akedat yitshak*, v. 28a–b.

[135] See Baer, *A History of the Jews in Christian Spain*, ii. 253–9; Heller-Wilensky, *Rabbi Isaac Arama and His Teaching* (Heb.), 16–26.   [136] Arama, *Akedat yitshak*, v. 28a–b.

founder of a false religion; Arama looked inwards and censured the philosophiz-
ing educated class in Jewish society.

Even if the authors were aiming to impart moral lessons, they still had to
study general history and select what they needed from the sources. The written
exempla, therefore, do not contain all the historical knowledge available to them,
but only those materials that served their purposes. For example, Isaac Nathan, a
leader of the Jews of Arles in the fifteenth century, claimed to be well versed in the
historical works of the Christian priests from Rome and France. He regarded
Christian political-historical writing (particularly on what he called the 'wars of
the knights') as a praiseworthy commemoration of great men and was particularly
interested in the history of ancient Greece and Rome. He discussed Alexander
the Great and mentioned the astuteness of Roman leaders, their advisers, and
sages. He used many exempla in *Me'amets koaḥ*, including one which describes
the siege of Athens during the reign of Philip II of Macedonia (382–336 BCE), the
father of Alexander the Great. Isaac Nathan claimed that he heard the story in
Provence. This, however, was not the product of some storyteller's imagination,
but a popular tradition that preserved an accurate historical testimony. Although
the exemplum refers to Alexander the Great's father, it was not included in the
literary corpus known as the *Alexander Romance*. It is found in Plutarch's *Lives*,
but that was unknown in western Europe until the end of the fourteenth century.[137] It is impossible to say whether Isaac Nathan learned the story from an
oral tradition that preserved it during the centuries when Plutarch's work was
unknown, or it found its way to local storytellers from the Aragonese translation,
which was made in the court of the pope at Avignon,[138] but his use of the exemplum reveals that Jews in the Middle Ages acquired historical knowledge through
various channels in addition to chronicles: family traditions, folk tales, exempla—
a fact that is also confirmed by the writings of Abraham ibn Daud and Elijah
Capsali.[139]

[137] Plutarch's *Lives* was translated into Aragonese in 1388, and some chapters were translated into
Latin in the early fifteenth century (see Bergua Cavero, 'El Príncipe de Viana'; Cary, *The Medieval
Alexander*, 267; Giustiniani, 'Sulle traduzioni latine delle Vite di Plutarco nell Quattrocento'; Green,
Spain and the Western Tradition, iii. 123; Lopez Ferez, 'La traducción castellana de las "Vidas"';
Luttrell, 'Greek Histories Translated and Compiled for Juan Fernández de Heredia'; Pade, 'The
Latin Translations of Plutarch's Lives in Fifteenth-Century Italy'; Rincón González, 'Los Reyes
Católicos y sus modelos plutarquistas'). Several excerpts were known earlier, as reflected in the writ-
ings of John of Salisbury (see *Policraticus*, col. 540).

[138] In 1395 an Italian translation was made on the basis of the Aragonese translation (see Luttrell,
'Greek Histories Translated and Compiled for Juan Fernández de Heredia', 405).

[139] MS Guenzburg 113/1 (Russian State Library, Moscow—Institute of Microfilmed Hebrew
Manuscripts, no. 6793), fo. 87*b*; see R. Ben-Shalom, 'Exempla and Historical Consciousness in the
Middle Ages' (Heb.); id., 'The Authorship of the *Me'ir nativ* Concordance' (Heb.); id., 'The Tortosa
Disputation' (Heb.). At about the same time, this exemplum was used as a political allegory by the

Abraham Zacut explicitly stated his position on the purpose of historiography in the 'Introduction to the Author' of chapter 6 of *Sefer yuḥasin*. He believed that knowledge of the history of the non-Jewish nations, as well as of that of the Jewish people, 'reinforces faith in God's power'.[140] In his view, God directed history, and anyone with knowledge of history would recognize the imprint of the invisible hand of God on the world. History also taught several important articles of faith, such as personal providence and reward and punishment. The examples that Zacut gave were all drawn from the biblical and Second Temple periods, including the Flood and earthquakes during the reigns of King Uzziah and King Herod, but they were only a small part of an overall historiographical and philosophical method that regarded the sequence of events from Creation until the End of Days as an ongoing expression of divine providence. Zacut stressed this in the very first sentence of the 'Introduction to the Author', in which he recommended 'knowledge about what happened at all times to every nation'.[141] The traces of God's hand are in every event, everywhere, and every nation. He was probably writing in opposition to another historiographical and philosophical approach prevalent among Jews which found the expression of divine providence only in the specific history of the Jews.[142] Zacut illustrated his method through an interpretation of the biblical commandment to 'remember the days of old' (Deut. 32: 7). Unlike earlier Bible commentators (Rashi, Ibn Ezra, Maimonides) who interpreted 'days of old' to refer only to the distant, biblical past, Zacut interpreted it as a commandment to acquire knowledge of all history.

Three of the five examples cited by Zacut in his 'Introduction to the Author' deal with earthquakes,[143] including one during the reign of King Uzziah (Amos 1: 1; Zech. 14: 5), which he had also mentioned twice earlier in *Sefer yuḥasin*, where he noted that its intensity was comparable only to the earthquake in the time of Herod.[144] Why did Zacut stress such a marginal event, mentioned only twice in the Bible, without any historical background or accompanying story? This is probably because of the historical significance that he ascribed to natural disasters. They are attributed to God's action and the positions of the stars, which are also directly under God's control.[145] Here, Zacut was in agreement with views prevailing in Europe among Jews and non-Jews alike.[146]

Castilian bishop Rodrigo Sánchez de Arévalo (1404–70) (*Suma de la política*, 287; see Edwards, 'Conversos, Judaism and the Language of Monarchy', 217).

[140] Zacut, *Sefer yuḥasin* (ed. Filipowski, 231*a*).   [141] Ibid.

[142] Profayt Duran's lost work, *Ma'amar zikhron hashemadot*, may have been an example of this.

[143] Zacut, *Sefer yuḥasin* (ed. Filipowski, 231*a*).   [144] See ibid. 9*b*, 91*a*.

[145] Ibid. 248*a–b*, 225*b*.

[146] See Rossi, *Meor einayim*, 'Kol elohim' (Vilna edn., 16; trans. Weinberg, 22–3); Ibn Daud, *Zikhron divrei romi* (Mantua edn., 22; ed. Vehlow, 110–13).

One of the many earthquakes that hit Constantinople illustrates the link that Zacut made between biblical exemplum and historical event:

In the year 5650, which is in truth 4211,[147] there was a great earthquake in the land, four months in Constantinople, and when a Jewish boy said: 'Holy, holy, holy, is the Lord of Hosts' [Isa. 6: 3], the quake subsided, and it was established that this verse should be recited.[148] And it seems to me this is the truth, as we found on the day of Uzziah's earthquake when Isaiah spoke this verse, and our rabbis of blessed memory said: 'Why does the world stand according to the sacred order, etc.? So that the world will not be destroyed.'[149]

The numerous earthquakes were an expression of God's anger with humanity. However, in the Jewish tradition there is a topos that recitation of the benediction can assuage God's anger and stop earthquakes. In a change to his usual practice, Zacut stressed his faith in the veracity of this story of how the Christians adopted the Jewish practice in their Sanctus benediction.

For Zacut, biblical events and later historical events merged to provide a model for human behaviour, on the one hand, and an understanding of God's actions, on the other. In this, he followed the sages of the Mishnah and the Talmud, who were not interested in the figures in the Bible as real historical people, but rather as moral examples.[150] However, Zacut also applied this method to the post-biblical period and included Herod among his subjects.

Along with the moral lessons that could be extracted from it, Zacut claimed that history could provide consolation for the heart and amusement for the mind, a view that even Maimonides, who rejected historiography, concurred with.[151] This is why the historical books of the Bible were read to the high priest on the eve of Yom Kippur. Some non-Jewish rulers wrote history, and in this they followed the biblical example of Ahasuerus, who recorded the events of Esther in the 'Annals of the Kings of Media and Persia' (Esther 10: 2). Apparently Zacut cited this biblical incident in order to provide the profession of historian with some respectability and to refute those Jews who argued that historiography was an imitation of non-Jewish ways.[152] He also included moral sayings of non-Jewish philosophers, such as Socrates, Pythagoras, Aristotle, Ptolemy, and, as a negative example, Epicurus.[153]

---

[147] The dates in *Sefer yuḥasin* are often incorrect due to copying errors. I have reproduced them as they appear in Filipowski's edition without attempting to provide the correct ones.

[148] Presumably by the Christians.

[149] Zacut, *Sefer yuḥasin* (ed. Filipowski, 247a); see also 9b; Rashi on Amos 1: 1; David Kimhi on Zech. 14: 5.   [150] Herr, 'The Sages' Concept of History' (Heb.), 134.

[151] Zacut, *Sefer yuḥasin* (ed. Filipowski, 232a).

[152] Ibid.   [153] Ibid. (ed. Filipowski, 239b, 238b, 240a–b, 245b–246a, 240a).

The moral approach to general and Jewish history was apparently accepted by many of the exiles from Spain. It was strikingly expressed, for example, by Abraham ben Jacob Gavison in *Omer hashikhehah*, a commentary on the book of Proverbs, in which he cited historical examples to illustrate numerous moral maxims. Gavison referred to the 'Annals of the Kings of Media and Persia' and also mentioned various stories from Muslim books of history and Spanish oral traditions about the relationships between Jewish courtiers and kings in Castile and Portugal.[154]

Viewing history as a source of exempla was not exceptional among Jews in the Middle Ages. Maimonides also perceived Jewish history as a moral lesson for the educated, and his approach was very influential.[155] It was also part of the general historiographical approach in Christian Europe, which was based on the writings of classical historians, such as Livy—who claimed that history was a means of teaching moral, practical, and political lessons through stories of rulers and wars—and Cicero—who applied the rules of rhetoric to history for didactic purposes. In the early Middle Ages, there was little interest in the past in itself. Although in the twelfth century, a clear historical awareness developed among Christian historians, they nonetheless saw little point in discussing past events at length, unless they contained some moral lesson. Most Jewish chronicles dealt with the chain of tradition and the order of the generations, but, in those too, moral lessons were widespread.[156] Christian exempla with historiographical or hagiographical content were enthusiastically imitated by Jewish thinkers in Spain and southern France, also using exempla from Jewish history. The phenomenon seems to have become more prevalent during the fifteenth century, so it is not surprising that Solomon ibn Verga praised the Christian custom of 'knowing of ancient things to take counsel from them',[157] and it was an accepted practice in at least one circle of fifteenth-century Spanish Jewry, not an innovation, as some scholars have argued.[158] In contrast to Ibn Verga's attempt to preserve and develop this historiographical trend, some exiled Spanish Jews rejected the reading of history books (even the *Book of Josippon*), because they were thought to be of no

---

[154] See Gavison, *Omer hashikhehah*, 72a, 55b; for the story about the Jewish noble in Toledo—probably Samuel Abulafia—see ibid. 14b; for the story about the plot of Portuguese aristocrats against the king and Isaac Abravanel's flight to Spain, see ibid. 21b–22a.

[155] See Baron, 'The Historical Outlook of Maimonides', 109, 113.

[156] See Bonfil, Introduction (Heb.) to Rossi, *Writings*, 66–7; Coleman, *Ancient and Medieval Memories*, 297–324; Gutwirth, 'The Expulsion from Spain and Jewish Historiography', 143, 158 n. 19; see also Bonfil, 'How Golden was the Age of the Renaissance in Jewish Historiography?', 89–90; Gutwirth, 'The Jews in 15th Century Castilian Chronicles', esp. 396.

[157] Ibn Verga, *Shevet yehudah*, 21, 30.   [158] Kochan, *The Jew and His History*, 1.

moral benefit. They tried to propose a spiritual alternative, mainly based on kabbalistic interpretations.[159]

HISTORICAL AND SCIENTIFIC INTEREST

The first signs of Jewish interest in historiography for scientific and cultural purposes appeared in the twelfth and thirteenth centuries. Jewish writers made frequent use of Christian historiographical sources, but the earliest statements about the virtues of historiography were made by Abraham Zacut and Isaac Abravanel at the end of the fifteenth century. Zacut found Christian historiography often contained important information that was missing from Jewish works. He stated that in such cases, Jews should be aware of the accomplishments of Christian historiography:

At times [the Christians] speak of things related in the Babylonian and Jerusalem Talmuds and the Midrash and write about them in greater detail. For instance, of King Bar Kokhba, the years of Titus the Wicked, the affairs of Hadrian the Oppressor, in whose time were the battle of Bethar and the ten martyrs, and after him, Antoninus the Good, his era and that of his good brother as well as many other affairs.[160]

The reader of *Sefer yuḥasin*, particularly chapter 6, could learn much about the work of dozens of ancient philosophers and writers, the founders of Greek philosophy and science, and when they lived, just as they could from Christian Spanish chronicles. In these parts Christian chronology often contradicted Jewish chronology, and Zacut needed to reconcile the two.[161] Like Ibn Daud and Joseph ben Tsadik, he dated Hippocrates, Euclid, and Plato to the time of Esther, and Ptolemy to the sixty-fifth year after the destruction of the Temple.[162] Like any historian, Zacut had to weigh the information from his sources; however, he

---

[159] See Shamir, 'On the Meaning of an Excerpt from Abraham Galante's Commentary on Lamentations' (Heb.), 226.　　　　　　　[160] Zacut, *Sefer yuḥasin* (ed. Filipowski, 231a–b).

[161] On the subject of chronology, see First, *Jewish History in Conflict*, esp. 19–20 on Zacut.

[162] Zacut, *Sefer yuḥasin* (ed. Filipowski, 238b–246a, 10b). Zacut mentioned Pythagoras, Anaxrasus (?), Myson, Anaximander, Anaximenes, Aesop, Anaxagoras, Hippocrates, Gorgias, Socrates, Isocrates, Plato, Epicurus, Demosthenes, Aristotle, Apollonius of Tyana, Damis, Cleistenes, Dinocratis, Archimedes, Philo of Alexandria, Manetho, Cato the Younger, Abraxas (Basilides?), Tully, Cicero and his son (?), Lucretius, Apollodorus, Cicero, Virgil, Livy, Ovid, Valerius, Grattius, Seneca, Lucan, Annaeus Cornutus, Pliny the Elder, and Pliny the Younger. Chapter 50 of Joseph ben Tsadik's *Kitsur zekher tsadik* is a chronicle of events from Jewish and general history, beginning with the Creation and ending in 1487, which also attempted to correlate the dates of Greek and Roman philosophers with those of biblical characters and talmudic sages. Following Ibn Daud, he dated Aristotle to the time of Shimon Hatsadik, Hippocrates to the time of Mordecai and Esther, Ptolemy to the time of R. Akiva's disciples, and Galen to the time of Judah Hanasi (see Joseph b. Tsadik, *Kitsur zekher tsadik* (ed. Neubauer, 88, 90); Ibn Daud, *Sefer hakabalah*, ch. 3, lines 47, 68–70; ch. 4, lines 101–2 (ed. Cohen: Heb. section, 21, 23, 30; Eng. section, 29, 30–1, 40).

rarely managed to reach an unequivocal conclusion. He claimed that the physician Galen lived at the same time as Judah Hanasi, the redactor of the Mishnah
(late second century), following Jewish sources, but also mentioned that Christian
historiography placed Galen seventy years after the destruction of the Temple,
without challenging its credibility or claiming that the Jewish tradition was preferable.[163] He also mentioned a chronological inconsistency between Jewish and
Christian traditions of the Egyptian exile and, again, did not decide which tradition he thought more reliable —although he was happy that the discrepancy was
only small:

The Egyptian exile began in 3541, after the death of Joseph. Isidore [of Seville] said that
it was 144 years after the death of Joseph, and Augustine said 145 years, and our sages
said, according to the tradition, about 140 years after the death of Joseph, and there is a
slight discrepancy between them of 4 years, if only it was so in all other reckonings.[164]

Zacut spared no criticism of Christian historiography, stating that it was not reliable from a religious standpoint (in the stories of the miracles), in its calculation
of dates, or its description of events. To substantiate this claim, he cited his own
experience: 'I have seen with my own eyes in my time many things, when after a
certain act took place [the Christians] wrote it in their books of history, and it was
not so.'[165] Consequently, Abraham Neuman, Ephraim Urbach, and J. L. Lacave
all claimed that Zacut had little regard for Christian sources, since on many
matters, particularly chronology, they were opposed to the Jewish tradition.[166]
However, Zacut also criticized Jewish historiography. He thought that the
authoritative *Book of Josippon* included exaggerated descriptions of events and
inaccurate dates: 'While everyone relies on Joseph ben Gorion Hakohen, nonetheless I do not rely on him, for he also speaks in hyperbole and in an arrogant
tongue and makes calculations that do not match the literal meaning of the
Torah.'[167] The phrase 'for he also' shows clearly that Zacut was comparing Jewish
and Christian historiography. He also mentioned chronological errors in Ibn
Daud's *Sefer hakabalah* and Maimonides' work. Zacut did not reject Christian
sources out of hand. If he had, he would hardly have made such extensive use of
them. However, he drew a distinction between absolute religious truth, found in

[163] Zacut, *Sefer yuḥasin* (ed. Filipowski, 198b–199a, 246a).
[164] Ibid. (ed. Filipowski, 234a). I have corrected Filopowski's version according to MS Hebrew
d.16 (Neubauer 2798) (Bodleian Library, Oxford), fo. 188a.
[165] See Zacut, *Sefer yuḥasin* (ed. Filipowski, 231a).
[166] See Neuman, 'Abraham Zacut, Historiographer', 604–5; Urbach, 'Eastern Jewish Literature'
(Heb.), 6; Lacave, 'Las fuentes Cristianas del Sefer Yuhasin', 96.
[167] Zacut, *Sefer yuḥasin* (ed. Filipowski, 231b); see Neuman, 'Abraham Zacut, Historiographer',
614–18.

the Bible, and relative truth, found in history books. He told his readers that by no means should they think 'that *everything* written in their history, things which I have cited, are entirely the truth like the books of our sacred Torah'.[168]

As mentioned, Zacut noted that Christian writers provided more detail than the Talmud of several historical events, and, thus, Christian historiographical traditions were sometimes more reliable than Jewish ones. Zacut cited several different Jewish versions of the number of generations between Boaz and David (Ruth 4: 21–2), but in all of them the members of the family would have had to have been blessed with miraculous longevity. Therefore, he preferred the Christian version, which included several more generations, although he assumed that the Christians received this information from the Jews: 'And the wise men of the Gentiles understood that there were other generations between them, perhaps they took that from the sages of Israel, and so it transpires.'[169] However, this assumption is problematic, because it is not known from any other source. Elsewhere Zacut stated explicitly that one should not resolve a chronological difficulty by holding that someone lived a miraculously long life.[170] He also criticized the accepted Jewish dating of the Bar Kokhba revolt—for example, in *Sefer hakabalah*—and, here too, preferred the Christian dating.[171]

In other cases, Zacut preferred Jewish chronology. For example, he found a wide discrepancy between Christian and Jewish dates for the Exodus and asserted that the Jewish date was the correct one. Christians and Jews agreed that the Exodus began 400 years after the birth of Isaac, but the Jews held that Isaac was born 2,448 years after the Creation, and Christians that he was born 3,283 years after the Creation.[172] The debate, then, centred on how events were calculated from the Creation. The same holds true for the birth of Abraham: the two traditions disagreed by 1,039 years. On the birth of King David, Zacut also decided in favour of the Jewish tradition.[173]

In his discussion of Abraham, Zacut cited a work called the 'Chronicles of the Christians':

[Abraham], of blessed memory, proclaimed that there is a sole [God] in the world, and from the pulpit in Egypt he preached the science of astronomy and astrology to demon-

---

[168] Zacut, *Sefer yuḥasin* (ed. Filipowski, 231a; see also 81a–81b); Neuman, 'Abraham Zacut, Historiographer', 611, 613; for criticism of the Hebrew and Christian chronology, see Zacut, *Sefer yuḥasin* (ed. Filipowski, 8b); Neuman, 'Abraham Zacut, Historiographer', 616–18.

[169] Zacut, *Sefer yuḥasin* (ed. Filipowski, 7b).   [170] Ibid. (ed. Filipowski, 87a).

[171] Ibid. (ed. Filipowski, 245b).

[172] Ibid. (ed. Filipowski, 234b, 6a; see also 233b). Christian historians, like their Jewish counterparts, tried to date the Exodus as early as possible, in order to establish the greater antiquity of their civilization; pagans dated it as late as possible (see Rokeah, *Judaism and Christianity in the Light of Pagan Polemic* (Heb.), 143–4 n. 143).   [173] Zacut, *Sefer yuḥasin* (ed. Filipowski, 233a–b, 236b).

strate the existence of the sole [God] from the movements of the heavenly bodies, and that he created them as is stated in the 'Chronicles of the Christians'.[174]

Later he cited another Christian tradition that 'in Egypt there was no wisdom at all and the king asked [Abraham] to teach him arithmetic, astronomy, and astrology, and then he taught everyone'.[175] Abraham the philosopher, astronomer, astrologer, and first monotheist was a key figure in the popular literary motif of the theft of wisdom from the Jewish sages, which first appeared during the Second Temple period. Stories of the Jewish patriarchs as the source of wisdom are prevalent in midrashic literature, and they can be found in the writings of Artapanus and Josephus.[176] They were also popular in Christian historiography. Eusebius, for example, followed Artapanus in stating that Abraham taught the king of Egypt astrology. In doing so, he represented a Christian historiographical trend that attempted to prove that the civilization, theology, and philosophy of Abraham and Moses preceded those of the Greeks and, hence, that the Greeks were plagiarists.[177] This trend continued in the Middle Ages: Cassiodorus followed Josephus in stating that Abraham introduced arithmetic and astronomy to the Egyptians, as did Isidore of Seville and Rabanus Maurus.[178] Abraham as civilizing hero was a major theme of Spanish historiography, in particular in the *Grande e general estoria* of King Alfonso X the Wise of Castile.[179] There Abraham is depicted as the culmination of a long process of religious development: at first humans worshipped stones; then religious faith advanced to higher levels: trees and plants, animals, the four elements (earth, water, air, fire) and the stars; the final stage was faith in a sole, omnipotent God. It was Abraham who understood

[174] Ibid. (ed. Filipowski, 5*a*).

[175] Ibid. (ed. Filipowski, 233*a*–*b*). Lacave tried to determine the identity of the writer of this chronicle and decided it was impossible ('Las fuentes Cristianas del Sefer Yuhasin', 96–8). However, its structure, its division into periods, and the chronology it cites suggest that the author was a pupil of Isidore of Seville. In Lacave's view, it was written in the fifteenth century.

[176] See Schalit, Introduction and notes (Heb.) to Josephus, *Jewish Antiquities*, vol. i, pp. xlviii–xlix. The view that the Jews are the source of all wisdom is a topos that recurred in many of the books written by Jews in Spain and Provence (see Idel, 'Studies in the Method of the Author of *Sefer hameshiv*' (Heb.), 233–4; Zinberg, *History of Jewish Literature* (Heb.), ii. 395–8).

[177] See Bar-Kochva, 'Jewishness and Greekness' (Heb.), 460–2; Gutman, *Hellenistic Jewish Literature* (Heb.), ii. 161–2; Rappel, *The Seven Wisdoms* (Heb.), 47, 62 n. 3; Rokeah, *Jews, Pagans and Christians in Conflict*, 187–91.

[178] Rappel, *The Seven Wisdoms* (Heb.), 47, 62 n. 5. According to Josephus, Abraham was not the source of wisdom but merely brought it from the Chaldeans to the Egyptians (*Jewish Antiquities*, 1.8.2).

[179] Alfonso commissioned two works of history: *Estoria de España* or *Primera crónica general de España*, a history of Spain, was written between 1260 and 1284, the date of his death; *Grande e general estoria*, a universal history, was begun later and interrupted work on the *Primera crónica general de España* (see Alfonso X, *Primera crónica general de España*; id., *Grande e general estoria*; see Fernández-Ordóñez (ed.), *Alfonso X el Sabio y las crónicas de España*; id., *Las 'Estorias' de Alfonso el Sabio*).

that the stars were not gods and that they had no power themselves but derived it from the one true God.[180]

This motif, in its Christian version, is found in *Sefer yuḥasin*: Abraham demonstrates on the basis of the movements of the stars the existence of the sole God who created them. Abraham's acknowledgement that the stars are limited in their power and are created entities was the highest stage of religious development. According to Zacut, the Christian historical information about Abraham in Egypt complements his depiction in the Talmud and the exegetical midrashic work *Genesis Rabbah*. In the Jewish sources, Abraham is described as the harbinger of belief in a world created *ex nihilo*. The Christian sources tell of his publicizing belief in Creation in Egypt. Combining the Jewish and Christian sources provides a fuller picture of biblical history and shows the biblical figures in a brighter light.

Similarly, Christian historiography confirmed that Job was Jobab son of Zerah, king of Edom (see Gen. 36: 33), and that Moses was the author of the book of Job.[181] In a discussion of Shimon Hatsadik, Zacut provided the Christian version of his name—'the Righteous'—which he earned because he was merciful and treated the people with compassion, unlike the high priests who preceded him.[182] The Christian sources also contained information about Shimon's meeting with Alexander the Great and about Alexander's war with the Samarians.[183]

Zacut's astrological writings also reveal a concern with the accurate dating of historical events. In his *Mishpat* (Prognosis) written in 1498, he elucidated his historical and astrological conceptions, which were based primarily on the writings of Abraham bar Hiyya. The work relates events of world history to the stars and the signs of the zodiac and embodies the view that history is predetermined and the future can be discovered through observation of the heavens. The *Mishpat* had three purposes: to explain past events using Abraham bar Hiyya's method, including those that affected Iberian Jews before and after the Expulsion; to foretell events of the near future, not necessarily those related to the fate of the Jewish people, also using Abraham bar Hiyya's method; and to calculate the end of the diaspora and the coming of the messiah, in which Zacut differed from Abraham bar Hiyya.[184]

---

[180] See Fraker, 'Abraham in the "General Estoria" '.

[181] Zacut, *Sefer yuḥasin* (ed. Filipowski, 6*b*). The origin of the information about Jobab son of Zerah is from the Greek version of the book of Job, which includes extra material after Job 42: 17 (see Mack, *Job and the Book of Job in Rabbinic Literature* (Heb.), 49–50).

[182] Zacut, *Sefer yuḥasin* (ed. Filipowski, 78*a*).   [183] Ibid. (ed. Filipowski, 12*b*).

[184] Zacut, *Mishpat*, 179–81; see Guttmann, Introduction (Heb.) to Abraham bar Hiyya, *Megilat hamegaleh*, pp. xxi–xxx.

The determination of the exact dates of the Exodus and the reign of King David in *Sefer yuḥasin* takes on special importance in light of the astrological and apocalyptic scheme in the *Mishpat*, as Zacut used these two dates and the visions in the book of Daniel to calculate the End of Days. According to his calculations, it would commence in 1504 and the war of Gog and Magog would take place in 1531.[185] In Isaac Abravanel's writings, the date of the Exodus is similarly important. He also accepted Abraham bar Hiyya's historical-apocalyptical approach and arrived at the same date as Zacut, but he deducted one year, for the 'fragmented years' and thought that the End of Days would start in 1503 and end in 1530. The date of the Exodus was the subject of a long-standing dispute with the Christians, and Abraham bar Hiyya mentioned debates he had had with Christian monks on the subject.[186]

Isaac Abravanel, who possessed a highly developed historical sense, greatly esteemed Christian chronological methods, which involved using a single continuous timeline to fix the date of each and every event, and he used them to criticize Jewish chronology and historical texts.[187] The introduction to his commentary on the books of Kings contains an example of a critical examination of the Talmud and the use of Christian historiography to resolve textual and interpretative difficulties.[188] He tried to present a historical survey of the times the Jewish people had been sent into exile according to the calculations in *Seder olam*. At the end of the list of exiles, he attempted to clarify the fate of the Jewish community of Alexandria, which dated from the time of the First Temple.[189] According to the Babylonian Talmud the Alexandrian community was destroyed by Alexander the Great, but, according to Abravanel, the Tosafists had already noted that Alexander lived before the destruction of the Second Temple, while the Alexandrian community disappeared afterwards,[190] and they preferred the account in the Jerusalem Talmud, which attributed the destruction of the community to Trajan—the solution accepted by modern scholars.[191] Abravanel was not satisfied with this and argued that the Babylonian version should not be rejected in its entirety, but only an error made by one scribe, who added the

---

[185] Zacut, *Mishpat*, 184.

[186] Abravanel, *Ma'ayenei hayeshuah*, 9: 7 (Jerusalem edn., 360–1); see Abraham bar Hiyya, *Sefer ha'ibur*, 45; see also Baer, 'The Messianic Movement in Spain at the Time of the Expulsion' (Heb.), 393; Netanyahu, *Don Isaac Abravanel*, 226; Silver, *A History of Messianic Speculation in Israel*, 120–1.

[187] Abravanel on 1 Sam. 13: 1 (*Perush linevi'im rishonim*, 232).

[188] For a comprehensive discussion on this subject, see Lawee, 'On the Threshold of the Renaissance', 313–14.

[189] Abravanel on Kings, Introduction (*Perush linevi'im rishonim*, 421); see Milikowski, '*Seder olam* and Jewish Chronology' (Heb.).

[190] This is not found in the Tosafot on *Sukah* printed in the Babylonian Talmud.

[191] See Kasher, *The Jews of Hellenistic and Roman Egypt* (Heb.), 310–11.

sobriquet 'Great' to Alexander's name. He asserted that the two Talmuds dealt with different events: the first (related in the Jerusalem Talmud) occurred during the time of Trajan, when many Alexandrian Jews were killed, but the community was not totally destroyed; the second (related in the Babylonian Talmud) was in the time of the Roman emperor Alexander Severus, who wiped out the community.

Abravanel's historical reconstruction is not very convincing. Alexander Severus was compelled to suppress several revolts in the empire, but nothing is known about his having taken any action against the Jews of Alexandria. Moreover, there is no known source that Abravanel could have used.[192] However, what is more important is Abravanel's criticism of the Tosafists. He stressed that they were mistaken because of their ignorance of historiographical sources: 'and all this happened to them because they did not see the chronicles of the kings of Rome'.[193] Here he expressed his belief that general historiography was an essential interpretative tool. The Spanish biblical commentator, Alonso Tostado (c.1400–55), levelled a similar criticism at Rashi and other Jewish commentators, arguing that their work was limited because they were not familiar with the history and literature of non-Jews. According to Solomon Gaon, Abravanel was influenced by Tostado.[194]

In this instance, historiography was able to resolve the contradictions in the sources, and, in Abravanel's view, save the honour of the Babylonian Talmud. Abravanel used legitimate methods of historical enquiry. He was aware of the contradictions in the Jewish sources and tried to reconcile them by using another source. The Tosafists, on the other hand, used only the Jewish sources, and, even though their solution is the one accepted by modern scholars, the method Abravanel used is superior and more likely to produce accurate results. Moreover, Abravanel took broader historical considerations into account. For example, in his discussion, he identified the emperor and showed concern for the history of the Alexandrian community, its institutions, economic status, and demographic strength.[195] Azariah de Rossi (1513/14–78) devoted an entire chapter of *Meor ein-*

[192] In *Primera crónica general de España*, there is a description of Alexander Severus, but there is no mention of his actions in Alexandria (Alfonso X, *Primera crónica general de España*, i. 160b). Abravanel may have relied on information he found in Paulus Orosius on Lucius Septimus Severus, who suppressed the revolts of the Jews (see Orosius, *Seven Books of History against the Pagans*, 7: 17).

[193] Abravanel on Kings, Introduction (*Perush linevi'im rishonim*, 421); see Melamed, 'The Perception of Jewish History in Italian Jewish Thought of the Sixteenth and Seventeenth Centuries', 162.

[194] See Gaon, *The Influence of the Catholic Theologian Alfonso Tostado on the Pentateuch Commentary of Isaac Abravanel*, 22.

[195] Abravanel on Kings, Introduction (*Perush linevi'im rishonim*, 425); see Lawee, 'On the Threshold of the Renaissance', 313–14; Veltri, 'The Humanist Sense of History and the Jewish Idea of Tradition'.

ayim to the end of the Jewish community in Alexandria. He rejected Abravanel's reconstruction, but used the same methodology to propose that the 'emperor' mentioned in the Babylonian Talmud was Tiberius Julius Alexander, prefect of Egypt.[196]

Abravanel also used the historical literature available to him to resolve problems with the Bible, although many of the problems he saw were the result of his historical thinking. For example, according to the Bible, when King Abijah of Judah triumphed over King Jeroboam of Israel, the number of casualties from the kingdom of Israel was 500,000 (2 Chr. 13: 17). In Abravanel's Latin copy of Josephus's *Jewish Antiquities*, the number was 50,000. Abravanel attempted to explain this large discrepancy by appealing to Josephus's historiographical motives. He asserted that Josephus, writing for a Roman readership, did not want to say anything they might find unreasonable. Hence 'when he found something large and strange that the Romans would have difficulty believing, he made an effort to write something pleasing to their ears as he thought best, and did not hesitate to deviate from what is written in the scriptures':[197] a conclusion consistent with those of modern scholarship.[198] Abravanel asserted the accuracy of the numbers in the Bible and justified them by comparing them to those given for similar events, both in the Bible and in other historical sources:

And I also have seen, in the stories of history and of the wars between the Trojans and the Greeks, and between the Romans and the Africans in the time of Hannibal, and between the nation of Edom in Spain with the Ishmaelites who conquered Spain, that in one war many, many more than 500,000 were slain on one side, and if that happened to them with a human force, why should we deny the testimony of the scriptures regarding what was done for Israel under divine providence.[199]

Comparing sources is an important historiographical method and, in this case, provided support for the Bible. However, the problem Abravanel raised did not stem from a difficulty in the Bible itself but from a contradiction with what he found in Josephus's writings.

Abravanel was also interested in Christian extra-biblical stories. For example, according to a Christian legend, Noah had a fourth son called Joniko, who 'invented tools of astrology after the flood . . . and who advised Nimrod on how to reign over the entire world'. Abravanel wished to remain faithful to the biblical

---

[196] Rossi, *Meor einayim*, 'Imrei binah', I: 12 (Vilna edn., 180–9; trans. Weinberg, 239–51, see esp. 243–4).

[197] Abravanel on 1 Kgs 15: 6 (*Perush linevi'im rishonim*, 569): 'And I saw in the book by Joseph ben Gorion that he wrote for the Romans on the wars of the Jews.' The Greek original of *Jewish Antiquities* has 500,000 dead as in the Bible (Josephus, *Jewish Antiquities*, 8.11.3).

[198] See e.g. Stern, 'Josephus's Historical Method' (Heb.).

[199] Abravanel on 1 Kgs 15: 6 (*Perush linevi'im rishonim*, 569).

account, which stated that Noah only had three sons and claimed that Joniko did in fact exist but that he was Noah's grandson: 'perhaps he was Eber who was wiser than all the men of his generation'.[200] In contrast, Zacut accepted the story of Joniko in its entirety, without trying to explain the contradiction between it and the Bible.[201] The Christian tradition about Abraham the astrologer also appears in Abravanel's writings: 'And it was already widely known among the nations, based on what is found in their ancient books, that Abraham was very accomplished in the science of the zodiac, and debated on it with Nimrod, who was a renowned expert, and that Abraham taught that wisdom in Egypt.'[202]

Jewish historiographers read more Christian history than was directly reflected in their writings. Sometimes this is evident in their chronological calculations. For example, a book on the different ways that Jews and non-Jews counted eras, written in 1513 by an anonymous exile from Spain who went to a Muslim country, mentions several Roman emperors and a king of Castile, but the author's generalized remark about the accuracy and authenticity of the books of Christian historiography is of particular interest. He preferred Christian writings on chronology for the Second Temple period and the following centuries and rejected the works of Maimonides, Sherira Gaon, and Ibn Daud.[203]

Another common interest of Abravanel and Zacut was Graeco-Roman mythology. I have already noted the polemical use of mythological material, but it could also serve interpretative purposes, and, in many cases, it was included out of intellectual curiosity. Zacut and Abravanel's work on mythological subjects was influenced by the historical and cultural writings of west European scholars in general and by Spanish humanism's particular interest in mythology.[204] The

---

[200] Abravanel on Gen. 9: 18 (*Perush al hatorah*, i. 168). The story about Joniko is found in Peter Comestor, *Scholastic History*, cols. 1088*c–d*. He may have heard it in conversations with the Jews of Troyes in the second half of the twelfth century (see Feldman, 'The Jewish Sources of Peter Comestor's Commentary on Genesis', esp. 120). The story also appears in Brunetto Latini's widely circulated *Book of the Treasure* (16). It appeared earlier, at the beginning of the twelfth century, in Yerahmiel b. Solomon, *Sefer hazikhronot*, 129–30; see Yassif, Introduction (Heb.), ibid. 26. On the origins of the Christian legend, see Gero, 'The Legend of the Fourth Son of Noah'.

[201] 'And after the flood [Noah] begot sons and daughters, and begot a fourth son named Joniko, a very wise man, and he began the science of astrology and taught it to the whole world, which are the four kingdoms from east to west, and he taught Nimrod how to reign over the sons of Ham' (Zacut, *Sefer yuhasin* (ed. Filipowski, 232*b*)).

[202] Abravanel on 1 Kgs 3: 12 (*Perush linevi'im rishonim*, 478). Abravanel also claimed that Plato studied with the prophet Jeremiah in Egypt, a view that was also accepted by Frat Maimon, Nethanel ben Nehemiah Kaspi of Provence and Messer David Leon of Italy (see Idel, 'Kabbalah and Ancient Philosophy in the Works of R. Isaac and Judah Abravanel' (Heb.), 77–8, 100–1 nn. 29–30).

[203] 'And thus it was in the chronicles of the Gentiles, as everything written in the chronicles from the destruction of the Second Temple and thereafter in the matter of the kings is all true' (*Sefer bitekufot umoladot*, 258). Later he rejected the Jewish traditions.

[204] See Lawrance, 'On Fifteenth-Century Spanish Vernacular Humanism', 78.

effects of the Renaissance were felt in Spain by the end of the fourteenth century, and the nobility, primarily the Mendoza family, had a marked Renaissance spirit.[205] Abravanel and Zacut breathed this intellectual atmosphere.[206] In Castile, Zacut established a relationship with the bishop of Salamanca, Gonzalo de Vivero (d. 1480), and practised astronomy at his court. After 1480 he was in the service of Don Juan de Zúñiga, head of the Order of Alcántara. After the Expulsion he worked in Portugal as astrologer to Juan II and Manuel I. Abravanel, while still in Portugal, became friendly with prominent representatives of the Portuguese Renaissance and at the start of his stay in Castile worked for Cardinal Pedro Gonzáles de Mendoza managing tax-farming operations. In 1490 he was appointed *contador major* to Mendoza's nephew, Iñigo López de Mendoza, the second Duke of the Infantado. Cardinal Mendoza and Iñigo López de Mendoza introduced the architectural style of the Italian Renaissance to Spain and also translated the *Iliad* and works by Virgil and Ovid from Latin into Castilian.

Within these circles there was much interest in Graeco-Roman mythology. For example, Enrique de Villena's *Los doze trabajos de Hércules* raised the profile of the Greek hero, and both Abravanel and Zacut discussed him.[207] The Trojan War was another popular subject and is discussed in *Sefer yuḥasin*:

In the year 3944 the Trojan War began.... Priam the king of Troy reigned in the days of Tola [1 Chr. 7: 2] for fifty-two years, and he had six sons, and Aeneas was his nephew. ... In 4010 Hector, son of the king of Troy, and his son Astyanax the hero, whom all the men of Greece feared came. Achilles the Greek killed Hector. Then there was Penthesilea, Queen of the Amazons. She taught the Trojans how to fight the Greeks: that was in 4012. When she heard about Hector, she desired him and went to the battlefield of the Greeks to see him. ... Achilles waged war against Troy and killed Hector. They asked their gods [lit. idols] whether to [fight] Troy and were told to go with Achilles....

That year the Trojan War began. The king was Priam. The cause of the war was that the king invited three beautiful women, who they called goddesses, to a feast. Then, an uninvited woman came in. In order to annoy them, Paris sent three apples for the women, with the best apple intended for the most beautiful woman, and they fought over who was the most beautiful.[208]

[205] See Cirot, *Les Histoires générales d'Espagne*, 38–40; Nadler, *The Mendoza Family*, 7–16, 77.

[206] See Cantera Burgos, *El Judío Salmantino Abraham Zacut*, 20–6; Nadler, *The Mendoza Family*, 1, 115, 119–21; Netanyahu, *Don Isaac Abravanel*, 14, 51–2; Cobos Bueno, *Un astrónomo en la academia rena-centista del maestre de Alcántara Fray Iuan de Zúñiga y Pimentel*.

[207] See De Villena, *Los doze trabajos de Hércules*; Lawrance, 'On Fifteenth-Century Spanish Vernacular Humanism', 71 n. 20, 75–8; see also Chapter 5 below.

[208] Zacut, *Sefer yuḥasin* (ed. Filipowski, 235*b*–236*a*). On the story of Penthesilea's love for Hector, see Boccaccio, *Concerning Famous Women*, 30: 14–15. The story also appeared in Castile, in great detail, in the mid-fifteenth century (see Pero Niño, *El victorial*, 92–3).

Zacut described the myth of Troy at some length for two reasons: first, because medieval Christian chronology assigned it so much importance—Christian chroniclers believed the sack of Troy was a firm chronological reference point from which the dates of other historical events could be calculated[209]—and, second, because the story of Troy played a key role in the historical consciousness of Christian Europe and especially Spain.

The history of Troy was known in the Middle Ages primarily through the rhymed French version *Roman de Troie*, written by Benoît de Saint-Maure in around 1160, and the Latin version, *Historia destructionis Troiae*, edited by Guido delle Colonne on the basis of Saint-Maure's book.[210] In Spain, the version of the story in *Primera crónica general de España* was known from the thirteenth century, as well as from translations of Saint-Maure's book in rhymed prose, such as *Historia troyana polimétrica*. From the fourteenth century, translations of delle Colonne's book (into Castilian in 1350 and Catalan in 1374) and many romances in Aragonese, Catalan, and Castilian were widely distributed. In the first half of the fifteenth century, the Converso Juan de Mena translated the *Ilias latina*, a Latin paraphrase of the *Iliad* into Castilian, the first translation of its kind. Towards the end of the century, Pedro Gonzáles de Mendoza's translation of Pier Candido Decembrio's literal Latin version of the *Iliad* appeared.[211]

The story of Troy was popular, because it was a rich source of heroic and romantic tales that provided courtly and chivalrous models and because it became the foundation myth of several countries, whose royal houses claimed descent from Trojan heroes fleeing to western Europe after the fall of the city.[212] These foundation myths were common in Spain,[213] and Zacut provides several of them. There are two about Aeneas, who founded a city in Italy and later became king;[214] one about the founding of France by Frankus;[215] and one about the foundation of Britain by Brutus:

---

[209] See Zacut, *Sefer yuḥasin* (ed. Filipowski, 236*b*); Alfonso X, *Primera crónica general de España*, i. 5*b*, 48*b*–49*a*, 92*a*, 7*a*.   [210] See C. D. Benson, *The History of Troy in Middle English Literature*, 3–6.

[211] See Deyermond, *A Literary History of Spain*, 160.

[212] See Beaune, *Naissance de la nation France*, 19–54; Bossuat, 'Les Origines troyennes'; Huppert, 'The Trojan Franks and Their Critics'.

[213] See e.g.: 'El el señor de Galiçia hera del linaje de Troya, que truxeran allí su padre niño pequeño, quando Troya fué destruydo' (Pero Niño, *El victorial*, 160). According to another tradition from Castile, based on the *Anales Toledanos* of 1219, Toledo was also founded by Trojans (see Lopez Torrijos, *La mitología en la pintura española del Siglo de Oro*, 191).

[214] 'Gaeta was built then by Aeneas who named it after his wet nurse' (Zacut, *Sefer yuḥasin* (ed. Filipowski, 236*a*)); 'Aeneas of Troy came to Italy and reigned there' (ibid. (ed. Filipowski, 236*b*; see also 232*b*)).

[215] 'That year [4082] they began to reign in France, which is called Gallia. Its first king was Franco and thus the people of France are called Franks' (ibid. 236*a*–*b*; see Beaune, *Naissance de la nation France*, 15–22).

The first king [of England] was Brutus, son of King Latinus. He killed his father the king of the Latins by mistake while hunting in the fields, and escaped from Ililia [Italy?] to England, the big island in the Western Sea, called Great Britain in the west. It has the shape of a triangle, like the island of Sicily. There were giants whom he defeated and reigned over. The longest day there is 17 hours. There are many riches there, gold, wool and hunting dogs. [Brutus's] mother died in childbirth.[216]

As far as we know, the earliest source for the myth of Brutus the Trojan (son of Aeneas), the founder of the kingdom of Britain, is a book by the English chronicler Nennius, written around 830 CE. The myth was greatly expanded by Geoffrey of Monmouth in his *History of the Kings of Britain*, written between 1136 and 1147, and later in the long verse history in French by Wace, *Roman de Brut*, written in 1155, and the English poem by Layamon, *Brut*, written at the end of the twelfth century.[217] Geoffrey of Monmouth's work rapidly circulated throughout England, France, Germany, and Italy and became very influential.

Zacut dedicated more space to this myth than to the foundation myths of any other country or city in western Europe, which may be a consequence of the growing interest in the history of England in Castile. In the thirteenth century, the myth of Brutus was briefly mentioned in the *Primera crónica general de España*. In the fifteenth century it was described in great detail in *El victorial* the chronicle of Captain Don Pero Niño of Castile and in three other chronicles: *Libro de las generaciones, Livro das linhagens*, and *Crónica de 1404*. In addition, Brutus's sea journey and several other episodes appear on a tapestry apparently woven in Tourney in the fifteenth century, which eventually found its way to the cathedral in Saragossa.[218] In the three chronicles, European history is integrated with biblical history, and, similarly, Zacut placed the story of Brutus after the period of the Judges, in the time of Eli.[219] Zacut's description of British geography and the

---

[216] Zacut, *Sefer yuḥasin* (ed. Filipowski, 236*b*); see Bossuat, 'Les Origines troyennes'.

[217] See Nennius, *History of the Britons*, 6, 7–9; Geoffrey of Monmouth, *History of the Kings of Britain*, §§6–7, 21–2.

[218] 'Bretanna poblo Brutho, que fue del linage de los Troya, e por essol puso assi nombre, ca enante auie nombre Siluaria e depues le camiaron el nombre Ynglaterra' (Alfonso X, *Primera crónica general de España*, i. 6*a*; see De Mata Carriazo, Introduction to Pero Niño, *El victorial*, pp. xxxiii–xxxiv; *Libro de las generaciones*, 246–8).

[219] 'And Eli the priest began in the year 51 and judged for forty years. . . . The English kingdom began in the year 83. The first king was Brutus. . . . In the year 4093 the ark was captured' (Zacut, *Sefer yuḥasin* (ed. Filipowski, 236*a*–*b*)). See: 'Esta sazon hera bispo Eli en Judea, e los filiestos prisieron la arca del testament en la batalla' (*Libro de las generaciones*, 248; see also *Livro das linhagens; Crónica de 1404*); 'En este tienpo era saerdote Eli de los Judios; e enton fue rrobada la archa del testamiento de los phyllisteus, quando Brutus entro en Bretaña' (*Libro de las generaciones*, 248).

famous wealth of the island were necessary details for non-English readers, and the version in *El victorial* began in a similar manner.[220]

Zacut also recorded that the Ottomans justified their attacks on the Byzantine empire by claiming that they were avenging the sack of Troy: 'The Turks, who are called *benei tomi* [lit.: 'sons of Tomi', Ottomans] said they sought revenge against Greece for the blood of their native Troy.'[221] The Ottoman manipulation of the myth was a subject of much discussion in Christian Europe, and Spain in particular, in the light of the threat the Ottomans posed after the fall of Constantinople in 1453. References to the Trojan origin of the Ottomans can be found in Latin chronicles from the early Middle Ages, but it became a popular subject among Italian humanists of the fifteenth century, primarily Giovanni Mario Filelfo, whose epic poem *Amyris* recounts the conquests of Sultan Mehmed II.[222] The theory also spread with the aid of a forged letter from Mehmed to the pope (*Epistolae magni turci*), in which the sultan justified his aggressive actions in Asia Minor with the claim of hereditary right and stated that he was not fighting for religious reasons. The letter was one of the earliest pieces of writing printed in Spain, possibly as early as 1475.[223] Intellectuals in western Europe made similar claims to justify the conquest of Byzantium by the Latins during the Fourth Crusade in 1204. Invoking the myth of the Trojan origin of the French, they asserted that the conquest of Byzantium was an act of revenge for the sack of Troy by the Greeks. There were also some who argued, using the same mythographical apologetics, that the Turks' claims were legitimate.[224] Zacut's brief comment on Ottoman claims to Byzantine territory attests to the literary and cultural milieu

---

[220] See De Mata Carriazo, Introduction to Pero Niño, *El victorial*, pp. xxxiii–xxxiv; see also: 'porque biben en tierra muy abastada de viandas e buíres, e rica de metales' (Pero Niño, *El victorial*, 142).   [221] Zacut, *Sefer yuḥasin* (ed. Filipowski, 236a).

[222] See Schwoebel, *The Shadow of the Crescent*, 148–9.

[223] See Heath, 'Renaissance Scholars and the Origins of the Turks'. The writer of the letter was the humanist Laudivio Zacchia from Genoa. It was widely printed in Europe from 1473 and thereafter (see Babinger, *Laudivius Zacchia*; Griffin, 'Spanish Incunabula in the John Rylands University Library'). The medieval basis for the claim of the Trojan origin of the Turks (and of the French too) is found in a seventh-century chronicle attributed to Fredegarius. He wrote that the Turks were linked to the hero Turkus, who was a member of a group of Trojan refugees that settled first in Macedonia and later moved to the banks of the Danube. Some of them, led by Francion, emigrated to the Rhine river and established New Troy there. This story was later repeated by important chroniclers, including Vincent de Beauvais. From the mid-fifteenth century several thinkers tried to challenge the myth. For various reasons, others, such as Johannes Angelus in *Opus Davidicum*, written between 1496 and 1498, held that it was true (see Linder, 'Ex mala parentela bona sequi seu oriri non potest', 502, 510–11).

[224] See Beaune, *Naissance de la nation France*, 21, 48–9, 360 n. 183. Turkus was thought to be Francion's cousin. Consequently, towards the end of the fifteenth century, all mention of Turkus was omitted from the French versions.

in which he moved. Like the intellectuals of his time, he connected events of ancient history—including mythological ones—to contemporary politics.

Abravanel also mentioned the Trojan War. He used it to support the biblical claim about the number of casualties in the war between Judah and Israel, as discussed above, and also to teach a historical lesson. According to Abravanel the total annihilation of the Trojans showed that the Jewish diaspora was intended to prevent the Jews from suffering a similar fate:

For as you know, the people of Troy were a great nation, and as they were all assembled together in one place, the Greeks attacked them and destroyed them, leaving them neither a name nor a vestige. And this happened to other nations too. Since the Jews were dispersed they were never totally annihilated. We have seen that the king of England destroyed all the Jews in the cities under his control. And at another time the king of France did the same to the Jews in his country. . . . And if all the Jews had been gathered there, not a single one of them would have remained alive . . . and for that reason the diaspora was a right and benevolent condition so that the [Jewish] people may survive and be saved.[225]

Abravanel used the Homeric tale to show God's concern for the Jews and to supply an explanation for the disapora: a method common in western Europe at the time.[226]

Abravanel also had access to classical works and Christian, as well as Jewish, biblical commentators who had made use of Latin historiography in their interpretations. In a comment on Daniel 4: 30 he disagreed with earlier commentators, who claimed that Nebuchadnezzar was turned into an ox.

For I have seen that the Christian sages as well as the last sages of our own people have said that because Nebuchadnezzar did not know his Creator . . . he turned into an ox . . . and they said that was similar to what was related in the chronicles of the Latins: that three sorceresses began practising the art of magic and trickery, and they call them Ioanna, Circe, and Medea, and that they knew how to turn men into beasts, so they would look exactly like an animal, and Ovid and Virgil and other wise men wrote about this . . . and afterwards they turned them back into men, as Ovid and others wrote.[227]

The earlier commentators compared the fate of Nebuchadnezzar to other transformations in Graeco-Roman mythology, particularly those recorded in Ovid's *Metamorphoses*. Vincent de Beauvais, for example, quoted Isidore of Seville as saying that Circe's spells were real, noting that in a number of documented cases human beings had been turned into animals and these should be regarded 'not as

---

[225] Abravanel on Deut. 32: 26 (*Perush al hatorah*, iii. 306).

[226] Guenée, *Histoire et culture historique dans l'Occident médiéval*, 275–6.

[227] Abravanel, *Ma'ayenei hayeshuah*, 6: 5 (Jerusalem edn., 320); see Dan. 4: 30.

fallacious legends but as proven history'.[228] Boethius, in describing Ulysses'
encounter with the Cyclops, acknowledged Circe's ability to transform humans
into animals. He also mentioned two possible types of metamorphosis: a change
of the body while the mind remained human and a change of both body and
mind.[229] Abravanel rejected the possibility that humans could be physically trans-
formed into animals and argued that the myths should be read allegorically. For
example, women describe men who pursue them as wild asses that are incapable
of controlling their passions.[230] In this Abravanel adopted the allegorical approach
to the tales of Ovid prevalent in European Christian thought from the eleventh
century.[231] In this context, it is worth noting that Ovid had a great influence on
Spanish literature in the fourteenth and fifteenth centuries.[232]

Similar historical subjects appear in the writings of Zacut and Abravanel,
because they read similar historical literature, from ancient myths to the political
and military history of the ancient world, in particular the Roman empire.
Apparently they never met, and there is no evidence that they were familiar with
each other's work. After the Expulsion Zacut went to Portugal, Tunisia, and
finally the Land of Israel and Abravanel went to Italy. It is probable that interest
in these subjects spread faster in the fifteenth century than earlier. Ideas can be
traced from one writer to another in the earlier period and lines of influence
discerned. However, in the fifteenth century historiography was developed by
several writers in parallel and signs of direct influence are harder to detect.

In the fifteenth century historiography was an important part of scientific
and cultural endeavours. As mentioned above, Zacut noted that Christian history
books contained many extra details about historical events referred to in the
Talmud. He included this in his 'Introduction to the Author', a section that would
be read with great attention, rather than simply citing the Christian sources in the
body of the work without emphasizing that they were preferable. In my opinion,
Zacut wanted to legitimize his use of Christian sources. Addressing historical
topics discussed in the Talmud could preclude critical readers from complaining
about the fact that Zacut wished to extend the Jews' historical knowledge: later he
makes it clear that he intended to use Christian sources to discuss subjects that
did not appear in Jewish texts at all.

---

[228] Vincent de Beauvais, *The Mirror of History*, 1: 95; see Bietenholz, *Historia and Fabula*, 146–7; on
the influence of *Speculum historiale*, see Guenée, *Histoire et culture historique dans l'Occident médiéval*,
305–6.   [229] Boethius, *The Consolation of Philosophy*, 4: 3.

[230] Abravanel, *Ma'ayenei hayeshuah*, 6: 5 (Jerusalem edn., 320).

[231] See Born, 'Ovid and Allegory'; Guthmüller, *Ovidio Metamorphoseos vulgare*, 78–80; on the very
influential work, *Ovide moralisé*, see Blumenfeld-Kosinsky, *Reading Myth*, 90–136.

[232] See Schevill, *Ovid and the Renaissance in Spain*, 6–86.

To satisfy the desires of those of our people who wish to know everything that [the Christians] wrote. I mean, the more general affairs: such as what happened in Jerusalem and in the Land of Israel, Italy, Greece, Egypt, Babylonia, and Turkey, places with a large Jewish population, and which were recorded in the Torah, such as 'Crowned Zor' (Tyre in the language of Christians), a day's walk from Acre, near Sidon and near the Land of Israel, where in ancient days the Venetians lived. Thus, many were misled to believe that Venice was Tyre.[233]

The implication is that Jewish readers should know the history of every place where Jews lived, and, therefore, they should be interested in all of human history, because Jews lived in nearly every place.

Zacut used the city of Tyre to illustrate his point. Crusader Tyre was known throughout the Jewish world, because it was one of the gateways to the Land of Israel and there was a large Jewish community there.[234] However, few knew that crusader Tyre was the Tyre mentioned in the Bible. Most Jews believed that the biblical Tyre was Venice. Zacut claimed that the epithet derived from the presence of Venetians in the city from the earliest times. He was, however, wrong: the name originated during the Crusades, when Venice was involved in the capture of Tyre and took the rights to a third of the city.[235] It is not, however, the solution that is important, but rather the problem that Zacut posed. The identification of biblical Tyre, crusader Tyre, and Venice aroused much interest among Jews, and the problems could only be resolved by the use of historiography.

Abravanel also discussed the problem. According to him, the mistake arose out of a misinterpretation of Isaiah and Ezekiel: 'What is the Tyre mentioned here? Many of our people thought it was the glorious city in the Italy of Greece, today called Venice. And they were led to believe this by what Isaiah and Ezekiel remembered about the descriptions of Tyre, and that [both cities were] built on the sea.'[236] Elsewhere he stated:

Tyre that was adjacent to the Land of Israel had already been destroyed a long time before. It was destroyed twice: once by Nebuchadnezzar and a second time by Alexander the Great. It was covered by the sea, and until today its foundations can be seen. But I

---

[233] Zacut, *Sefer yuḥasin* (ed. Filipowski, 231*b*).

[234] See Gil, *The Land of Israel during the First Muslim Period* (Heb.), i. 205–12, 344–6, 606–26; Prawer, *The Crusaders* (Heb.), 317–23; see also Benjamin of Tudela, *Sefer masaot*, 20–1.

[235] See Chéhab, *Tyr à l'époque des croisades*, ii. 160–97. 'Communis Venecie in Tyro' appears in some documents (see ibid. 197). Zacut referred to Venetian control of Tyre in connection with the war between Venice and Genoa, and, in order to remove any doubt, stressed: 'Tyro, which is Tyre in the Land of Israel' (Zacut, *Sefer yuḥasin* (ed. Freiman, p. xlv)).

[236] Abravanel on Ezek. 26: 1 (*Perush al nevi'im aḥaronim*, 540). Italy was called Greece because of the long Byzantine control of the area: 'Italy is one of the districts of Greece, but her inhabitants are not Greeks' (Abravanel on Ezek. 26: 2 (ibid. 542)). See also: 'And Tyre that is mentioned here is not Venice, which we today call Tyre' (Abravanel on 2 Sam. 5: 11 (*Perush linevi'im rishonim*, 405)).

have already made it known many times that the glorious city of Venice was built from
the seed of the people of Tyre: after Tyre was destroyed, they went many years from bad
to worse, and many of them settled in the land of Venice and its area to hunt for fish
there and built houses and made a large city. And after many years, the king of France
attacked them from the sea, and, out of fear of him, the people of the city fled to that
place called the Rialto, where no ship can enter. And then they built the glorious city of
Venice. All this is written in their chronicles.[237]

Abravanel found his historical information about Venice in Christian history
books, and, although the underlying motives for his commentary were eschatological, he used what he believed to be reliable historical information.[238] Like
Zacut, he wished to correct the mistaken belief among Jews that the biblical Tyre
was Venice. According to him, the Venetian chronicles reveal a gap of more than
1,000 years between the time of Isaiah and Ezekiel and the foundation of the
city.[239] He ascribed the confusion to two related causes: that Venice was founded
by the inhabitants of Tyre (as Zacut contended) and that it was also a city built on
water (as an anonymous traveller of 1522–3 also described it):[240] '[Venice] was not
called Tyre in those days, for Venice had not yet been built in the time of these
prophets, but rather she was built in Tyre's image and by her inhabitants after
Tyre was destroyed.'[241] The biblical Tyre is on the border of the Land of Israel,
is called Tyre by the Christians, and the ruins of the ancient city can still be
seen under the sea.[242] According to the testimony of Greek and Latin historians it
was first built on the shore, but after it was destroyed by Nebuchadnezzar, it was
founded again in the sea, 'like Venice is today'. It was destroyed again by Alexander

---

[237] Abravanel on Zech. 9: 4 (*Perush al nevi'im ukhetuvim*, 225); see also Abravanel on Amos 1: 3
(ibid. 81); Zacut mentions the tradition about the fishermen (*Sefer yuḥasin* (ed. Filipowski, 247*a*)).

[238] Abravanel anticipated that Zechariah's prophecies about Tyre would soon be fulfilled, but in
relation to Venice (see Abravanel on Zech. 9: 4 (*Perush al nevi'im ukhetuvim*, 225)). Prophecies about
Tyre had an apocalyptic importance, because Tyre was the 'head of Edom' (Rashi on Zech. 10: 11; see
Abravanel on Zech. 10: 12 (*Perush al nevi'im ukhetuvim*, 230)).

[239] 'Both Isaiah and Ezekiel prophesied about Tyre, and now 2,000 years have passed according to
the time each prophesied in his generation, and Venice, according to the testimony of her chronicles,
was founded and built by fishermen no more than 1,000 years ago, and from this it is clear that the
city of Tyre whose destruction the prophets foretold was another (city), more ancient than Venice by
more than 1,000 years (Abravanel on Isa. 23: 1 (*Perush al nevi'im aharonim*, 132)).

[240] 'Travels in the Land of Israel by an Anonymous Sage' (Heb.), 131. There is a more reliable
description by Capsali, who stated that the first inhabitants of Venice were among those who settled
in Italy and Lombardy and fled the barbarian invasions (*Seder eliyahu zuta*, 'The Stories of Venice'
(ed. Shmuelevitz, Simonsohn, and Benayahu, ii. 218)).

[241] Abravanel on Zech. 9: 4 (*Perush al nevi'im ukhetuvim*, 225).

[242] 'And that Zor [Tyre] drowned in the sea and its foundations and buildings can be seen from
afar, and the Gentiles called her Tirus' (Abravanel on Isa. 23: 1 (*Perush al nevi'im aharonim*, 131)).
Abravanel could have learned this from Benjamin of Tudela (see *Sefer masaot*, 21).

the Great after a long siege and buried in the sea.[243] Venice in Italy is the typological Tyre, whose eschatological destruction, like that of Rome, the typological Edom, is approaching.

Zacut and Abravanel both contended that Jews needed 'new' historiographical information. In the case of Tyre, they both explained to their readers why, on the one hand, Venice should not be identified with Tyre, and, on the other, what the symbolic link between the two cities was. They tried to familiarize their readers with the historical reality, while leaving them in the symbolic field with which they were familiar. Zacut, as we noted, did not hesitate to prefer Christian historiographical traditions to Jewish ones, when the Jewish ones were incorrect. The same was true of Abravanel. He disagreed with the legends in midrashic literature which identified Tyre with Rome.[244] 'If it is the tradition, we accept it', he wrote, but 'according to the literal meaning of the words, Zor is neither Rome nor Venice, but rather the city that the Christians call Tyre'.[245]

The writings of Abraham bar Hiyya, Abravanel, and Zacut show that chronological precision was not meant solely to justify the Jewish dating of events, it was also an attempt to link historical events and chronology into one uniform overarching historical-apocalyptical scheme. Zacut preferred Christian chronology when it was more consistent with his astrological computations. However, many Jews found the questioning of the Jewish tradition and the preference for the Christian tradition audacious, amounting, in effect, to a legitimization of Christianity. In his 'Introduction to the Author', Zacut followed a conventional apologetic trend intended to deflect this criticism. He also tried to satisfy the intellectual needs of those Jews who were interested in general history because they were part of human culture, who 'wish[ed] to know everything [the Christians] wrote . . . the more general affairs', and who were not satisfied merely with Jewish sources. Abravanel also tried to fill that same cultural lacuna and provide his readers with the historical information they desired.

---

[243] 'As I have seen from the testimony of the ancient Greek and Latin writers, who wrote about Alexander the Great and accepted the fact that, after Nebuchadnezzar destroyed Tyre, it was resettled, not on the seashore as before, but it was built in the sea, as it is today . . . and that afterwards it was attacked by Alexander the Great, and a long time passed until he conquered it, because it was in the sea, but nonetheless he did conquer it, and breached it, so that the sea entered into the city, swept over it, and it sank into the sea' (Abravanel on Ezek. 26: 2 (*Perush al nevi'im aḥaronim*, 533)).

[244] Abravanel on Ezek. 26: 1 (ibid. 540).

[245] See Abravanel on Isa. 23: 1 (ibid. 131); on Ezek. 26: 2 (ibid. 542).

CHAPTER TWO

Rome: Images and Influence

THE CHRISTIANS OF the Middle Ages had a great interest in the Roman
empire. At that time history was not perceived of as a separate discipline: it
was studied either within the framework of biblical studies; for its theological or
moral lessons; or as part of classical literature, as exemplars of good writing.
Roman literature was regarded as wisdom literature and used to educate children
from both higher and lower social classes.[1] Even the writings of Livy, who was
not particularly popular, were distributed to the monks of Cluny in the mid-
eleventh century to be read during the forty days of Lent. There was interest in
the past, although people's ideas of it were often imprecise and sometimes contained gross errors.[2] People believed that the Roman empire still existed and
regarded Saxon and Salian rulers as direct descendants of Julius Caesar or
Augustus. They also imagined contemporary rulers to be similar to the emperors
of ancient Rome. As far as they were concerned, despite the religious difference,
there was no break between the classical period and their own time. Cassiodorus
(c.483–583) contributed to this idea by drawing an unbroken line from the beginning of Rome to the Ostrogoth kings (a period of 5,721 years) in his *Chronicle*.[3]
The notion of 'transfer of empire' (*translatio imperii*), which first developed at the
court of Charlemagne and was popular with the Ottonian emperors, also supported this view of history. According to it, the Roman empire passed from Rome
to Constantinople, from there to the Franks, from the Franks to the Lombards
and from there to the Germans—the Holy Roman Empire.[4]

In the Middle Ages, the concept of the Roman empire was shaped by
Charlemagne's. symbolic use of Rome, which was fostered afterwards by Otto II
(955–83), who frequently used the title 'Emperor of the Romans' and Otto III
(980–1002), who made Rome the capital of his kingdom, and announced the

---

[1] See M. Bloch, *Feudal Society*, 88; Guenée, *Le Métier d'historien au Moyen Âge*, 277–8.

[2] M. Bloch, *Feudal Society*, 91; cf. Gurevich, *Categories of Medieval Culture*, 129–32.

[3] See M. Bloch, *Feudal Society*, 91; Breisach, *Historiography*, 90; Weiss, *The Renaissance Discovery of Classical Antiquity*, 3.

[4] See Folz, *The Concept of Empire in Western Europe*, 16–29, 61–74, 98–101; Gurevich, *Categories of Medieval Culture*, 131; Ne'eman, *The Birth of a Civilization* (Heb.), 202; on other approaches, in particular those of Gregory of Tours and Isidore of Seville, see Breisach, *Historiography*, 90–1.

'renewal of the Roman empire'. Later German emperors, such as Conrad III and Frederick Barbarossa, also stressed the continuity of Roman rule. A typical example of this can be found in Otto von Freising's *Chronical or History of the Two Cities* (1143–5). Von Freising placed the German kings, including those of his own time, in his list of Roman emperors. The ideology of the 'transfer of empire' developed alongside and in combination with the idea of the 'transfer of wisdom': enlightenment and wisdom originated in the east or Greece, from there they passed to Rome, and from there to the Franks.[5]

The cultural renaissances of medieval Europe—Carolingian, Ottonian, and the twelfth-century renaissance—exalted the values and concepts of Roman culture long before the Italian Renaissance.[6] Although it was mainly the educated who came into contact with those cultural values, ordinary people also encountered the Roman empire, through the ruins across Europe that testified to the accomplishments and glory of the past. Legends about Rome and her history were to be found in guide books, such as *Marvels of the City of Rome* (1140s) on the topography of ancient Rome, written by a canon of Saint Peter's named Benedict, and chronicles, such as William of Malmesbury's *Deeds of the English Kings* (1125–7) and John of Salisbury's *Policraticus* (1159). *Marvels of the City of Rome* was more than a simple guide to Rome. It perpetuated the ideology of the city's divine and imperial destiny as the centre of the world, which was a key element in the ideology of the Holy Roman Empire from the time of Otto III. That same ideal of Rome also existed in other works, such as the English traveller Magister Gregorius's *On the Marvels of the City of Rome* (late twelfth century) and the *Description of the Golden City of Rome* (1155), a composite work including a re-ordering of material from the *Marvels of the City of Rome*.[7] One of the most striking depictions of ancient Rome as the ideal state is in Dante's *On Monarchy*, apparently written in 1312–13. Dante's idea of one universal secular kingdom for all human beings was realized in the Roman empire. The second volume deals entirely with the traits of the Roman empire and the Roman people and offers various reasons for the superiority of Rome.[8]

[5] See Folz, *The Concept of Empire in Western Europe*, 98–101, 174; R. L. Benson, 'Political Renovatio'; H. Bloch, 'The New Fascination with Ancient Rome'; Gurevich, *Categories of Medieval Culture*, 131; Ne'eman, *The Birth of a Civilization* (Heb.), 202.

[6] See Guenée, *L'Occident aux XIVe et XVe siècles*, 124; Haskins, *The Renaissance of the Twelfth Century*; Weiss, *The Renaissance Discovery of Classical Antiquity*, 3–4; cf. Beaune, *Naissance de la nation France*, 293–4.

[7] '[The] obvious conclusion is that much more antique material was available during the Middle Ages than at any time up to the nineteenth century' (Greenhalgh, *The Survival of Roman Antiquities in the Middle Ages*, 248; see also R. L. Benson, 'Political Renovatio', 351–5; H. Bloch, 'The New Fascination with Ancient Rome, 630–3; Weiss, *The Renaissance Discovery of Classical Antiquity*, 7–8).

[8] See Dante, *De Monarchia*, 2: 1–11; Folz, *The Concept of Empire in Western Europe*, 140–4.

In the Middle Ages the Roman empire was familiar to Jews as well. In Arles, for example, which had an important Jewish community, columns from the forum temple were still visible, people lived in the ancient amphitheatre, and the Roman baths served as a paddock.[9] This everyday contact with ancient Rome is reflected in a comment by Isaac Abravanel: 'And here, in all the lands of Italy, and in Spain too, wherever the Romans set foot in the time of their greatness and glory, you will find even today many monuments left by the ancients.'[10] Jewish merchants would spend many days on roads which followed the courses of Roman ones. Jews also knew about the city of Rome through hearsay and letters or from reading historiographical literature, such as Abraham ibn Daud's *History of Rome*, and travel literature, such as Benjamin of Tudela's *Book of Travels* (*Sefer masaot*). Ibn Daud provided admiring descriptions of the statue of Romulus and the Vatican obelisk, which at the time was believed to be Julius Caesar's tomb.[11]

Benjamin of Tudela, the famous Jewish traveller who made his journeys between 1165 and 1173, devoted much space in his book to Rome. He described its buildings, palaces, and castles in the style of the *Marvels of the City of Rome*, combining a description of real ruins with myths and legends.[12] He wrote that Saint Peter's cathedral was in 'the palace of the great Julius Caesar'. He described Vespasian's palace and the Colosseum and recounted a tale of a brutal battle that had occurred there.[13] He also described statues and sculptures, including those of biblical figures, an ancient battle, and Constantine on his horse.[14] His enthusiasm and admiration for the monuments of ancient Rome are palpable. For example, he lists eighty palaces in the ruins of ancient Rome outside the smaller part inhabited during the Middle Ages, and added that it was settled by 'eighty kings . . . called imperators [emperors], from the kingdom of Tarquinus . . . until the kingdom of Pepin the Short, the father of Charles Martel, who first conquered the land of Spain from the Ishmaelites'.[15] Here he reflects the prevalent Christian view that the Roman empire had been transferred to the Carolingian empire, and Pepin the Short (d. 768) was an emperor just like the ancient Roman emperors.

---

[9] See Stouff, *Arles à la fin du Moyen-Âge*, 66–7; on similar situations in other cities, see Greenhalgh, *The Survival of Roman Antiquities in the Middle Ages*, 37–118.

[10] Abravanel on Josh. 8: 30 (*Perush linevi'im rishonim*, 44).

[11] Ibn Daud, *Sefer hakabalah*, ch. 4, lines 69–72, 85–8 (ed. Cohen: Heb. section, 28–9; Eng. section, 37–8). Christians of that period wrote similar descriptions (see G. D. Cohen, Introduction and notes, ibid. 37, notes to lines 93–4; 38, notes to lines 116–19).

[12] Benjamin of Tudela, *Sefer masaot*, 7–8.   [13] Ibid. 7.

[14] Ibid. 8. In actual fact, the statue is of Emperor Marcus Aurelius and is now in the Capitol. In the Middle Ages it stood before the Lateran Palace and was thought to be Constantine (see Magister Gregorius, *On the Marvels of the City of Rome*, 21–2).

[15] Benjamin of Tudela, *Sefer masaot*, 7.

Benjamin of Tudela's descriptions are accurate, realistic, and very similar to those of Magister Gregorius, who visited Rome at about the same time.[16]

A series of letters between Zerahiah ben Isaac She'altiel Hen from Barcelona, who lived in Rome from 1277 to 1291, and his relative Judah ben Solomon also reveals Jewish interest in the Roman empire and the ruins of Rome.[17] The discovery of some huge bones in Rome and nearby Castellana evoked great excitement in scholarly circles and led to a debate about the possibility that giants had existed in the past.[18] Judah ben Solomon doubted that bones could have been preserved for so long. Zerahiah Hen, however, insisted that these were indeed ancient bones, from a period prior to the construction of Rome. He argued that if those giants had lived in the time of Rome, their existence would have been written about and depicted in the buildings of Rome, particularly in the palaces and temples, in keeping with Roman custom.[19] This indicates that he was well acquainted with the Roman ruins, inscriptions and works of art. Later he dealt with the reason why the teeth of giants could have been preserved for so long without decaying. He compared them to the copper and lead in the buildings of ancient Rome, which, he claimed, unlike the large stones and marble, showed no sign of decay.[20]

Rome, then, was not forgotten by Jews in the Middle Ages. Considerable segments of Roman history were included in books about the Second Temple period, such as the *Book of Josippon* and Ibn Daud's *Sefer hakabalah*; there were books dedicated to Rome, such as his *History of Rome*; and additional historical information is found in chronicles, such as Joseph ben Tsadik's *Kitsur zekher tsadik* and Abraham Zacut's *Sefer yuḥasin*. Rome was also mentioned in works outside the genres of historiography and travel literature—in ethical books and biblical commentaries, such as Isaac Nathan's *Me'amets koaḥ* and the writings of Isaac Abravanel.

Before discussing the images of Rome in these books, I should like to discuss its image in the talmudic and midrashic literature. According to Yosef Hayim Yerushalmi, the images, symbolism, and vocabulary of the Talmud determined the content of the collective memory of medieval Jews.

THE IMAGE OF ROME IN THE SECOND TEMPLE, MISHNAIC AND TALMUDIC PERIODS

The Habakkuk Pesher found among the Dead Sea Scrolls is probably the earliest extant Hebrew document that expresses hatred of Roman imperialism, and

[16] See Borchardt, 'The Sculpture in Front of the Lateran'.

[17] On Zerahiah Hen, see Ravitzky, 'The Teachings of Zerahiah ben She'altiel Hen' (Heb.), 66–94; Zinberg, *History of Jewish Literature* (Heb.), i. 381–7.

[18] Zerahiah b. She'altiel Hen, *Igeret*, 121. [19] Ibid. [20] Ibid.

Jewish anticipation of the downfall of Rome first appeared in the Nahum Pesher.[21] The symbolic interpretation of Rome as the fourth kingdom, or the fourth beast of Daniel's visions, appeared in Josephus and was apparently widely accepted. These images were common in the Talmud and Midrash, and derogatory terms were added to them: 'the evil reign', 'the wicked kingdom', 'Edom', 'Zor', 'Amalek'.[22] Many Jews were unwilling to bend to the Roman yoke, and hatred of Rome was deeply rooted and widespread and at times led to rebellion. From the plethora of sources hostile to Rome, it is obvious that this hatred did not diminish over time.[23] However, hatred of Rome cannot be separated from parallel phenomena that were widespread throughout the empire. The Jews were not the only ones who resisted Roman occupation and world-view: such attitudes were prevalent among pagans and later Christians.[24] Concentrating only on the negative image of Rome among Jews distorts its historical significance.

The early sages were well informed about Roman culture, and this knowledge found various expressions in literature.[25] Some of them spoke in favour of Rome: the earliest expression of praise is found in 1 Maccabees, where Judas Maccabee forms an alliance with the Romans. The author describes the Romans' military valour and discipline, their rulers' lack of airs, and the intelligent manner in which the senate conducted public affairs. Although this testimony is exceptional, later in the Second Temple period there were signs that some Jews reconciled themselves to Roman rule and acknowledged the advantage it offered of orderly lives, peace, security, and justice.[26] We can find such positions in the works of the Jewish philosopher Philo of Alexandria and Josephus, and these can be compared to a similar assessment by many Greek historians, such as Strabo, Dionysus of Halicarnassus, Plutarch, and Dio Cassius. They all lauded Rome's military power, her administrative accomplishments, and the prosperity and

[21] See Flusser, 'Rome in the Eyes of the Hasmoneans and the Essenes' (Heb.). On the first Jewish attitudes expressed in Greek, see De Lange, 'Jewish Attitudes to the Roman Empire', esp. 258–60.

[22] Josephus, *Jewish Antiquities*, 10.4.209–10; see I. Ben-Shalom, *The House of Shammai and the Zealots' Struggle against Rome* (Heb.), app. 1, 277–8; Schalit, Introduction and notes (Heb.) to Josephus, *Jewish Antiquities*, i. 161 n. 326; see also e.g. *Genesis Rabbah* 2: 4, 16: 4, 99: 2 (ed. Albeck, i. 16–17, 147–8, iii. 1273–4); Herr, 'Rome in Rabbinic Literature' (Heb.), col. 774.

[23] See I. Ben-Shalom, 'Rabbi Judah bar Ilai and His Attitude to Rome' (Heb.), 11 n. 8; Kasher, 'The Causal and Circumstantial Background to the Jews' War against the Romans' (Heb.); Oppenheimer, 'The Bar Kokhba Revolt' (Heb.), 10; see also Avi-Yonah, *In the Days of Rome and Byzantium* (Heb.), 61–7. The discussion of Rome also belongs within the broader issue of the Jewish attitude to foreigners (see Y. Cohen, 'The Image of the Non-Jew in the Tannaitic Period' (Heb.)).

[24] See Fuchs, *Der geistige Widerstand gegen Rom in der antiken Welt*; Gruen, *The Image of Rome*.

[25] See Krauss, *Persia and Rome in the Talmud and the Midrash* (Heb.).

[26] 1 Macc. 8: 1–16; see Alon, 'The Attitude of the Pharisees to Roman Rule and the House of Herod' (Heb.), 319–22; Flusser, 'Rome in the Eyes of the Hasmoneans and the Essenes' (Heb.), 154–7.

security that the Pax Romana bestowed on the entire world.[27] In the Mishnah, this view is reflected in the words of Rabbi Hanina, the assistant high priest: 'Pray for the welfare of the government [Rome], for if not for fear of it a person would swallow his fellow alive.'[28] There were, however, disagreements among the rabbis regarding Roman culture and its achievements:

Rabbi Judah bar Ilai commenced by observing, 'How fine the deeds of this nation! They have built bridges, they have erected baths.' Rabbi Yose was silent. Rabbi Shimon bar Yohai answered and said: 'All that they made, they made for themselves; they built market-places, to set harlots in them; baths, to rejuvenate themselves; bridges, to levy tolls for them.'[29]

The majority of rabbis thought Rome's values and institutions were reprehensible and frequently emphasized its abuses. They were even harshly critical of Roman jurisprudence, an area in which the Romans were famous, and found their laws capricious and arbitrary.[30] Moses David Herr drew a distinction between the Jews' evaluation of Rome during the period of the sages of the Mishnah, when Jews were on equal grounds with Romans, at least from the spiritual standpoint, and the period of the sages of the Talmud, when Judaism was on the defensive. He claimed that most of the talmudic sages believed that Rome was hypocritical and robbed and cheated while pretending to be merciful and just.[31] While this describes the picture in general, Herr's position needs refining, as the talmudic sages in the Land of Israel had different attitudes from those in Babylonia.[32]

THE IMAGE OF ROME IN THE EYES OF MEDIEVAL JEWS

In the light of the enormous influence of talmudic and midrashic literature on the Jewish world-view, one might have expected that the hostile view of Rome would

---

[27] See Delling, 'Philons Enkomion auf Augustus'; Gernentz, *Laudes Romae*; Hallewy, *Biographical-Historical Legends in the Light of Greek and Latin Sources* (Heb.), 510–11; Stern, 'Josephus's *Jewish War* and the Roman Empire' (Heb.); on the perception of Rome in Plutarch, see C. P. Jones, *Plutarch and Rome*. [28] Mishnah *Avot* 3: 2.

[29] BT *Shab.* 33*b*; see Ankar, 'Rabbi Judah ben Ilai (Heb.), 208–37; I. Ben-Shalom, 'Rabbi Judah bar Ilai and His Attitude to Rome' (Heb.); Meir, *The Poetics of Rabbinic Stories* (Heb.), 11–34; Rokeah, 'On Rabbi Judah bar Ilai and His Attitude to Rome' (Heb.).

[30] Krauss, *Persia and Rome in the Talmud and the Midrash* (Heb.), 101–6.

[31] Herr, 'Rome in Rabbinic Literature' (Heb.), col. 774; see also col. 775; id., 'The Historical Significance of the Dialogues between Jewish Sages and Roman Dignitaries', esp. 145; see also De Lange, 'Jewish Attitudes to the Roman Empire', 275–81.

[32] See Baron, *A Social and Religious History of the Jews*, ii. 176–80, esp. the quote from Rabbah bar Hana (ibid. 176).

have been retained or that the issue would become moot with the collapse of Rome. One might also expect to find a negative attitude to Rome as a consequence of Christian claims about the relationship between Rome and the Church. According to Christian theology, it was no accident that Jesus appeared during the time of Augustus and the Pax Romana. The peace during Augustus's reign enabled the spread of Christianity, and, at the same time, the empire needed the Church, as its members were the only people who had no local commitment and were, hence, the true and natural citizens of the empire.[33]

According to Yosef Hayim Yerushalmi, Rome was not a historical reality for Jews. Although the memory of the destruction of the Temple was preserved, the typological understanding of Rome predominated, and Jews took no interest in the historical details. They remembered the day and month on which the destruction took place, but it is doubtful that they knew the year. The image of Rome in Jewish eyes was extremely negative.[34] According to Gerson Cohen, for Jews in the late Middle Ages, even more than for contemporary Christians, Rome was very much alive, and her image was that of a wicked kingdom. It made no difference that the religion of the empire was replaced by Christianity: 'Esau can replace the eagle with the cross, nonetheless he is still Esau.'[35] Haim Hillel Ben-Sasson agreed that Jews had a consistently negative attitude to Rome. In his view, the roots of Jewish attitudes to Christianity and the peoples of Europe can be found in the legacy of hatred and antithesis between Jerusalem and Rome. Although this legacy of opposition to Rome was also shared by other peoples in the ancient world, it was sharpest and most extreme among the Jews.[36]

These claims need to be examined in the light of a number of historical sources that have not previously been taken into account. In a number of cases, Jews showed a great deal of interest in various periods of Roman history. In the following section, I will describe these sources and examine the writers' motives, sources, and attitudes to Rome.

The Foundation Myth of Rome

Medieval and Renaissance thought was much concerned with the foundation of Rome. The *Description of the Golden City of Rome* refers to several urban settlements within the boundaries of Rome that preceded Romulus. It was Romulus who finally built a wall around all of these cities and called it Rome after him-

---

[33] See Breisach, *Historiography*, 80–8; Funkenstein, *Theology and the Scientific Imagination*, 256–61.

[34] Yerushalmi, *Zakhor*, 43. In Yerushalmi's view, the main indicator of the Jews' attitude towards Rome was their lack of any interest in the Romans' military tactics and weapons.

[35] Ibid.   [36] H. H. Ben-Sasson, *Essays on Medieval Jewish History* (Heb.), 243.

self.[37] Niccolò Machiavelli devoted an entire chapter to it and tried to prove that Rome was founded by free men, regardless of whether they were foreign (Aeneas) or native (Romulus).[38] Intellectuals discussed the multiple traditions not only out of historiographical interest but also because of the importance and sanctity of foundational acts: the two major acts of foundation in Europe—of Rome and of the Catholic Church—were believed to be somehow connected.[39]

Medieval Jewish historiographical works also often contained a chapter dealing with the founding of Rome. Ibn Daud, for example, dealt with the myth of Rome's construction in *Sefer hakabalah*.[40] It is also the event with which he, logically, chose to begin his *History of Rome*:

The great city of Rome was built by two generals who were brothers. The elder was named Romulus, and the other Remus. They built it in the sixth year of Hezekiah king of Judea, and they added two months to the solar year: May, which means large, and June, which means small, for before then the solar year was divided into eight months. And the older, Romulus, conspired against his brother, Remus, and struck him down, and he died, and after the death of Romulus, powerful kings ruled it for about 210 years, until the year of the construction of the Second Temple.[41]

As he did elsewhere, Ibn Daud tried to synchronize the history of Rome with the history of the Jews. As we have seen, this was a common historiographical method, but in this instance Ibn Daud was following the *Book of Josippon*.[42] According to Gerson Cohen, Ibn Daud's motives were polemical. He wanted to sever the symbolic link—so often emphasized in Christian chronicles—between the decline of Babylon and the rise of Rome and to make the Jewish people part of the cycle of world history.[43]

Ibn Daud ignored an earlier event mentioned in the *Book of Josippon*, in which (another) Romulus, who feared King David, built a wall around 'the buildings of the kings who reigned before him . . . and he called the city Rome after the name of Romulus'.[44] Following Cohen's interpretation, dating the foundation of Rome to the time of David did not fit into Ibn Daud's historiographical schema, according to which glorious periods for the Jewish people coincided with the

---

[37] See Flusser, *The Book of Josippon* (Heb.), ii. 135.

[38] Machiavelli, *The Discourses*, i: 1. The founding of Rome was a major interest of humanists and intellectuals in Europe until the beginning of the nineteenth century (see Bietenholz, *Historia and Fabula*, 288–310, 416–22; Grandazzi, *The Foundation of Rome*, esp. 177–211).

[39] See Arendt, 'What was Authority?'

[40] See Ibn Daud, *Sefer hakabalah*, ch. 4, lines 66–72 (ed. Cohen: Heb. section, 28; Eng. section, 36–7).   [41] Ibn Daud, *Zikhron divrei romi* (Mantua edn., 21–2; ed. Vehlow, 98–9).

[42] See *Sefer yosipon*, 6: 34 (ed. Hominer, 145); see Flusser, *The Book of Josippon* (Heb.), ii. 25–6, n. 64; Dönitz, *Überlieferung und Rezeption des Sefer Yosippon*, 223–39.

[43] See G. D. Cohen, Introduction and notes to Ibn Daud, *Sefer hakabalah*, 226–9.

[44] *Sefer yosipon*, 1: 3 (ed. Flusser, 18–19; ed. Hominer, 6).

waning of Rome. However Cohen's messianic interpretation has been challenged recently, and more local polemical concerns have been suggested as the reasons behind his historiography.[45]

In the 1480s Joseph ben Tsadik, who, unlike Ibn Daud, was not constrained by polemical considerations, was cognizant of these two events, which the *Book of Josippon* placed at very different points in time. In order to reconcile them, he created a distinction between the construction of Rome by 'the other Romulus' in the time of David, and the construction of 'the great city of Rome' by the brothers Romulus and Remus, in the time of Hezekiah.[46]

Abravanel and Zacut gave a different account of Rome's foundation. While Ibn Daud and Joseph ben Tsadik remained close to the *Book of Josippon*, Abravanel and Zacut used other historical sources as well. Abravanel wrote at length on the subject in an attempt to identify Rome with Edom.[47] His discussion was underpinned by a passage in the *Book of Josippon*, which relates how Zepho, son of Eliphaz, son of Esau (Gen. 36: 11) went to Italy. Zepho founded the Roman dynasty and his sons reigned after him. Consequently, Rome can be identified as Edom, since a member of Esau's family founded Rome.[48] This provided pseudo-historical support for the allegorical interpretation of Rome/Edom in the Talmud and Midrash.[49] However, Jews who were aware of Roman historiography knew that it was not the case, so Abravanel tried to identify Edom and Rome on the basis of Isidore of Seville's discussion in *Etymologiarum*:

For it is accepted by all in the Talmud and Midrash, without any disagreement, that the Romans came from Chief Magdiel, who was one of Esau's chiefs, and he is Edom. And the Christian interpreters of the Holy Scriptures and above all Nicholas of Lyra, their great interpreter, have accepted that the Romans issued from Magdiel, the chief of Edom. And due to the long time that has passed, there may be nothing found in the history books of the Romans about the manner in which the sons of Edom settled in Rome and in the land of Italy, but this does not contradict the words of our holy sages in their tradition, for Isidore the ancient, great sage of the Christians, has already written in chapter 5 of his *Etymologiarum*, a statement worth remembering, in which he says: 'It is not proper to denounce and deny the words of the ancient storytellers regarding the beginnings of the nations and the peoples of the lands and how they replaced one another. For we do not truly know the genealogy of the people of Rome, the large, heav-

---

[45] Krakowski, 'On the Literary Character of Abraham ibn Da'ud's Sefer Ha-Qabbalah'; Vehlow, Introduction to Ibn Daud, *Zikhron divrei romi*, 41–4.

[46] Joseph b. Tsadik, *Kitsur zekher tsadik* (ed. Neubauer, 87).

[47] G. D. Cohen, 'Esau as Symbol in Early Medieval Thought'; see also David Kimhi on Joel 4: 19.

[48] Flusser, *The Book of Josippon*, ii. 10–20.

[49] See G. D. Cohen, 'Esau as Symbol in Early Medieval Thought'; Rosenthal, 'Interest from the Foreigner' (Heb.), 280–96.

ily populated city—whether the Trojans came and settled there, as Sallust said, or the people of Evander built it, as Virgil said, or Romulus's men, as others say. And if in that notable metropolis, the finest of all metropolises, no one truly knows until today the genealogy of her people, what will come to pass in other metropolises, for the passage of many years will give rise to errors and folly in this regard.' And these are [Isidore's] words.[50] So we can say that the peoples of the nations are constantly on the move, shifting from here to there. And as Italy at first was the land of the Kittim and of the sons of Greece, from the beginning of the Creation and the time of the Flood, who, then, over time, could prevent peoples who are the sons of Edom from coming and settling there, all the more so since we have found much support for this in the words of Joseph ben Gorion who wrote: 'When Joseph arose . . . and captured Zepho, son of Eliphaz, son of Esau. . . . Afterwards Zepho escaped and came to Italy, the land of the Kittim . . . and when the Kittim saw his great successes in war, and all of his heroic deeds, they made him their king and gave him the name Zepho-Janus. . . . And he was the first king of Italy . . . and after him his son reigned, and all the following kings were of his seed.' And according to the tradition of our sages, one of them was Chief Magdiel, who was the first to settle the state of Rome, before Romulus came and built her walls. . . . And here we have clear evidence from the words of Josippon, who was the chief of the storytellers, that the sons of Edom ruled over the land of the Kittim. And there is no doubt that when they reigned there, many peoples from the land of Edom came to settle in Italy because the Edomite kings reigned there, so they multiplied . . . and the land of Italy was filled with them. And Rome was built from them.[51]

Abravanel noted the existence of various traditions regarding the foundation of Rome, which he exploited to prove the connection between Edom and Rome. He cited Isidore of Seville, who compiled some of the legends and pointed out that it was impossible to decide which was the true one, to show that the Romans did not have a clear idea of who founded their city: according to Sallust, it was Aeneas and a band of refugees from Troy;[52] according to Virgil, it was Evander (a Greek), known as the 'builder of the walls of Rome' or 'founder of the fortress of Rome';[53] while for others, it was Romulus, who was born with his twin Remus to the god Mars and the daughter of the king of Alba Longa;[54] and, in the talmudic

[50] Isidore of Seville, *Etymologiarum*, 15: 1. The discussion is in ch. 15, not 5 as Abravanel claimed.

[51] Abravanel, *Mashmia yeshuah*, 3: 7 (Jerusalem edn., 461–3); see the more extensive parallel (Abravanel on Isa. 35: 10 (*Perush al nevi'im aharonim*, 169–73)); see also Rosenthal, 'Interest from the Foreigner' (Heb.), 286–90.   [52] Sallust, *The War with Catiline*, 6: 11.

[53] Although it is clear that Aeneas the Trojan was the true founder of Rome (see Virgil, *Aeneid*, 8: 411). Evander was given those epithets because he built Pallantium on the Palatine Hill (ibid. 8: 65–9). On the myth of Evander, see Ogilvie, *A Commentary on Livy*, 51–2; Papaioannou, 'Founder, Civilizer and Leader'.

[54] For example, the ancient Roman analyst Fabius Pictor (Plutarch, 'Life of Romulus', *Lives*, 5: 1; Virgil, *Aeneid*, 1: 385–90; see Ogilvie, *A Commentary on Livy*, 46–55).

tradition, it was the twins Romulus and Remus.[55] The Romans had already felt the need to harmonize their various traditions, and, according to the revised legend found for the first time in Cato and later in Livy, Ascanius, son of Aeneas, founded the city of Alba Longa, and his offspring reigned there, and the twins Romulus and Remus were born twelve generations later.[56]

This confusion of traditions provided Abravanel with plenty of opportunity to connect Edom and Rome. However, the traditional identification of Italy with the land of the Kittim posed difficulties.[57] Abravanel was not satisfied with the genealogical tradition of the *Book of Josippon*, because it left too many questions open, such as: 'Does the identity of a people change merely on the basis of the dynasty of kings that rule it?' and 'Should Rome no longer be identified with Edom, because of the change that took place in the Roman royal dynasty?' Abravanel argued that Esau's grandson, Zepho, escaped to Italy and so impressed the Kittim that they made him their king. Other Edomites then settled there, because Rome was now ruled by Edomite kings.[58] Another problem with the account in the *Book of Josippon*, was the identification of Zepho with Janus (Zepho-Janus), the first king of Rome, since the name Zepho was not known among the Romans.[59] To address this problem, Abravanel cited an additional tradition from 'the history books of the Romans' and appealed again to the confusion and incompleteness of the sources:

> Know that in the history books of the Romans there is a mention of Janus, and it is written that he was the first king in Italy and was called the father of the divinity, the god of gods, and the gate of heaven. . . . And [in order] to signify the abundance of the planet Saturn, who in their language was called Janus, they named [Janus] after [Saturn], and called him a gate of heaven, but they did not mention anything about his family, his people, or the land of his birth, as they did for the other kings of Italy. And in addition, they said that Janus came from a land in the east, and that also shows the truth of the words of Josippon, for [as he tells us, Janus] came from Egypt and from the land of Edom first.[60]

According to Virgil, Saturn brought civilization to the savage people who lived in Latium after he was expelled from Olympus by his son Jupiter. Virgil also men-

---

[55] See Krauss, *Persia and Rome in the Talmud and the Midrash* (Heb.), 14–19; Rieger, 'The Foundation of Rome in the Talmud'.

[56] Livy, *The History of Rome*, 1: 1–6; see Ogilvie, *A Commentary on Livy*, 32–5; see also Bietenholz, *Historia and Fabula*, 46–61.

[57] According to Gen. 10: 4, the Kittim were the Greeks; in the Dead Sea Scrolls, they were identified as the Romans.   [58] Abravanel, *Mashmia yeshuah*, 3: 7 (Jerusalem edn., 163).

[59] Janus, the ancient god of the Romans, was, according to one legend, the first king of Rome (see Flusser, notes (Heb.) to *Sefer yosipon*, 1: 51, 55 (pp. 13–14)).

[60] Abravanel, *Mashmia yeshuah*, 3: 7 (Jerusalem edn., 63); cf. Abravanel on Isa. 35: 10 (*Perush al nevi'im aharonim*, 171).

tioned Janus in this context, and they are depicted as the builders of two ancient cities on the site of what would become Rome.[61] Plutarch, however, ascribed the bringing of civilization to Janus.[62] In other Roman legends, Janus was the first king of Rome, and Saturn reigned after him.[63] The identification of Janus with Saturn seems to be unique to the *Book of Josippon*, but it is reasonable to assume that the lack of clarity in the various Roman traditions easily allowed the first two Roman kings to be fused into one. Abravanel took the statement that Janus came from the east and the absence of any other information about his origin and family as support for the claim that he was Zepho, Esau's grandson, who, according to the *Book of Josippon*, came to Italy through Egypt from Edom.[64] In his commentary on Isaiah, Abravanel added chronological calculations to prove that Zepho and Janus lived at the same time.[65]

Abravanel also ascribed an Edomite origin to the Roman king Latinus. He based this on the etymological similarity between the names Latinus and Lotan, an Edomite chief mentioned in the Bible (Gen. 36: 29). In his view, the fact that the names have a similar sound showed that the name Latinus was common among the Edomites.[66]

I think that Latinus, who was also one of the kings of Italy and was said to have invented the Latin language, and the [Latin] alphabet came from the Edomites, because among [the Edomites] this was a common name as the scripture says: chief of Lotan.[67]

Abraham Zacut also attempted to resolve the confusion of traditions about the foundation of Rome. He found no fewer than seven figures called Janus, only a few of whom had any connection to Roman history.[68] In contrast to the *Book of Josippon*, Zacut asserted that Janus and Saturn were two different people. Janus was the first king of Rome and was the same as the biblical Zepho; Saturn came to Italy from Crete and reigned after him. Zacut also stated that one ought not to confuse, as the author of the *Book of Josippon* did, Janus the first king of Rome with the seventh Janus who is associated with the city of Genoa.[69]

[61] Virgil, *Aeneid*, 8: 418–30, 464–9.   [62] Plutarch, 'Life of Numa', *Lives*, 19: 119.

[63] Flusser, notes (Heb.) to *Sefer yosipon*, 1: 55, 57, 60 (p. 14).

[64] *Sefer yosipon*, 1: 56–8 (ed. Flusser, 14); Flusser, notes (Heb.) to *Sefer yosipon*, 1: 19 (p. 11); id., *The Book of Josippon* (Heb.), ii. 23–4; Grant and Hazel, *Gods and Mortals in Classical Mythology*, 201, 306.

[65] Abravanel on Isa. 35: 10 (*Perush al nevi'im aharonim*, 171).

[66] See Gen. 36: 20; 1 Chron. 1: 38. Joseph ben Tsadik and Abraham Zacut also wrote about King Latinus and, following the *Book of Josippon*, credited him with the invention of Latin. Joseph ben Tsadik placed him between the time of Eli the priest and that of King David (*Kitsur zekher tsadik* (ed. Neubauer, 86–7)). Zacut placed him at the time of the judge Yair (*Sefer yuhasin* (ed. Filipowski, 235*b*); see *Sefer yosipon*, 2: 63–4 (ed. Flusser, 14); Flusser, note (Heb.), ibid.).

[67] Abravanel, *Mashmia yeshuah*, 3: 7 (Jerusalem edn., 463).

[68] Zacut, *Sefer yuhasin* (ed. Filipowski, 234*b*).

[69] Ibid. 237*b*; see *Sefer yosipon*, 2: 53–62 (ed. Flusser, 14); Flusser, note (Heb.), ibid.

Abravanel and Zacut's attempts to reconcile Jewish, Christian, and pagan historiographical traditions indicate their positive attitude to non-Jewish historiography, an attitude that was reflected elsewhere in their writings. Unlike other Jewish commentators, who ignored non-Jewish sources, Abravanel and Zacut tried to reconcile the traditions as far as possible and sometimes clearly preferred non-Jewish ones. Abravanel tried to show that the *Book of Josippon* was compatible with pagan traditions and came up with a 'realistic' explanation of the identification of Janus and Saturn: the king-god Janus was the source of miraculous bounty and therefore people associated him with the planet Saturn—a planet that provides abundance. Zacut, on the other hand, emphatically rejected the identification of Janus with Saturn and stated that these were two distinct people, thereby challenging an important Jewish historiographical tradition. But he did not reject the identification of Janus with Zepho (although he had some reservations about it—'and they say he was Zepho') and thus remained faithful to the central mythic perception that identified Rome with Edom.

Although they disagreed about Janus, Abravanel and Zacut were of the same opinion on the role of Romulus and Remus in the founding of Rome. They believed the twin brothers built Rome but did not found it. In this regard, they followed the *Book of Josippon*.[70] The myth of Romulus and Remus, as it appeared in the long version of the *Book of Josippon* and as it was adapted by Ibn Daud in his *History of Rome*, was certainly well known among Jews. However, the first part of the story, the adventures of the twins before the establishment of the city, is missing. Although one could surmise that this important part of the myth was not known, Jews who studied the Torah must have been familiar with an abridged version of it which appears in *Midrash tehilim*.[71]

Joseph ben David, a fourteenth-century *dayan* (judge) from Saragossa, provided another version of the myth:

It is told in *Midrash tehilim* about Romulus and Remus, that at the time of their birth, their father dreamt that two lights would come out of his nostrils and burn the city that he ruled, and when he awoke he was informed that his wife had given birth to twins, and he judged that they were the lights he had dreamt of and ordered that they be left to die in the forest. A female bear came along and suckled them, and when they grew up

---

[70] Abravanel, *Ma'ayenei hayeshuah*, 8: 2 (Jerusalem edn., 330); Zacut, *Sefer yuḥasin* (ed. Filipowski, 237*b*–238*a*); *Sefer yosipon*, 2: 108–23 (ed. Flusser, 18–19). The Christian tradition on the construction of Rome in the time of Ahaz is found, for example, in the Additions to Peter Comestor, *Scholastic History* (ed. Migne, col. 1406) (see G. D. Cohen, Introduction and notes to Ibn Daud, *Sefer hakabalah*, 226, esp. n. 16; Merhavia, *The Talmud in Christian Eyes* (Heb.), 199).

[71] *Midrash tehilim* on Pss. 10: 6; 17: 12 (ed. Buber, 35, 81–2). The *midrash* was known as far back as the mid-eleventh century (see Zunz, *Haderashot beyisra'el*, 131–2; Albeck, comment (Heb.) ibid.).

they burned their father's city and built Rome, and from them come the great families of Rome and they are the Bears.[72]

This version differs in several details from the one in *Midrash tehilim*. In this particular *midrash*, Romulus and Remus are twins who were suckled and raised by a female wolf and grew up to build Rome. It does not say why or how they were orphaned or how they came to be cared for by the wolf. Joseph ben David also relates the father's dream, his interpretation of it, and his attempt to kill his two sons. The dream is not mentioned in any of the versions collected by Livy or Plutarch, and the king who ordered the brothers to be killed was their mother's uncle, not their father.

The she-wolf (*diba* in Aramaic) was replaced by a she-bear (*duba* in Aramaic), a mistake that appears in the *midrash* and some of the later commentators.[73] Joseph ben David's comment on the genealogical dynasty of the 'Bear' families in Rome, which goes as far back as Romulus and Remus, is particularly interesting. He was probably referring to the Orsinis (*orso* is Italian for 'bear'), a noble Roman family, which provided many popes and other religious and political figures.[74]

Zacut presents the myth in its entirety:

In that same year reigned Amulius Silvius. . . . He exiled his elder brother and killed the son of his elder brother. He forced his niece into seclusion [as a Vestal Virgin], but she gave birth to Remus and Romulus. The brothers killed Amulius Silvius and restored their exiled grandfather to the throne. Nobody knows who lay with the mother of Remus and Romulus, but she gave birth to twin boys. When the king learned of it, he killed the mother by burying her alive. He ordered that the twins be cast into the river, but as the river was vast, they were not cast where the king ordered, but on the riverbank. A shepherd found them and took them home to his wife. She was a harlot and nursed them. Some people say they were taken and nursed by wolves. Maybe it is an allegory for a harlot who nursed them as a she-wolf would. . . . [Rome] was built in twenty-two years. In it there were seven hills and seven towns on them. It was built by Remus and Romulus; they gave the city their name and reigned for thirty-eight years. Some say their father was Mars; others say it was the uncle of their mother—that is the opinion of our sages of blessed memory in *Midrash tehilim* on the verse 'You have ever been the orphan's help' [Ps. 10: 14].[75]

Zacut's account is similar to that in Plutarch, who collected various traditions about Romulus and Remus, some of which were contradictory.[76] Zacut cited two versions of the twins' paternity: the more well-known version, that their father

---

[72] See Joseph b. David on Gen. 37: 1–40: 23.

[73] See *Targum*, Isa. 11: 6; *Genesis Rabbah* 99: 2 (ed. Albeck, iii. 1273–4); *Genesis Rabbati* 49: 27 (ed. Albeck, 253); Abraham ibn Ezra on Dan. 7: 5 (*Mikra'ot gedolot*).

[74] Or perhaps he intended to underscore the viciousness of the great families of Rome, since bears were noted for their savagery. [75] Zacut, *Sefer yuḥasin* (ed. Filipowski, 237*b*–238*a*).

[76] See Plutarch, 'Life of Romulus', *Lives*, 4: 32–3; see also Livy, *History of Rome*, 1: 4.

was Mars; and the other, that he was Amulius Silvius himself. Zacut tried to verify one of the Roman versions on the basis of *Midrash tehilim* that the brothers were orphans. He claimed that the *midrash* was more compatible with a human father: perhaps because of the use of the word 'orphans', even though Amulius was alive at the time. An inconsistency Zacut apparently did not notice.

Abravanel also used what he found in non-Jewish sources on the foundation of Rome for biblical exegesis. His use of Latin sources and the distinction he drew between the builders of Rome and the founders of Rome enabled him to criticize Nahmanides' typological interpretation of the ten 'chiefs of Esau' (Gen. 36: 40) and the ten horns of the fourth beast (Dan. 7: 7), according to which nine kings would rule over the fourth kingdom (Edom) before the tenth (Magdiel) came to reign over Rome.[77] Abravanel explained that Nahmanides was referring to ten kings 'who reigned in Italy prior to the building of Rome, since the last one ruled over Rome'. He commented: 'With all due respect, that is not the case, for in the books of the Gentiles it is written that there were twenty-one kings in Italy, and the last of them was Romulus who built the walls of Rome.' This is also the number given in the *Book of Josippon*. Thus, Abravanel argued that it was impossible to understand what Nahmanides wrote unless one assumed that he accepted Rashi's interpretation of the ten horns.[78] Abravanel wrote:

I do not know the intention of [Nahmanides] because if he said this regarding the kings that reigned there when the city was first settled, before the leadership of the elder and his advisers,[79] then there is no doubt that there were no more than seven, and here are their names: Romulus, the first, who built her walls; and Numa Pompilius, the second; and Tullus Hostilius, the third; and Ancus Marcius, the fourth; and Tarquinius Priscus, the fifth; and Servius Tullius, the sixth; and Tarquinius Superbus the Wicked, the seventh, was the last. And based on these we cannot interpret the ten horns. And if we say that [Nahmanides] referred to the emperors who reigned in Rome, since in our language their real name is 'kings', here too the count of ten is not correct, for from Julius Caesar, the first emperor, until today there have been more than 200 emperors in Rome and how can these be ten horns?[80]

---

[77] Nahmanides on Gen. 36: 43 (ed. Chavel, 204–5); see Sperber, 'Chief Magdiel' (Heb.). As mentioned above, Abravanel accepted the identification of Magdiel and Rome and also stated that this was the interpretation of Christian scholars, in particular Nicholas of Lyra (see Funkenstein, *Perceptions of Jewish History*, esp. 111).

[78] Abravanel, *Ma'ayenei hayeshuah*, 8: 2 (Jerusalem edn., 336). Zacut also noted that there were twenty-one kings of the Latins in Italy before Rome was built. According to Rashi, the last of the ten kings was Titus (Rashi on Dan. 7: 24).

[79] The 'elder and his advisers' are the *princeps senatus* (head of the senate) and the 300 senators. 'Senate' is derived from the Latin *senex*, 'old man'. See the section on Isaac Nathan below, where the origin of the error in the *Book of Josippon* is discussed.

[80] Abravanel, *Ma'ayenei hayeshuah*, 8: 2 (Jerusalem edn., 336).

Abravanel was correct about the order of the kings of Rome and very nearly correct about the number of Roman emperors—working on the accepted premise that the Roman empire had never stopped existing and the medieval German emperors should be included.

Abravanel also rejected Gersonides' interpretation of 'the chiefs of Esau' as a reference to Constantine, the tenth emperor, who imposed Christianity on the Roman empire, as Constantine was the thirty-ninth emperor. Furthermore, Abravanel claimed that he had attempted to find an answer in Christian commentaries on Daniel, but without success. His solution apparently corresponded to Rashi's, although Rashi simply claimed that the last of the ten kings was Titus, while Abravanel used a list of emperors from Julius Caesar to Vespasian, who was emperor when Titus conquered Jerusalem.[81] Although Abravanel attempted to demonstrate his innovativeness and erudition, his commentary here is not actually any different from Nahmanides'.[82] Nahmanides was not referring to the ten kings who reigned before Rome was built, as Abravanel thought, but to the ten emperors who preceded Titus, and hence Abravanel's criticism is groundless. Despite this, Abravanel reveals a sound historical and exegetical method, which embraces non-Jewish sources and uses them to reconcile different interpretations.

The use of non-Jewish sources enabled Abravanel and Zacut to present a more complete picture of the myth of the foundation of Rome, each according to his purpose. Abravanel used the proliferation of incompatible versions to prove that Edom was Rome and to criticize earlier Jewish biblical interpretation; Zacut incorporated the myth into his chronicle as a significant historical event and as part of his attempt to synchronize Roman and Jewish history. They both dealt with Roman history because of exegetical needs or intellectual curiosity, not, or not only, for polemical purposes. At times, they both made polemical points in their discussions, but in general their examinations of the issue were based on accepted historical 'facts', with no attempt to defame or distort the reputation of the Roman empire. Much historical knowledge was provided without any other reason than an interest in Roman history in itself and a scientific approach to history.

It is not possible to determine whether a positive image of Rome existed continuously from the talmudic period to the fifteenth century or whether it was

---

[81] 'And these are the names of the emperors. The first, Julius Caesar, the second Octavius Augustus, the third Tiberius Caesar, the fourth Gaius Caligula, the fifth Claudius, the sixth Nero, the seventh Caesar Galba, the eighth Salvius Otho, the ninth Sergius [*recte* Aulus] Vitellius, and the tenth Vespasian, who we call Aspasianus: in his time and under his orders, Jerusalem was captured by Titus' (Abravanel, *Ma'ayenei hayeshuah*, 8: 2 (Jerusalem edn., 336)).

[82] As proven in another work, in which Nahmanides made the same point: 'And ten horns . . . because ten kings reigned in Rome prior to Titus the destroyer' (Nahmanides, *Sefer hage'ulah*, 3 (ed. Chavel, 286)).

suppressed for centuries and re-emerged (or perhaps was created) in the Middle Ages. Nonetheless, one can say that this favourable image of Rome gained some support when the *Book of Josippon* became the 'official' Jewish history of the Second Temple period.[83] The popularity of the *Book of Josippon* among the Jews of Spain and southern France and the numerous citations from it in the texts they produced mean that an examination of their image of Rome must take into account the image of Rome in the *Book of Josippon*.

THE IMAGE OF ROME IN THE *BOOK OF JOSIPPON*

Many positive characteristics of Rome and her inhabitants are presented in the *Book of Josippon*. This can be traced back to Josephus's view of Rome, which was also carried over into a free adaptation into Latin of the *Jewish War*, written in the fourth century and falsely attributed to Hegesippus.[84] In many cases, however, the author of the *Book of Josippon* went further and described the Romans with superlatives and sweeping images that he did not get from his sources. In Yitzhak Baer's opinion, a central theme of the *Book of Josippon* is its favourable view of the Jews' submission to each of the four kingdoms in turn and in particular to Rome. The doctrine of submission is already found in Josephus, and Pseudo-Hegesippus added his own Christian ideas, but the author of the *Book of Josippon* rejected some things and changed others to fit his purposes. He believed that the Jewish people were wrong to rebel against Rome, since the Roman empire was divinely ordained.[85] On the other hand, according to David Flusser, he did not subscribe to a philosophy of exile and redemption, nor did he try to explain the role of the fourth kingdom.[86] Even if Flusser is right, it is important to clarify how readers would have understood this. In addition to the idea of submission to the fourth kingdom, the *Book of Josippon* portrayed Rome as an empire committed to the pursuit of justice and peace, desiring only amicable relations with the people of Israel.[87]

The *Book of Josippon* contains details of the founding of Rome and her ancient kings. It deals with the wars between Hannibal and Rome, praises Scipio's victory,

---

[83] Apparently this was already the case in the first half of the eleventh century (see Flusser, *The Book of Josippon* (Heb.), ii. 63–74; Baer, 'The Hebrew *Sefer yosipon*' (Heb.), 101–6; Neuman, 'Josippon', 637–9).

[84] See Dönitz, 'Historiography Among Byzantine Jews'; id., *Überlieferung und Rezeption des Sefer Yosippon*. On the images of Rome in Josephus, see Stern, 'Josephus's *Jewish War* and the Roman Empire' (Heb.); Flusser, *The Book of Josippon* (Heb.), ii. 173.

[85] Baer, 'The Hebrew *Sefer yosipon*' (Heb.), 108–14; see Flusser, *The Book of Josippon* (Heb.), ii. 32.

[86] Flusser, *The Book of Josippon* (Heb.), ii. 169–70.

[87] See Bowman, 'Sefer Yosippon', 286–9; G. D. Cohen, Introduction and notes to Ibn Daud, *Sefer hakabalah*, 222.

and describes Rome's enormous power and her rule over distant peoples.[88] The Romans are depicted as good friends of the Jews ('And now it is a pleasure to tell of the love of the Roman generals who loved our forefathers for their strength, their heroism and their faith'[89]), and it is claimed that Julius Caesar sent letters to all of the procurators throughout the empire, informing them of 'the love of the peoples of the Romans and the peoples of Judea'.[90] Although the author admired the resistance and heroism of the Jews who fought against the Romans, he regarded the revolt as an irresponsible act that led to the diaspora. In contrast to the talmudic tradition, which blamed Rome for the destruction of the Temple and denigrated her rulers, the *Book of Josippon* describes Vespasian and Titus as men of good will and also repeated Josephus's claim that Titus did not want the Temple destroyed and that he (and Pompey) greatly esteemed Jerusalem.[91]

For medieval Jews, the *Book of Josippon* was a reliable history of the Jewish people and of Rome. In the Middle Ages, therefore, many Jewish writings that dealt with the history of Rome made no attempt to present it in an unfavourable light. The image of Rome found in the *Book of Josippon* was not contested,[92] and tempered the more negative image in the talmudic literature. To illustrate this, I have chosen to focus on Titus, because unlike other figures and events in the *Book of Josippon*, he is mentioned in the Talmud and Midrash on a number of occasions.

Titus

The image of Titus in the Talmud and Midrash is that of a rebel against God, an all-out enemy of the Jews, 'a wicked man, a son of a wicked man, descendant of Esau the Wicked',[93] in the same league as Pharaoh, Sisera, and Sennacherib. According to tradition, Titus entered the holy of holies when the Temple was on fire, blasphemed God, and had sexual relations with whores lying on a Torah scroll. He also stabbed the ornamental curtain covering the Torah until blood spurted out and believed he had killed the God of the Jews.[94] He was the worst of all the enemies of Israel, the man who showed insolence towards God, looted his most sacred objects, and brought about the Jewish diaspora.

---

[88] See *Sefer yosipon*, 2: 1–145; 21: 1–57 (ed. Flusser, 9–20, 91–5); Bowman, 'Sefer Yosippon', 287–8; Flusser, *The Book of Josippon* (Heb.), ii. 171.

[89] *Sefer yosipon*, 21: 66–7; 40 (ed. Flusser, 96, 174–7); see Bowman, 'Sefer Yosippon', 288.

[90] *Sefer yosipon*, 40: 18–19 (ed. Flusser, 175).

[91] See ibid. 84: 17–18 (ed. Flusser, 396–7); Flusser, *The Book of Josippon* (Heb.), ii. 172.

[92] Ibn Daud, *History of the Kings of Israel, History of Rome, Sefer hakabalah*; Joseph b. Tsadik, *Kitsur zekher tsadik*; Zacut, *Sefer yuḥasin*; the writings of Abravanel; and others (see Solomon b. Moses b. Yekutiel, *Edut hashem ne'emanah*, 413–14).   [93] See BT *Git.* 56*b*.

[94] See Hasan-Rokem, 'Within Limits and Beyond'; Herr, 'Titus Flavius Vespasianus' (Heb.); Yuval, 'History without Wrath and Bias' (Heb.), 368–70.

In the Middle Ages a totally different image of Titus emerged, based on a twelfth-century adaptation of the *Book of Josippon*.[95] There Titus is depicted as having offered the Jews autonomy under Roman protection and the leadership of Joseph the priest. He also ordered that all Jewish slaves be freed and ransomed them from their owners. Vespasian, Titus, and Augustus are called 'kings of mercy and compassion for Israel'.[96] The adaptation contains an entire section on Titus's reign, which is not in the original *Book of Josippon*, including a description: 'Titus the king was very wise, well versed in the languages of Greece and Rome, and he wrote many books of science in Greek and Roman. Titus was a righteous, honest man, and all of his judgements were just. And he was forced to destroy and demolish Jerusalem.'[97] According to another version, Titus also transferred the Jewish prisoners to Spain and issued orders that they not be mistreated.[98]

In his *History of Rome*, Ibn Daud repeated the praise of Titus,[99] and, in *The History of the Kings of Israel*, he adapted the excerpt about the three 'kings of mercy and compassion for Israel': 'For Emperor Nero alone hated Israel. And had [the Jews] suffered his yoke until the day of his death, Vespasian and Titus would have ruled them with kindness as Octavian Augustus had done and would have set up Jewish kings over them.'[100] He also accepted the claim of the *Book of Josippon* that the blame for the destruction of the Temple lay with the rebels and described how Titus tried to put out the fire that his soldiers had started.[101] Ibn Daud depicts Titus as a wise emperor, who was fluent in Greek and Latin, engaged in science, wrote books, and judged fairly. According to Gerson Cohen, Ibn Daud totally abandoned the rabbinical view of Vespasian and Titus and even of Hadrian. He blamed the Jewish zealots for the calamity more harshly than his sources did and consistently defended the Roman emperors.[102]

This positive image of Titus also found its way into sermons and biblical

---

[95] This adaptation was published in several versions (see *Sefer yosipon* (ed. Hominer)); on the time and sources of the version, see Flusser, *The Book of Josippon* (Heb.), ii. 25–38.

[96] *Sefer yosipon*, 6: 79 (ed. Hominer, 295).

[97] Ibid. 6: 97 (ed. Hominer, 404); see Flusser, *The Book of Josippon* (Heb.), ii. 38, n. 96; Hallewy, *Biographical-Historical Legends in the Light of Greek and Latin Sources* (Heb.), 441; Suetonius, *Lives of the Caesars*, 274–9.

[98] See Appendix B, in *Sefer yosipon* (ed. Flusser, 432–3); Flusser, notes (Heb.), ibid., nn. 7, 8.

[99] Ibn Daud, *Zikhron divrei romi* (Mantua edn., 22; ed. Vehlow, 106–9).

[100] Ibn Daud, *Divrei malkhei yisra'el* (Mantua edn., 53–4; ed. Vehlow, 314–15).

[101] Ibid. (Mantua edn., 53–4; ed. Vehlow, 336–9).

[102] The only emperor Ibn Daud used a derogatory term for was Hadrian ('may his bones be crushed') (*Zikhron divrei romi* (Mantua edn., 61; ed. Vehlow, 110–11)). He also wrote: 'Neither Nebuchadnezzar nor Titus had dealt with them as harshly as Hadrian did' (ibid. 22; see Joseph b. Tsadik, *Kitsur zekher tsadik* (ed. Neubauer, 90)). In *Sefer yuḥasin*, the epithet 'wicked' was also reserved for Hadrian (Zacut, *Sefer yuḥasin* (ed. Filipowski, 244*b*–245*a*)).

commentaries, such as those by Gersonides,[103] Isaac Arama, and Abravanel. Abravanel regarded Vespasian and Titus as peace-seekers, in contrast to the Jews, whom he depicts as more interested in strife and war. Here, Abravanel differed from the *Book of Josippon* and Arama, who blamed only the rebels.[104] According to Abravanel, Titus proposed to the Jews that they stop fighting and reconcile themselves to Roman rule. He was prepared to exempt them from all taxes and even from subjugation, as long as it did not dishonour Rome. In order to achieve this, he offered to enter into an alliance with them, and it was their refusal that led to the destruction of the city and the Temple.[105]

Abravanel also used Josephus's *Jewish Antiquities* as a source for his depiction of Titus,[106] although he was aware of Josephus's pro-Roman bias: 'like a slave standing before stern masters, who speaks in keeping with their desires'.[107] In several instances, he was harshly critical of Josephus (whom he referred to as Ben Gorion) for failing to speak the truth and deliberately introducing historical errors into his books. Despite this, and the sages' attitudes to Titus, Abravanel adopted the favourable image in its entirety without any criticism. Titus is described as a man possessed of lofty (Stoic) personality traits who was capable of restraining his anger even when the Jews responded badly to his favourable attitude towards them. As I will show below, this was related to the general image of Rome in Abravanel's writings.

Elsewhere, however, Abravanel included Titus in a list of the enemies of Israel, together with Sennacherib and Nebuchadnezzar, and foresaw that at the End of Days they would be resurrected to be punished and to see the eschatological destruction of the nations.[108] On the historical plane, however, he depicted Titus as he appears in the *Book of Josippon*, absolved him of the blame for the destruction and the exile, and assigned all of the guilt to the zealots.[109]

Titus was similarly described in Solomon ibn Verga's *Shevet yehudah* and David Gans's *Sefer tsemaḥ david*. Gans was apparently the first to explicitly mention the disparity between Titus's image in the Talmud and how he was depicted in the *Book of Josippon*.[110] Although *Sefer tsemaḥ david* was published much later, in 1592, it casts light on the historiographical techniques of the earlier works:

---

[103] See Gersonides on Dan. 9: 26–7.   [104] Arama, *Akedat yitsḥak*, v. 101*b*.

[105] Abravanel, *Ma'ayenei hayeshuah*, 10: 6 (Jerusalem edn., 374).

[106] Abravanel on 1 Kgs 3: 2 (*Perush linevi'im rishonim*, 478); see Josephus, *Jewish Antiquities*, 18.2.5.

[107] Abravanel, *Ma'ayenei hayeshuah*, 10: 7 (Jerusalem edn., 375).

[108] Abravanel on Joel 4: 9 (*Perush al nevi'im aharonim*, 75).

[109] Abravanel on Deut. 28: 49 (*Perush al hatorah*, iii. 269).

[110] See Ibn Verga, *Shevet yehudah*, 41–3; Gans, *Sefer tsemaḥ david*, 84–5. Another criticism, close to the time, was from Judah Loew ben Bezalel, the Maharal of Prague, in *Sefer netsaḥ yisra'el*, written in 1600 (see Baer, 'The Hebrew *Sefer yosipon*' (Heb.), 112 n. 15). This criticism was probably inspired

If some of the words [in the *Book of Josippon*] regarding Titus seem to somewhat contradict the words of our revered rabbis . . . you should know that, since he was great in wisdom and reason, a righteous, honest man, and he lived several centuries before the sages of the Talmud, and saw all that happened in his own lifetime, we do not regard him as an unreliable author, and for that reason, well-known scholars joined together his stories and the stories of our revered rabbis in such a manner that they do not contradict one another, and nothing more need be said here.[111]

The 'well-known scholars' were Abraham Zacut and Isaac Abravanel, whose writings were Gans's main sources for this part of his book and whom he referred to as 'the two great mountains'.[112] In general, Zacut and Abravanel tried to reconcile contradictions between the Talmud and other sources, but sometimes, when they were unable to do so, they preferred the non-talmudic tradition. In the second part of his book, Gans depicted Titus similarly to the *Book of Josippon* and Ibn Daud and added that some 'who wrote about him [said] that he regretted the blood that was shed and throughout his reign as emperor, he justly ruled his people'.[113]

The openness of these authors to general historiography was probably the main reason they could reject the Talmud's depiction of Titus. Unquestionably, the *Book of Josippon* made it easier for them to accept the image of Titus in non-Jewish sources and to regard them as more accurate. The positive image of Titus did not completely expunge the negative one, however. Joseph ben David included him in a list of the haters of Israel, together with Sisera, Sennacherib, and Hadrian, and some sages, who were familiar with the revolt and the destruction of Jerusalem, called him Titus the Wicked.[114] Judah Loew ben Bezalel (the Maharal of Prague), a native of Gans's own city, also had a very negative image of Titus.[115]

THE IMAGE OF ROME ACCORDING TO
ISAAC NATHAN

Several events from Roman history are mentioned in Isaac Nathan's *Me'amets koah*. Most of them are popular traditions and lack any firm historical basis. But

by the polemic about Azariah de Rossi's *Meor einayim* (see Rossi, *Meor einayim*, 'Imrei binah', 2: 16 (Vilna edn., 308–18; trans. Weinberg, 296–304)).

[111] Gans, *Sefer tsemah david*, 85.   [112] Ibid. 26.

[113] Ibid. 218. Breuer explained Gans's attitude to Titus as part of his attitude to kings in general. For Gans, a corrupt king was one who hated scholars. Hence, a ruler like Titus who loved learning could not possibly have been hostile towards the Jews (see Breuer, Introduction (Heb.) to Gans, *Sefer tsemah david*, 19).

[114] Joseph b. David on Gen. 41: 1–44: 17; see Arama, *Akedat yitshak*, v. 101a; David Kimhi on Joel 4: 19; Nahmanides, *Sefer hage'ulah*, 3 (ed. Chavel, 268); Zacut, *Sefer yuhasin* (ed. Filipowski, 231b).

[115] Judah Loew b. Bezalel, *Sefer netsah yisra'el*, 5: 19–20.

sometimes the exempla, which primarily convey moral lessons, also contain accurate historical details.

It is told that when Rome ruled over all the states, the elder with his 300 advisers[116] constantly oversaw the administration of his government, was a prince and commander of nations, and he would divide his time into three: one third on the strategies and conduct of his wars and sending soldiers to the regions where he feared rebellion; the second third in dispensing justice among the provinces and their people . . . to establish peace among the peoples under them and their men; the last third was spent on the studies of religions and customs. . . . And one day, one of his advisers said: 'There is no doubt that throughout all time the hearts and minds of men . . . have turned to their God.' . . . And hence [the elder] asked: 'Which of all the attributes is most fitting to him, may he be blessed?' The elder asked his query of four factions: the scholars, masters of learning; the cavalrymen, governors of the provinces; the tillers of the soil; and the merchants. The scholars replied that the attribute most suitable to God was wisdom and knowledge. . . . The cavalrymen replied that it was more fitting to attribute heroism to him. . . . The tillers of the soil replied that the most fitting for him was that he fed and provided for his creatures. . . . The merchants replied that it was most worthy to attribute to him righteous guidance and fairness in trial. . . . And the arguments among these factions intensified. . . . And they asked a wise philosopher, who lived close to Rome in one of the caves, an ascetic hermit, to give his judgement and decide among them. They placed their four opinions before him, and it took him some time to reply to them. And when he came to answer their query . . . he said, none of these four attributes are fitting for God nor do they refer to him, for the possessors of each of them can use them wrongly, but the true attributes of God are mercy, amnesty, and compassion, for within them there is no possibility of using them for ill purposes.[117]

Isaac Nathan set this exemplum during the Roman republic, after the monarchy was overthrown and the state was ruled by 'the elder with his 300 advisers'. This slightly confused information about the Roman senate comes from the *Book of Josippon*, in which it was written:

And that day the Romans swore no king would reign over them in Rome, and they chose from the elders of Rome one elder and with him 320 advisers and they placed them to rule over them and to run the kingdom, and the elder and his 320 advisers ruled and conquered the entire west.[118]

Isaac Nathan identified the rule of the elder with Rome's period of glory when it dominated the world. The Roman approach to warfare and the administration of

[116] i.e. the head of the senate and the 300 senators, see n. 79 above.
[117] Isaac Nathan, *Me'amets koaḥ* (MS Guenzburg 113/1 (Russian State Library, Moscow—Institute of Microfilmed Hebrew Manuscripts, no. 6793)), fos. 62a–63a.
[118] *Sefer yosipon*, 2: 131–5 (ed. Flusser, 19–20). The author of the *Book of Josippon* learned this from 1 Macc. 8: 15–16.

the Pax Romana are mentioned as two of the major aspects of the Roman political system: 'strategies and conduct of his wars' and 'peace among the peoples'. The ideology of the Pax Romana is based, on the one hand, on the art and tactics of war, since a powerful army is required to deter rebellion; and, on the other, on the establishment of a government that dispenses justice and promotes equality. The third part of the Roman political system concerns abstract questions of ethics, science, physics, and metaphysics. In particular, the elder was occupied with 'profound, moral, scholarly, natural, divine questions'.[119] The division of Roman society into four classes (scholars, soldiers, farmers, and merchants) reflects the conditions of the late Middle Ages, when the bourgeois middle class evolved alongside the traditional triple division of clergy, soldiers, and peasants. The replacement of the clergy by scholars was clearly more suitable to ancient Rome, although the pagan Romans seem to have a monotheistic world-view and are concerned with the attributes of God, which did not trouble the Roman philosophers but was an important part of medieval philosophy. However, for medieval readers, the elder's religious attitude would seem reasonable for one described as devoting a third of his time to 'the studies of religion'.

This exemplum reveals how medieval Jews perceived ancient Rome. It is described in terms that were familiar to Jewish readers and not as a remote country from the distant past. The elder—an accepted figure in contemporary Jewish historiography—is depicted as the ideal Roman ruler. At the height of its power, Rome controlled the entire known world. The Pax Romana was based on moral principles of equality, justice, and integrity, and the Roman ruler also aspired to perfection. Although anachronistic, the division of study into four fields—ethics, science, physics, and metaphysics, characteristic of medieval scholasticism—also highlights Rome's perfection. From all angles, Rome is given an ideal representation here.

It could be argued that this exemplum represents Isaac Nathan's personal view, rather than general Jewish attitudes to Rome. However, *Me'amets koah* is meant to be a popular moral work, and there would be no point in locating the exemplum in ancient Rome if his intended readership was antagonistic towards Rome.[120]

A favourable image of Rome is also found in another exemplum:

It is told that a Roman scholar painted Justice as a virgin with a golden crown upon her head. A beauty, whom no man had known, blind, and without hands. Another scholar saw her thus depicted and wrote on the margins of the painting: 'Beautiful you would be

[119] Isaac Nathan, *Me'amets koah* (MS Guenzburg 113/1), fos. 62a–63a; see Samuel ibn Tibbon, *Perush hamilot hazarot*, 50–2, 61–2.

[120] See R. Ben-Shalom, 'Isaac Nathan, "The Light of Our Exile"' (Heb.), 230, 420–1.

if you had eyes.' And another scholar wrote on the margins: 'You would be more beauti-ful if you had hands.' And a third scholar wrote on the margins: 'Far more beautiful if you had not those flaws.' Afterwards the maker of the painting came and wrote on the margins: 'Blind she is beautiful, and more beautiful for she has no hands, and even more beautiful with her flaws.' And his intention was that he made her a virgin, pure of all the limitations of contradictory thoughts or base musings, which would obstruct the pub-lic's acceptance of her truth. He also placed a golden crown upon her head, to show she is the queen of all the virtues. . . . And he made her blind, so she would not be biased. And he gave her no hands, so she would take no bribes.[121]

According to classical aesthetic principles, the subject of a work of art should be perfect and the work composed according to strict rules of symmetry and pro-portion.[122] The painter also contravened the Socratic principle that the good, the true, and the beautiful are one and the Platonic concept that the idea of beauty is identical with the idea of the good.[123] However, the contravention is only apparent: the principles of justice are consistent with very different aesthetic prin-ciples. The lack of hands and eyes may mar the perfection of the human body, but it preserves moral perfection—by making bias and the taking of bribes impossible.[124]

The only way the reader knows this exemplum is set in Rome is because it says that the painter was a 'Roman scholar', and, in fact, there is no need for the exemplum to be set in Rome, since the moral is valid regardless of the place or time. However, Isaac Nathan included this detail, presumably because Roman scholars had an aura of importance and wisdom in medieval Europe and Rome was famed for its law and jurisprudence.

The creation of moral exempla was common in medieval Europe. The famous collection *Gesta Romanorum* claimed to describe the deeds of the Romans, but it contains very few exempla that fit its title. Most of them are fictional narratives unconnected with Rome, Roman history, or the Roman people. It has been argued that the person who compiled the *Gesta Romanorum* may have set the stor-ies in Roman contexts in order to compensate for the disparity between the title and the contents;[125] however, in my opinion, the Roman context was intended to give the exempla moral weight in a society which held that age implied authority. Nonetheless, it seems that the collection originally reflected its title. During the thirteenth century, a number of collections of stories from Roman history were

---

[121] Isaac Nathan, *Me'amets koah* (MS Guenzburg 113/1), fo. 55.

[122] See Speigel, 'Plotinus's Thought' (Heb.), 108–9. [123] See Pappas, 'Plato's Aesthetics'.

[124] See R. Ben-Shalom, 'Christian Art in the Intellectual World of Jewish Scholars'; Speigel, 'Plotinus's Thought' (Heb.), 108–13.

[125] Swan, Introduction to *Gesta Romanorum*, pp. xxxi–xxxii; see Weiske, *Gesta Romanorum*, i. 9–126.

compiled and adapted as morals for sermons. Over time other stories were added to the collection, and when the *Gesta Romanorum* we now know was printed at the end of the fifteenth century the original Roman stories had been swamped by later additions.[126] A similar process was at work here to the one that prompted Isaac Nathan to artificially locate his two exempla in a Roman context. Isaac Nathan and the compiler of the *Gesta Romanorum* were trying to use the prestige of Rome to add weight to their moral lessons.

Jewish use of exempla set in ancient Rome supports my conclusions about their attitude to Roman history and challenges the earlier picture of implacable Jewish hostility to Rome in the Middle Ages. If the image of pagan Rome was so unfavourable and she was regarded as a kingdom of evil, why did Jews choose to use exempla set in Roman contexts? They could have set them anywhere: Persia, Greece, or some imaginary place. Their use of exempla set in Rome and the unambiguous language which they contain indicates they had a favourable image of Roman culture. This image drew upon very different historical sources from those which reinforced the negative image of Rome and undermines the scholarly consensus that Rome had no real historical substance for medieval Jews.

THE IMAGE OF ROME IN *SEFER YUḤASIN*

Zacut's treatment of the founding myth of Rome demonstrates his scholarly interest in Roman history. There are, however, other Roman myths in *Sefer yuḥasin*, including the story of Nicostrata, King Latinus's wife, who invented the Latin alphabet; the abduction of the Sabine women; the founding myths of several Italian cities; Jupiter and the ancient Roman household divinities, the Penates; and the Cumaean Sybil, who sold her books of prophecy to Tarquinius Superbus. In addition, Zacut dealt with the Roman royal dynasty and the overthrow of Tarquinius Superbus, the last Roman king; the replacement of the monarchy with a republic and of the republic with an empire; the Second Punic War and the struggle between Scipio and Hannibal; Diocletian's abdication; and more—all very matter-of-factly.[127] Following the *Book of Josippon*, Zacut stressed the peace treaties entered into between Rome and the Jews—first in the time of Judah and Simon Maccabee and later in the time of Jonathan Maccabee. He blamed the Roman conquest of Jerusalem entirely on Hyrcanus II and noted Pompey's respect for the Temple. He also tried to identify the Emperor Antoninus

---

[126] See Hooper, Preface to *Gesta Romanorum*, p. xiii; Bourne, 'Classical Elements in the Gesta Romanorum'.

[127] Zacut, *Sefer yuḥasin* (ed. Filipowski, 235*b*, 236*a*–*b*, 238*a*, 239*a*–*b*, 241*b*, 246*a*); see R. Ben-Shalom, 'Graeco-Roman Myth and Mythology in the Historical Consciousness of Medieval Spanish Jewry' (Heb.), 457–8.

who appears in the Talmud and midrashic literature as a 'friend' of Judah Hanasi and emphasized his piety and wisdom.[128]

Sefer yuḥasin contains a list of Roman emperors from Julius Caesar (100–44 BCE) to the Byzantine Constans II Pogonatus (630–68 CE). For the first seventeen emperors, Caesar to Commodus in 180 CE, the list is quite accurate and relatively complete. After Commodus it becomes fragmentary.[129] Zacut's greater interest in the period before 180 CE is probably linked to his concern with the history of the Jewish people. The end of the Second Temple period and the period of the Mishnah provided him with historical material that was interesting from a political and religious standpoint, and he tried to find correspondences with the events of world history. For the Byzantine empire, he was accurate only in relation to the first emperors (from Constantine's moving of the capital to Constantinople in 330 CE to the death of Jovian in 364) because of his interest in the Christianization of the Roman empire. A comparison of Zacut's list with that in the *History of Rome* shows that Ibn Daud's list was better for the emperors after Commodus.[130] This is because Ibn Daud was concerned primarily with the transfer of dominion over Europe from Rome to the Spanish Visigoths,[131] and he needed to show how rule passed from one emperor to another until the Gothic conquests.

Zacut was generally faithful to the historical facts he found in the Christian writings; however, in several places, he distorted matters for polemical purposes. One of these is his discussion of Julian the Apostate (332–63), who interested him mainly because of his attempt to stop the spread of Christianity and return the empire to paganism.[132] Zacut wrote at length about his attempt to rebuild the Jerusalem Temple:

The third king [in Constantinople] was Julian the Apostate . . . who reigned for two years and five months. Valentinus reigned for eleven years.[133] In his second year there was a worldwide earthquake that came from the sea and entire lands sank into the depths. . . . The Temple of Israel was then standing in Jerusalem, having been built by Jews at great expense four years earlier in the days of Julian the Apostate. It collapsed in that earthquake and many Jews were killed. The next day fire burned the whole Temple,

---

[128] Zacut, *Sefer yuḥasin* (ed. Filipowski, 242*a–b*, 245*b–*246*a*).

[129] Ibid. (ed. Filipowski, 243*b*–248*a*). David compared the five lists of Roman emperors, including those in *Sefer yuḥasin* and Ibn Daud's *Sefer hakabalah* ('The Historiographical Work of Gedaliah ibn Yahya' (Heb.), 240–6).

[130] See David, 'The Historiographical Work of Gedaliah ibn Yahya' (Heb.), 240–1.

[131] G. D. Cohen, Introduction and notes to Ibn Daud, *Sefer hakabalah*, pp. xxxii–xxxiv.

[132] On Julian, see Bidez, *La Vie de l'empereur Julien*; Browning, *The Emperor Julian*; on his struggle against Christianity, see Levy, *Worlds Meet* (Heb.), 221–54, esp. 243–6; Rokeah, *Judaism and Christianity in the Light of Pagan Polemic* (Heb.), 36–40, 195–201.

[133] Valentinian I (emperor, 364–75) confused with his brother Valens (emperor in the east, 364–78). Valens was an Arian and persecuted the Catholic Christians (discussed below).

even the iron utensils. They say this horror caused 300 Jews to become Christians. Emperor Valentinus [*recte* Valens] was against Christians. He returned Jews to Jerusalem and ordered them to rebuild the Temple, he gave them permission and helped defray their expenses. He said there was to be no sacrifice but in Jerusalem. Then the Jews were anxious to rebuild an even more magnificent temple than the previous one.[134]

There is no mention in Hebrew sources before Zacut of the rebuilding of the Temple during Julian's reign.[135] The Church Fathers considered it an attempt to contradict Jesus' prediction about the Temple: 'the days will come when not one stone will be left upon another; all will be thrown down' (Luke 21: 6; see also Matt. 24: 2; Mark 13: 2).[136] According to Yochanan Levy, Julian's decision to rebuild the Temple was based on Porphyry's criticism of the book of Daniel and Jesus's prophecy: 'Its intent is not merely to disprove one of the Christian proofs, but to undermine the foundations of their entire historical theology. The Temple in Jerusalem was meant to serve as an example to refute the claim of the Christians that they had inherited the title "the true children of Israel".'[137] According to the usually reliable historian Ammianus Marcellinus, fire broke out from the foundations of the building and caused the death of several of the workmen, stopping work on the rebuilding. The Christians gloated over this failure, and Christian sources mention a cross of fire appearing in the heavens and black crosses appearing on the clothing of Jews—phenomena that caused many Jews to convert to Christianity.[138]

Zacut does not say where he got the information that the Temple was rebuilt during the reign of 'Valentinus' from, although Valens did treat the Jews with tolerance and sympathy and enacted several laws in their favour.[139] In any case, a lack of critical acumen is evident here: it is not clear from the rest of his chronicle—nor, of course, from any other source—how and when the Temple was destroyed again. The story serves to refute Christian claims that God destroyed the Temple during Julian's reign and that, as a result, masses of Jews converted.[140] According

---

[134] Zacut, *Sefer yuḥasin* (ed. Filipowski, 246*b*).

[135] Ibn Daud only wrote about Julian's apostasy: 'And he was succeeded by Julian Caesar who reigned for two years and restored the worship of idols as was custom formerly and did not accept the doctrine of Edom and died' (*Zikhron divrei romi* (Mantua edn., 24; ed. Vehlow, 122–3); see David, 'The Historiographical Work of Gedaliah ibn Yahya' (Heb.), 42).

[136] See Levy, *Worlds Meet* (Heb.), 224 n. 14; Wilken, *John Chrysostom and the Jews*, 129–38.

[137] Levy, *Worlds Meet* (Heb.), 225–6; Wilken, *John Chrysostom and the Jews*, 157.

[138] See Geiger, 'The Revolt in the Time of Gallus and the Construction of the Temple in the Time of Julian' (Heb.), 208–17 and bibliography; Levy, *Worlds Meet* (Heb.), 223–4; Wilken, *John Chrysostom and the Jews*, 145–8.

[139] See David, 'The Historiographical Work of Gedaliah ibn Yahya' (Heb.), 43.

[140] See Wilken, *John Chrysostom and the Jews*, 153–8, esp. 157. According to John Chrysostom, Julian's failure to rebuild the Temple was proof of Jesus's divinity. Historical events proved Jesus's prophecy to be accurate, and he triumphed, with his words alone, over Emperor Julian and the entire Jewish people.

to Christian historiography, Julian's attempt to abolish Christianity was the cause of his death, and his attempt to rebuild the Temple failed because of God's intervention. According to the counter-history in *Sefer yuḥasin*, the rebuilding of the Temple was finally completed in the time of Julian's successor, and hence there is no basis for the Christian claim that God wanted to prevent the construction of the Temple. In the Christian version, the earthquake and the fire were divine punishment; in Zacut's version, it was just a natural disaster, the damage from which was immediately repaired.

THE IMAGE OF ROME ACCORDING TO ISAAC ABRAVANEL

Abravanel's attitude to Rome is complex. On the one hand, he tried to establish the traditional identification of Rome with Edom, the 'place of wickedness'.[141] This idea was central to the messianic hopes of his time, and he anticipated Rome's imminent destruction. On the other hand, he used the history, culture, laws, and leaders of Rome as models to illustrate his political theories, to support his historiographical approach, and to provide moral lessons.

Rome as Edom and the End of Days

Abravanel tried various ways to substantiate the symbolic identification of Rome and Edom. For this, he used Jewish sources, such as Midrash and the *Book of Josippon*, and non-Jewish sources that included Christian historiography and theology. He read Jewish and Christian authors who rejected the identification of Edom and Rome and attempted to refute their claims, particularly those of Abraham ibn Ezra and the convert Pablo de Santa María (the archbishop of Burgos, formerly the rabbi of Burgos, Solomon Halevi).[142]

First, he attempted to ascertain what Edom–Rome referred to: the city of Rome; Italy, the land of the Romans; the Holy Roman Empire; or the entire Christian world? According to Abravanel, Rome united the religious and the

---

[141] Abravanel, *Sefer yeshuot meshiḥo*, 21*b*.

[142] See Lifschitz, 'The Interpretation of Prophecy according to Abraham ibn Ezra and Isaac Abravanel' (Heb.). On the debate with Pablo de Santa María, see Abravanel on Isa. 35: 10 (*Perush al nevi'im aḥaronim*, 170–3). His perception of Rome as Edom was shaped by a polemic with Christian commentators who claimed that the biblical prophecies of the destruction of Edom were about the Jews. They countered the Jewish symbol Edom–Rome with a parallel symbol Edom–Jews: 'And the commentators of the nations were undecided . . . until they said that we, the Jews, were the sons of Edom based on the wickedness of our deeds, and that it was about us that the prophecies and curses were uttered, and some of them said that R. Meir was the founder of the Talmud, and because our holy rabbi [Judah Hanasi] who established the Mishnah received [the halakhah or wisdom] from him [*kibel mimeno*], and R. Meir was an Edomite proselyte, we who adhere to his teachings are called Edom by the prophets' (Abravanel, *Mashmia yeshuah*, 3: 15 (Jerusalem edn., 492)).

political spheres, it was the seat of the emperors and the popes, and therefore 'Rome' meant 'Christianity'.[143]

Abravanel's eschatology envisaged a war between Christians and Muslims, in which most of them would be killed, but about a third (mainly Muslims) would survive.[144] Rome would be totally destroyed by the surviving Muslims immediately after the war, removing the religious centre of Christianity.[145] Abravanel's generation had already witnessed the fall of Constantinople (the 'daughter of Edom') and looked forward to the destruction of Rome itself, which they expected to be more thorough than Constantinople's.[146] According to Abravanel, anyone reading the history of Rome could already see that many troubles had befallen it, and that it had been destroyed several times by various peoples. However, none of these disasters was the fulfilment of the biblical prophecies of its destruction. The final, absolute destruction of Rome was yet to come, and it would be soon.[147] The whole Christian world was also due for destruction, not, Abravanel stressed, because of the evil deeds or corrupt morals of Christians, but rather because of the Christian faith itself, which was idolatrous. He also asserted that Rome would be punished in this world and in the next.[148]

According to Israel Yuval there were two understandings of the fate of non-Jews at the End of Days: destruction or conversion.[149] Both of these could be found among the Jews of twelfth-century Spain, as can be seen from the writings of Abraham bar Hiyya and Judah Halevi,[150] and both can be found in Abravanel's works. The destruction of Christianity, Rome, and Islam has been outlined above.[151] Elsewhere, however, he says that 'Edom' only applies to the city of Rome, Italy, France, and Spain. Germany, England, Hungary, Poland, and

---

[143] Abravanel, *Ma'ayenei hayeshuah*, 2: 3 (Jerusalem edn., 290).

[144] Abravanel, *Mashmia yeshuah*, 14: 3 (Jerusalem edn., 566).

[145] Abravanel on Isa. 34: 6–14 (*Perush al nevi'im aharonim*, 167–8); see id., *Ma'ayenei hayeshuah*, 11: 8 (Jerusalem edn., 394); id., *Mashmia yeshuah* 2: 7 (Jerusalem edn., 459–60).

[146] Abravanel, *Ma'ayenei hayeshuah*, 11: 10 (Jerusalem edn., 400–1); on Joel 2: 20 (*Perush al nevi'im aharonim*, 70). According to Netanyahu, Abravanel was influenced by Girolamo Savonarola's prophecies of the destruction of Rome (see Netanyahu, *Don Isaac Abravanel*, 245–7).

[147] Abravanel on Obad. 1: 5 (*Perush al nevi'im aharonim*, 113).

[148] Abravanel, *Ma'ayenei hayeshuah*, 8: 8 (Jerusalem edn., 346–7).

[149] Yuval, *Two Nations in Your Womb*, 92–115; id., 'Vengeance and Damnation, Blood and Defamation' (Heb.), 34–50; see also Berger, 'On the Image and Destiny of Gentiles in Ashkenazi Polemical Literature' (Heb.); Kimelman, *The Mystical Meaning of* Lekhah dodi *and* Kabalat shabat (Heb.).

[150] Abraham bar Hiyya believed that all non-Jews would be destroyed at the End of Days (see *Megilat hamegaleh*, 3: 76; 4: 102, 110). In contrast, Judah Halevi, despite his complete faith in the superiority of the Jews, did not rule out the possibility that non-Jews would be rewarded in the next world (*The Book of the Kuzari*, 1: 111 (trans. Hirschfeld, 52–3); see Guttmann, Introduction (Heb.) to Abraham bar Hiyya, *Megilat hamegaleh*, p. xxii).

[151] Abravanel, *Mashmia yeshuah*, 3: 15 (Jerusalem edn., 492).

Scotland are not included,[152] and Christians from those nations would be converted.[153] The final act of the Jewish diaspora, which had served to bring non-Jews closer to the Torah of Israel, would be all the non-Jews witnessing the redemption of the Jews and the conversion of many non-Jews to Judaism.[154] After that there would still remain a political system of separate nations, kingdoms, and empires, but Israel would be the greatest.[155]

Rome in Reality and History

Abravanel's use of general historical information and Christian sources is particularly interesting in his commentaries on the books of the Prophets and Daniel. It is interesting to see how these interpretative discussions enabled him to place before his readers his overall historical perception of world history. Rome is one of the central axes around which human history revolves, and he tried to explain in his own way, like Augustine before him (and Edward Gibbon later), the decline and fall of the Roman empire:

I shall inform you, by way of a story, of what has been written in the chronicles of the Romans, and especially, what is told by those who wrote on Roman history: that Titus conquered Jerusalem, while Vespasian, his mother's husband, was already emperor of Rome. After Vespasian's death, Titus became emperor, and thus continued the line of Roman emperors, and they ruled over the world, and the Jews were their subjects in their own land. The Christian faith had so far spread among only a few people, and they always had one man at their head, whom they called a pope, who replaced Peter, the head of the disciples, and who lived in Rome in poverty and misery and preached to the people of his religion. The emperors persecuted the Christians and would order the execution of the pope and all who followed the religion, so that the popes would hide in caves and in crannies in the rocks. And this situation continued until the great king Constantine, the first one of that name, who ruled as emperor for thirty-eight years in Rome. He was the son of Queen Helena, the daughter of the king of England, and she was enticed by the violent men of Christianity to follow the Christian religion, and she persuaded her son, and they both became Christians. Constantine granted Sylvester, the pope of his time, control

---

[152] Abravanel on Ezek. 32: 30; 32: 26 (*Perush al nevi'im aharonim*, 560, 559).

[153] Various precedents for Abravanel's view can be found among Spanish Jews. For example, Hayim ibn Musa included the German empire, France, and Spain in the concept of Rome (*Magen varomah*, 87). As I noted, elsewhere in Abravanel's writings, the Holy Roman Empire is included in the symbol of Rome.

[154] Abravanel, *Ma'ayenei hayeshuah*, 10: 6 (Jerusalem edn., 372); see id. *Mashmia yeshuah*, 3: 12 (Jerusalem edn., 480).

[155] Abravanel on Mic. 4: 20 (*Perush al nevi'im aharonim*, 140). Revenge would be meted out to those nations who had caused harm to the Jews and not to those who had treated them well (on Mic. 5: 14 (ibid. 144)). Berger comments that medieval Jews believed that the Jewish nation would preserve its uniqueness even after the End of Days ('On the Image and Destiny of Gentiles in Ashkenazi Polemical Literature' (Heb.), 86).

over the city and government of Rome, and he himself went to Greece, where he founded the great Constantinople and called it after his own name, and moved the seat of the empire there, and from there ruled over all the lands, in the east and the west. And his sons reigned after him, and after them other kings in Constantinople, where the seat of the emperors was located, until a king called Ino Morio [Honorius?] reigned. And in his time a nation arose known as the Goths, who came from beyond the land of Ashkenaz [Germany], and many men came forth from their lands, fierce, warlike men, and they came to Italy, besieged Rome, and captured it, and burned it to the ground. And, although they did not believe in Christianity, they respected the popes and the priests in Rome, and treated them well, for they regarded them as worshippers of a higher power, but they denied them the right to rule. And all of the priests who had been tonsured, for there were then many in number, were subjugated to them. The capture and burning of Rome took place 405 years after the destruction of the Temple. And the Goths continued to rule over all of Italy for seventy-eight years, but the emperor [Justinian I] twice sent his general [Belisarius] to fight against the Goths and drive them out of Italy because it was part of the empire. And the soldiers of the emperor, and all the people of Italy who aided them, finally overthrew the Goths, so that they had to leave Italy and the rule of the empire. And Rome and the land of Italy remained under the empire, while the Goths spread to France and Spain [*sefarad*] and the other countries of the west, and those kingdoms were no longer subjugated to Rome. And seventy-two years later, Muhammad the prophet of the Ishmaelites arose and declared himself a ruler, and then most of the world rebelled against Rome, and the entire land of the east was no longer under her rule for they adopted the religion of Muhammad. And the Goths held France and Spain, which were no longer enslaved to Rome. And in this manner, the yoke of Rome was removed from most of the world, and the kingdoms remained each in its own right. And this is the entire, true story, that all of their books of history agree on.[156]

For Abravanel, the period of the Flavian emperors, Vespasian and Titus, and those who followed them was one of Rome's highest points. However, several centuries later the empire had collapsed. Abravanel tried to pinpoint the crises that led to the fall of Rome. The first occurred during the reign of Emperor Constantine, who adopted Christianity and moved his capital to the east. Roman hegemony over the world was maintained, but the transfer of rule to Constantinople was the beginning of the end, perhaps because Constantine left control of Rome to the popes. The second crisis was the Gothic invasion of Italy. They captured and sacked Rome[157] and ruled Italy for seventy-eight years and

---

[156]   Abravanel, *Sefer yeshuot meshiḥo*, 45a.

[157]   Abravanel dated the sack of Rome to 405 years after the destruction of the Second Temple. The Jews of the Middle Ages believed this occurred in 68 CE (not 70 CE), so he arrived at the date 473 CE. This actually seems to be the date of the deposition of Emperor Romulus Augustulus by Odoacer in 476 (the traditional date of the end of the Roman empire) and not of the sack of Rome by Alaric in 410 during the reign of Honorius. See Gibbon, *The Decline and Fall of the Roman Empire*.

were very sympathetic towards Christianity (Abravanel did not know that they were Arian Christians). The third crisis was the reconquest of Rome in the time of Justinian I, which dispersed the Goths throughout western Europe, and that part of the empire was lost forever. The final crisis was the appearance of Muhammad seventy-two years later[158] and the conversion of the Arabs to Islam. The eastern parts of the empire were also no longer under Roman control. Abravanel described the historical process as a worldwide rebellion against Rome, at the end of which most of the lands of the east were under Muslim control, and the kingdoms of the west never came under Roman rule again. Thus the fall of Rome was complete.

Abravanel attempted to date the crises precisely. Although his main motive was an apocalyptic interpretation of history, it is also further evidence of the historical knowledge he had. To round out the picture, Abravanel provided details that are not directly required for an understanding of the historical process or for his apocalyptic interpretation. He mentions that Helena, Constantine's mother, was the daughter of the king of England; that the emperors who reigned after Constantine were members of his family, but later his dynasty was replaced; that Justinian failed in his first attempt to conquer Italy; and that the Italian people supported him in the war against the Goths.

Abravanel identifies two types of historical source: Roman writings from the period ('the chronicles of the Romans') and later Christian writings ('those who wrote on Roman history'). Abravanel followed these sources and the only detail from Jewish sources he introduced was his reference to Vespasian as the 'husband of Titus' mother' rather than as his father. In rabbinic literature Titus is described not as Vespasian's son, but as the 'son of Vespasian's wife', a detail Abravanel repeated in other places as well.[159]

Abravanel praised Roman law, Roman political practices, Roman administration, the heroism of the Roman soldiers, and even the physiognomic traits of the Romans. In his view, they were endowed with rare physical beauty: 'and the sons of Japheth, from whom came the Greeks and Romans, how fine the deeds of this nation were and their laws and customs, policies and modes of governance, all were becoming and handsome, they were whiter than milk, they were more ruddy in body than rubies'.[160] 'How fine the deeds of this nation' are the words of Judah

---

[158] Abravanel tried to arrive at the year of the Hegira (633 CE), but his calculations came to 623 (*Sefer yeshuot meshiho*, 45*b*).

[159] See *Sifrei* on Deut. 32: 38 (ed. Finkelstein, 378–9); *Avot derabi natan*, B, 7 (ed. Schechter, 10*b*); see Finkelstein, *Introduction to Tractates* Avot *and* Avot derabi natan (Heb.), 112, 200–3; Lieberman, *Greek and Hellenism in the Land of Israel* (Heb.), 126–7.

[160] Abravanel on Gen. 10: 1 (*Perush al hatorah*, i. 171). In general, European Jews felt physically and aesthetically inferior to Christians. In some cases, the Jews' ugliness and physical flaws were

bar Ilai in the talmudic passage cited above.[161] One would have expected readers
of the Talmud to reject the opinion of Judah bar Ilai, since the hero of this passage
is Shimon bar Yohai, who held that all the deeds of Rome were harmful. Shimon
bar Yohai was forced to flee from the Romans and hide in a cave, where a miracle
involving a carob tree showed that divine providence was on his side. Furthermore,
Judah bar Ilai was described as 'the chief spokesman on all topics and occasions',
which was interpreted, from the context and Rashi's commentary, to mean that
he co-operated with the Romans and spoke on their behalf.[162] Finally, in another
talmudic story, the Romans present Judah bar Ilai's arguments to God to prove
that they behaved admirably; however, God rejects the Romans' arguments, preferring those of Shimon bar Yohai.[163] Despite all this, Abravanel chose to quote
Judah bar Ilai's words of praise for Rome.[164]

In chapter 8 of *Ma'ayanei hayeshuah*, Abravanel dealt with several apocalyptic
interpretations of the fourth beast of the book of Daniel. Unlike Abraham ibn
Ezra, but following Rashi, Nahmanides, and Maimonides, Abravanel adopted the
sages' view that the fourth beast was Rome.[165] In support of this interpretation, he
listed the traits of the fourth beast and attempted to show that they matched the
characteristics of the Roman empire. He also described at length and in detail
the qualities of the Roman political and military leadership that enabled the
Romans to create the strongest empire in the world. The fourth beast is said to be
'dreadful and terrible, and strong exceedingly' (Dan. 7: 7). Abravanel wrote:

Rome's success and her control over other nations depended on three things: great brutality to terrify peoples' hearts so they would not revolt against her, great reason and
wisdom in the mode of governance, and heroism to triumph over their enemies. About
the brutality, it says 'dreadful'; about the wisdom it says 'terrible' [*eimetani*] from the
word 'cautious' [*metunim*]—'be cautious in judgement'; and about the heroism, it says
'strong'. And since these traits are also found among the other nations compared to the
earlier beasts, here it says 'exceedingly'. In other words, these traits were found in
exceeding measure in this beast.[166]

regarded as the price they had to pay for their moral and spiritual superiority (see Berger, 'On the
Image and Destiny of Gentiles in Ashkenazi Polemical Literature' (Heb.), 75–8).

[161] BT *Shab.* 33*b*; p. 69 above.

[162] Rashi on *Shab.* 33*b*, *rosh hamedabrim*; *Men.* 103*b*, *rosh hamedabrim*; see Alon, *The Jews in the
Land of Israel during the Mishnaic and the Talmudic Periods* (Heb.), ii. 75 n. 142; see also Zacut, *Sefer
yuḥasin* (ed. Filipowski, 44*a*); Gans, *Sefer tsemaḥ david*, 93).   [163] BT *AZ* 2*b*.

[164] Perhaps he was influenced by the image of Judah bar Ilai as a key figure among the talmudic
sages following the Bar Kokhba revolt. On the honour and esteem bestowed on Judah bar Ilai in the
Middle Ages, see Zacut, *Sefer yuḥasin* (ed. Filipowski, 44*a*–45*a*, 67*a*).

[165] On why Ibn Ezra did not interpret the fourth beast as Rome, see G. D. Cohen, 'Esau as
Symbol in Early Medieval Thought', 257–61; see also e.g. BT *AZ* 2*b*.

[166] Abravanel, *Ma'ayenei hayeshuah*, 8: 5 (Jerusalem edn., 334).

Abravanel made a special hermeneutic effort to ascribe wisdom to the Romans. Most commentators interpreted *eimetani*, based on the literal meaning of the biblical text and the grammatical structure of the word, to mean 'dreadful'.[167] In contrast, Abravanel interpreted it to mean 'caution' (from the Hebrew word *metunim*). This contrived and unsatisfactory interpretation enabled him to link the word *eimetani* to the expression 'be cautious in judgement',[168] and conclude that it meant 'wise'. Abravanel used this hermeneutic tactic in order to make the book of Daniel support his own opinion of the Roman empire.

Characterizing nations by a single basic trait was a widespread literary technique in the Middle Ages: Jews were miserly, Persians treacherous, Greeks wise, Gauls lecherous, Franks arrogant, Bretons hot-tempered, Huns ruthless, and so on. Nations tended to view themselves in a positive light, while their neighbours viewed them slightly differently: the Germans described themselves as courageous, noble, and generous, while the English, French, and Italians regarded them as haughty, boastful, and quick-tempered.[169] This tendency was also observable among Jewish writers: Solomon ibn Verga, for example, asserted that Jews were clever and stubborn and Germans handsome and heroic.[170] Abravanel also wrote about the basic characteristics of nations, which he traced back to the three sons of Noah: Shem, Ham, and Japheth. The Cushites (Ethiopians), Egyptians, and Canaanites, the offspring of Ham, inherited bestial passions, physical ugliness, and poor morals. In contrast, the Greeks and the Romans, the descendants of Japheth, inherited beauty, heroism, and political acumen. Wisdom was a characteristic of the descendants of Shem—Elam, Asshur, Arpachshad, Lud, Aram, Babylon, Hodu, and the Israelites.[171] This raises the question of how Abravanel could attribute wisdom to the Romans so often. According to Abravanel, the Edomite kings of Rome, beginning with Zepho, Esau's grandson, were descendants of Shem and transferred wisdom to the Romans—'and due to that, wisdom was not found in other nations of the sons of Japheth'.[172] The Romans were therefore the only non-Semitic nation to possess wisdom. The secret of the empire's strength was the combination of Semitic wisdom with the other traits of the descendants of Japheth.

Like Isaac Nathan, Abravanel saw the republic as the apogee of Roman history and the senate as the embodiment of all the virtues of Rome: resoluteness,

---

[167] See e.g. Rashi on Dan 7: 7; Sa'adiah Gaon on Dan. 7: 7. [168] Mishnah *Avot* I: I.

[169] See Guenée, *Le Métier d'historien au Moyen Âge*, 132.

[170] See Ibn Verga, *Shevet yehudah*, 154.

[171] Abravanel on Gen. 10: 1 (*Perush al hatorah*, i. 171).

[172] Ibid. Later Abravanel added the myth of the theft of wisdom from the Jews to the myth of the transfer of wisdom to Rome (see Rappel, *The Seven Wisdoms* (Heb.), 46–66; N. Roth, 'The "Theft of Philosophy" by the Greeks from the Jews').

heroism, brutality, and wisdom.[173] He found proof of this in the book of Daniel: '[It had] great iron teeth—that devoured and crushed, and stamped the remains with its feet. It was different from all the other beasts which had gone before it; and it had ten horns' (Dan. 7: 7). Abravanel rejected the Christian interpretation that regarded the beast's teeth as a parable for Roman machinations:[174]

In my view, it is correct that the teeth allude to the advisers of Rome, who are called senators, for it is already known that after Rome became a superior state, she passed through three types of leadership. The first was the leadership of the kings who ruled her. Second, after the Roman people cast off the yoke of the kings, the overall leadership was placed in the hands of one elder and 300 advisers,[175] the finest in Rome, and they continued to lead for 465 years, as all of their scholars wrote in their history books, although Josippon did not write this [length of] time. Afterwards, there were emperors in Rome, and they ruled. And it is known that in the time of the kings Rome did not rule [other countries], only over her own kingdom, nor over many peoples and distant countries, and even the kings of Greece ruled over them. But after the leadership of the advisers was installed, then Rome did great things and conquered vast kingdoms. And the emperors in their times did likewise.[176]

In contrast to Ibn Daud's view of the greatness of Rome during the monarchy, Abravanel believed that Rome was then a powerless nation. Her fortune changed for the better only when the Romans overthrew the tyrant Tarquinius Superbus and abolished the monarchy.[177] During the republic and the empire, Rome became the greatest nation in the world: 'It is written in their books of history, that there was no nation or language that was not under the yoke of the Romans, either in the time of the advisers or the time of the emperors.'[178] Hence the fourth beast in the book of Daniel was post-monarchic Rome, and its iron teeth were the senators and emperors, who set aside their self-interests and aspired to achieve the greatest good for the state:

Thus were the senators, the advisers of Rome, such as the Scipiones, Tully [Cicero], Quintus Fabius, Mark Antony, and Pompey, and also Julius Caesar when he was a consul, and the other heroes, excellent men of fame, for they were special men in Rome, not kings, but men who served the general good. They conquered lands, fiercely attacked insubordinate, troublesome peoples, and brought them under the rule of Rome. They

[173] See Baer, 'Don Isaac Abravanel's Attitude to History and the State' (Heb.), 411 n. 29.

[174] 'And the Christian interpreters wrote that the teeth were a parable for the Romans' machinations by means of which they conquered the world, and that is a trivial statement' (Abravanel, *Ma'ayenei hayeshuah*, 8: 5 (Jerusalem edn., 334)).   [175] See n. 79 above.

[176] Abravanel, *Ma'ayenei hayeshuah*, 8: 5 (Jerusalem edn., 335).

[177] On Jewish philosophical currents opposed to the Platonic political theory of monarchy, see Melamed, *Wisdom's Little Sister*; on Abravanel, see ibid., esp. 9–11, 60, 69–74; on Tarquinius, see Grant and Hazel, *Gods and Mortals in Classical Mythology*, 321–2.

[178] Abravanel, *Ma'ayenei hayeshuah*, 8: 5 (Jerusalem edn., 335).

enjoyed no advantages from their work in the government, but always eschewed any benefit, and rather chose to seek the general good. As for the teeth, their entire function is to prepare the food for the body, to keep it healthy and temperate. So they too are likened to the teeth for their function is to counsel and to speak well of Rome.[179]

Abravanel included in his list those who he thought served the overall interest of Rome. Some were famous military commanders, who conquered vast territories, such as the Scipiones, who provided six consuls including Scipio Africanus,[180] Pompey, and Julius Caesar; others, such as Mark Antony and Cicero were known for their oratorical prowess.

Abravanel distinguished between Julius Caesar as a consul and as an emperor. Although he praised both the consuls and the emperors, things he wrote elsewhere suggest that he regarded the reign of the emperors as a period of decline that led to the collapse of the empire.[181] Abravanel was opposed to monarchy and preferred a republic ruled by an elected body, like the Italian republics of his own time. His ideal form of government combined Cicero's legislative model, Venice's constitution, and institutions from the days of the Judges and the Second Temple period.[182] The title emperor was merely a means of circumventing the commitment the Romans had undertaken not to have any more kings, and hence the empire was an inferior political institution.[183]

The Roman republic was, therefore, an exemplary model, and one that both Christian and Jewish nations should emulate. For Christians, this had immediate implications: to support the republican regimes of the Italian cities or to strive to replace monarchic regimes elsewhere.[184] For the Jews, the implications lay in the

[179] Ibid.

[180] On Scipio Africanus as a moral and political model in the writings of Mossen Diego de Valera, chronicler and courtier to Ferdinand and Isabella (*Doctrinal de príncipes*, 1476; *Valeriana*, 1481), a few years before the arrival of Abravanel from Portugal to the same courtly milieu in Castile, see Moya García 'El *Doctrinal de príncipes* y la *Valeriana*', esp. 233–5.

[181] Abravanel stressed this in his commentary on 1 Sam. 8: 4–8 (*Perush linevi'im rishonim*, 206); see Ravitzky, 'On Kings and Statutes in Jewish Thought in the Middle Ages' (Heb.), 476–9. Ravitzky compared Abravanel's view to that of Thomas Aquinas. However, he noted that Aquinas did not draw any anti-monarchic conclusions.

[182] See Baer, 'Don Isaac Abravanel's Attitude to History and the State' (Heb.), 412–13; Netanyahu, *Don Isaac Abravanel*, 158–73. These institutions were organized within a theocratic framework (see ibid. 186–94). Melamed notes that Abravanel's attitude to Venice and the form of its government was already established when he was in Spain, but it developed following his stay in Venice ('Wisdom's Little Sister' (Heb.), 284–8; id., 'The Myth of Venice in Italian Renaissance Jewish Thought').

[183] Abravanel, *Ma'ayenei hayeshuah*, 6: 2 (Jerusalem edn., 310).

[184] See Baer, 'Don Isaac Abravanel's Attitude to History and the State' (Heb.), 399. Baer thought that Abravanel's hatred of autocratic regimes may have inspired him to join the rebellion of the nobles against John II in Portugal in 1483. Netanyahu disagreed and accepted Abravanel's claim that he did not take part in the conspiracy based on Abravanel's theoretical opposition to the overthrow of monarchic regimes or subversive activities against them (see Netanyahu, *Don Isaac Abravanel*, 263–4, 314 n. 165).

future, at the End of Days, which according to Abravanel's calculations was imminent.[185] The destruction of Christian Rome was a central part of the plan of redemption; however, her political and cultural achievements would remain, as the Jewish government at the End of Days would be modelled on that of Rome. Abravanel reveals an ambivalent attitude to Rome here: Rome the eschatological symbol was evil and had to be destroyed; the achievements and culture of Rome the historical entity he held in high esteem.

Although Abravanel favoured a republican form of government, he did not ignore the reality of his own time and asserted that the institution of monarchy ought not to be overthrown, even if kings were tyrannical and corrupt.[186] However, kings ought to follow those Roman leaders who promoted the general good rather than their own personal interests. For example, in commenting on Jotham's parable (Judg. 9: 7–15), Abravanel wrote that the king should regard his position as a burden not as a privilege, supporting his claim with a quotation from Augustus:

We see then that the king is the slave of his people. When they brought Emperor Octavian [Augustus] a coronet to crown him in Rome, he took the coronet in his hands and said: 'Coronet, Oh Coronet, if men knew the labour and pain that lie under you, if they found you outside thrown to the ground, they would not take you up', as the statesman Valerius Maximus wrote in his book, and that is the meaning of the olive tree.[187]

In Jotham's parable the olive tree refused to be anointed king, because it knew that if it were it would have to give up many things. That is also what Augustus meant. At the conclusion of his discussion on Rome and the rule of the consuls, Abravanel stated:

As for the moral here, there is no doubt that the kingdom of Rome was not like the other nations: not in wisdom nor reason, for these were found in abundance among the Romans; nor in heroism, for what is the chaff to the wheat; nor in the perfection of the people or in the length of their rule and in other such things. For, just as the heavens are far from the earth, so the ways of Rome are far from their ways.[188]

Abravanel's admiration for Rome is mirrored in many Christian works from Italy of the fourteenth and fifteenth centuries,[189] but the most striking is the simi-

[185] See Netanyahu, *Don Isaac Abravanel*, 225–6. Abravanel believed the End of Days would take place between 1503 and 1530.

[186] See ibid. 186–9; see also Funkenstein, 'The Image of the Ruler in Jewish Thought in the Late Middle Ages' (Heb.), 183–6; Ravitzky, 'On Kings and Statutes in Jewish Thought in the Middle Ages' (Heb.), esp. 480–1 n. 8.

[187] Abravanel on Judg. 9: 14 (*Perush linevi'im rishonim*, 124). Baer notes that the quote from Augustus is not in Valerius Maximus ('Don Isaac Abravanel's Attitude to History and the State' (Heb.), 403 n. 13).   [188] Abravanel, *Ma'ayenei hayeshuah*, 8: 5 (Jerusaelm edn., 335).

[189] Among them Petrarch, Leonardo Bruni, and Flavio Biondo (see Coleman, *Ancient and Medieval Memories*, 558–62).

larity to Nicholas of Lyra's commentary on the book of Daniel, written in Paris in 1309–10 and re-edited in 1328.[190] The virtues of Rome were also a popular subject in Spanish literature: Alonso de Cartagena's 'Response to the Marqués de Santillana', regarded as the first essay in Castilian, dealt with the obligations of aristocrats using Rome as a model;[191] Juan Alfonso de Baena, a courtier of King Juan II of Castile, argued that it was the aristocrats' duty to study the military campaigns of the Roman emperors.[192] Aviezer Ravitzky has pointed to the similarities between Abravanel's comments on the Roman republic and those of Thomas Aquinas.[193] However, his overall image of Rome is closer to Dante's, despite Dante's preference for monarchy as the best form of government: both stressed the Romans' genetic traits, using the founding myth to support their theories;[194] both ascribed special importance to the Roman government's attempts to promote the general good and its leaders preparedness to forgo their personal interests;[195] and both saw the guiding hand of God in the greatness of the Roman empire.[196]

Dante regarded the Holy Roman Empire as the direct continuation of ancient Rome, even though by his time the emperors had fallen from their lofty position, and the empire had lost much of its splendour.[197] Abravanel also regarded the emperors from Julius Caesar to his own time as one sequence: 'And all the emperors who were in Rome until the present day have an eagle drawn on their flag.'[198] However, unlike Dante, Abravanel subscribed to a version of the 'transfer of empire': the Roman empire was transferred to Constantinople by Constantine, moved from Constantinople to the Franks during the reign of Charlemagne, and then to the Holy Roman Empire under the German emperor Otto the Great

---

[190] See Zier, 'Nicholas of Lyra on the Book of Daniel', 188.

[191] See Díaz-Esteban, 'Jewish Literary Creation in Spanish' (Heb.), 338; Nadler, *The Mendoza Family*, 65–6, 83, 132, 186–8, 200–1. The marqués of Santillana posed the question to Alonso de Cartagena in 1444, after reading Leonardo Bruni's *De militia* (see Amador de los Rios, *Études historiques, politiques et littéraires sur les juifs d'Espagne*, 339–59; Cantera Burgos, *Álvar García de Santa María y su familia de conversos*, 416–64, esp. 452–3).

[192] See Alfonso de Baena, *Cancionero*, i. 7–15; Lawrance, 'On Fifteenth-Century Spanish Vernacular Humanism', 69.

[193] See Ravitzky, 'On Kings and Statutes in Jewish Thought in the Middle Ages' (Heb.), 476–9; on Aquinas's influence on Dante, see Merhavia, 'Dante and His Political Essay' (Heb.), 38–40; on Bruni, see Coleman, *Ancient and Medieval Memories*, 558–62.

[194] Dante made much use of Virgil's story of Aeneas to demonstrate the nobility of the Roman people and their right to rule (*De Monarchia*, 2: 6, 9).

[195] See ibid. 2: 5; cf. Machiavelli, *The Discourses*, i: 2.

[196] As mentioned, for Abravanel the divine plan was already evident in the stories of Noah's sons (the prototypes of humankind) (see Dante, *De Monarchia*, 2: 7–10).

[197] See Merhavia, 'Dante and His Political Essay' (Heb.), 25–9; Sabine, *A History of Political Theory*, 243–8.   [198] Abravanel on Ezek., Introduction (*Perush al nevi'im aharonim*, 437).

and his descendants.[199] Abravanel combined this with the astrological notion of the twelve conjunctions of the planets, each of which represented a nation. The transfers of the empire were part of a chain of twelve changes of kingdoms.[200] It began with the Jews and the Exodus from Egypt, continued with the Trojans, and ended with the twelfth, the change from the German Holy Roman Empire to the Ottoman sultanate.[201] Thus Abravanel used Christian political and theological methods to support his messianic views about the imminence of the End of Days and the Ottomans' role in bringing it closer.

The complex image of Rome in Abravanel's writings was assimilated into the work of Isaac Nathan, Abraham Zacut, and other Jews, who were also influenced by the positive depiction of Rome in the *Book of Josippon*. Therefore, the claim that Rome was not a historical reality for Jews is unfounded. The sources discussed in this chapter show that the prevailing view of how medieval Jews perceived Rome must be revised. Although Gerson Cohen's conclusions are still valid—Rome did have a negative image, expressed in Jewish hopes for its destruction—at the same time Rome had another positive image as an exemplary model of politics, culture, and ethics. The image of Rome also left its imprint on Jews' overall evaluation of Christian culture, since many kingdoms of western Europe were, in their own eyes, the direct heirs of Rome. Derogatory statements about ancient Rome might be expected to reflect a negative image of those who claimed to be its heirs. However, negative images of Rome are found mainly in eschatological contexts, and the overall image of Rome was positive. According to Yitzhak Baer, Abravanel 'approaches the beauties of Greece and the heroic greatness of Rome, with all the enthusiasm of the humanist—an enthusiasm, to be sure, that never affects his bitter hatred towards the Rome of the popes'.[202] It should be stressed, however, that Abravanel's hatred was directed at Christianity and channelled towards the End of Days. This complex attitude was apparently shared by several Jewish thinkers, who were attracted by the charms of Roman culture and rejected the Christian religion that was perceived as its successor.

[199] 'There is a tradition among the Ashkenazi Jews that when the seat of the empire is [in Germany], the messiah will come' (Abravanel on Zech. 2: 1 (*Perush al nevi'im aharonim*, 201); see id., *Ma'ayenei hayeshuah*, 12: 4 (Jerusalem edn., 410); id., *Mashmia yeshuah*, 14: 1 (Jerusalem edn., 573)).

[200] This approach was influenced by Abraham bar Hiyya (see Barkai, *Science, Magic, and Mythology in the Middle Ages* (Heb.), 31–3).

[201] See Abravanel, *Ma'ayenei hayeshuah*, 12: 4 (Jerusalem edn., 409–10).

[202] See Baer, *Galut*, 63.

CHAPTER THREE

Jesus and the Origins of Christianity

T HE SECOND TEMPLE period was often the subject of debate between Jews and Christians in the Middle Ages, and the reason is clear: Christians regarded it as the time of their messiah, while Jews rejected their claims and continued to await the messiah's coming. Polemicists, Christian and Jewish alike, believed that clarifying the history of the period would support their positions. Abraham ibn Daud, for example, examined the events of the Second Temple period to see if the messiah had come and the prophecies been fulfilled or if the Jews still had to wait for him.[1] Around 1414 Joseph Albo studied what the rabbis of the Talmud had said about the period and the time of the messiah in order to prove that the period was only a step towards redemption.[2] Between the twelfth and fifteenth centuries Jews held a variety of opinions on the life of Jesus and the beginnings of Christianity, which can reveal much about how they saw Christian culture during the Middle Ages.

THE LIFE OF JESUS

The life of Jesus was a common subject in medieval Jewish historiography.[3] Early mentions occurred in the twelfth century, but the question of Jesus's life and the stories about him in the Talmud played a key role in religious disputes from the thirteenth century.

The height of the discussion was the Disputation of Paris in 1240. During it, Nicholas Donin, a Jewish convert to Christianity, tried to prove that the Talmud contained blasphemy against Jesus and Christianity. Scholars are divided on how the disputation was conducted and whether it was an inquisitorial procedure;[4]

---

[1] See G. D. Cohen, Introduction and notes to Ibn Daud, *Sefer hakabalah*, pp. xxxiv–xxxv, 171–2.

[2] See Y. Ben-Sasson, 'R. Joseph Albo's Idea of History' (Heb.), 503–9; Ehrlich, *The Thought of R. Joseph Albo* (Heb.), 61–7.

[3] See Talmage, Introduction (Heb.) to Profayt Duran, *Polemical Writings*, 16 n. 30; id., Appendix (Heb.), ibid. 68–9.

[4] See e.g. Baer, 'On Criticism of the Disputations of Yehiel of Paris and Nahmanides' (Heb.), 135–8; Berger, 'On the Uses of History in Medieval Jewish Polemic against Christianity'; J. Cohen, *The Friars and the Jews*, 60–76, esp. 63 n. 22; Maccoby, *Judaism on Trial*, 23–4; Merhavia, *The Talmud*

however, the Jews of the Middle Ages accepted the Hebrew record of it as accurate.[5] In his response to Donin, Yehiel of Paris stated that the Christian Jesus was not mentioned in the Talmud.[6] Two other people mentioned in the Talmud— Ben Stada (or Stara) and Jesus, the son of Pantera—were also sometimes claimed to be the Christian Jesus but both were different people.[7] Yehiel, following Rabbenu Tam, argued that the man whom the sages hanged on the eve of Passover was Ben Stada, not the Christian Jesus.[8]

In Spain and southern France, most Jewish scholars accepted that the Jesus mentioned in the Talmud was the Christian Jesus; however, they rejected Christian claims about the date of his birth. This topos appeared in the writings of Judah ben Barzillai al-Bargeloni, Abraham ibn Daud, Levi ben Abraham ben Hayim, Nahmanides, Shimon ben Tsemah Duran, Hayim ibn Musa, Joseph ben Tsadik, Solomon ibn Verga, and Abraham Zacut:[9]

in *Christian Eyes* (Heb.), 227–90; Rosenthal, 'The Talmud on Trial'; Eisenberg, 'Reading Medieval Religious Disputation', esp. 90–106.

[5] Yehiel of Paris, *Vikuaḥ rabenu yeḥi'el mipariz*.

[6] According to Baer, the Jewish references to Jesus at the Disputation of Paris are contradictory. There is a general statement that the Jesus whom the Christians regard as their God is not mentioned in the Talmud; however, at one point, Yehiel admitted that the Talmud does refer to the Christian Jesus (see Baer, 'On Criticism of the Disputations of Yehiel of Paris and Nahmanides' (Heb.), 131). However, it is not necessary to view these, as Baer does, as 'overt additions'. It is possible that in the one instance where Yehiel agreed that the Jesus in the Talmud was the Christian Jesus (BT *San.* 43*a*), he may not have had an answer ready and had to agree with Donin (see J. Cohen, *The Friars and the Jews*, 71). Berger shows that in fact Yehiel referred to three men called Jesus, two of whom came from Nazareth ('On the Uses of History in Medieval Jewish Polemic against Christianity', 33; see also Eisenberg, 'Reading Medieval Religious Disputation', 30–89.

[7] BT *Shab.* 104*b*; *AZ* 27*b*; see M. Goldstein, *Jesus in the Jewish Tradition*, 57–62, 281 nn. 4–5; Rokeah, 'Ben Stara is Ben Pantera' (Heb.), esp. 17–18; Murcia, 'Ben Stada (ou Ben Stara) n'est pas Jésus'.

[8] Yehiel of Paris, *Vikuaḥ rabenu yeḥi'el mipariz*, 8; see Margaliot, note (Heb.), ibid.; *Tosafot* on *Shab.* 104*b*, *ben stada*; see also Maccoby, *Judaism on Trial*, 27–30; Merhavia, *The Talmud in Christian Eyes* (Heb.), 316–17.

[9] Judah b. Barzillai, *Perush sefer yetsirah*, 239; see Baer, 'On Criticism of the Disputations of Yehiel of Paris and Nahmanides' (Heb.), 131 n. 3; Talmage, Introduction (Heb.) to Profayt Duran, *Polemical Writings*, 16 n. 30; see also Joseph b. Tsadik, *Kitsur zekher tsadik* (ed. Neubauer, 89); Ibn Musa, *Magen varomaḥ*, 63, 65–7; Shimon b. Tsemah Duran, *Keshet umagen*, 46. In *Sefer hakabalah*, Ibn Daud cited two contradictory traditions. One identified Jesus as the student of Joshua ben Perahya (*Sefer hakabalah*, ch. 2, lines 64–77 (ed. Cohen: Heb. section, 15–16; Eng. section, 20–2)), the other stated that he was born in the thirty-eighth year of the reign of Augustus (ibid., ch. 4, lines 94–5 (ed. Cohen: Heb. section, 30; Eng. section, 39)). According to Gerson Cohen, in discussing Augustus, Ibn Daud was faithful to his Arabic source (Introduction and notes, ibid. 39, notes to lines 127–8; p. 246). In the *History of the Kings of Israel*, he mentioned that at the time of Pompey and the war between the brothers Aristobulus and Hyrcanus 'Jesus the Christian was captured' (Ibn Daud, *Divrei malkhei yisra'el*, 34). The topos also appeared in Levi ben Abraham's *Sefer hatekhunah*, according to Profayt Duran (*Kelimat hagoyim*, 11 (ed Talmage, 62)); Nahmanides, *Vikuaḥ haramban*, 8 (ed. Chavel, 303); and Ibn Verga, *Shevet yehudah*, 68, 106.

The truth is that the Nazarene was born in the fourth year of the reign of Jannaeus II, also called Alexander, which is year 263 after the rebuilding of the Temple and year 51 of the Hasmoneans, which is 3671 of the Creation. But the Christians claim that he was born in the time of Herod, servant of the Hasmoneans, in the year 3760 of the Creation and that he was hanged at the age of 32, thirty-five years before the destruction of the Temple. They say so in order to shame us and to tell us that [we were punished] immediately and swiftly for our iniquity, within forty years, through the destruction of the Temple for what we did to him. This is not so, since his birth was eighty-nine years earlier than what they claim.

The truth is that he was born in the year 3671, and in year 299 after the rebuilding of the Temple he was arrested and he was 36 years old in the third year of Aristobulus son of Jannaeus. That is why the sages of Israel wrote in a dispute with the Christians that there is no reference in the Talmud to the Nazarene to whom they refer. In the chronicles of the Christians, there is also a controversy among them regarding which year he was born. We know about him and his disciples from the talmudic tractates *Shabat*, *Sotah*, and *Sanhedrin*.[10]

In keeping with the general Jewish position, Zacut placed Jesus's life earlier in order to disprove the Christian claim that the Temple was destroyed as punishment for his Crucifixion. Based on the Talmud he calculated that Jesus was born 150 years before the destruction of the Temple and crucified 114 years before it.

Following other scholars, in particular Shimon ben Tsemah Duran, Zacut rejected the argument that Jews should refrain from arguing with Christians about the life of Jesus because there was no common ground for such a dispute. According to this position, which emerged at the Disputation of Paris and in the talmudic glosses of the Tosafists, if one rejects the identification of Ben Stada with the Christian Jesus, then it is possible to accept the Christian version of Jesus's life.[11] Menahem Me'iri, Moses Hakohen of Tordesillas, and Isaac Abravanel agreed with this position.[12] By accepting that Ben Stada was Jesus, Zacut opened up the possibility of a dispute about when he lived. Zacut found an opening in Christian controversies over the date of Jesus's birth, which he thought weakened the Christian position and allowed Jews to introduce the talmudic position as a legitimate solution. Zacut's argument reflects an advanced stage in

---

[10] Zacut, *Sefer yuḥasin* (ed. Filipowski, 15*a–b*). The date that Zacut gave for Jesus's arrest is consistent with what Ibn Daud wrote in *Sefer hakabalah* and the *History of the Kings of Israel*.

[11] Yom Tov Lipmann Mülhausen also shared this view (*Sefer nitsaḥon*, 192). According to Zacut, Mülhausen arrived independently at the same conclusions as Shimon ben Tsemah Duran (Zacut, *Sefer yuḥasin* (ed. Filipowski, 86a–87a); see Shimon b. Tsemah Duran, *Keshet umagen*, 18–19; id., fragments from *Ḥeshev ha'efod* and *Magen avot* in Talmage, Appendix (Heb.) to Profayt Duran, *Polemical Writings*, 68–9; M. Goldstein, *Jesus in the Jewish Tradition*, 57–62).

[12] Me'iri, *Beit habeḥirah al masekhet avot*, 28; Moses Hakohen, *Ezer ha'emunah*, ii. 141; Abravanel, *Ma'ayenei hayeshuah*, 10: 8 (Jerusalem edn., 378).

Jewish polemic, in which Jews could use dates from Christian historiography to question details of Jesus's life.

In *Megilat hamegaleh*, Abraham bar Hiyya accepted the Christian dates of Jesus's birth and Crucifixion without comment.[13] He repeated the dates in *Sefer ha'ibur*, but noted there that they were according to the Christians. He also discussed Jesus's age at the time of his Crucifixion and the day of the week on which it took place.[14] Jacob ben Reuben also regarded the Christian date as the most acceptable. However, in his view, the Christian date was contradicted by some of the Christological interpretations of the New Testament, but he made no effort to propose an alternative. He cited the Christian date as a fact, accepted by Jews and Christians alike ('everyone knows it is true').[15]

In *Shame of the Gentiles*, Profayt Duran often turned his opponents words against them, using the rhetorical formula: 'as the speaker said'.[16] He accepted the Christian date of the birth of Jesus and used it to refute the Christians' claims about the connection between Jesus's death and the destruction of the Temple. The Christians used a talmudic passage about signs that appeared in the Temple forty years before its destruction to link it with Jesus's Crucifixion.[17] However, according to Duran's calculations, even in the Christian version, Jesus's death preceded the destruction of the Temple by fifty years. Hence, there was no need to exaggerate the gap between the two events: the Christians were already out by ten years:

All of the misleaders [Christians] agree that Jesus was born three years before the death of Herod; and that Herod lived in the time of Emperor Augustus, the emperor of Rome, who made him a leader; and that [Herod] ruled over Galilee in the tenth year of [Augustus's] reign; and that he ruled for thirty-three years, and that he was an Edomite who converted to Judaism out of his love and desire for a Jewess who would not marry him until he was circumcised and became a Jew. And Emperor Augustus reigned for fifty-six years; and after him came Emperor Tiberius, who reigned for twenty-three years; and after him was Emperor Gaius, who reigned for four years; and after him Emperor Claudius, who reigned for thirteen years; and after him Emperor Nero, who reigned for fourteen years, and in the second year of his reign Peter and Paul came to Rome, and in the last year of his reign he put them on trial for their faith in Jesus ... and after Nero came Emperor Vespasian and he reigned [ten years]; and after him came Titus his son who destroyed the city and the Temple and reigned for two years.

---

[13] Abraham bar Hiyya, *Megilat hamegaleh*, 4: 98.

[14] Abraham bar Hiyya, *Sefer ha'ibur*, 109–10; Talmage, Appendix (Heb.) to Profayt Duran, *Polemical Writings*, 69.   [15] Jacob b. Reuben, *Milḥamot hashem*, 87–8.

[16] See Talmage, Introduction (Heb.) to Profayt Duran, *Polemical Writings*, 16; Katz, *Between Jews and Gentiles* (Heb.), 114; see also Kozodoy, 'The Hebrew Bible as Weapon of Faith'.

[17] BT *Yoma* 39*b*.

And according to what is said and known about him, Jesus lived around thirty years. For Luke wrote in Chapter 3 that Jesus was about 30 when he began to do his work [Luke 3: 23]. And according to this, he was hanged about fifty years before the destruction, in the fifteenth year of Tiberius's reign for Tiberius began to reign in the sixteenth year after Jesus's birth according to what they say, and reigned for twenty-three years. And all this was written by . . . Vincent [de Beauvais] in a famous book of theirs on the history of Rome. And this is in the seventh, eighth, and ninth parts of that book.[18]

In order to support his chronological calculations, Duran listed the Roman emperors from Augustus (the birth of Jesus) to Titus (the destruction of the Temple). Dating Jesus's Crucifixion to the fifteenth year of Tiberius's reign means that it occurred about fifty years before the destruction of the Temple, which contradicts the Christian claim that there was a connection between the two events. Duran summed up his discussion by affirming the identification of the talmudic Jesus and the New Testament Jesus, and stating that 'the date is not known for certain, but in their books there is proof that it was about fifty years earlier'.[19] For his list of Roman emperors, Duran used Christian histories of the Second Temple period, in particular Vincent de Beauvais' *Mirror of History*, a work which he regarded highly.[20] The use of Christian sources added greater force to his conclusions.

Profayt Duran's method was adopted by Shimon ben Tsemah Duran and Hayim ibn Musa, who did not mention him as their source, but referred directly to Vincent de Beauvais.[21] Zacut, as mentioned earlier, used a similar method. It seems then, that Jewish disputants were making use of Christian historiography in the debate over the life of Jesus from the end of the fourteenth century, a development that should be credited to Profayt Duran.

---

[18] Profayt Duran, *Kelimat hagoyim*, 11 (ed. Talmage, 60–1); on corrections in counting the years, see Talmage, notes (Heb.), ibid. 60 nn. 1, 4.

[19] See Profayt Duran, *Kelimat hagoyim*, 11 (ed. Talmage, 62–3). Nonetheless, it is not clear how Duran reconciled the talmudic claim that Jesus was a disciple of Joshua ben Perahya with the date of his birth.   [20] Ibid. 3–5 (ed. Talmage, 23, 26, 30, 32).

[21] See Shimon b. Tsemah Duran, *Keshet umagen*, 47, 51. The only two places where Shimon ben Tsemah Duran referred to De Beauvais are also in *Shame of the Gentiles*, and hence it is reasonable to assume that he did not read the Christian source (see Profayt Duran, *Kelimat hagoyim*, 5, 11 (ed. Talmage, 32, 61–2)). Hayim ibn Musa wrote: 'According to Vincent's calculations in his book Jesus died fifty years before the destruction [of the Temple] or, according to the lower calculation, forty years. . . . Also in their book of history of the kings of Rome, between the time of Herod until Titus there were many years. For their scholars agree that three years before the death of Herod, Jesus was born. And Herod reigned in the tenth year of Caesar Augustus' (*Magen varomah*, 79–81). Later he followed more or less the calculations of Profayt Duran.

THE ORIGINS OF CHRISTIANITY

Profayt Duran

Medieval Jewish writers and polemicists also discussed who Jesus was and what he did: issues that were linked to the origins of the new religion. Jews and Christians agreed that Christianity originated in Judaism, and Jews tried to explain the connection between Judaism and its offshoot and to determine when that separation occurred. To do this they had to define Jesus's place in Jewish society, the relationship between Jesus and his disciples, and the connection between the medieval 'Church triumphant' and early Christianity. Although several other writers preceded him, Profayt Duran's *Shame of the Gentiles* is a monumental response to these questions.

Profayt Duran attempted to prove that contemporary Christianity had diverted from and misrepresented the intentions of Jesus and his disciples. In his view, the Christianity of his time was the outcome of a series of theological adaptations and distortions made by the leaders of the Church over a long period. He devoted the fourth and fifth chapters of *Shame of the Gentiles* to this subject, under the rubrics: 'For Jesus never meant to dispute the divine Torah, but very much desired its existence and eternality, and his disciples also believed it was eternal' and 'What did those who came after them, the believers in Jesus, hope to achieve by disputing the Torah and destroying it?'[22]

Duran divided the history of Christianity into two stages: the first being the period of Jesus and his disciples. At this stage, Christianity was a flawed form of Judaism, a product of the misunderstandings of ignorant people, whom Duran called the 'misled'. However, Jesus and his disciples adhered to the Torah, and there was no dispute about its eternality. In the second stage, Christian theology was founded. At this stage an attempt was made to undermine the Torah. The leaders of Christianity were no longer lower class or uneducated like the Apostles, but rather intellectuals, who employed logic and philosophy to destroy the Torah and prove the truth of their faith—these Duran called the 'misleaders'.[23]

Eleazar Gutwirth stressed the link between religious disputation and apologetics, on the one hand, and the development of the critical trend in Christian historical thinking, on the other. He pointed to a similar development in Spanish Jewry in the fifteenth century, which grew out of Duran's *Shame of the Gentiles*. Gutwirth showed that Duran developed new methods of criticizing Christianity,

[22] Profayt Duran, *Kelimat hagoyim*, 4, 5 (ed. Talmage, 24, 30); see Talmage, Introduction (Heb.) to Profayt Duran, *Polemical Writings*, 19–25.

[23] Profayt Duran, *Kelimat hagoyim*, Dedication (ed. Talmage, 4).

including comparing the texts of the New Testament, the Vulgate, and the Hebrew Bible. Like Yitzhak Baer and Ephraim Talmage, Gutwirth presented Duran's new approach against the background of the fourteenth-century schism in the Church and the criticisms of the Conciliarists, who wanted to weaken the papacy in favour of the Council of Cardinals.[24]

Jeremy Cohen has recently offered another interpretation. He asserts that Duran's writings do not reveal any influence of the Conciliarists. While the Conciliarists mainly attacked the ecclesiastical establishment, Duran concentrated on theological issues, the divinity of Jesus, the Trinity and original sin, which the Conciliarists did not challenge. In addition, Cohen pointed out that the division of Christian history into stages and the distinction between new and old (false and true) Christianity was not an invention of the Conciliarists. Such a distinction was present in the writings of the Church Fathers, and in the thirteenth century it re-emerged at the University of Paris in the controversies around mendicant poverty.[25] Cohen suggested that Duran acquired all of his tools of historical criticism from the anti-Jewish polemic of the mendicant friars, in particular Raymundus Martini's monumental work, *Dagger of Faith*, and showed the similarities between Martini's view of Judaism and Duran's depiction of Christianity.

Raymundus Martini distinguished between the Jews of the Bible and the Jews of the post-biblical period. The turning point in Jewish history was, in his opinion, the development of talmudic Judaism at the time of Jesus. The talmudic rabbis created a new, satanic religion while deliberately ignoring the Christological evidence in the Bible. Duran adopted the same tactics: he divided the history of Christianity into two stages (Jesus and his disciples, the later followers) and presented the Christianity of his own time as a deviation from the ancient Christianity of Jesus. He showed that the Church Fathers maliciously distorted the biblical text and clung tenaciously to their errors.[26]

Talmage had in fact already noted that Duran's approach was not new and mentioned a number of precedents; however, in his view, the method gained greater impetus from the appearance of the Conciliarists.[27] Gutwirth went further and attributed particular importance to the critical tools that Duran

[24] See Gutwirth, 'History and Apologetics in XVth Century Hispano-Jewish Thought', 231–8.

[25] See J. Cohen, 'Profiat Duran's "The Reproach of the Gentiles"', 78–9; on the polemical shift in the writings of Profayt Duran and Hasdai Crescas, see id., 'Towards a Functional Classification of Jewish Anti-Christian Polemic in the High Middle Ages', esp. 109–12.

[26] J. Cohen, 'Profiat Duran's "The Reproach of the Gentiles"', 81–3; see id., *Living Letters of the Law*, 342–58; Szpiech, 'Translation, Transcription, and Transliteration in the Polemics of Raymond Martini'; Vose, *Dominicans, Muslims and Jews in the Medieval Crown of Aragon*.

[27] Talmage, Introduction (Heb.) to Profayt Duran, *Polemical Writings*, 19 n. 50.

developed under Christian influence, asserting that he was particularly innovative in this area.[28] Although Cohen noted the precedents mentioned by Talmage, he chose to emphasize the influence of Maimonides' understanding of Christianity in his *Epistle to Yemen*, which, according to Abraham Halkin, was the understanding accepted by Jewish intellectuals in the Middle Ages.[29] Despite these precedents, Cohen argued, Duran wrote his book in response to the widespread conversions to Christianity in Spain following the riots of 1391. Cohen accepted Benzion Netanyahu's view that *Shame of the Gentiles* was intended for converts and argued that Duran's use of Martini's method, which was intended to convince Jews to convert, turned out to be a very effective counter-measure.[30]

Abraham bar Hiyya

As mentioned earlier, Abraham bar Hiyya differed from other Jewish writers on the life of Jesus. He took no position on the date of his birth: in *Sefer ha'ibur* he accepted the date according to the Christians and merely noted that it was the Christian date. The reasons for this become clear in *Megilat hamegaleh*:

It is said that this conjunction of the planets began under the sign of Virgo . . . and that an omen foreshadowed the emergence of a new religion in the world . . . and that the religion would be established by worthless people, who are contemptible in the eyes of the world, and [the religion] was not adhered to in their own area but in places distant from their land, to the north. And since the sign was of two colours, this religion was favourably regarded by many people, who all joined together to invent it through words of sorcery and illusion . . . and this caused them to be brought to death in various ways, by the sword, by hanging, and by the other harsh deaths that Mars is responsible for. . . . And Mars too, which looked upon them, was a strong sign that attested to their error and their evil rites, which will be observed by the wicked men who believe in them for a very long time. . . . And they say that in the year 3793 of the Creation [33 CE], one year before this conjunction, Jesus son of Pandera—may his bones be crushed—was hanged, and a year after that his evil, lawless disciples went forth to mislead the world. And you do not find in this conjunction or the one that went before any omen of the birth of this hanged Jesus, because in the eyes of his people he was worthless and loathsome, and he had no great standing in the world all the days of his life, but those wicked disciples of his revived his memory after his death. It is written about them that 'the lawless sons of your people will assert themselves to confirm the vision, but they will fail' [Dan. 11: 14]. And it was not said that they will assert themselves to confirm a vision for themselves

[28] Gutwirth, 'History and Apologetics in XVth Century Hispano-Jewish Thought', 235. Gutwirth mentioned several precedents for the textual comparisons that Profayt Duran made between the Vulgate and the Hebrew Bible and his attempt to describe the Jewish background of Christian customs (see also ibid. 236 nn. 23, 25).

[29] Maimonides, *Epistle to Yemen*, 120–1; Halkin, Introduction and notes, ibid. 14–15.

[30] J. Cohen, 'Profiat Duran's "The Reproach of the Gentiles"', 79, 83.

but will try to confirm it for another, and they shall fail in this issue, as did the evil disciples of the hanged Jesus, for he died in his sin and iniquity and they bore his shame and wickedness and revealed his infamy and disgrace, and after him they all died like him a bad, horrible death. And after their failure, nothing more is written to recall them.[31]

Abraham bar Hiyya believed that each of the nations of the world had a corresponding sign of the zodiac and that all historical events were primarily the consequence of the conjunction and separation of Saturn and Jupiter.[32] According to him, Jesus's birth was of no importance, since it had no relevance to Christianity. The relevant date is that of his Crucifixion, and the importance of this event does not derive from Jesus, but from the activity of his disciples afterwards. The disciples were the founders of Christianity, and the astrological signs attest to the fact that with their activity a change occurred in the world.[33] But the heavens were absolutely indifferent to Jesus's birth, since he was a marginal figure, and the stars only give omens in relation to the births of great men. Therefore, debate on the subject is superfluous, and the Christian version of the date can be accepted.

Abraham bar Hiyya's distinction between the two stages of early Christianity was undoubtedly one of the precedents for Profayt Duran's approach. His view that Christianity was founded by Jesus's disciples and not by Jesus is quite prevalent in modern scholarship. It is, however, reasonable to assume that he arrived at his conclusions for polemical reasons: he wanted to denigrate Jesus and his disciples in order to disparage Christianity, and he wanted to create a sense of superiority among the Jews, the followers of the original religion.[34]

Abraham ibn Daud

One of the precedents suggested by scholars for Duran's approach is Abraham ibn Daud's understanding of Christianity.[35] In the *History of Rome*, Ibn Daud states that Christianity developed in two stages: from Jesus to Constantine and from Constantine onwards.

[31] Abraham bar Hiyya, *Megilat hamegaleh*, 5: 135–6.

[32] See Barkai, *Science, Magic, and Mythology in the Middle Ages* (Heb.), 31. Abraham bar Hiyya took the fundamentals of his approach from the Muslim astrological tradition, in which astrology was a means of interpreting the past and predicting the future of communities and nations. An example of this from Spain is the *Kitāb al-tibyān* (1094–5) of Abdallah ibn Buluqqin, the last Ziri ruler of Granada who used this method against Jews and Christians alike (see Barkai, *Science, Magic, and Mythology in the Middle Ages* (Heb.), 26–30; Zomeño Rodríguez, 'Abdallāh ibn Buluqqin').

[33] Abraham bar Hiyya, *Sefer ha'ibur*, 109.

[34] Contempt for Christianity is a striking aspect of Abraham bar Hiyya's writing, but it was less pronounced in other authors (see Flusser, *Judaism and the Origins of Christianity* (Heb.), 425).

[35] See G. D. Cohen, Introduction and notes to Ibn Daud, *Sefer hakabalah*, p. xxxiii n. 81; Talmage, Introduction (Heb.) to Profayt Duran, *Polemical Writings*, 19–20 n. 50; Falbel, 'On a Heretic Argument in Levi ben Abraham ben Chaim's Critique on Christianity', 39–41.

And Constantine Caesar reigned in his place. He established the doctrine of the Christians and converted to their religion and teachings 300 years after Jesus by their calculation, but according to our calculation more than 420 years. And in order to make it known, we composed [*ḥibarnu*] this on the history of Rome. [Constantine] left Rome and gave it to the priests of Edom to this very day and built *kostantiniyah novella*, which means the noble [city of] Constantinople. And during his reign lived Arius, who wrote a book containing answers and proofs about their doctrine, but Constantine did not heed him. And Constantine died in the twenty-first year of his reign. And his son Constans [Constantius II, r. 337–61] succeeded him as Caesar. And he listened to Arius and he corrupted the doctrine of Edom and reigned thirty-four [*recte* twenty-four] years and died. And he was succeeded by Julian Caesar who reigned for two years and restored the worship of idols as was the custom before and did not accept the doctrine of Edom and died.[36]

According to Gerson Cohen, the *History of Rome* was primarily a polemical work, and here Ibn Daud had two purposes in mind. In the first place he wanted to show that there was a gap of at least 300 years between Jesus's Crucifixion and the composition of the New Testament. Secondly he argued that, even if the Christians had faithfully observed what was written in the Gospels from their composition until the twelfth century, that was not a reliable foundation for their tradition, since the claim that the Gospels reflected Jesus's teachings could not be maintained. The New Testament was a fabrication by Emperor Constantine, a fact which was known to Arius who wrote a refutation of its doctrines.[37]

A passage from *Sefer hakabalah* supports the interpretation of the *History of Rome* as a polemical work: 'The *History of Rome* is intended to inform [its readers] of when the Gospels were written.'[38] However, in my opinion, the polemical aspects of the *History of Rome* are marginal. If Ibn Daud wanted to demonstrate the gap between Jesus and Constantine, he did not need to begin with Romulus and Remus, nor did he need to end with the rise of Islam and the spread of Christianity to Spain. In the excerpt above, he wrote: 'And in order to make it known, we composed [or put together or wrote: *ḥibarnu*] *this on* the history of Rome', referring supposedly to the claim that Constantine wrote the Gospels. But the structure of the sentence raises some doubts. Why did Ibn Daud not write 'We have written the history of Rome' or just 'We have written this' without adding the Hebrew letter *bet* ('in' or 'with'): *bezikhron romi*, '*with* the history of Rome'? In my view, the sentence should be translated 'in order to make it known, we composed *this with* the history of Rome', explaining why he included a discussion of the origins of Christianity in a book about the kings of Rome. In a similar

---

[36] Ibn Daud, *Zikhron divrei romi* (Mantua edn., 23–4; ed. Vehlow, 120–3).

[37] See G. D. Cohen, Introduction and notes to Ibn Daud, *Sefer hakabalah*, pp. xxxii–xxxiii.

[38] Ibn Daud, *Sefer hakabalah*, ch. 7, line 438 (ed. Cohen: Heb. section, 74; Eng. section, 103).

manner Abraham Zacut explained why he added chapter 6 to *Sefer yuḥasin*: 'And hence I composed [*ḥibarti*] this with the book of the holy ones, *Sefer yuḥasin*, that I composed [*ḥibarti*] to recount . . . all the events that have come to pass since the Creation.'[39]

The claim that Ibn Daud thought that Constantine wrote the Gospels is based on the sentence: 'Constantine . . . *established* [*ḥakak*] the doctrine of the Christians and converted to their religion and teachings.' According to this interpretation, *ḥakak* is to be understood as 'wrote', and Constantine converted to Christianity and wrote the Gospels. However, unlike the Mantua edition, the De Rossi manuscript of 1409 includes the phrase: 'Constantine . . . *strengthened* [*ḥizek*] the doctrine of the Christians and converted to their religion and teachings'.[40] These may be Ibn Daud's original words, which fit precisely with what we know about Constantine's actions. However, even if we reject this possibility and prefer the printed version, we can assume that Ibn Daud's choice of *ḥakak* rather than *katav* (wrote) was not accidental.

Although Ibn Daud stated in *Sefer hakabalah* that he wrote the *History of Rome* 'to inform [its readers] of when the Gospels were written', it is possible that he found no confirmation for the view that Constantine wrote the Gospels in any of the historiographical sources at his disposal. Hence, he chose to use the ambiguous word *ḥakak* which can also mean 'enacted [a law]'.[41] According to this interpretation, Constantine did not write the Gospels, but rather legalized Christianity. Ibn Daud may have been referring to Christianity becoming the state religion. This is not what happened, but it could have been acceptable in the light of the far-reaching implications of the Edict of Tolerance published by Constantine and Licinius in Milan in 313 CE. Possibly, Ibn Daud meant to ascribe authorship of the Nicene Creed, the theological formula established at the Council of Nicaea in 325, to Constantine. This interpretation is more consistent with the historical reality

[39] Zacut, *Sefer yuḥasin* (ed. Filipowski, 232*a*).

[40] See MS De Rossi 1409/2 (MS 2420, Palatina Library, Parma—Institute of Microfilmed Hebrew Manuscripts, no. 13285), fo. 17*b*. For comparison, see the phrase 'He strengthened [*ḥizek*] it' (ibid., fo. 18*a*). 'He established the doctrine of the Christians' is in MS 28/25 (London Beth Din and Beth Hamidrash—Institute of Microfilmed Hebrew Manuscripts, no. 139), fos. 139*b*–140*a*; MS Guenzburg 1420/5 (Russian State Library, Moscow—Institute of Microfilmed Hebrew Manuscripts, no. 48486), fos. 38*b*–39*a*. On MS De Rossi 1409/2 and MS 28/25, see G. D. Cohen, Introduction and notes (Heb.) to Ibn Daud, *Sefer hakabalah*, 16, 4, 6. In Cohen's view, MS 28/25 precedes MS De Rossi 1409/2 (ibid. 19), although they both belong to the same branch, which was edited for style and content (at least of *Sefer hakabalah*). For this reason, I have refrained from unequivocally stating a preference for *ḥizek* over *ḥakak*. An editor may have corrected the 'error', just as names in *Sefer hakabalah* were corrected in this branch and additions were made according to the Talmud and other medieval traditions.

[41] See Ben-Yehuda, *Dictionary of the Hebrew Language* (Heb.), iii. 1724. Constantine played an active role in the Council of Nicaea (see Barnes, 'Emperor and Bishops').

and the image of Constantine (especially, as they could have been interpreted in the twelfth century). The belief that Constantine opened a new period in the history of Roman legislation was widespread in medieval thought and is also found in the writings of Isidore of Seville, one of Ibn Daud's sources.[42] In addition, there is nothing in this scenario that implies anything about the Gospels. Even if Jews attributed a decisive role in the creation of Christianity to Constantine, they never claimed that he wrote the Gospels, but generally tried to show that he caused a deviation from the religion of the Gospels.

I do not totally reject the interpretation of *ḥakak* in the sense of 'wrote', but I prefer 'enact'. The precise meaning of *ḥakak* in the Bible is not clear, and in several cases commentators were unsure whether it referred to writing or law-making.[43] One also has to take into account the way in which a contemporary reader would have understood what was written, and from this standpoint 'wrote' is preferable. Nonetheless, even if we interpret *ḥakak* in the sense of 'wrote' and accept the view that Constantine (according to Ibn Daud) was the author of the Gospels, we have to reject the claim that Constantine was depicted as having falsified the Gospels.

Nothing in what Ibn Daud wrote suggests that he thought the Gospels were not a faithful representation of Jesus's doctrine, nor that he attributed any falsification to Constantine. He also did not claim that Arius was aware of any falsification by Constantine and hence formulated an opposing doctrine. According to Ibn Daud, Arius composed 'a book containing answers and proofs about their doctrine', and Constantine rejected his view. This can be understood in two ways depending on how 'their doctrine' is understood. Either Arius wrote about the doctrine of the New Testament, or he wrote against the doctrine of the Council of Nicaea, the doctrine that Constantine 'established'. In neither case is Arius depicted as acting against Constantine, but simply as a theologian whose views were not accepted by the emperor. Here Ibn Daud was faithful to his source, Paulus Orosius.[44]

---

[42] See Isidore of Seville, *Etymologiarum*, 5: 1/7; see also G. D. Cohen, Introduction and notes to Ibn Daud, *Sefer hakabalah*, 162 n. 16; Linder, 'The Myth of Constantine the Great', 44, n. 5; on Ibn Daud's reliance on Orosius in this part, see Klein and Molner, 'Rabbi Abraham ben David' (Heb.), *Hatsofeh lehokhmat yisra'el*, 8 (1924), 33.

[43] See e.g. Abravanel on Judg. 5: 9 (*Perush linevi'im rishonim*, 110).

[44] See: 'His diebus Arrius, Alexandrinae urbis presbyter, aueritate fidei catholicae deuians, exitiabile plurimis dogma constituit' (Orosius, *Seven Books of History against the Pagans*, 7: 28). Klein and Molner pointed out the similarity to Orosius ('Rabbi Abraham ben David' (Heb.), *Hatsofeh lehokhmat yisra'el*, 8 (1924), 33). Cohen, however, rejected their assumption that Ibn Daud had made direct use of the books of Orosius or Isidore of Seville. In his view, the similarities only proved that the ideas of Orosius and Isidore had penetrated Jewish writings, but that this was probably through mediating historiographical works (Introduction and notes to Ibn Daud, *Sefer hakabalah*, 162 n. 16). I should note here too that, because of Augustine's historiographical influence, Orosius did not glamorize

Ibn Daud's descriptions of historical events from the time of Constantine to the reign of Julian were also fairly accurate: Constantine convened the Council of Nicaea and passed theological laws (325 CE), later converted to Christianity (337), established the city of Constantinople (330), acted against Arius, and died after a reign of twenty-one years (actually thirty-one). He was succeeded by his son Constans (Constantius II), who supported Arianism. After him, Julian became emperor for two years (360–2) and attempted to reinstate paganism as the religion of the empire.[45]

Finally, in the excerpt from the *History of Rome* above, there is no attempt to divide Christian history into two stages: the Christianity of Jesus and the religion of Constantine.[46] For this reason too, Ibn Daud cannot be regarded as a precedent for Profayt Duran. Arius is depicted as having proposed an alternative to Catholic Christianity, and hence Constans, who supported him, 'corrupted the doctrine of Edom'. However, this does not refer to a return to the 'primitive' religion of Jesus and his Apostles, but a deviation from the Nicene Creed. Even if we adopt the view that Ibn Daud is claiming that Constantine wrote the Gospels, he still says nothing about a break between Christianity before Constantine and Christianity afterwards. Constantine 'converted to their religion', which was already in existence. He may have been a crucial figure in the history of Christianity, and he may have composed the Gospels, but nothing here suggests that he created anything new or different from the Christianity that preceded him. He converted and accepted the doctrine of the Christians as it was.

Maimonides

As Maimonides was greatly esteemed by the Jewish scholars of Spain and Provence, his views on Christianity were also highly regarded, and some modern scholars see him as representative of medieval Jews.[47] He referred to Jesus and Christianity in several of his works. In his *Epistle to Yemen*, he wrote:

Constantine as Eusebius did (see Chesnut, 'Eusebius, Augustine, Orosius, and the Later Patristic and Medieval Christian Historians', 698).

[45] See Klein and Molner, 'Rabbi Abraham ben David' (Heb.), *Hatsofeh leḥokhmat yisra'el*, 8 (1924), 33–4. Vehlow suggests that 'Constans' is probably Constantine II; however, it was Constantius II, the son of Constantine, who supported semi-Arianism and became sole ruler of the empire (introduction and notes to Ibn Daud, *Zikhron divrei romi*, 52–6, 123 n. 79). See also Fernández Urbina and Targarona Borrás, 'La historia romana', 337. On these events in the life of Constantine, see Barnes, *Constantine and Eusebius*, 208–23, 260–73; A. H. M. Jones, *The Later Roman Empire*, i. 112–19, 337–61; Hunt, 'Constantius II in the Ecclesiastical Historians'.

[46] See Falbel, 'On a Heretic Argument in Levi ben Abraham ben Chaim's Critique on Christianity', 39–41.

[47] See J. Cohen, 'Profiat Duran's "The Reproach of the Gentiles"', 78; Halkin, Introduction and notes to Maimonides, *Epistle to Yemen*, 14 n. 15.

After that there arose a new sect [Christianity] . . . and it believed that its approach would be more effective in wiping out every trace of the Jewish nation and Torah. It, therefore, resolved to lay claim to prophecy and to found a new Torah, contrary to our divine law, and to contend that it was equally God-given, according to his word and true law. Thereby it hoped to raise doubts and to create confusion, since one is opposed to the other, and both emanate from the same God, which would lead to the destruction of both religions. For such is the remarkable plan contrived by a very wicked man. He will strive first to kill his enemy and to save his own life, but when he finds it impossible to attain his objective, he will devise a scheme whereby they will both be slain.

The first to adopt this plan was Jesus the Nazarene—may his bones be ground to dust. He was a Jew. . . . He compelled people to believe that he was a prophet sent by God to clarify perplexities in the Torah, and that he was the messiah who was predicted by each and every prophet. He interpreted the Torah in such a way as to lead to its total annulment, to the abolition of all its commandments, and to the violation of its prohibitions, according to his intention. . . . God had already notified us of this in the book of Daniel when he presaged that a wicked man and a heretic among the Jews would endeavour to destroy the law, claim prophecy for himself, deal with weighty matters, and say he was the messiah and that God would cause his downfall. And it is written: 'the lawless sons of your people will assert themselves to confirm the vision, but they will fail' [Dan. 11: 14]. . . . Long after, a religion came forth from the sons of Esau, and it was attributed to him, but it had not been his intention.[48]

Maimonides divided the history of Christianity into two stages: Jesus's founding of a new religion and the development of another new religion in Rome that regarded Jesus as its source, but in fact had nothing to do with him. This division was the basis for Profayt Duran's method. But although the two approaches were similar, there was also much disparity between them.

According to Duran, no new religion was founded during the lifetimes of Jesus or his disciples. Jesus's faith was a distorted, erroneous form of Judaism, based on magic techniques learned in Egypt and allegorical exegesis. The uneducated disciples misinterpreted Jesus's allegories, taking them out of context and understanding them literally.[49] The nature of Christianity during Jesus's lifetime is a key subject of *Shame of the Gentiles*, as Duran's dedication to Hasdai Crescas attests: 'You have asked me, Your Highness, to inform you of what I have learned about the intent of the false messiah and his disciples or apostles in general, and whether they intended to destroy the divine Torah in whole or in part, as it was widespread and followed by those who believed in him and followed him';[50] and

[48] Maimonides, *Epistle to Yemen*, 120–1, 159.

[49] Profayt Duran, *Kelimat hagoyim*, 2 (ed. Talmage, 13); see Talmage, Introduction (Heb.) to Profayt Duran, *Polemical Writings*, 21–3.

[50] Profayt Duran, *Kelimat hagoyim*, Dedication (ed. Talmage, 3).

his reply is unequivocal: Jesus and his disciples did not intend to diverge from the Torah.[51]

Maimonides was of a different opinion. Although there was a vast difference between the Christianity of the time of Jesus and the Christianity of Rome, Jesus did play a crucial role in creating the new religion. He was the founder of Christianity, and his intent was to destroy Judaism by abolishing the Torah. Earlier scholars claimed that Maimonides believed Jesus did not wish to harm the Jewish people, based on the statement that '[Jesus's] deeds did not harm Israel, as neither individual nor groups followed him, since his inconsistencies became clear to them, and [also] his defeat when he fell into our hands, and his fate is well known.'[52] However, he did not say that Jesus did not intend to harm the Jews, but rather that he did not succeed in harming them because his doctrine was confounded.[53]

Unlike other nations, who tried to destroy the Jews by violence or to refute the Torah by intellectual argument,[54] Jesus attempted to use prophecy. He claimed that the God of Israel would give a new Torah. This new Torah was in fact an 'anti-Torah', whose purpose was to abolish the real Torah and its commandments. The idea that both doctrines referred to the same God was also a trick meant to sow doubt and confusion and to destroy Judaism.

In *Mishneh torah* there is a similar passage: '[Jesus] plotted to destroy Israel by the sword and to disperse and debase those among them who remain, to replace the Torah and to mislead most of the world into worshipping a god other than the God [of Israel].'[55] Here also, the accusation is directed at Jesus and not at his disciples or the 'sons of Esau'. It was Jesus who wanted to replace the Torah with another doctrine and to substitute another god for the God of Israel. It was Jesus

---

[51] Ibid. 4 (ed. Talmage, 24–6).

[52] Maimonides, *Epistle to Yemen*, 120. Falbel, for example, argued that 'Maimonides . . . recalls that Jesus did not have the intention of either teaching his doctrine to the Gentiles or to hurt Israel' ('On a Heretic Argument in Levi ben Abraham ben Chaim's Critique on Christianity', 41). Leibowitz states that 'in the *Epistle to Yemen*, Maimonides writes that Jesus never intended to found a new religion. He clears him completely of that accusation' (*On a World* (Heb.), 62).

[53] It seems many were misled by Boaz Cohen's English translation: 'Quite some time after, a religion appeared the origin of which is traced to him by the descendants of Esau, albeit it was not the intention of this person to establish a new faith' (Maimonides *Epistle to Yemen*, 120; see Halkin, Introduction and notes, ibid. 14–15; R. Ben-Shalom, *Facing Christian Culture* (Heb.), 163–4 n. 56).

[54] As examples, Maimonides cites a list of enemies, including Nebuchadnezzar, Titus, and Hadrian, as well as Persian and Hellenist scholars.

[55] Maimonides, *Mishneh torah*, 'Laws of Kings', 11: 4. This excerpt, which was excised from most of the printed versions by the censor but still exists in the first Rome printing, was well known in western Europe, as is clear from Nahmanides' sermon, *Torat hashem temimah*, 'The Torah of the Lord is Perfect' (Chavel, notes (Heb.) to Nahmanides, *Torat hashem temimah*, 144 n. 34) and Bernard Gui's *Inquisitors' Manual* (see Yerushalmi, 'The Inquisition and the Jews of France', 353).

who misled the nations, and because of him Jews were exiled, dispersed all over the world, and killed.

Salo Baron assumed that Maimonides had Abraham bar Hiyya's *Megilat hamegaleh* in mind when he described the historical development of Christianity.[56] However, Abraham bar Hiyya had different intentions entirely from Maimonides. It is true, as Baron argued, that they both interpreted Daniel 11:14 as a reference to Christianity, but in doing so they were adhering to an interpretative approach already widespread among rabbinic Jews and Karaites. Abraham bar Hiyya was preceded by Sa'adiah Gaon.[57] In contrast to Maimonides, who ascribed the verse to Jesus, Abraham bar Hiyya noted that it is actually in the plural and therefore interpreted it to mean that the disciples of Jesus would found the new religion, not Jesus himself.[58] Later Abraham ibn Ezra also used this interpretation.[59]

According to Amos Funkenstein, Maimonides believed history was a gradual development towards monotheism, and Jesus and Christianity (as well as Islam) were weapons in the war waged by polytheism against monotheism. According to Maimonides, the worldwide polytheistic religion was declining, and, in order to save itself, it tried to create a false monotheistic religion and substitute it for the true monotheistic religion. However, it failed to induce the Jews to convert and turned out to have been part of the divine plan all along. By taking over the world, Christianity and Islam promoted monotheism. Jesus had attempted deliberately and maliciously to destroy the true monotheistic religion, but, in doing so, he unwittingly bolstered it.[60]

In the light of this, it is clear that Profayt Duran did not base his approach to Christianity on the *Epistle to Yemen*. Although both Maimonides and Duran divided the development of Christianity into stages, they differed on the figure of Jesus, his purpose, and his intentions. Maimonides regarded Jesus as the founder of a new religion, whose purpose was to destroy the Jews and their religion; Profayt Duran depicted him as a man who erred and blundered, but whose intentions were good and whose basic aim was legitimate. From the viewpoint of medieval Jews, there was a substantial difference between the two.

---

[56] Baron, 'The Historical Outlook of Maimonides', 9–10 n. 6; see also n. 8. Guttmann rejected the view that Maimonides was familiar with *Megilat hamegaleh* (see Introduction (Heb.) to Abraham bar Hiyya, *Megilat hamegaleh*, pp. xxiii–xxiv).

[57] See Abraham bar Hiyya, *Megilat hamegaleh*, 4: 98; Rosenthal, 'Religious Tolerance in Medieval Biblical Commentary' (Heb.), 204.

[58] Abraham bar Hiyya, *Megilat hamegaleh*, 4: 95.

[59] Abraham ibn Ezra on Dan. 11:14 (*Haperush hakatsar al daniyel*, 13).

[60] Funkenstein, *Nature, History and Messianism in Maimonides* (Heb.), 51–2; see also Benin, *The Footprints of God*; Hartman, *Leadership in Times of Distress* (Heb.), 104–6, 117–20.

Levi ben Abraham ben Hayim

As mentioned above, the approaches of Ibn Daud and Maimonides differed from that of Abraham bar Hiyya. Levi ben Abraham ben Hayim of Provence (1245–1315) had similar views on Jesus and early Christianity to Abraham bar Hiyya:[61]

And some [Christian scholars] made [Jesus] only a messiah. But [Jesus] did not intend that, nor did he intend to abolish the commandments, as is clear from their Gospels. But others, his disciples, tried to do damage to the essence [of Judaism]. But [another MS: 'But perhaps'] [Jesus] did not wish to mislead, but his fantasies and delusions caused him to speak and act. And Maimonides wrote, about the end of the book of Judges, that Jesus the Nazarene also imagined he was the messiah, but the vast majority [of Christian scholars] did not want to speak of it. . . . In the end [the Christians] interpreted all the parts of their faith by allegory and typology to support the [doctrine of the Incarnation]. The first ones might have intended to; the last ones, in particular King Constantine, inverted all the things about God himself and gave him a corporeal form and imposed upon him sayings which are not true.[62]

Levi ben Abraham described Jesus as a man with messianic pretensions, but stressed that he did not intend to abolish the commandments or establish a new religion. The commandments were annulled by his disciples. He cited this as the view of some Christians and not as his personal opinion. According to him, Jesus did not intend to mislead his disciples or the people, but his messianic pretensions disrupted his mind. A similar idea occurs in *Mishneh torah*: 'Jesus the Nazarene, who imagined he was a messiah.'[63]

Levi ben Abraham also claimed that, in contrast to heretical Christian views that emphasized Jesus's humanity, the normative Christianity of his time accepted the doctrine of the Incarnation: that God became flesh in Jesus. He tried to identify the turning point in the history of Christianity and distinguished between two groups of Christians—'the first ones' and 'the last ones'. The first ones were apparently Jesus's disciples and the next few generations. The last ones were the Church Fathers until the time of Constantine, who, Levi ben Abraham held, changed Christianity by introducing the doctrine of the Incarnation. Constantine, although he was not a theologian, had a major role in this, probably because he convened the Council of Nicaea, which adopted Athanasius's position—that the Father and the Son were of the same substance—and rejected the Arian one—that Jesus was not divine by nature and that his divinity emanated from God

---

[61] See Halkin, 'Why was Levi b. Hayyim Hounded?'; Kreisel, Introduction (Heb.) to Levi b. Abraham, *Livyat ḥen*; Schwartz, 'The Controversy about Astral Magic in Fourteenth-Century Provence' (Heb.), 162–9, 173–4; Sirat, 'Les Différents Versions du Liwyat Hen'.

[62] Levi b. Abraham, *Livyat ḥen*, 6: 12 (ed. Kreisel, 288–91).

[63] Maimonides, *Mishneh torah*, 'Laws of Kings', 11: 4.

the Father. Constantine participated in the council and took an active role in the theological debates.[64] Levi ben Abraham noted that most Christian scholars were aware of Jesus's real, human essence, but they kept that knowledge secret. Later in *Livyat ḥen*, he tried to refute the doctrine of the Incarnation on the basis of philosophical evidence.

Nachman Falbel discussed precedents for Levi ben Abraham's belief that Jesus did not intend to damage Judaism and his distinction between a pure, early form of Christianity and a debased, later one in Ibn Daud's *History of Rome* and Maimonides' *Epistle to Yemen*. He regarded these as a continuation of the Jewish tradition about Jesus's Jewishness, reflected in the Talmud and *Toledot yeshu*.[65] In the Talmud Jesus is described as a pupil of Joshua ben Perahya who strayed from the right path.[66] Consequently, medieval scholars could stress Jesus's Jewishness and argue on the basis of a critical analysis of the Gospels that he did not wish to annul the commandments or to found an alternative religion. The very fact that Jesus was described as a Jew in the Talmud created the basis for understanding Christian history as a two-stage process.[67] In *Toledot yeshu*, Jesus is portrayed as a deviant, rebellious Jew, but it is explicitly stressed—unlike in the Talmud—that he and his disciples did not try to leave Judaism or propose a new Torah. Only after Jesus's death did the Christians separate from Judaism, but because the Jews cast the Christians out, rather than—as the medieval traditions had it—because the Christians wanted to go. In order to achieve this, the Jews sent one of their sages to the Christians disguised as an apostle, and he introduced new laws and customs. In opposition to the 'historical truth', the Christians now perceived Jesus as an enemy of the Jews, who had wanted to separate from them from the beginning, and had therefore abolished the sabbath and festivals, introduced new prayers, and forbidden marriage between Christians and Jews.[68]

It is possible that medieval Jewish scholars could have accepted the history of early Christianity as it appears in *Toledot yeshu* and that it is the source of the two-stage history of Christianity. However, not one of them suggested that the Jews wanted to separate from the Christians. They all wrote that the Christians separated from the Jews because of Paul and the disciples. Most of the writers also stressed Constantine's role in changing Christianity, a fact that is not mentioned

---

[64] See Barnes, 'Emperor and Bishops'.

[65] Falbel, 'On a Heretic Argument in Levi ben Abraham ben Chaim's Critique on Christianity', 41.   [66] BT *San.* 107*b*; see Klausner, *Jesus* (Heb.), 8–41.

[67] Baron, *A Social and Religious History of the Jews*, v. 118–19; cf. Rembaum, 'The New Testament in Medieval Jewish Anti-Christian Polemics'.

[68] See *Toledot yeshu*, 8–85; see also R. Ben-Shalom, 'The Converso as Subversive'; Horbury, 'A Critical Examination of the Toledoth Jeshu'; Schlichting, *Ein jüdisches Leben Jesu*; Schäfer, Meerson, and Deutsch (eds.), *Toledot Yeshu ('The Life Story of Jesus') Revisited*.

in *Toledot yeshu*. I agree with Falbel, who rejected the idea that Levi ben Abraham was continuing in this tradition and suggested that his understanding of early Christianity came from internal Christian polemics. Falbel pointed to heretical Christian movements, such as the Waldensians and heretical leaders such as Gerardo Segarelli and Dolcino, who claimed that the true Church had existed only until the time of Pope Sylvester. According to them, Constantine's gift of Rome to the papacy under Sylvester marked the end of the spiritual Church and the beginning of the temporal Church.[69]

It is also possible that in emphasizing Constantine's role, Levi ben Abraham and others were influenced by his near mythical status in medieval Europe. The story of his miraculous conversion to Christianity led to him being perceived in the Christian collective consciousness as the founder of Christian Europe. This was one reason for Jews' negative perception of him, as were the anti-Jewish attitudes attributed to him in the Christian myth.[70] Heretical Christian movements whose opinions had been rejected at the Council of Nicaea also had a poor opinion of Constantine, and Levi ben Abraham appears to be referring to them when he says: 'some [Christian scholars] made [Jesus] only a messiah'. This raises the question of which heresy it was.[71]

Scholars have already noted that the Jews in Provence in the twelfth and thirteenth centuries were familiar with the theological doctrines of Arians, Cathars, and other heretics.[72] For example, the Jewish disputant erroneously identified as the grammarian and Bible commentator David Kimhi may have used the claims of Christian heretics to advance similar arguments about Jesus to Catholic Christians. An anonymous thirteenth-century polemicist stated explicitly that the Albigensians rejected the Incarnation, and the Jewish scholar Menahem, in a dispute with Paul Christiani, praised those who left Catholicism and joined the Albigensians because they could not accept the doctrine of the

[69] Falbel, 'On a Heretic Argument in Levi ben Abraham ben Chaim's Critique on Christianity', 42–5. The distinction between later Christianity and the religion of Jesus was not an invention of the heretical movements: its roots lay in pagan criticism of the New Testament (see Julian the Apostate, *Against the Galileans*, 351a–356c, esp. 351d, in Rokeah, *Judaism and Christianity in the Light of Pagan Polemic*, 241–2. Constantine gave Rome to the Church under Pope Sylvester according to a forged edict known as the Donation of Constantine, which was created between 750 and 760 CE (see Folz, *The Concept of Empire in Western Europe*, 10–12).

[70] See Linder, 'Ecclesia and Synagoga in the Medieval Myth of Constantine the Great'; id., 'The Myth of Constantine the Great'.

[71] It is unlikely that Levi ben Abraham is referring to Sa'adiah Gaon's *Emunot vedeot*. Although Sa'adiah Gaon described the fourth sect of Christians (who he said 'had appeared recently') as believing that Jesus was one of the prophets, he had no two-stage conception of Christianity (see Sa'adiah Gaon, *Sefer hanivhar be'emunot uvedeot*, 2: 7 (ed. Kapah, 94–5)).

[72] See Shatzmiller, 'The Albigensian Heresy in the Eyes of Contemporary Jews' (Heb.).

Incarnation.[73] It is possible that Levi ben Abraham was referring to the Cathar belief that the term 'son of God' was only a metaphor and that Jesus and God did not have a shared essence but only a spiritual resemblance.[74] However, many of the Cathars totally rejected the Old Testament, regarding the God of the Old Testament as a demon,[75] and Levi ben Abraham was hardly likely to attribute a favourable attitude to the commandments to them. He may also have come across Adoptionism—the doctrine that Jesus, who was human in nature, was adopted by his father, God—from Arians, Nestorians, or ancient Christian writers.[76] However, it is hard to accept any of these, since Levi ben Abraham included details of the messiah that are not found in Arian theology, Adoptionism, or Catharist doctrines.

Another heretical movement that may have been the source of Levi ben Abraham's views were the Passagini. Unlike the Cathars, the Passagini were very sympathetic towards biblical law and tried to follow it. For this they were even accused by the Catholic Church of Judaizing. They claimed Jesus was not equal to God the Father but was created by him and, hence, was lower in rank. They also rejected the doctrine of the Trinity and argued that the Father, the Son, and the Holy Spirit were not of one substance.[77] The Passagini were centred in Lombardy, around the city of Milan, but several groups of them spread to Languedoc, near where Levi ben Abraham lived. This may well be the heresy he was referring to.

Maimonides' view of the development of Christianity, as given by Levi ben Abraham, was very similar to that of the Passagini. However, Maimonides and Levi ben Abraham differed greatly in their attitude towards Christianity. Levi ben Abraham explained Jesus's messianic pretensions in purely Jewish terms, not as a malicious attempt to destroy Judaism. The decisive break from Judaism—the abolition of the commandments—he blamed on Jesus's disciples. He also dated the formulation of Christian doctrine to a third stage, in which the Church Fathers and Constantine played key roles. It is possible that Levi ben Abraham

---

[73] *Vikuaḥ haradak*, 95–6; see Berger, 'Christian Heresy and Jewish Polemic in the Twelfth and Thirteenth Centuries', 297, 303; Shatzmiller, 'The Albigensian Heresy in the Eyes of Contemporary Jews', 335; on Menahem, see ibid. 340–1.

[74] See Talmage, 'A Hebrew Polemic Treatise', 332; id., Introduction (Heb.) to Profayt Duran, *Polemical Writings*, 17.   [75] See Duvernoy, *Le Catharisme*, i. 44–8, 107, 118.

[76] See ibid. 301–2; Cavadini, *The Last Christology of the West*.

[77] See Alphandéry, 'Sur les Passagiens', esp. 356; Newman, *Jewish Influence on Christian Reform Movements*, 240–302, esp. 268 n. 22. Alphandéry connected the Passagini with the Waldensians. The Passagini lived in Lombardy, around the city of Milan, but several groups of them or similar heretics also moved to Languedoc (see ibid. 256–7, 271–3; see also: 'Dicunt quod lex Judaeorum melior est quam lex Christianorum' from the Inquisition files in Carcassonne (cited ibid. 258 n. 8)).

misunderstood Maimonides, or perhaps he deliberately misrepresented him so that he could claim him as an authoritative support.

Falbel's claim that Levi ben Abraham's two-stage history of Christianity has its source in heretical Christian movements is reasonable. However, the closest Jewish parallels are not found in the *History of Rome* or the *Epistle to Yemen* as Falbel asserted. The *History of Rome* shows that Ibn Daud did not divide Christian history into periods. Although he attributed a decisive role to Constantine, he did not distinguish between an authentic, primitive Christianity and a later, corrupted Christianity. Maimonides did make such a division, but Falbel erred when he stated that Maimonides believed that Jesus did not intend to harm Israel. As mentioned above, in *Mishneh torah*, Maimonides wrote '[Jesus] plotted to destroy Israel . . . and to replace the Torah and to mislead most of the world into worshipping a god other than the God [of Israel].'[78] In this regard, Levi ben Abraham's approach was the very opposite of Maimonides' and resembled that of Profayt Duran, who regarded Jesus as a Jewish phenomenon and not as an enemy of Israel. The closest parallel, however, is the work of Abraham bar Hiyya. He did not ascribe any malicious intentions to Jesus and divided the history of Christianity into stages. As mentioned above, the date and events of Jesus's life were of no importance to him, because, according to Abraham bar Hiyya, Christianity had nothing to do with Jesus: it was the creation of his disciples. Moreover, Abraham bar Hiyya asserted that Constantine's reign marked a key turning point in the history of the Church: 'Constantine . . . added an error to an error, and came to believe in the false words of the wicked disciples of Jesus'; 'wicked Constantine adhered to the faith of the disciples of Jesus'.[79]

It is not certain, however, that heretical Christian movements could have influenced Abraham bar Hiyya. Levi ben Abraham lived in Provence at a time when heresies were rife in the region, and Provençal Jews had contact with heretics and disputed with them on matters of faith and theology. Abraham bar Hiyya also spent the years of his literary activity in Provence, but, since apparently he died in 1136, it is doubtful whether he could have encountered any of these movements. Segarelli and Dolcino lived at the end of the thirteenth century, and the Waldensians first emerged at the end of the twelfth. The Cathar movement (called the 'Good Men' by the people in southern France) was earlier, and early sounds of heresy (perhaps Catharist) were heard in southern France in the early 1140s; however, signs of real Catharist activity were evident only in the 1160s. Nonetheless, we cannot rule out the exposure of Jews to heretical ideologies even

[78] Maimonides, *Mishneh torah*, 'Laws of Kings', 11: 4.
[79] Abraham bar Hiyya, *Megilat hamegaleh*, 4: 95; 5: 137.

before the appearance of the Cathar movement, since the roots of heresy in southern France went back a long way.[80]

Falbel did not mention the Cathars as a possible influence on Levi ben Abraham. However, they preceded the Waldensians and the Pseudo-Apostles in their two-stage understanding of Christian history. They regarded Pope Sylvester as the Antichrist and the Donation of Constantine as the event that led to the deterioration of the Church. They also dated the creation of the Mass and the doctrine of the Incarnation to the time of Constantine and Sylvester.[81] If Abraham bar Hiyya encountered Christian heresy in the first half of the twelfth century, it would be similar to Catharism and not the later heretical movements. It remains possible that he developed his ideas from Jewish sources (the Talmud or *Toledot yeshu*) or Karaite sources known in Spain.[82] However, there is no denying that the two-stage model of Christian history with Constantine as the turning point was prevalent among Jews at the end of the thirteenth century and was also a central tenet of many Christian heresies.[83]

CONSTANTINE

Abraham bar Hiyya described Constantine in the most derogatory terms:

And in the time of the conjunction [of the planets], Constantine the wicked adopted the faith of the disciples of the hanged Jesus, and forced his people to adhere to that faith and he took the hanged Jesus's error to establish a kingdom and greatness in the city of Constantinople, and did not live long after his error. . . . And that wicked man

---

[80] See Dossat, 'La Répression de l'hérésie par les évêques', 222; Duvernoy, *Le Catharisme*, i. 13–26; Lansing, Epilogue to Strayer, *The Albigensian Crusades*, 186–7, 192–5; Moore, *The Foundation of a Persecuting Society*, 19–24; id., 'When did the Good Men of the Languedoc become Heretics?'; Shahar, 'The Idea of Chosenness in Heretical Movements in the Middle Ages' (Heb.), 179–90; Pegg, *The Corruption of Angels*.   [81] See Duvernoy, *Le Catharisme*, i. 227.

[82] On the spread of Karaism in Spain, see G. D. Cohen, Introduction and notes to Ibn Daud, *Sefer hakabalah*, pp. i–xlvi. In Abraham bar Hiyya's time, there were many Karaite books available in Spain, including works by Al-Qirqisani (see ibid., p. xlix), who was explicitly mentioned by Ibn Daud (*Sefer hakabalah*, ch. 2, line 97 (ed. Cohen: Heb. section, 17; Eng. section, 24). Al-Qirqisani divided the history of Christianity into three phases: the time of Jesus, the founding of Christianity in the time of Paul, and the Christianity of his own time. He recorded several rabbinic and Karaite opinions of Jesus but regarded him as an internal phenomenon that belonged only to the history of the Jews. He also stated that some Karaites believed that Jesus was a 'good man' who followed the ways of Zadok and Anan but that the rabbis plotted against him and killed him (see Al-Qirqisani, *The Book of Lights and Watch-Towers*, 364–6; Lasker, 'Karaism and the Jewish–Christian Debate', 323).

[83] I do not mean to suggest that the heretics influenced Jewish views, since criticisms of this kind could have emerged in parallel. Nonetheless, we cannot reject this possibility out of hand (see R. Ben-Shalom, 'The Converso as Subversive', 272–4; G. D. Cohen, 'Esau as Symbol in Early Medieval Thought', 268 n. 95).

when he held to the error of the hanged man, proceeded to abolish the idols of the men of his nation and the people of the land. He did not live for long, stumbled and fell. . . . And that wicked man replaced one insolence with another and put an end to [one] disgrace and [at the same time] brought on another disgrace.[84]

Although Abraham bar Hiyya believed that Christianity was founded by Jesus's disciples, this passage suggests that he also assigned an important role to Constantine. In his view, it was Constantine who imposed Christianity on pagan Rome and in doing so became one of the three founders of evil religions alongside Mani and Muhammad.[85]

Earlier in *Megilat hamegaleh*, Abraham bar Hiyya credited Constantine with the establishment of Constantinople and the division of the Roman empire into eastern and western halves. He noted that new states were founded in Europe—the Gothic kingdoms—but he regarded the transfer of the capital to Constantinople as a decisive event and one that was accompanied by harsh edicts against Jews. It is in the context of these edicts that he first mentions Helena, Constantine's mother, and he clearly sees a connection between them.[86] He states that Constantine forbade Jews to visit the Temple mount and pray at the ruins of the Temple. In contradiction to statements made by some Church Fathers, Abraham bar Hiyya asserted that in the days of pagan Rome Jews were not prohibited from going to the Temple mount. He also believed that Constantine, unlike the pagan emperors who preceded him, acknowledged the sanctity of the Temple mount and wanted to build a church on it.[87]

Abraham bar Hiyya also dated some later events to the time of Constantine. During the Crusades, Christian attitudes to the Temple mount changed, and they claimed that it was the site of Mount Moriah (in the Byzantine and Muslim periods, traditions connected with the Temple mount were transferred to the Church of the Holy Sepulchre) and built the Templum Domini on the site of the Dome of the Rock. Abraham bar Hiyya attributed this to Constantine. However, the Crusaders themselves believed that the church was built by Helena or another Christian emperor, such as Justin or Heraclius, so this is not necessarily Abraham bar Hiyya's error.[88]

Amnon Linder makes it clear in his discussion of Roman legislation during Constantine's reign that Constantine did not maintain the consistent anti-Jewish policy which might be expected of an emperor under strong Christian influence.

---

[84] Abraham bar Hiyya, *Megilat hamegaleh*, 5: 137–8.   [85] See ibid. 137–9.   [86] Ibid.

[87] See ibid. 4: 99–100. On the statements by the Church Fathers, see Ir-Shai, 'Constantine the Great's Prohibition of the Entry of Jews into Jerusalem' (Heb.), 129–37.

[88] See Kenaan-Kedar, 'Symbolic Significance in Crusader Architecture' (Heb.), 174; Shine, 'Jerusalem in Christian Spirituality' (Heb.), 238–9.

Jeremy Cohen explained this by looking at earlier Roman legislation. He showed that, although Constantine spoke about Jews in very offensive terms, he did not deviate from the basic legislative policies of his predecessors. Shlomo Simonsohn believes that changes in the status of Jews did occur in Constantine's time, but they were not as dramatic as they are usually described. Recent scholarship has revealed that it was not the emperor himself who forbade the entry of Jews to Jerusalem but rather the Christians of Jerusalem and the local representatives of Roman rule. The prohibition was ascribed to Constantine in the hagiographical literature about him which flourished in Constantinople in the ninth century.[89]

Nonetheless, it is not surprising that Abraham bar Hiyya thought Constantine was responsible for draconian anti-Jewish edicts. As Linder showed, the new and, even more so, the traditional historiographies, credited Constantine with the change in policy towards Jews. Many scholars have assumed that the policy was personally determined by the emperor and that the various stages of it reflect the stages of his conversion to Christianity. At the beginning of his reign, he was tolerant; at the end of it, he supported fanatical persecutions, which formed the basis for persecution of Jews in Europe for centuries. However, these assumptions were not necessarily based on a detailed analysis of the historical documentation but rather on the myth that surrounded the emperor and established him as the enemy of Judaism.[90]

According to Linder, the myth that developed around Helena was conflated with the one surrounding Constantine and added further anti-Jewish elements to it. Helena was held to be responsible for giving the state a role in religious polemic with Jews and instigating compulsory disputations, conducted like trials of Judaism, with all Jews, not only those actively involved, being made to accept the verdict of the Christian judge, including forced conversion, torture, starvation, expulsion, and burning.[91] The Christians themselves believed that Constantine was responsible for the enactment of anti-Jewish laws and edicts, and medieval Jews accepted this as fact. The strong anti-Jewish element explains why Jews had such a negative opinion of Constantine.[92]

---

[89] See J. Cohen, 'Roman Imperial Policy toward the Jews', esp. 5–9; Ir-Shai, 'Constantine the Great's Prohibition of the Entry of Jews into Jerusalem' (Heb.), 164–70; Linder, 'Roman Rule and the Jews in the Time of Constantine' (Heb.), esp. 142–3; Simonsohn, *The Apostolic See and the Jews*, vi. 6–7.

[90] Linder, 'Roman Rule and the Jews in the Time of Constantine' (Heb.), 96–8; see J. Cohen, 'Roman Imperial Policy toward the Jews', 1–2.

[91] Linder, 'Ecclesia and Synagoga in the Medieval Myth of Constantine the Great', 1051–2.

[92] 'Because of the harsh edicts against the Jewish people in the time of [Constantine] and his mother' (Abravanel, *Ma'ayenei hayeshuah*, 11: 5 (Jerusalem edn., 369)). Abravanel relied on Abraham bar Hiyya and a Christian historiography that he called 'Tales of Constantine'.

The anti-Jewish aspects of the myth of Constantine were also completely in accord with the missionary ideology of the mendicant friars from the thirteenth century onwards[93] and found their way into religious theatre in the *Legend of Saint Sylvester*. Religious theatre was an influential institution in European cities, especially in the fourteenth and fifteenth centuries, which could inflame anti-Jewish sentiments among the Christian inhabitants and sometimes led to acts of violence against Jewish communities.[94] In *Moreh tsedek*, the convert Abner of Burgos, who lived from about 1270 to 1340, mentioned Titus, Hadrian, and Constantine as the Roman emperors responsible for the worst persecutions of Jews. According to Abner, the Jews repented after each persecution but did not gain redemption. This proved that the only way to redemption open to Jews was through Jesus. Abner regarded ('gentle') persecutions as a legitimate—and perhaps essential—tool in the redemption of the Jews.[95]

To counter the Christian myths, Jews developed their own. These took elements of the Christian ones and adapted them. In the Christian myths, Constantine was the founder of Christian Europe; the Jewish myths concurred, but depicted Constantine as forcing the new religion on the pagan Romans against their will. Pope Sylvester played a major role in the Christian myths as the man who convinced Constantine to convert; in the Jewish myths, Sylvester was given only a marginal role, and Constantine filled his place as the religious representative of Christianity, so that he not only founded Christian Europe but also the Christian religion itself. The Jewish myths implied that the Christians had distorted and falsified original Christianity. Indeed, Abner of Burgos tried to reverse this and prove that the Jews had distorted history.

The Jews of Spain and southern France accepted Abraham bar Hiyya and Levi ben Abraham's opinion of Constantine and his role in the foundation of Christianity. In Spain, polemical letters were exchanged between Abner of Burgos and the Jewish scholar and mathematician, Joseph Shalom.[96] In reply to

[93] See J. Cohen, *The Friars and the Jews*; for a different view of the mission of the mendicants, see Vose, *Dominicans, Muslims and Jews in the Medieval Crown of Aragon*; see also Ir-Shai, 'Constantine the Great's Prohibition of the Entry of Jews into Jerusalem' (Heb.), 164–70; Simonsohn, *The Apostolic See and the Jews*, vi. 6–7 n. 24.

[94] See Delumeau, *La Peur en occident*, 279–80; on ritual violence towards Jews, see Nirenberg, *Communities of Violence*, 200–30.

[95] Abner of Burgos, *Moreh tsedek*, cited in Baer, *A History of the Jews in Christian Spain*, i. 353–4; see Szpiech, *Conversion and Narrative*; id., 'From Testimonia to Testimony', esp. 293–304.

[96] Abner of Burgos sent his letters to three Jews; Joseph Shalom wrote all the replies, instructed by the physician Hayim Israel of Toledo. Abner kept the letters he received, and replied to Joseph Shalom's letters in a special work called *Teshuvot hameshuvot*. In it, he repeated his previous arguments in greater detail (see Abner of Burgos, 'The First Letter' (Heb.); id., 'Polemical Letters' (Heb.); id., 'The Second Letter' (Heb.); id., 'The Third Letter' (Heb.)). On the translation of the letters into Castilian, apparently by Abner of Burgos himself, see Alba Cecelia and Saínz de la Maza,

Abner's first letter, Shalom wrote that 'Constantine forced all the people in his land to adhere to the faith that he had invented, along with the priest [Sylvester]'.[97] He saw no need to explain Constantine's action and wrote about it as if it were an irrefutable historical fact. However, it would seem to be contradicted by something he wrote earlier in the letter: 'And after Constantine had reigned for some time, he left the faith of his fathers and believed in the Trinity [at the urging of] an Edomite priest or was himself an Edomite—as you said in your letter—and from that time onwards the whole nation was Edom.'[98] This implies that the Christian religion already existed and accordingly it was not founded by Constantine. Possibly Shalom was undecided about which of the two versions of events was historically accurate.

However, the contradiction can be reconciled by assuming that Shalom took a similar stance to Levi ben Abraham: 'the last ones, in particular King Constantine, inverted all the things about God himself and gave him a corporeal form and imposed upon him sayings, [and] this is not true'.[99] In other words, Christianity existed in some form or other before Constantine, but he was the one who introduced the crucial theological change: the doctrine of the Incarnation. Shalom's second letter also implies that he thought Constantine was the founder of Christianity. He interpreted verses from Daniel that, in his view, prophesied the beginning of Christianity and stated that the new religion was created about 300 years after the destruction of the Temple, which would be during the reign of Constantine.[100]

Joseph Shalom mentioned Constantine in response to a letter Abner of Burgos sent to a scholar named Abner ab Seregna. Shalom began by quoting a passage from Abner of Burgos's letter:

For it is not right to say: 'the Romans are Edomites, because a man from the land of Edom reigned over them', as [the Jews] do. Just as they do not call the Jews Edomites nor Romans, even though Herod, an Edomite or Roman, ruled over them. For not all matters go according to the names, but the names should go according to the essence of the matters.[101]

This passage reflects the Jewish view that Constantine was of Edomite origin, and hence the whole Roman empire should be considered Edom. Some scholars

'La primera epístola de Alfonso de Valladolid'; eid., 'La segunda epístola de Alfonso de Valladolid'; Del Valle, 'La tercera carta apologética de Abner de Burgos'; see also Baer, *A History of the Jews in Christian Spain*, i. 327–54; Saínz de la Maza, 'El converso y judío Alfonso de Valladolid', 75.

[97] Joseph Shalom, 'Parma MS no. 553 (Reply to Abner)' (Heb.), 29.   [98] Ibid. 11.
[99] Levi b. Abraham, *Livyat ḥen*, 6: 12 (ed. Kreisel, 288–91).
[100] Abner of Burgos, 'The Second Letter' (Heb.), 503–4.
[101] Abner of Burgos, 'The First Letter' (Heb.), 9.

think Abner is making this claim, but that is not the case.[102] A careful reading shows it was the Jews who made the claim, and that Abner refuted it by pointing out that it leads to the absurd conclusion that Israel too should be regarded as Edom, because in the past it had an Edomite ruler, Herod.[103] As far as Abner was concerned, both conclusions were wrong and should be rejected.

According to Yehuda Shamir, Abner of Burgos recounted the legend that Constantine was converted by an Edomite priest.[104] However, this is also not the case, the source was Shalom, who claimed that that was what Abner wrote. As mentioned above, Shalom explicitly ascribed to Abner the claim that Constantine was an Edomite or converted under the influence of an Edomite priest: 'Constantine . . . left the faith of his fathers and believed in the Trinity [at the urging of] an Edomite priest or was himself an Edomite—*as you said in your letter*'.[105] However, it would be very surprising if this is what Abner did say, since claims of this sort were not put forward by Christians. As we do not have Abner's original letters but only the fragments contained in Shalom's letters, it seems that the version in our possession was inaccurately edited, falsified, or misunderstood by Shalom. Moreover, in *Teshuvot hameshuvot*, Abner explicitly denied having said what Shalom ascribed to him: 'If you have testified about what you have not seen, whether deliberately or mistakenly, such as what you said at the beginning of your words, that you found in the wording of his [*recte* my] letter that King Constantine was an Edomite, then that is clearly a false testimony.'[106]

It is unlikely that Joseph Shalom deliberately falsified what Abner of Burgos wrote. Instead, he misunderstood that Abner was inveighing against the claim that 'the Romans are Edom, because the king who reigned over them was from the land of Edom', which was widespread among Jews, and assumed that it was Abner's own opinion. The prevalence of this argument among Jews may have led Shalom to assume that even Abner, an erstwhile Jew, accepted it as valid.

In reply to Shalom's main polemical claim—that Constantine founded Christianity—Abner provided the 'official' version of Christian history: Christianity was founded by Jesus and disseminated by Jesus and his disciples. Constantine converted to Christianity, and later the entire Roman empire accepted Christianity as 'one doctrine' without any changes. Afterwards the Romans

---

[102] See Shamir, *Rabbi Moses Ha-Kohen of Tordesillas*, 56.

[103] Here Abner used the polemical technique 'as the speaker said'. Although he did not accept the Jews' claim that Constantine was an Edomite, he was prepared to adopt it as a point of departure for the purpose of the debate. Afterwards he proved that even on that basis, it is impossible to accept the Jews' conclusion that Edom is identical with Rome.

[104] Shamir, *Rabbi Moses Ha-Kohen of Tordesillas*, 56.

[105] Joseph Shalom, 'Parma MS no. 553 (Reply to Abner)' (Heb.), 11.

[106] Abner of Burgos, 'Polemical Letters' (Heb.), 329.

were called Christians, not Edomites.[107] Abner's reply makes it clear that he was aware that Shalom's version was not his own invention but the prevailing understanding among the Jews.

This raises the question of whether Jews were familiar with this version of Christian history or Abner was relating something he himself had learned only after he had converted. In my opinion, the Jews were well acquainted with the 'official' version, but nonetheless some of them stuck to the Jewish one. In one of his two versions of events, Shalom revealed some knowledge of the Christian narrative. However, in the twelfth century, a variation appeared in Abraham ibn Ezra's commentary on the book of Daniel: 'Constantine was a great king over Babylonia and Persia and Egypt and Africa, and converted Babylonia to his religion. And his friends also converted the Persians and the Sabaeans and Egypt and Africa to his religion. And he abandoned the doctrine of Aram [Rome].'[108] Ibn Ezra did not ascribe any theological activity to Constantine: he praised him for the size of the Roman empire, his ability to impose the Christian religion within its boundaries, and for abandoning idolatry. Ibn Ezra was apparently the first Jewish scholar who did not distort the Christian narrative about Constantine, but used it as he found it. Elsewhere he interpreted it at greater length:

'The king will do as he pleases': that is great Constantine who built Constantinople and who spread the fame of the religion of the hanged man. 'He will prosper until [the divine] wrath is spent' over Israel, 'and what has been decreed is accomplished'. '[He will not have regard] for the God of his ancestors' and shall not seek after women. And to 'the god of the fortresses', he said: if you place the form of the hanged man on your flags, you shall succeed. And to 'the gods his ancestors worshipped': they are the sinners [*kedeshim*] of Edom. And 'on his stand' means that he will abandon Rome for the sake of his God. 'He will deal with fortified strongholds': they are Constantinople and its surroundings. The people of 'an alien god': they are their abominations. 'Those who acknowledge him' and convert to his religion, 'he will heap honour on' them and 'make them master over many'.[109]

Ibn Ezra's version is close to the Christian one: Constantine did not found Christianity, he converted and helped it grow; he left Rome for religious reasons ('for the sake of his God', an allusion to the Donation of Constantine) and founded Constantinople; there he erected churches ('abominations') and gave official positions to those who accepted Christianity. As far as I know, Ibn Ezra

---

[107] Abner of Burgos, 'Polemical Letters' (Heb.), 339.

[108] Abraham ibn Ezra on Dan. 11: 36 (*Mikra'ot gedolot*). On the substitution of Aram for Rome, see Lifschitz, 'The Interpretation of Prophecy according to Abraham ibn Ezra and Isaac Abravanel' (Heb.), 135 n. 19.

[109] Abraham ibn Ezra on Dan. 11: 36–9 (*Haperush hakatsar al daniyel*, 13–14); see Benjamin of Tudela, *Sefer masaot*, 8.

was the only writer to allude to the appointment of members of the new Christian nobility in Constantinople to government positions.[110]

His discussion contains another important historical detail that was not mentioned again until the time of Isaac Abravanel: that Constantine was told he would succeed if he placed the image of the 'hanged man' on his standards. The reference is to Constantine's revelation on the Milvian Bridge in Rome before his decisive battle with Maxentius in 312 CE. Following the revelation, Constantine inscribed the Christogram (a combination of the first two letters of 'Christ' in Greek) on the standards of his army, and his victory in the battle was credited to the Christian God.[111]

Following Ibn Ezra, Nahmanides described Constantine's actions at length in *Sefer hage'ulah*:

We are today living in the exile of Edom ... and they are the main subject here ⟨for the Edomites were the first to err in following the man who claimed he was the messiah, and they also attributed divinity to him, and they came to the land of Edom and their error spread to nearby Rome⟩. And in the time of King Constantine, [the error] took hold, established there by the Edomite Roman [Sylvester], for he founded for them ⟨the trickeries [rituals or doctrines] of the priests of⟩ Rome and their faith in [Jesus]. . . . Hence, Rome and Edom are regarded as one kingdom although they are different nations, nonetheless they are close and became as one people and one land, for they are of one mind.[112]

Nahmanides divided Christian history into three stages: in the first, Jesus claimed to be the messiah; in the second, his Edomite followers regarded him as divine; and, in the third, Constantine established Christianity as the religion of the Roman empire. As discussed above, most versions of Christian history that divided it into stages had two. Nahmanides' three-stage model allows for a distinction between the religion of Jesus and the religion of his followers, but also allows Constantine's role to be making Christianity the religion of the empire not creating it or making any theological changes to it.

The Jewish perception of the Edomites as the first Christians has already been explained by a number of scholars. Judah Rosenthal saw it as an attempt to support the identification of Rome with Edom. Gerson Cohen suggested it was to allow Islam to be identified as the fourth kingdom.[113] Nahmanides' interpretation

---

[110] On the Christian nobility, many of whom were pretending to be Christians in order to advance their status at the court, see Rubin, *The Christianization of Europe* (Heb.), 37.

[111] See ibid. 22–7.

[112] Nahmanides, *Sefer hage'ulah*, 3 (ed. Chavel, 284–5). The words in angle brackets are from MS Hebrew 27 (Bibliothèque nationale, Paris), which was not censored by the Christians.

[113] See Rosenthal, 'Interest from the Foreigner' (Heb.), 282–90; G. D. Cohen, 'Esau as Symbol in Early Medieval Thought', 259–61, 268 n. 96.

reflects the hermeneutic needs of the thirteenth century, when the Spanish Reconquest was at its peak.[114] Although he rejected the notion that pagan Rome was ethnically connected with Edom, he categorically identified the Rome of his time with Edom.

Nahmanides' description of Christian origins is more complete than those of most earlier writers. He described Constantine's conversion in great detail, following the Christian version of events, and also related the legend about Sylvester and the Donation of Constantine, which he interpreted in his customary manner: the gift of Rome and the adoption of Christianity by the Roman empire were Sylvester's and the Christians' reward for having cured Constantine of leprosy ('and he divided his land for the price of a cure').[115] Here Nahmanides interpreted Daniel 11: 36–9: the king who 'will not have regard for the God of his ancestors' is Constantine, who converted to Christianity;[116] 'He will deal with fortified strongholds with the help of an alien god' refers to the Donation of Constantine; he 'will make them master over many' means he will make the Christian religion rule in Rome and dominate the entire world; and the one who 'will not have regard for … the desire of women' is Pope Sylvester, who, as a priest, was celibate.[117]

Gersonides also clearly distinguished between Constantine's actions as a Christian emperor and the theological development of Christianity. In his view, Constantine was the emperor who rose to power after ten Roman emperors and forced many kingdoms to 'believe in a new Torah', fulfilling another of Daniel's prophecies. He did not, however, invent the doctrine of the Incarnation, create the concept of the Virgin Birth, or change the commandments and festivals of the Torah. During his reign, Christianity spread throughout the empire, but it had been created earlier.[118]

Abraham ibn Ezra, Nahmanides, and Gersonides were aware of Christian historiography, and they took their information about Constantine's conversion from it. The positions they expounded and the images they used reflect how early Christianity was perceived between the twelfth and fifteenth centuries. As Jews started reading Christian historiographical sources seriously, they also began to accept the Christian version of events. Extreme polemical arguments, like Joseph Shalom's claim that Constantine had invented Christianity or Abraham ibn Daud's that Constantine wrote the Gospels (if in fact he did make that claim), were no longer used or at least became rarer. This process is evident in the works

---

[114] G. D. Cohen, 'Esau as Symbol in Early Medieval Thought', 261, 269 n. 101.

[115] Nahmanides, *Sefer hage'ulah*, 3 (ed. Chavel, 285).

[116] Here Nahmanides followed Abraham ibn Ezra, who regarded the 'king' as a metaphor for Constantine, unlike Abraham bar Hiyya, who regarded Constantine as the 'prince'.

[117] Nahmanides, *Sefer hage'ulah*, 3 (ed. Chavel, 287).   [118] Gersonides on Dan. 7: 25.

of Profayt Duran, Shimon ben Tsemah Duran, and Shem Tov ibn Shaprut, who wrote during the transitional period of the fourteenth and fifteenth centuries.

In *Shame of the Gentiles*, Profayt Duran attempted to refute a number of claims made by Nicholas of Lyra, including that all idolatry in the world had ceased with the coming of Jesus, fulfilling Jeremiah's prophecy about non-Jews: 'they shall no longer follow the wilfulness of their evil hearts' (Jer. 3: 17). Duran used Vincent de Beauvais' *Mirror of History* to prove that the pagans stopped practising idolatry, not in the time of Jesus, but when forced to by Constantine:

And Nicholas thought the verse in the Bible provided incontrovertible proof of the replacement of the Torah and that [the Torah] would have an end with the coming of the false messiah and his corporeality. . . . For with his coming, idolatry ceased—so they assumed. But that is a lie, for Constantine, the Roman emperor who forced Rome and Italy to accept faith in Jesus, lived more than 200 years after him. . . . And this is made clear in the history of the Romans; and Vincent wrote this in his book about the times of the emperors.[119]

Here, again, Constantine is presented as a purely political figure who forced Christianity on to his subjects but was not a theologian. Following Profayt Duran, Shimon ben Tsemah Duran also stressed the element of coercion in the acceptance of Christianity by the Roman empire,[120] and in 1385 Shem Tov ibn Shaprut made a similar charge in *Even boḥan*. He was more precise than Profayt Duran and Shimon ben Tsemah Duran about the time of Constantine, and—as a polemical provocation—described the imposition of Christianity on the Romans as an act of violence: few would have accepted Christianity otherwise.[121]

Isaac Abravanel's survey of the decline of the Roman empire discussed in Chapter 2 provides another example of the growing trend of focusing on Constantine's actions as a ruler and not as a theologian. Abravanel summarized a centuries-long historical process, using Roman and Christian sources, a fact he mentioned twice. He devoted a major section to the early history of Christianity, and, like many others, he divided it into two stages: before and after Constantine. Christianity before Constantine was a small, persecuted sect. The pope had established himself in Rome, but his situation was poor.[122] The conversion of the emperor, under the influence of his mother, Helena, marked a major change. Constantine granted Pope Sylvester control of the city of Rome and moved his own capital to Constantinople.

---

[119] Profayt Duran, *Kelimat hagoyim*, 5 (ed. Talmage, 32; see also 60–3).

[120] Shimon b. Tsemah Duran, *Keshet umagen*, 51.

[121] Ibn Shaprut, *Even boḥan*, 1: 12 (ed. Niclós, 407); on the dating and editing of the book, see Frimer and Schwartz, *Philosophy in the Shadow of Terror* (Heb.), 34–6.

[122] Abravanel, *Ma'ayenei hayeshuah*, 8: 5 (Jerusalem edn., 336).

Abravanel's account of Constantine's conversion differed from those of earlier writers, who followed the majority of Christian sources and attributed it to Pope Sylvester's influence. Abravanel relied on a marginal stream of Christian historiography which claimed that Helena was a British princess and that the Christians managed to convince her of the truth of Christianity: she persuaded her son, and they both converted to Christianity.[123] A story about Helena, daughter of King Cole of Britain, marrying Emperor Constantius Chlorus and giving birth to Constantine appears in three fifteenth-century Spanish chronicles—*Libro de las generaciones*, *Livro das linhagens*, and *La crónica de 1404*—which deal with it at length in a number of chapters.[124] Helena almost certainly came from Asia Minor, and the legend first appears in Henry of Huntingdon's *History of the English People* (*c*.1154) and Geoffrey of Monmouth's *History of the Kings of Britain* (*c*.1136).[125] The belief that Helena played a major role in Constantine's conversion also came to Spain and can be found in a fourteenth-century prayer book.[126] Abravanel also had access to a version of *Primera crónica general de España*, which contains no information about Helena's origin and attributes Constantine's conversion to Sylvester.[127] Therefore, Abravanel knew both traditions and preferred to report the British one: probably because he preferred the idea of a mother enticing her son to accept Christianity than attributing a miraculous cure of leprosy to the divine powers of a pope. Abravanel repeated the story of Constantine's conversion in *Ma'ayanei hayeshuah*, and there too Helena was assigned the leading role.

Abravanel also reported the story of the Donation of Constantine, although doubts had already arisen among Christian scholars as to its reliability.[128] In Abravanel's account, Constantine found Sylvester hiding in a cave, brought him to Rome, and crowned him pope, telling him that he and his successors would rule in Rome forever, which Abravanel believed fulfilled the prophecy: 'A new little horn sprouted up among them; three of the older horns were uprooted to make

---

[123] See Linder, 'The Myth of Constantine the Great', 89. The legend about Sylvester appears in the *Golden Legend*. According to Theodoret's *Ecclesiastical History*, written in 440 CE, Helena raised her son a Christian from an early age. Eusebius's version, according to which Helena converted after Constantine, is probably the most reliable (see Drijvers, *Helena Augusta*, 35–8, 107).

[124] See *Libro de las generaciones*, 239, 266–8, 300. Both *Libro de las generaciones* and *Livro das linhagens* state that it was actually Sylvester—and not Helena—who was responsible for Constantine's conversion (268, 300). *La crónica de 1404* does not mention who was responsible.

[125] See Linder, 'The Myth of Constantine the Great', 91–3. Geoffrey of Monmouth's work was known in Castile in the fifteenth century, as is evident from Pero Niño, *El victorial*, 142.

[126] Linder, 'The Myth of Constantine the Great', 89 n. 266.

[127] See Alfonso X, *Primera crónica general de España*, i. 175a; id., *Crónica general de España de 1344*, 7 (ed. Catalán and Soledad de Andrés, 7).

[128] See Dorman, *Marsilius of Padua* (Heb.), 87–8; Folz, *The Concept of Empire in Western Europe*, 65–6, 186–8; Valla, *De falso credita et ementita Constantini donatione*.

room for it' (Dan. 7: 8). Sylvester was the wicked 'little horn', and the previous three types of Roman ruler—kings, consuls, and emperors—were replaced by popes.[129] This interpretation is similar to that of the Cathars, the Waldensians, and the Pseudo-Apostles, who also had negative attitudes to the Donation of Constantine and thought Sylvester was the Antichrist.[130] Abravanel and the heretical movements agreed that the Donation of Constantine marked a turning point in world history—for the heretical movements it represented the end of the spiritual Church and the beginning of the temporal Church. In the time of the spiritual Church, when Christians were persecuted and lived in poverty, the Roman empire was at the height of its glory. The heretical movements believed that persecution, poverty, and martyrdom were external manifestations of the essence of the spiritual Church, whereas Abravanel understood them politically: Christianity was not yet strong or wealthy enough to gain control of the centres of power. Constantine's gift of Rome to the papacy was a negative moment in the history of both the Church and the empire. From the viewpoint of the heretical movements, it represented the corruption of the pope and of the Church, which became the 'synagogue of Satan' (Rev. 2: 9).[131] From Abravanel's viewpoint, it represented Rome's abandonment of imperial rule in favour of religious rule and the beginning of the empire's decline, as it hastened its fall to the Goths. Abravanel also included two other details: the date of Constantine's conversion—about 300 years after the death of Jesus—and the inscription of the Christian symbol on Constantine's standards ('the image of Jesus horizontally and vertically on his pennant'). Abravanel was the first scholar after Abraham ibn Ezra to mention this.[132]

Abravanel also wrote about religious changes that occurred after Constantine:

'He will head back to the strongholds of his own land, but will stumble and fall [Dan. 11: 19]. [Abraham bar Hiyya] did not interpret this at all, and I think it best to interpret it according to what I found in the 'Tales of Constantine': that he had two sons and, in his old age, attempted to make them into emperors, so that one would rule in Rome with the pope and the other would rule in Constantinople, but he did not succeed in his lifetime, for his time came. 'His place will be taken by one . . . who will raise taxes' [Dan. 11: 20]. This can be interpreted to mean his son, called Constantine after him

---

[129] Abravanel, *Ma'ayenei hayeshuah*, 8: 5 (Jerusalem edn., 337). Abravanel rejected the Christian notion that the little horn was a symbol of the Antichrist (ibid. 8: 6 (Jerusalem edn., 338–41)).

[130] See Dorman, *Marsilius of Padua* (Heb.), 87–8; Duvernoy, *Le Catharisme*, i. 227; Shahar, 'The Idea of Chosenness in Heretical Movements in the Middle Ages' (Heb.), 179, 188.

[131] Duvernoy, *Le Catharisme*, i. 227–33.

[132] Abravanel, *Ma'ayenei hayeshuah*, 11: 5 (Jerusalem edn., 389). Constantine was only baptized on the eve of his death in 337. However, according to the *Golden Legend*, he was baptized after his victory at the Milvian Bridge in 312 (see Jacobus de Voragine, *Legenda aurea* (Leipzig edn., 271–2)).

[Constantius II]. It is said that he was an apostate in his religion, drawn to Arianism, which denied the principles of the religion of Jesus, and whereas his father forced all men to believe in [Jesus] and ordered the Jews not to build synagogues, his son was just the opposite. And he raised taxes in the land, so that every man could believe in and worship any God he wished, and he gave the Jews permission to build synagogues, and the son of his son, Emperor Julian, did the same.[133]

Abravanel followed Abraham bar Hiyya, providing his own interpretation of verses that were not interpreted in *Megilat hamegaleh*. However, Abravanel had a richer knowledge of Christian historiography than Abraham bar Hiyya and included many historical details that were absent from *Megilat hamegaleh*. Ibn Daud had mentioned the Arian shift at the time of Constantius II and the return to paganism in the time of Julian in the *History of Rome*, but Abravanel added several details, connecting the religious changes in the empire to changes in the emperors' attitude to the Jews. But in this instance he erred: Constantius did not alter his father's policy, and, from the standpoint of the Jews, things actually got worse.[134] Abravanel was probably projecting the reality of Julian's time, when a noticeable change did take place in attitudes to the Jews, on to the earlier period.[135]

Elsewhere Abravanel addressed the contradictions and errors in Jewish versions of early Christian history. He rejected the ascription of the founding of Christianity to Constantine, although he was obviously familiar with the emperor's importance and his achievements:

And in this interpretation of mine, [the reader] should note that there were two beginnings to the faith of Edom: the first related to Jesus, whose fame grew with the destruction of the Second Temple and who rose [to greater heights] when the daily offering was abolished. The second related to Emperor Constantine who, nearly 300 years after the death of Jesus, became a Christian and was baptized, as I noted, and gave Rome and the entire land to the priests, and he went to Greece and built the great city of Constantinople. . . . Constantine ruled over the whole world and forced all the lands of the west and Italy and Greece and the lands of the south and Egypt and northern Assyria and Babylonia, from India to Cush, to believe in the religion of Jesus. And he made it known far and wide throughout the world that [Jesus] was God, the possessor of heaven and earth, and they accepted and upheld his divinity. Hence this faith had two heads, as it had two beginnings. The first head was Rome, the seat of the pope, in memory of Peter and Paul, the first disciples of their master Jesus. And the second head was Constantine, as I noted.[136]

---

[133] Abravanel, *Ma'ayanei hayeshuah*, ii: 5 (Jerusalem edn., 389–90).
[134] See J. Cohen, 'Roman Imperial Policy toward the Jews', 8–10.
[135] Geiger, 'The Revolt in the Time of Gallus and the Construction of the Temple in the Time of Julian' (Heb.), 208–17.
[136] Abravanel, *Ma'ayenei hayeshuah*, ii: 10 (Jerusalem edn., 400).

Abravanel offered a simple solution to the differences between the versions: there were two beginnings to Christianity. Jesus was responsible for the first, and Constantine for the second. In this manner, Abravanel was able to credit Constantine with founding Christianity, without divesting Jesus of his historical role and without deviating from the accepted historical facts. The existence of two separate Churches, Greek and Roman, with two territorial centres, Constantinople and Rome, supported his notion of two beginnings. The Church in Rome, headed by the pope, symbolized the first founding of Christianity by Jesus, since the two major Apostles, Peter and Paul, were linked to Rome; the Church in Constantinople symbolized the second beginning because of its links to Constantine.

A historical event, the destruction of the Second Temple, led to the dissemination of Jesus's message, albeit in a limited fashion. It took the power of a Roman emperor to spread Christianity throughout the world. According to Abravanel, Jesus became well known after the abolition of the daily offerings, apparently a reference to his prophecy about the destruction of the Temple (Matt. 24: 1–2): only after the prophecy proved to be accurate, did he gain support and fame.[137] Constantine was famous, because he was the emperor, and he could therefore impose Christianity on the empire. Constantine did not invent the doctrine of the Incarnation—as Levi ben Abraham had claimed—but only made it widely known. How ideas are promulgated was important to Abravanel, and it is discussed in different contexts in his other books.[138]

Abravanel was not the first to discuss the spread of Christianity. There were traces of it in Abraham ibn Ezra's *Short Commentary on Daniel* (*Haperush hakatsar al daniyel*): 'It was Constantine the Great who built Constantinople, through whom the religion of the hanged man became known far and wide.'[139] However, Abravanel was influenced by Renaissance attitudes and critical-historical approaches, which developed in Spain from the fourteenth century. Similar ideas were expressed by Profayt Duran and Machiavelli. Abravanel was a courtier and adviser at the court of King Ferdinand II of Aragon, who served as the model for *The Prince*, and did not need to read Machiavelli's writings in order to understand realpolitik. Machiavelli described Constantine as the ideal prince, or 'armed

[137] Abravanel claimed that the destruction of the Temple was a decisive event in the spread of Christianity in his interpretation of Deut. 28: 51, a passage that was censored from the Venice edition of *Perush al hatorah* (1579), which served as the basis for all later editions. The passage is extant in the Sabbioneta edition (1551), p. 97 (see Leiman, 'Abarbanel and the Censor', esp. 59).

[138] See his discussion of the messianic movements (Abravanel, *Sefer yeshuot meshiho*, 20*b*). A precedent was set with Maimonides' statements about Christianity and Islam as religions that paved the way for the coming of the messiah (*Mishneh torah*, 'Laws of Kings', 11: 4).

[139] See Abraham ibn Ezra on Dan. 11: 3 (*Haperush hakatsar al daniyel*, 13–14).

prophet', who used violence and coercion as well as propaganda to spread his message.[140] Abravanel also held that Constantine forced Christianity on the empire but made the new faith appealing through theological tenets such as the Trinity, the Incarnation, the Virgin Birth, and the Eucharist.[141] Here he followed Levi ben Abraham and in particular Profayt Duran, who claimed that Constantine and his advisers, took 'the faith of Jesus and shrewdly brought it closer to reason in order to instil it in the heart of the masses', although, 'since they themselves erred, they came to mislead others'.[142]

Similar realistic images of Constantine also appear in Abraham Zacut's writings:

Constantinople was founded in the year 4536 . . . and its name was Byzantium. King Constantine enlarged and broadened it almost 1,000 years later and renamed it Constantinople after himself. It is called the Second Rome, for 301 years after the birth of That Man, Constantine began to reign, and he built the city up. He accepted the Christian faith 318 years after the birth of That Man in the days of [Pope] Sylvester and he built the city. . . . Galerius reigned in 5055 for two years with Constantine the Great. Afterwards Constantine the Great reigned alone in 5507—which is seventy-eight years after the birth of That Man—for thirty years. In the tenth year of his reign he became a Christian because, they say, Pope Sylvester healed him of leprosy. . . . And then the emperor decreed that they would no longer hang [men] on wood in a crosswise manner.[143]

Constantine extended the wall of Byzantium and renamed it Constantinople after himself. It has been called the Second Rome because of its greatness and from that time until our own time Rome [belonged] to Pope Sylvester and his followers.[144]

Zacut's version of events is historically accurate. Constantine co-ruled Rome with Galerius and later reigned alone over the entire empire.[145] He converted to Christianity under the influence of Sylvester, built Constantinople, abolished crucifixion, and gave Sylvester and all the popes after him rule over Rome.[146] The important change during Constantine's reign was that Christianity gained political power, rather than any theological or ideological development.[147] Prior to that,

---

[140] Profayt Duran, *Atsat ahitofel vehushai ha'arki*, 206–7; Gutwirth, 'Duran on Ahitophel', 73 n. 19; Machiavelli, *The Prince*, 6: 16–18; 18: 49–51; 16: 46; on Ferdinand of Aragon, see ibid. 21: 63–6; on Abravanel's courtly milieu in Portugal, see Gutwirth, 'Hercules Furens and War'.

[141] Abravanel, *Ma'ayenei hayeshuah*, 8: 5; 11: 8 (Jerusalem edn., 337, 393).

[142] Ibid.; Profayt Duran, *Kelimat hagoyim*, Dedication (ed. Talmage, 4); see also Gutwirth, 'History and Apologetics in XVth Century Hispano-Jewish Thought', 231–8.

[143] Zacut, *Sefer yuhasin* (ed. Filipowski, 238a).   [144] Ibid. 246a.

[145] Zacut's dates are wrong, probably, as mentioned, due to copyist errors (see Ch. 1, n. 147 above). Galerius died in 311, and Constantine reigned alone only after the defeat of Lycinius in 324 (see Barnes, *Constantine and Eusebius*, 28–39, 76–7).

[146] Zacut, *Sefer yuhasin* (ed. Filipowski, 246a).   [147] Ibid. (ed. Filipowski, 200a).

Christianity had merely been a heresy: its members were called 'apostates' by the sages, because they practised baptism, and the sages of Yavneh introduced the curse on apostates into the daily prayers.[148]

Another tradition about Constantine was preserved in Elijah Capsali's *Seder eliyahu zuta*, which was written in 1523 and contained popular historical traditions he learned from the exiles from Spain:

And 390 years after the construction of the Second Temple, the religion of the Nazarene Jesus came about, and a few people believed in his religion, some here and some there. After many days had passed Constantine, ruler of the world, was induced to believe in this religion by an Edomite priest who cured him of leprosy, and this religion was made known far and wide by Constantine, who sent forth a message throughout his kingdom saying that all who do not believe in this religion would be put to death and their house would be made a dunghill [see Dan. 2: 5]. And all the kings of the nations obeyed him, for they were his subjects, and then Rome and all the worshippers of the sun and moon and stars and all the inhabitants of Spain converted and believed in the religion of Jesus, and the stories about him seemed to them to be sown in light [see Ps. 97: 11]. And then they turned on the Jews, deprived them of the right to wear head coverings and shawls, and decreed that they must become Christians, and many died to sanctify the name of God. Later they entered into a covenant with the Jews on condition that when there was a drought and the earth provided no harvest, the Jews would pray to God for rain, both the first and the last rain, for among the Jews then there were pious men whose voice God heard, and the non-Jews knew the deeds of God. And they wrote an eternal covenant with them, and God made all those who hated and banished them feel mercy, and God said: 'They have suffered enough.' And the Christians ruled safely in Spain, and no one made them afraid.[149]

The description of Constantine's conversion is similar to the popular version in Christian Spain: Constantine converted to Christianity after Sylvester cured him of leprosy, Christianity already existed, although its members were few in number, but it became widely known after Constantine imposed it upon the empire by force.

Two different historical events are probably conflated here: Constantine's conversion and the enactment of edicts against Jews after the Visigothic kings of Spain converted to Christianity. After the empire became Christian, the status of Jews did change, but it was a gradual process. Later generations tended to place all the blame on Constantine. Later improvements in the situation of Spanish Jewry are explained by their ability to petition God for rain.[150] This was why the

---

[148] Ibid. (ed. Filipowski, 15*a*).

[149] Capsali, *Seder eliyahu zuta*, 2: 40 (ed. Shmuelevitz, Simonsohn, and Benayahu, i. 145).

[150] On the myth of rainfall brought about by the Jews of Spain, see Ibn Verga, *Shevet yehudah*, 142;

Jews of Spain were spared Constantine's anti-Jewish decrees, and how the special relationship between Jews and Christians in Spain was established.

Profayt Duran, Shimon ben Tsemah Duran, Abravanel, Zacut, and the Spanish traditions preserved by Capsali, all confirm that a more realistic perception of Constantine gradually developed among the Jews of Spain from the end of the fourteenth century as a result of closer acquaintance with Christian historiography. However, even after this more realistic image of Constantine entered their historical consciousness, Jews still needed to adapt it for polemical purposes, as Christians continued to use the myth in their arguments. One good example is provided by the convert Gerónimo de Santa Fe at the Disputation of Tortosa in 1413–14. During the fifty-fourth session, Santa Fe delivered a historical survey of the creation and development of the Mishnah and the Talmud. He attempted to show how a 'second Torah' had been created by the Jews as a reaction to the emergence and spread of Christianity. The Mishnah, in his view, was a reaction to the success of Jesus's doctrines and Christian interpretation of the Bible. However, after the creation of the Mishnah, Christianity continued to spread, many Jews converted to Catholicism along with the pagans of Italy and 'Helena, the mother of the emperor', and the Christians became a majority. Fearing that their Torah would be lost, the Jews invented another one, which they called the Talmud.[151]

Although the old Jewish myth of Constantine the theologian and founder of Christianity was rejected by those Jews who knew the Christian historiographical tradition, another polemical tradition of Constantine and Helena surfaced. It concerned the finding of the holy cross, a piece of which can be found in most churches in Spain, where its discovery is celebrated every May. Here too both figures were linked. In some versions of the story, the emperor instructs Helena to find the cross, and hence her success—or failure—was regarded as his. One such example is from Abraham Zacut, who discussed Christian saints and relics out of historical curiosity, although he often added a polemical slant. According to Zacut, 'Constantinople, the head of the kingdom of Greece was captured by the Ottoman king. . . . And in that year, they burned in Constantinople the tree from which the Christians say their messiah was hanged.'[152] Zacut did not deny that a tree was burned by the Ottomans, but he did not think it was the holy cross. In another part of *Sefer yuḥasin*, he explained why the Christian tradition about the holy cross is not credible:

Sambari, *Sefer divrei yosef*, 93–5 (ed. Shtober, 259–61); Yassif, *The Hebrew Folktale* (Heb.), 456–9. I will elaborate on this issue in my forthcoming article 'How to Remember a Leader?' (Heb.).

[151] See Pacios López, *La disputa de Tortosa*, ii. 453–4.

[152] Zacut, *Sefer yuḥasin* (ed. Filipowski, 226*b*); see R. Ben-Shalom, 'Polemic Historiography in *Sefer yuḥasin*' (Heb.), 124–7; Fernández Conde, 'Religiosidad popular y piedad culta', 302, 315.

Constantine's mother, whose name was Helena, went to Jerusalem. Filled with great hatred of Jews, she threatened to kill them unless they gave her the tree That Man was hanged on. Then they prayed and learned where it was 300 years after the Crucifixion. And they said they had found three crosses [lit.: 'pieces of wood, length and breadth'], one of which bore the inscription of That Man in Hebrew, Greek, and Latin. And, because of that, the emperor abolished crucifixion. And one Jew, whose name was Judah, [found the cross and] became a Christian. [Helena] made him the bishop of Jerusalem, but later he was killed, and the cross was taken to Rome. [Helena] gave her son one of the nails of the cross, and he put it into the bridle of his horse to go to war. According to their version, she cast the second nail into the sea. The whereabouts of the third nail are unknown [in another version: 'She put the third nail in the saddle'].[153]

Christian myths about the discovery of the cross took many different forms. The earliest versions did not contain any supernatural or miraculous elements. In the early fifth century Rufinus introduced a miracle: the identification of the holy cross from among the three that were found through the resurrection of a dead woman. The early Christian historiographers Eusebius and Jerome accused pagans of maliciously hiding the cross, but other Christian versions of the myth blamed the Jews. According to Linder, the legend was meant to depict Jews as obstinately refusing to see the light and trying to preserve their religion even though they clearly realized that Jesus was the messiah and that their ancestors had committed deicide. Consequently, Jews could never be forgiven or tolerated. The legend provided legitimacy for forced conversion and anti-Jewish violence.[154] Jews appeared in the story for the first time in a version by Paulinus of Nola written in 403.[155] However, scholars have recently noted an earlier version: Gelasius of Caesarea's lost continuation of Eusebius's *Church History*, written around 390, which included oral traditions from Christians living in Jerusalem at the end of the fourth century.[156] In this version, Helena was credited with the discovery of the cross. This tradition entered Spanish historiography in several different forms, as we can see from *Libro de las generaciones* and *Livro das linhagens*, which relate that after his conversion, Constantine came to Jerusalem with Helena.

[153] Zacut, *Sefer yuḥasin* (ed. Filipowski, 246a). I have corrected some parts according to MS Hunt. 504 (Neubauer 2202) (Bodleian Library, Oxford).

[154] Linder, 'Jerusalem as a Focus of Conflict between Judaism and Christianity' (Heb.), 20–1.

[155] See ibid. 18.

[156] See Borgehammar, *How the Holy Cross was Found*, 7–55; Drijvers, *Helena Augusta*, 96–9, 138–9, following Winkelmann, 'Charakter und Bedeutung der Kirchengeschichte des Gelasios von Kaisareia'. According to Jan Willem Drijvers, 'soon after the origin of the legend it gradually changed from a story invented to explain the presence of the True Cross in Jerusalem and to underline the special status of the Jerusalem bishopric, into a narrative which was particularly striking for its anti-Judaism' (*Helena Augusta*, 145).

There she gathered all the Jews, and some of them showed her where the holy cross was. Consequently, the feast of the discovery of the holy cross was established.[157] The legend about Helena and Judah (known as Cyriacus after his conversion) originated in Jerusalem or Syria in the first half of the fifth century, was soon translated into Latin, and in the early sixth century was already known in Rome. From there it spread throughout western Europe and was even introduced into the liturgy of the Roman Church.[158]

Toledot yeshu contains a version of the story that served as a historiographical response to the anti-Jewish developments in the legends of the holy cross from the fifth century. Helena decided to find the holy cross in order to cure the leprosy that had afflicted her son. She demanded that the Jews of Rome give it to her and threatened to have them killed if they refused. The Roman Jews told her to go to the Jews of Jerusalem, and, using similar threats, she demanded they give her the cross. The elders appealed to Rabbi Judah for help, and Rabbi Judah promised Helena that he would show her where the cross was. He told the elders to 'take three very old pieces of wood and bury them in a certain place and cover them so it will not look as if they are new'.[159] After showing the Christians where the three pieces of wood were, Rabbi Judah resurrected a dead man with the help of the name of God and was thus able to 'tell' which of the three was the true cross. Finally Rabbi Judah converted to Christianity in order to annul the harsh edicts against Jews which Constantine had proclaimed. In the Christian version, Judah was baptized after he observed the miracle wrought by the cross and thus became a type of the eschatological Jewish convert. In the Jewish legend, Rabbi Judah remained faithful to his religion and only converted to protect the Jews, even though it meant sacrificing himself.

Zacut's version has many differences from *Toledot yeshu*. In fact, he followed a later mixture of Syrian, Byzantine, and Hellenistic traditions that Jacobus de Voragine incorporated into the *Golden Legend* in the mid-thirteenth century, which is closely related to an anonymous Spanish version of the tenth century

[157] 'Quoando ouo Constantin conquerida Rroma, mouio se d'i con su madre e paso a Jherusalem. E Elena aplego todos los judios de Jherusalem, e tanto lis fezo, que ouieron de mostrar la vera cruz en que Dios priso muert e passion por nos' (*Libro de las generaciones*, 268). 'O emperador Costamtim, quamdo ouue Rroma comquista, moueosse com sa madre e passousse a Jerusalem. E a rrainha frez ajumtar todollos homeès e todollos judeus velhos, e tamto lhes fez e tanto lhes disse, quie lhe ouuerom a mostrar a vera cruz. E poremde fazem a festa a tres dias amdados de mayo "de inventione sancte crucis" ' (*Livro das linhagens*, 268).

[158] See Borgehammar, *How the Holy Cross was Found*, 188–95, 204–10; Drijvers, *Helena Augusta*, 174–84; Linder, 'Ecclesia and Synagoga in the Medieval Myth of Constantine the Great', 1035–44; id., 'Jerusalem as a Focus of Conflict between Judaism and Christianity' (Heb.), 17–19.

[159] *Toledot yeshu*, 142; see R. Ben-Shalom, 'The Converso as Subversive'; Krauss, 'Eine judische Legende von der Auffindung des Kreuzes'.

and the one in *Primera crónica general de España*.[160] He added nothing from *Toledot yeshu*.[161] The version in the *Golden Legend* recounts how Judah/Cyriacus, the representative of the Jews, dug and found three crosses buried in the ground where the temple of Venus had stood. The temple had been built by Emperor Hadrian on the site of the Crucifixion, so that Christians coming there to honour Jesus would pay homage to Venus as well. Zacut's version does not mention a search for the cross, any digging, or its being found in any specific place. According to him, the Jews prayed to their God (a motif lacking from the *Golden Legend*), and afterwards 'they said they had found' a piece of the cross—in other words, they did not tell Helena the truth: by omitting several motifs and adding 'they said', Zacut changed the meaning of the story.[162] From that point onwards, the story reads ironically: the Christians used the piece of the cross as a talisman, but in fact it was a forgery and would have been of no benefit.[163] This is counter-history, which seeks to distort the opponents' self-image and identity by disrupting their collective memory using sources they accept as their own against them and producing as different and contradictory an interpretation as possible.[164]

A similar story by Isaac Abravanel suggests that Zacut may have used an existing tradition.

[Constantine] went to Greece where he built the great city of Constantinople. And from there sent his mother to Jerusalem, to search for the tree from which Jesus the Nazarene was hanged, and the Jews, bitter at heart, deceived her, told her falsehoods, gave her a large tree and told her that it was the tree. And she brought it to Constantinople, and a fine building was erected there for it called Hagia Sophia.[165]

Abravanel's version lacks many of the details of Zacut's: Helena's threats against the Jews, how the Jews forged the piece of the cross, Judah's conversion, how the Christians were persuaded that it was the holy cross. Moreover, Abravanel mistakenly stated that Hagia Sophia was erected to mark the discovery of the cross and its arrival in Constantinople. In fact, it was built many years later (532–7 CE),

---

[160] The Jews of Spain and Provence also chose not to present the life of Jesus and his disciples based on *Toledot yeshu* but used the New Testament. Examples of this can be found in Profayt Duran and Shimon ben Tsemah Duran.

[161] See Jacobus de Voragine, *Legenda aurea* (Leipzig edn., 269–76); on the Latin versions that preceded the *Golden Legend*, see Borgehammar, *How the Holy Cross was Found*, 146–95; Linder, 'Ecclesia and Synagoga in the Medieval Myth of Constantine the Great', 1036; for the tenth-century Spanish version, see *Pasionario Hispánico*.

[162] In various places, Zacut quoted statements by Christians ('they said that . . .'; 'the Christians say . . .') and, in doing so, expressed his doubts. However only in the story of the cross is the subject of 'they said' the Jews (see e.g. *Sefer yuḥasin* (ed. Filipowski, 244*a–b*, 246*a–b*, 247*a*)).

[163] On the talismatic importance of the remnants of the cross, see Linder, 'The Myth of Constantine the Great', 66–7.   [164] Funkenstein, *Perceptions of Jewish History*, 36–40.

[165] Abravanel, *Ma'ayenei hayeshuah*, 11: 10 (Jerusalem edn., 400).

during the reign of Justin. Abravanel presented only the essence of the story and erred in some of the details, but he did stress what Zacut only implied: that the Jews deceived Helena and gave her any old piece of wood.

Gerónimo de Santa Fe's historical explanation of the invention of the Talmud is also a type of counter-history. In his view, the Talmud was not the product of internal developments in Jewish law and an organic continuation of the writings of the Second Temple period, but a malicious reaction to the Christianization of the Roman empire, a process symbolized in the myth of Constantine and Helena. This claim may not have elicited a direct response from Zacut or Abravanel, but their attempts to denigrate Constantine's and Helena's religious actions through the story of the finding of the holy cross may be an indirect response to Santa Fe. The legend of the holy cross in its Christian version, with Jews, knowing the Christians were right and recognizing Jesus's divinity, obstinately holding on to their erroneous faith, conformed nicely with the negative image of Jews in Santa Fe's story. In both instances, the Jews tried to thwart the Christians, either by creating a new anti-Christian doctrine or by concealing holy relics, making the point that the Jews knew the truth of Christianity but attempted to conceal the fact.[166] The Jewish counter-history denied that the Jews knew that Christianity was the true religion. However, the knowledge they did possess exposed the spuriousness of the Christian myth: all the religious truths that it ostensibly expressed (the discovery of the holy cross, the use of the nails, the erection of Hagia Sophia) were shown to be illusions, devoid of any religious implications. While Gerónimo de Santa Fe argued that the Jews knew that the Christians possessed the religious truth and nonetheless denied it, Zacut and Abravanel came forward to show that historical claims of this sort were baseless.

The polemical potential of the life of Jesus, the origins of Christianity, the writings of the New Testament, and the development of Christian doctrines evoked an interest in the history of the Second Temple period and the early years of Christianity. Contrary to the view that the Jesus mentioned in the Talmud was not the Christian Jesus, the majority of scholars and polemicists agreed that he was one and the same man. As for when he lived, two trends developed—one attempted to challenge Christian chronology and the New Testament on the basis of the Talmud; the other accepted the Christian version of Jesus's life. Both trends used methodical historical criticism to try to show that Jesus had remained within Judaism, albeit a deviant form of Judaism. There were also two approaches to the development of Christianity after Jesus. According to one, he founded a new religion in order to destroy Judaism. According to the other, he was a

---

[166] See Limor, 'Christian Sacred Space and the Jews', esp. 58–63; id., 'Christian Sanctity, Jewish Authority' (Heb.).

well-intentioned Jew who wanted to preserve Judaism but was misguided in his actions: medieval Christianity was the product of either his disciples or Constantine.

Constantine had a major role in most Jewish versions of Christian history. In some, he invented the religion; in others, he merely imposed it on the empire. In addition he was responsible for harsh measures against Jews, which, although not historically accurate, were part of the Christian myth built around him. Therefore, early Jewish versions of Constantine's life presented him in very negative terms and claimed that the Christianity he imposed on the Roman empire was a corruption of the original faith of Jesus. A more balanced perception of Constantine developed from the end of the fourteenth century among Jews who were familiar with Christian historiography. Some of them preferred to follow the Christian version and ignore the anti-Jewish elements of the myth.

Maimonides, who lived all his life in a Muslim environment, made no serious attempt to grapple with the heritage of Christianity. Although Jewish anti-Christian polemic first made its appearance in Muslim areas,[167] criticism of the Gospels largely developed in Christian Europe.[168] This difference is apparent when one compares Maimonides' discussions of early Christianity with those of twelfth- and thirteenth-century Jews from Christian Spain and southern France, who had acquired critical tools from Jewish sources (rabbinic and Karaite) and from heretical Christian movements. In contrast to Maimonides, Jews from Spain and southern France did not see any attempt to undermine the Jewish foundations of Jesus's religious activity, and this may be because they had learned about Jesus's life and sayings from the Gospels. For example, Profayt Duran, following Levi ben Abraham, perfected critical methods of reading Christian sources.[169] In his writings, the polemical trend in Spain and southern France reached its peak.

Duran was also influenced by Raymundus Martini's *Dagger of Faith*, which was used by the mendicant orders in their missions to the Jews. The mendicants' attitude to the sacred Hebrew texts and the Jewish critical approach of Christianity have some common theoretical roots in Muslim anti-Jewish polemic, particularly the work of the most important Muslim biblical critic, Ibn Hazm of Cordova, who died in 1064. In *Kitab al-Fisal fi al-Milal wa al-Ahwa' wa al-Nihal* (The

---

[167] Lasker, 'Jewish–Christian Polemic and Its Origins in the Lands of Islam' (Heb.).

[168] See Rembaum, 'The New Testament in Medieval Jewish Anti-Christian Polemics', esp. 212–19. The *Polemic of Nestor the Priest*, which originated in the Arabic east, is an exception (see Lasker, 'Jewish–Christian Polemic and Its Origins in the Lands of Islam' (Heb.), 5–6; Rembaum, 'The Influence of "Sefer Nestor HaKomer" on Medieval Jewish Polemics').

[169] See Profayt Duran, *Kelimat hagoyim*, 11 (ed. Talmage, 62–3); see Gutwirth, 'History and Apologetics in XVth Century Hispano-Jewish Thought', 234–5.

Distinctions between the Religions, the Views, and the Sects), he drew a distinction between the Judaism of the Second Temple period and the original Jewish religion, which was based on the revelation at Mount Sinai. He claimed that Ezra falsified the original text of the Torah and that Ezra and other rabbis introduced prayers as a substitute for sacrifices in the Temple, in effect creating a new Jewish religion.[170] These views could have reached the Christian world as far back as the twelfth century, through converts such as Peter Alfonsi—born Moses Sephardi, converted to Christianity in 1106—who was well-versed in Muslim writings and the works of Ibn Hazm, who died in 1175.[171] Jews in Spain were aware of these claims and adopted the principle of religious development by stages for their own purposes.[172]

The Jews' historical approach to early Christianity developed in parallel with new polemical methods, including the criticism of the New Testament, in such works as Joseph Kimhi's *Sefer haberit*, Jacob ben Reuben's *Milḥamot hashem*, *Vikuaḥ haradak*, Joseph ben Nathan Official's *Sefer yosef hamekane*, Meir ben Shimon Hame'ili's *Milḥemet mitsvah*, and Yom Tov Lipmann Mülhausen's *Book of Victory* (*Sefer nitsaḥon*). David Berger observed that the Christian attitude to the Talmud was similar to the Jewish attitude to the New Testament: each group exposed the sacred literature of its adversaries to severe criticism and exploited it to refute the beliefs of its adherents.[173]

Jesus's activities and intentions became important in the discourses of Jews, Christians, and Conversos, as is evident from Profayt Duran's 'Letter of Dedication' in *Shame of the Gentiles*, a work apparently aimed at Conversos. According to Duran, his main motive for writing was to address the question of whether or not Jesus and his disciples intended to destroy Judaism. Duran cleared Jesus of any malicious intent, and the blame was placed on others (the disciples, Christian scholars, Constantine).[174] Shimon ben Tsemah Duran, who used Profayt Duran's method, totally exonerated Jesus and argued that all of his activity was a misguided attempt to protect the Torah.[175] The founders of Christianity were Paul, Jerome, and Augustine, who interpreted Jesus's words allegorically.[176]

---

[170] See Lazarus-Yafeh, *Intertwined Worlds* (Heb.), 151; see Perlmann, 'The Medieval Polemics between Islam and Judaism', esp. 108–11.

[171] See Lazarus-Yafeh, *Intertwined Worlds* (Heb.), 153–4; J. Cohen, *Living Letters of the Law*, 210–18; Tolan, *Petrus Alfonsi and His Medieval Readers*, esp. 19, 24.

[172] See Lasker, 'Jewish–Christian Polemic and Its Origins in the Lands of Islam' (Heb.).

[173] See Berger, Introduction to *Nizzahon vetus*, 30.

[174] Profayt Duran, *Kelimat hagoyim*, Dedication (ed. Talmage, 3); Berger, 'On the Uses of History in Medieval Jewish Polemic against Christianity'.

[175] Shimon b. Tsemah Duran, *Keshet umagen*, 40.

[176] Ibid. 38, 40. Although elsewhere in this book Duran blames Jesus for inciting Jews to adultery (see Berger, 'On the Uses of History in Medieval Jewish Polemic against Christianity', 34–5).

These approaches were also consistent with Maimonides' view that Christianity and Islam advanced monotheistic ideas in the world.

This raises the question of whether interpreting Jesus as well-intentioned but misguided created a favourable and more tolerant attitude to Christians. The answer is not simple. Abraham bar Hiyya, for example, certainly intended to denigrate Jesus and Christianity, but this trend is less obvious in other writers. On the one hand, the purpose of creating a discrepancy between Jesus's Jewish faith and later Christianity was to attack contemporary Christianity; on the other, the very 'acceptance' of Jesus suggested that the two religions had some common basis. Even if there was no conscious intention to demonstrate an affinity, from a broad and long-term perspective, some common ground might have been found, perhaps even movement towards an easier coexistence of Jews and Christians.

CHAPTER FOUR

History of the Church

IN THE MIDDLE AGES, the Church had a significant place in Jewish life. The fragile coexistence of Jews and Christians was based on the Augustinian idea of 'tolerance', which left room for Jews in the Christian world. However, Jews were marked out, isolated, ostracized, and abused. The Church burned the Talmud and censored rabbinical literature, but it also issued orders protecting Jews in times of crisis (such as during the Black Death in 1348 or after blood libels), and Jews frequently appealed to the pope for protection (for example, at the conference of Jewish communities of Catalonia and Valencia in Barcelona in 1354).[1] Jews encountered the Church as an integral part of their daily lives, and some served it directly: we know of Jews who were physicians and tailors to popes.[2] The cultural and social encounter with the Church made a strong impression, which was manifested in various forms. In contrast to Ashkenazi Jewry, which constantly expressed a strong aversion to the Church, the Jews of Spain and southern France acknowledged the positive aspects of their contact with Christian culture.[3] For example, they regarded Christian universities and other educational institutions as praiseworthy temples of knowledge and bastions of science, and some Jews even tried to gain entrance to them or studied privately with teachers from the universities.[4] The works of Christian theologians, philosophers, logicians, and scholars were admired, studied, and translated by Jews.[5]

---

[1] See Baer, *A History of the Jews in Christian Spain*, ii. 25–8; Simonsohn, *The Apostolic See and the Jews*, vi, esp. 287–99.

[2] See e.g. Grayzel, 'The Avignon Popes and the Jews'; on Jews serving popes, see Benjamin of Tudela, *Sefer masaot*, 6–7.

[3] See A. S. Abulafia, 'Invectives against Christianity in the Hebrew Chronicles of the First Crusade'; H. H. Ben-Sasson, 'The Spanish Exiles Speak of Themselves' (Heb.), 232–8; Katz, *Between Jews and Gentiles* (Heb.), 95–101; id., *Exclusiveness and Tolerance*, 114–28.

[4] See Leon Joseph of Carcassone's introduction to Gerard de Solo's commentary on Al-Razi's *Book of Medicine for Mansour* (Renan, *Les Écrivains juifs français du XIVe siècle*, 427–8) and Abraham Avigdor ben Meshullam's introduction to his translation of Albert Bernat's *Introduction to the Practice of Medicine* (ibid. 372–3), where he claimed that he studied in Montpellier with Gerard de Solo and translated his work on fevers (see also Shatzmiller, 'Étudiants juifs à la faculté de médecine de Montpellier').

[5] See R. Ben-Shalom, 'Between Official and Private Dispute', 67–71; id., 'Me'ir Nativ', 232–8; Shirman, *The History of Hebrew Poetry in Christian Spain and Southern France* (Heb.), 636–7;

Spanish and Provençal Jews admired the Church for other reasons as well. Solomon Alami ibn Lahmish enthusiastically lauded the Church's success in collecting tithes. He wrote after the Disputation of Tortosa in 1413–14 and stated that, in contrast to the Jews, the Christians, in particular the rich, paid their Church taxes willingly, thus contributing to the glorification of the Church, the studies of its scholars, and the honour of the houses of worship.[6] Joel ibn Shuaib, who lived in Tudela at the end of the fifteenth century, praised Christian methods of atonement and penitence, which involved a sanctified 'special house and a special man' who forgave and granted atonement. Menahem Me'iri of Perpignan (1249–1315) also admired Christian methods of obtaining atonement and the literature that dealt with it and wrote *Ḥibur hateshuvah* to make up for the lack of such literature in Judaism.[7]

Jews did not need to pore over books in Latin or Romance languages to gain familiarity with the religious and cultural symbolism of Christianity. Many of these symbols were conspicuously displayed in medieval architecture and visual arts. It was impossible to ignore the huge cathedrals with their splendid sculptures, constantly projecting a visual, ideological message about the size and power of the Church. Nor was it possible to deny the profound religious message of the monasteries. Their walls concealed everything going on inside, but the sound of the monks' prayers, which carried to the outside world in the late hours of the night, conveyed awe, majesty, and religiosity.

Jacob ben Reuben, who lived among Christians in 'lower Gasikoya' (probably Gascony) became friendly with a monk, 'one of the great men of the city and the scholars of the generation . . . well-versed in the art of rhetoric and in all the internal wisdoms', and became his pupil.[8] In 1170 he recorded that, in one lesson, the priest posed a question to him: How long would the Jews continue to reject Christianity, since they were growing few in number and living in base conditions in comparison to the glory and greatness of the Church? To prove the truth of Christianity, the priest cited his own life. He described his asceticism, his black woollen garment, the harsh weather conditions in which he carried out his worship of God, and his participation in nocturnal chants. He argued that all of these

García-Ballester, Ferre, and Feliu, 'Jewish Appreciation of Fourteenth-Century Scholastic Medicine'; Zonta, 'Latin Scholastic Influences on Late Medieval Hebrew Physics'.

[6] Alami ibn Lahmish, *Igeret musar*, 48. Alami's intent was actually to criticize Jewish society for its shortcomings, but the counter-image, drawn from Christian society to serve as a moral lesson, is nonetheless relevant.

[7] See Ibn Shuaib, *Nora tehilot*, 42: 97a; quoted in H. H. Ben-Sasson, 'The Spanish Exiles Speak of Themselves' (Heb.), 224; see Me'iri, *Ḥibur hateshuvah*, 2.

[8] Jacob b. Reuben, *Milḥamot hashem*, 4–5, 10; see Berger, 'Gilbert Crispin, Alan of Lille, and Jacob ben Reuben'; Rosenthal, Introduction (Heb.) to Jacob b. Reuben, *Milḥamot hashem*, pp. ix–x, xix.

maintained and strengthened faith in the Trinity.[9] Jacob ben Reuben agreed that the monastic way of life entailed a great effort, but he firmly stated that, although they lived in this upright manner, they were misled in their belief in the Trinity.[10] The monk's stringent lifestyle and great awe of God was seen as a legitimate argument in religious disputations, and Jews struggled to find a satisfactory retort to it. They regarded the monks' nocturnal prayers as a commendable custom, and for some it also served as an incentive for more fervent worship. After hearing some Franciscan vigils Todros ben Judah Halevi Abulafia (1247–c.1300), wrote:

> The Minorites sing to the satyrs
> And shall I not sing to the God of all creatures?
> Shall they arise at midnight and at dawn
> Without speech and sing unto other gods
> And I will not rise to sing to a living God
> The foundation and the secret of all things?
> Oh, my heart, rise up and praise my Lord
> The master of the earth and the heavens,
> Who brings low and lifts up high.[11]

Jews encountered the material and spiritual Church nearly everywhere they turned.

Exempla played an important role in promulgating the lessons and symbols of the Church, and numerous sources document Jewish exposure to them. Some Jews encountered them in Christian books; others heard them from Christian preachers who delivered their sermons in public to Christian audiences or to Jews in Jewish neighbourhoods and even synagogues. A number of fifteenth-century sources relate that Jews listened to Christian sermons.[12] Moreover, Solomon Alami ibn Lahmish censured the lack of attentiveness of Jewish audiences in the synagogue during sermons, describing how they fell asleep, how the men chatted and the women murmured. In contrast, he praised the way Christians listened to their preachers and how they put their words into practice,[13] which suggests a close acquaintance with Christian sermons.

---

[9] Jacob b. Reuben, *Milḥamot hashem*, 5, 10.   [10] Ibid. 12.

[11] Todros b. Judah Abulafia, *Gan hameshalim vehaḥidot*, 983 (668) (ed. Yellin, Pt. 2, vol. ii. 199–200). The Arabic title is 'To him upon hearing the sound of a bell' (Yellin, note (Heb.), ibid. 47; see Baer, 'Todros ben Judah Halevi' (Heb.), 270; Ishay, 'On the Oedipal Rebellion of Todros Abulafia' (Heb.). The Minorites, or Friars Minor, are the Franciscans.

[12] See J. Cohen, *The Friars and the Jews*, 13, 82–4; Chazan, *Daggers of Faith*, 38–48; Baer, *A History of the Jews in Christian Spain*, i. 155–7; Adret, *Teshuvot harashba*, 35 (ed. Dimitrovsky, 108)—Roth was correct in saying this was a Christian, not a Muslim, preacher (N. Roth, 'Forgery and Abrogation of the Torah', 225–6; see R. Ben-Shalom, 'Between Official and Private Dispute', 30; id., 'The Tortosa Disputation' (Heb.), 35–8; Pachter, 'The Homiletic and Ethical Literature of the Safed Sages' (Heb.).   [13] Alami ibn Lahmish, *Igeret musar*, 49.

Christian preachers who actively proselytized among Jews were instructed not to make their sermons antagonistic and to use 'material that will draw them to the faith and not . . . words that may act as obstacles'.[14] Exempla were an important part of this material. Isaac Arama tried to cope with the attractions of Christian sermons by introducing exempla of his own into his weekly sermons in the synagogue,[15] and Isaac Nathan frequently used exempla in *Me'amets koah*. Although Jews were exposed to a great number of Christian exempla in the fifteenth century, they had been forced to listen to sermons in Aragon and Provence as far back as the thirteenth century, and they probably listened to Christian sermons even when they were not compelled to. The chronicler from Arles, Bertrand Boysset, who described Vincent Ferrer's sermons in that city in 1400, wrote that the Jews of the city came to hear all his sermons, which generally included numerous exempla.[16] In the fifteenth century many Aragonese Jews came to hear Christian sermons of their own free will, because they were attracted by their philosophical and theological content.[17]

This chapter will focus on stories of saints and popes as presented by Jews. Their comments and observations, based on a large and varied number of Christian sources, provide a lot of information about the Church's impact on the Jews' historical consciousness. A considerable portion of the historical information about the Church was acquired from Christian exempla and hagiography, and it is interesting that Jews often used this material in their own exempla.

STORIES OF SAINTS

Igeret ya'akov mivenetsiah, Jacob ben Elijah's letter to the convert Paul Christiani—provides impressive evidence of the use of exempla. Jacob ben Elijah claimed that he was familiar with Christian legends from reading books and listening to Christian scholars.[18] The letter, which reveals a broad knowledge of Christian hagiography, tried to prove that it was possible to attack Christian writings in the same way that Christiani attacked the Talmud. This method was used

---

[14] From a 1419 order by Alfonso V of Aragon (see Baer, *Die Juden im christlichen Spanien*, doc. 527 (ii. 849)).

[15] On Arama, see H. H. Ben-Sasson, 'The Spanish Exiles Speak of Themselves' (Heb.), 223; Heller-Wilensky, *Rabbi Isaac Arama and His Teaching* (Heb.), 29–31.

[16] See Almazan, 'L'Exemplum chez Vincent Ferrier', 318–32 (including 183 exempla); R. Ben-Shalom, 'Between Official and Private Dispute', 37–9; id., 'The Tortosa Disputation' (Heb.), 36–7, esp. n. 72; Cátedra García, *Sermón, sociedad y literatura en la Edad Media*; Gorce, *St. Vincent Ferrier*, 74–5.

[17] Arama, *Akedat yitshak*, i. 1*a*; id., *Hazut kashah*, 4: 1; see R. Ben-Shalom, 'Between Official and Private Dispute', 30; id., 'A Minority Looks at the Mendicants'.

[18] Jacob b. Elijah, *Igeret ya'akov mivenetsiah*, 11.

primarily by the mendicant orders and gained prevalence after the Disputation of Paris: Christian scholars sought to show that the legends in the Talmud and the Midrash were irrational, deviant, and vulgar.[19] In response, Jacob ben Elijah focused on Christian hagiographical legends.

Apart from a brief mention by Nahmanides, *Igeret ya'akov mivenetsiah* is the only source of information about Paul Christiani's missionary activity prior to the Disputation of Barcelona in 1263.[20] According to Jacob ben Elijah, Christiani attacked the Talmud by focusing on irrational material in it.[21] He does not mention Christiani's other novel approach, adopted at the Disputation of Barcelona, of attempting to prove that Jesus was the messiah from talmudic legends.[22] Jewish scholars in Provence and Spain had reacted to the attack on the Talmud in various ways, which were, however, mainly defensive and apologetic.[23] Jacob ben Elijah went on the attack and cited a list of stories of Christian saints that contained irrational phenomena similar to those mentioned by Christiani.

The use of exempla in sermons by Dominicans was initiated by Dominic de Guzmán (1170–1221), the founder of the order. In the first generation after him, Stephen de Bourbon (1195–1261) compiled an important collection of exempla containing some 2,857 stories. Humbert of Romans, Vincent de Beauvais, Frère Lorens, who wrote *Somme de roi*, Jordan of Saxony, and many other Dominicans developed the genre.[24] Around the same time that *Igeret ya'akov mivenetsiah* was written the Dominicans created the first alphabetical anthologies of exempla, which proved an excellent tool in their preaching.[25]

Jacob ben Elijah was not content merely to present the irrational aspects of the legends about Christian saints. He recounted them in great detail, as the Christian preachers did. Previous scholarship has concentrated on the historical,

---

[19] See J. Cohen, *The Friars and the Jews*, 51–99; Chazan, *Daggers of Faith*, 33–7; Funkenstein, *Perceptions of Jewish History*, 183–96; Merhavia, *The Talmud in Christian Eyes* (Heb.), 227–360.

[20] See Nahmanides, *Vikuaḥ haramban*, 8 (ed. Chavel, 303). Nahmanides wrote that before the disputation Christiani preached in Provence and elsewhere, attempting to prove Jesus's divinity from the Talmud (see Chazan, *Barcelona and Beyond*, 26–7; J. Cohen, *The Friars and the Jews*, 108–9, 125, 127–8; id., *Living Letters of the Law*, 334–42; Shatzmiller, 'Paulus Christiani').

[21] Jacob ben Elijah cited two talmudic legends that were attacked by Christiani (*Igeret ya'akov mivenetsiah*, 12–13).

[22] See J. Cohen, *Living Letters of the Law*, 206, 216–17; Funkenstein, *Perceptions of Jewish History*, 196–8.

[23] See Chazan, *Daggers of Faith*; Saperstein, *Decoding the Rabbis*, esp. 198–207; Kreisel, Introduction (Heb.) to Moses ibn Tibbon, *The Writings of R. Moses ibn Tibbon*, esp. 57.

[24] See Almazan, 'L'Exemplum chez Vincent Ferrier', 289–91; Van Engen, 'Dominic and the Brothers'; Vose, *Dominicans, Muslims and Jews in the Medieval Crown of Aragon*, 13 n. 34.

[25] See Berlioz and Polo de Beaulieu, *Les 'Exempla' médiévaux*; Bremond, Le Goff, and Schmitt, *L'Exemplum*; Schmitt, 'Recueils franciscains d'"Exempla"', esp. 17, 20; Welter, *L'Exemplum dans la littérature religieuse et didactique du Moyen Âge*.

bibliographical, and polemical aspects of the letter and less on its literary and didactic features. However, Jacob ben Elijah's attitudes to the exempla and Christian hagiography call for a broader analysis. On the one hand, he used the exempla in a polemical context, and his intent was to show their negative aspects;[26] on the other, he was aware of their didactic potential for Christians and Jews alike, and hence he also found some good in them.

Jacob ben Elijah divided the legends into two types: stories about virtuous figures, whose examples should be followed, and 'obscure' stories that could be interpreted literally by the masses but allegorically by scholars.[27] He wanted to expose the flaws of Christiani's method, not the shortcomings of the exempla and legends themselves. He pointed out (in an approach that sounds 'modern' in its openness and sensitivity) that using Christiani's method one could impugn Christian holy scriptures and other fundamental tenets of Christian culture. All religions, not only Judaism, contain absurd and irrational elements. Jacob ben Elijah believed that the Jewish and Christian legends had much in common. The educated members of both societies, he noted, interpreted them non-literally, so that they were consistent with acceptable values. At the same time, they were cognizant of the important social role of the legends in reinforcing the faith of the common people.

Jacob ben Elijah placed special emphasis on the legends of saints and their miracles. He gave six examples: the first is set during the time of the Apostles; the second during the reign of Emperor Decius in the third century; the third involved Jerome at the beginning of the fifth century; the fourth describes the meeting between the monks Paul and Anthony at the end of the third century; and the last two deal with or involve the founders of the mendicant orders, Saints Dominic and Francis, at the beginning of the thirteenth century. Only the fourth story is out of chronological order.

Saint James of Compostela

The first legend in the letter is a story about one of the most important saints in Europe and in Spain in particular—Saint James of Compostela:

It is written in your book that one day one of your saints slept on a slab on the beach at Jaffa, and he could not stand for the wind pushed him, and he walked erect as the vulture swoops and passed serenely as he who swims spreads out his hands to swim; and

---

[26] Jacob b. Elijah, *Igeret ya'akov mivenetsiah*, 3.

[27] Ibid. 4–5, 11; see Chazan, *Barcelona and Beyond*, 142–57; see also Frimer and Schwartz, *Philosophy in the Shadow of Terror* (Heb.), 62–4; Schwartz, 'Philosophical Commentary on the Bible and the Aggadah' (Heb.).

over the water he flew with the slab, like any winged bird that flies in the air, and he went to the end of Spain, and he awakened from this sleep and descended there.[28]

The legend tells how Saint James—Jesus's twin brother according to one tradition—arrived at Compostela in Galicia in the north-western corner of Spain.[29] This was one of the central myths of the Spanish Church. The cult of Saint James attracted pilgrims from western Europe, and the miracles that he wrought along the pilgrimage routes to Compostela were famous throughout the Christian world. The legend explains how James, who was known to have preached and been martyred in the Holy Land, arrived in Spain and how his bones came to be buried there. Two answers were offered: according to the first, James's missionary journey to Spain was the result of a direct order from Jesus; according to the second, his body floated to Spain in a marble coffin, which came ashore near Compostela where it was later discovered.[30] At a certain stage, these two stories were merged in the popular consciousness. Jacob ben Elijah's version has the saint fall asleep on 'a slab' (perhaps the marble coffin) and thus being transported to Spain.

Christian pilgrimages to Compostela peaked in the thirteenth century, when Jacob ben Elijah was writing, and legends about Saint James had already appeared in guidebooks for pilgrims such as the *Liber Sancti Jacobi* in the twelfth century.[31] It is not surprising then that he was familiar with the main points of the myth and, because of its importance in Spain, chose to begin with it. Although his summary of the legend is brief, Jacob ben Elijah provided the reader with details such as the points of departure (Jaffa) and arrival ('end of Spain', Compostela) of the miraculous journey. Although in this case the details are negligible, in the stories that follow, his literary style is more elaborate.

The Seven Sleepers

The second story begins with the persecution of Christians during the reign of the Roman Emperor Decius:

[28] Jacob b. Elijah, *Igeret ya'akov mivenetsiah*, 5.

[29] On the myth of Saint James and its significance in the history of Spain, see Barkai, *Science, Magic, and Mythology in the Middle Ages* (Heb.), 85–8; Castro, *Santiago de España*; id., *The Spaniards*; Gonzalez-Lopez, 'The Myth of Saint James and Its Functional Reality'. According to the popular myth adopted by the bishopric of Compostela, James was sent by Jesus to Christianize the inhabitants of the Iberian peninsula. He returned to the Holy Land, where he died a martyr's death, but his body walked over the sea to Compostela (see also Moralejo and Lopez Alsina, *Santiago de Europa*).

[30] The 'marble coffin' (*arca marmorica*) is possibly a corruption of a detail from an apocryphal Greek source that told of the transfer of St James's body to Achaia Marmarica—Greece (see Chelini and Branthomme, *Les Chemins de Dieu*, 162).

[31] See Vielliard, *Le Guide du pèlerin de Saint Jacques de Compostelle*, pp. ix–xi; Van Herwaarden, 'The Origins of the Cult of St James of Compostela'; *The Pilgrim's Guide to Santiago de Compostela*.

It is written in the 'Book of Agonies' that Emperor Decius offered sacrifices to other gods, was from the seed of evildoers, and all of his servants were wicked. And seven men came to him to urge him to abandon his iniquity . . . and he became enraged, and, when the men saw how furious the emperor was, they became alarmed and left urgently. The king ordered that they be arrested, but they escaped from him, for they were afraid of him, and hid in a small cave where they slept for 700 years. And at the end of that time, they awoke from their sleep, and one said to the other: 'We are afraid of the emperor, but if we sit here we shall die, for how shall we get food from this rock and how will we assuage our hunger? One of us should risk his life, take care to avoid the emperor and his anger, and go slowly and innocently with the money, and then we shall live and not die.' And one of them did volunteer to go, and took all the money they had with them, and the amount was 5 dinars—The writer of these words spoke with wisdom and knowledge [and said 4 or 5 dinars], for he could not know for certain if there were 4 or 5 dinars, and he avoided speaking a direct lie—Now we shall return and complete our story. He took the money, and went to the city, where he saw the sign of his God engraved on the doors and on the corners of the altars, and all the people genuflecting to [Jesus] and kneeling at his feet, falling upon their faces and coming to him in time of trouble. And the man was greatly fearful and he said: 'Just yesterday anyone who uttered the name of my God [Christ] was persecuted like a leaf driven to and fro, and now all of the people hear what he says and heed his words.' And then he went to the market and found a woman who had bread and he bought it, taking the money from his pocket and placed it in the woman's hand, and he heard her cry out in anguish: '. . . he took out a coin which did not belong to the lord of the land'. And the servants of the bishop took him and brought him before him, and he said: 'What were you thinking . . . to take out a coin, in this place where you are now, that does not bear my name?' And the man replied: 'Here now I consent to speak to my lord. . . . I am not to blame. I did not make this coin. It was Decius who made it, and on it is his name, and yesterday I could use it to buy bread to eat and clothes to wear, with my six friends who remained in the cave, for we escaped from the emperor's wrath. . . . He ordered that we be arrested, and with bitter hearts we ran to the cave, and slept the whole night through, and we awoke in the morning, and there was light.' The bishop took the coin, and read the letters that were on it, and said: 'Be of calm mind and do not fear, arise and take us to the cave.' And the bishop went with all of the crowd, and the bishop called out to the people in the cave: 'My brethren, arise from this place and go out, peace unto you and do not be afraid.' And they went with the bishop and told him their story and everything that happened to them, and when they came to the church [*bamot*: high place for idolatrous worship], they turned into a heap of bones.[32]

This is a version of the well-known Christian story 'The Seven Sleepers', which recounts how seven Christians from Ephesus hid in a cave because of the decrees of Decius, fell asleep, and awoke after several hundred years in order to prove to Emperor Theodosius II and all the Christians the true version of the resurrection

---

[32] Jacob b. Elijah, *Igeret ya'akov mivenetsiah*, 5–7.

of Jesus. This legend was widespread throughout the Christian East, and its various versions are preserved in Syriac, Coptic, Arabic, Ethiopic, and Aramaic. It was brought to the Latin West in the sixth century by Gregory of Tours and appears in both ecclesiastical and secular Latin literature.[33] Jacob ben Elijah's Hebrew version closely resembles the one in the *Golden Legend*. The *Golden Legend* was an immediate success, so although it was completed at about the same time that he wrote *Igeret ya'akov mivenetsiah*, he may already have been familiar with it.[34] There are, however, some small differences between the two stories, and Jacob ben Elijah refers to another source, which he calls the 'Book of Agonies' (*Sefer yisurim*), apparently an ancient martyrology.[35]

Jacob ben Elijah's attitude to his Christian source is especially striking when he interrupts the story to mention the writer's uncertainty about the exact number of coins. The source he used probably said '4 or 5 dinars'. He chose—as did the *Golden Legend*—the number 5, but he found it necessary to tell his readers that his source was not certain. Expressing uncertainty about matters that were marginal to the story was often used to make the author appear more trustworthy, so readers would not question the veracity of the story as a whole.[36] It seems Jacob ben Elijah fell for it.

Jerome and the Lion

Jacob ben Elijah also found the next legend in the 'Book of Agonies'. It is about Jerome removing a thorn from a lion's paw. The Greek original involved a monk called Gerasimus,[37] but in the Latin West Jerome became the hero, probably because of the similarity of the names.

---

[33]   See Gregory of Tours, *Sufferings of the Seven Martyrs*; Heller, 'Éléments parallèles et origine de la légende des sept dormants'.

[34]   See Jacobus de Voragine, *Legenda aurea* (New York edn., 382–6). The term *legenda* was then understood as synonymous with *lectio*, which means a reading or a lesson (see Boureau, *La Légende dorée*; Reames, *The Legenda Aurea*; Ryan and Ripperger, Foreword to Jacobus de Voragine, *The Golden Legend*, pp. vii–viii); on the use of the *Golden Legend* by Christian preachers, see D'Avray, *The Preaching of the Friars*, 70–1.

[35]   A certain similarity is evident in the rhetoric of the two versions. For example, Jacob ben Elijah wrote about the martyr's wonder at the change that had taken place in Ephesus: 'Just yesterday anyone who uttered the name of my God was persecuted like a leaf driven to and fro, and now all of the people hear what he says and heed his words.' The parallel passage in the *Golden Legend* has: 'quid est, inquit, quod heri nemo Christum audebat nominare, et nunc omnes Christum confitentur' ('How is it', he asked, 'that yesterday no man dared to utter the name of Christ, and now all confesses him'?) (*Golden Legend* (Leipzig edn., 436)). The dates given in the two versions differ. In the *Golden Legend*, it is the time of Theodosius II and mention is made of the religious debates about the resurrection of the dead; Jacob ben Elijah claimed that the martyrs slept for 700 years and mentioned neither Theodosius nor the religious debates.

[36]   On this device in Ibn Daud, *Sefer hakabalah*, see G. D. Cohen, 'The Story of the Four Captives', 169–70.   [37]   See John Moschus, *Life of Abbot Gerasimus*; Kelly, *Jerome*.

In that same book, the story is told about what once happened to Jerome, who knew our language and translated the words of our prophets, from the tongue of gold and the goodly garment to stammering lips and another tongue. When he repented his sins and iniquities, he left his home and turned his face to the desert, and his brothers went with him, and he went at their head, to a land that no man had passed through and where no man lived. . . . And one day when he stood at his lodge, a lion came forth from his den, seeking prey . . . and a thorn had stuck in his paw and caused him much pain, and the lion came to Jerome, enraged and in great distress. . . . He stood before him in despair and extended his foot in pain, and Jerome removed the thorn from his foot, and he was cured. The lion was greatly pleased, his heart softened, and he thought to himself: 'I shall stay here and serve him.' . . . And Jerome had an ass grazing in the mountains, and the lion stayed in secret places, walked nearby to know whither he would go, and went in circles until the ass returned to his manger, and he was given a meal by Jerome every day. One day a caravan of merchants came over the mountains, and their asses bore clothing and all manner of precious things. And one [of their] asses fell under his burden and did not arise or move. . . . The merchant raised his eyes and saw Jerome's ass before him . . . and he took it. . . . And the lion did not hear because he lay asleep. And Jerome's servant boy went to look for the ass and could not find him; he called out to him, and he did not reply. And he went to the lion and found him asleep. . . . And he called out to the lion and said unto him: 'Awaken, why have you fallen asleep?' . . . And the lion awoke from his sleep and hastened to search for the ass and did not find him and returned to his home and was not satisfied. And Jerome said to him: 'Listen, you stony heart, in the morning you will eat straw. . . . You have done much wrong, and you will eat the food of your friend.' And the lion was ashamed and did not roar but remained silent, and went forth from his den and did not return, but went to seek the ass in the mountains, and searched in the forests. . . . And he lifted his eyes and saw the merchants coming from a far-off land. . . . He cast upon them the fierceness of his anger, like a lion roaring after his prey, and the merchants fled, leaving their animals and goods, running for their lives, and the lion led the animals back to his lodge. Jerome gathered them all to his home and the merchants came towards him and said: 'We are to blame [for taking] your ass. . . . Do as you see fit. You, our master, may even take it all.' . . . And Jerome said: '. . . For you did not fear my God, what is this deed you have done? I shall return half to you and you go back to your land, and the other half I shall take as a reward for my service [lit.: your service (see Num. 18: 31)].'[38]

This exemplum also appears, with slight differences, in the *Golden Legend*.[39] Jacob ben Elijah added his own introduction, noting that Jerome had translated the Bible into Latin and incidentally emphasizing the superiority of Hebrew. The historical background he supplied is somewhat faulty, since, according to the tradition, Jerome's conversion was not connected to his going into the desert.

[38] Jacob b. Elijah, *Igeret ya'akov mivenetsiah*, 7–9.
[39] See Jacobus de Voragine, *Legenda aurea* (New York edn., 589–91).

However, it attests to knowledge of other stories about Jerome. Jacob ben Elijah knew that Jerome was not alone in the desert, but was accompanied by several monks. He also added several details of his own, such as the merchandise carried by the merchants.

Paul and Anthony

The fourth legend describes the meeting between the first two Christian monks: Paul the Anchorite and Anthony the Great:

It is written in your books that Paul [lit.: 'Peninfio'] left his sisters and brothers and stayed in the desert … and there prepared a tabernacle. … No grass grew there, and each day a cake, the size of a small hand, fell from the heavens, a portion of food for Paul, and on the day of his death a double portion fell, and his heart melted and became as water. He stood there, troubled and wondered: 'Why is this day different from the others?' And he lifted his eyes and saw his friend [Anthony] coming, bending his knee and kneeling before him, and he was much gladdened to see him and said to him: 'Who brought you here?' And the two greeted one another, and each consoled the other, and they sat together to eat bread, and when the two had eaten, Paul's soul failed as he spoke. His friend had broken loins and limp hands and was unable to dig a grave. And a lion that had been hidden in the thicket of the forest came forth and dug the grave. And he took Paul and covered him with earth.[40]

The source of this story, which also appears in the *Golden Legend*, is Jerome's influential work, *Life of Paulus the First Hermit* (late 370s) on the fictitious Saint Paul the Anchorite.[41] Jacob ben Elijah adapted the story and wrote it in rhyme, and although there are a few differences between the Hebrew and the Latin versions, it is obvious that he knew the main details and none of them is lacking. He naturally stressed the miracles that attended the meeting: the bread falling from the sky and the lion digging Paul's grave. These were key motifs in the story and were similarly emphasized in the *Golden Legend*. Other details that appear in Jerome's version of the story were also omitted or played down in the *Golden Legend*.

Saint Dominic and the Heretics

The fifth story is about a miracle that occurred to Saint Dominic during a public disputation with the Cathars. Dominic is called the Master of the Preachers (after the formal name of the Dominicans, the Order of Preachers):

[40] Jacob b. Elijah, *Igeret ya'akov mivenetsiah*, 9.

[41] Jerome, *Life of Paulus the First Hermit*; see Jacobus de Voragine, *Legenda aurea* (New York edn., 89–90); see also Kelly, *Jerome*, 60–3; Kleinberg, *Flesh Made Word*, 151–63.

We speak about the Master of the Preachers when he was persecuting the foolish heretics and the wretched apostates. . . . And the Master of the Preachers disputed with them, he marched to battle to dissuade them from their evil ways and the abomination of their idols, spoke to them with rightful expressions and with words of reproof. And they did not heed his words, nor did they listen to his counsel. And he said to them: 'Take good counsel together. Behold here the fire and the wood, take the book of your faith in the name of your god, and we the Order of Preachers will take our book in the name of our God, and we shall throw them into the fire and see which shall prosper, either this or that, and God, who will reply in fire, is our glory and our Lord.' And the heretics answered and said: 'Let it be as you say, do whatever seems good to you.' And they took the two books and cast them into the fire, and the book of the Preachers did not remain in the fire but was swept up on the wings of the wind, and it had scarcely gone forth and the book fell intact to the ground, while the book of the heretics was burned, devoured [by the fire].[42]

Joseph Shatzmiller has shown that this refers to a miracle that reportedly happened during Saint Dominic's struggle with the Catharist heresy in Provence. According to the Cistercian monk and chronicler Pierre des Vaux de Cernay, writing in about 1213, the miracle took place in 1207 in Montreal. Dominic wrote down his arguments against heresy in a letter and gave it to the Cathars. The heretics gathered around a fire in a house to discuss it, and one of them suggested that the letter should be tested by being thrown into the fire. It was not consumed, although they repeated the test several times: each time the letter sprang into the air. Shatzmiller noted that 'a comparison between the Cistercian story and the Hebrew version reveals several disparities between the two: Jacob ben Elijah mentioned two "books", not one. He did not know about the private Cathar gathering, and believed that the miracle occurred in the presence of both parties. But they undoubtedly refer to the same event.'[43] However, as early as the thirteenth century there were several versions of this miracle, and Jacob ben Elijah apparently knew a different one. A similar miracle that occurred in Fanjeaux during a public disputation with heretics was recorded by Jordan of Saxony in *A Treatise on the Principles of the Order of Preachers* in 1233–4. In this case, three arbiters were chosen and each side gave them their book. The arbiters threw the two books on to the fire and Saint Dominic's book emerged unscathed. In the second half of the thirteenth century many believed that two different miracles had occurred, one at Montreal and the other in Fanjeaux.[44] Jacob ben Elijah does not mock this,

---

[42] Jacob b. Elijah, *Igeret ya'akov mivenetsiah*, 10.

[43] See Shatzmiller, 'The Albigensian Heresy in the Eyes of Contemporary Jews' (Heb.), 339.

[44] See Dossat, 'Le Culte de Saint Dominique à Fanjeaux en 1325'; Jacobus de Voragine, *Legenda aurea* (New York edn., 414). Dossat dated the notion of two different miracles to 1739 and attributed it to the historian A. Touron ('Le Culte de Saint Dominique à Fanjeaux en 1325', 203). However, he apparently did not notice the version in the *Golden Legend*.

the most famous of Saint Dominic's miracles. On the contrary, he uses biblical quotations to draw a parallel with Elijah's confrontation with the prophets of Baal (1 Kgs 18). He called the Cathars 'foolish heretics and wretched apostates'[45] and favourably depicted Dominic as the emissary of the 'good men', who attempted to persuade the 'bad men' to recant their erroneous views. Dominic tried to persuade the heretics to repent with rational arguments (perhaps in contrast to the Albigensian crusade), of which Jacob ben Elijah approved. Nonetheless, elsewhere in his letter, he seems to favour physically annihilating heretics.[46]

Saint Francis and the Birds

The last story describes the deeds of Saint Francis:

It is written in your books that one day the Master of the Friars Minor saw a flock of birds upon the highway. . . . Among them there was one bird, large and handsome, pleasant to the sight. And he called out and said to them: 'Hark unto me, my brothers, as I stand before you. Lift your eyes to the heavens, and give thanks to your God. For all of us have one Father, for one God has created us all, and he has given you a good part, your soul is like a watery garden. See how you fly upon the wings of the wind, you roam to all the lands and walk upon the earth, and he has clothed you with fancy clothing. Hence, you must praise and exalt his name, for he is the only one in his world.' And when they heard his words, they did not tremble nor were they stricken, but lowered their heads and spread their wings. And he said to the largest among them: 'Do you and your brothers as I have commanded you.' And they all chirped and said: 'Yes, yes.'[47]

This famous legend is found in Thomas de Celano's 'Vita prima Santi Francisci' and in *The Little Flowers of Saint Francis*, which was apparently written by an anonymous Franciscan based on the collection of Ugolino da Santa Maria and translated into Italian.[48] The story appears in an abridged version in the *Golden Legend.*[49]

The content of Francis's sermon in Jacob ben Elijah's story is very similar to that in the Christian source he used. Francis asked the birds to praise God for

---

[45] See Shatzmiller, 'The Albigensian Heresy in the Eyes of Contemporary Jews' (Heb.), 339–40.

[46] 'With what shall the cursed heretics be trampled upon and their believers put to tribute, with what shall they be annihilated, with what destroyed, with what shall they be lost, their towers overthrown, their cities made a heap forever, how shall they and their sons be burned? By the great bishops, who come to them from afar to hear their judgements' (Jacob b. Elijah, *Igeret ya'akov mivenetsiah*, 16–17).   [47] Ibid. 10–11.

[48] See Thomas of Celano, 'Vita prima Santi Francisci', 1: 21; *The Little Flowers of St. Francis*, 16 (trans. Gurney-Salter, 29–30); for a similar version of this legend, see Bonaventure, *Life of St. Francis* (trans. Gurney-Salter, 378); see also McKay, Introduction to *The Little Flowers of St. Francis*, pp. v–ix; Bequette, *The Eloquence of Sanctity*.

[49] See Jacobus de Voragine, *Legenda aurea* (New York edn., 604–6).

having given them splendid clothing,[50] and the freedom to fly everywhere.[51] The birds' reaction is also similar: they lowered their heads, spread their wings, and gladly accepted the words of Saint Francis.[52] In the Christian version of this exemplum, Francis does not address a specific bird in the flock, and the source for this may be another exemplum, in which Francis showed a particular affection for the lark.[53]

As in the other stories, Jacob ben Elijah did not fix his attention only on the conversation with the birds, the irrational and miraculous part of the story. He also described the content of the conversation in detail: Francis's words of praise for God and his sense of brotherhood with all creatures. The emphasis is on God's uniqueness and grandeur, which Jacob ben Elijah accepted, as did Francis and all Christians. In my view, the fact that he cited the legend in its entirety, without omitting the content of the conversation, shows that he identified with the ideas expressed in it, and this is consistent with his overall approach to legends—both Jewish and Christian—a readiness to accept a certain degree of irrationality for the sake of the religious and social message.

Jacob ben Elijah cited legends of saints with miraculous and irrational elements in order to show that such elements existed in Christian literature, as they did in Jewish literature. However, it is abundantly clear that he took an interest in the Christian stories themselves. The legends were told as they might have been by a Christian preacher, and there is no attempt to distort their contents or stress the negative aspects. He did not see the irrational aspects of the stories as a reason to reject them, and, as we noted, he appreciated the didactic and moral use that the Christians made of them. His polemical method was not to scorn the stories, but rather to point out that similar trends existed in Christian and Jewish society. In some instances—for example, in the legends of Dominic and Francis—he clearly agrees with the story's ideological messages.

[50] 'Fratres mei, volucres, multum debetis laudare creatorem vestrum et ipsum diligere semper, qui dedit vobis plumas ad induendum, pennas ad volandum' (Thomas of Celano, 'Vita prima Santi Francisci', 1: 21); 'Much are ye beholden to God your Creator, and always and in every place ye ought to praise Him for that He hath given you a double and a triple vesture' (*The Little Flowers of St. Francis*, 15 (trans. Gurney-Salter, 29–30)).

[51] 'He hath given you freedom to go into every place . . . but ever strive to praise God' (*The Little Flowers of St. Francis*, 15 (trans. Gurney-Salter, 30)).

[52] Ad haec aviculae illae, ut ipse dicebat et qui cum eo fuerant frates, miro modo secundum naturam suam exsultantes, coeperunt extendere collum, protendere alas, aperire os et in illum respicere' (Thomas of Celano, 'Vita prima Santi Francisci', 1: 21); 'all those birds began to open their beaks, and stretch their necks, and spread their wings, and reverently to bow their heads to the ground, showing by their gestures and songs that the holy father's words gave them greatest joy' (*The Little Flowers of St. Francis*, 15 (trans. Gurney-Salter, 30)).

[53] See *The Mirror of Perfection*, 12: 113 (trans. Gurney-Salter, 289); see Kleinberg, *Flesh Made Word*, 206–24.

Jacob ben Elijah was familiar with a number of hagiographical stories from Christian history, and this is consistent with his knowledge of general history reflected in the copious material he cited in his letter. He acquired some of this knowledge from listening to Christian sermons, but he read most of the legends of saints in Christian books, mainly in sources similar to the *Golden Legend*. He introduced the exempla into his writing in order to contend with the mendicant orders' new polemical technique, which disparaged Jewish legends. It is striking in this context that the last two stories deal with Dominic and Francis, the founders of the first two mendicant orders.

In the Middle Ages stories of saints were seen as part of ecclesiastical and universal history, and there was very little distinction made between biography and hagiography.[54] Along with tales of religious figures, such as Dominic and Francis, and kings, they were part of contemporary oral traditions.[55] An interesting attitude to these historical legends can be found in the words of Immanuel ben Jacob Bonfils, who lived in Orange and Tarascon in the mid-fourteenth century and translated the *Historia de praeliis* ('The History of the Battles', a life of Alexander the Great) into Hebrew: 'Most people believe the words [of this book], but I do not, although everything is possible.'[56]

There is no way of knowing how medieval Jewish readers reacted to the story of Dominic's confrontation with the Cathars in *Igeret ya'akov mivenetsiah*. They may have reacted with total disbelief (like Immanuel Bonfils), or, perhaps because of a negative attitude to heresy, they believed in its possibility (like the majority of readers of *Historia de praeliis*). But even if they did not believe in the miracle, the meeting between Dominic and the heretics—a description based on oral traditions[57]—remained part of their historical consciousness. Jacob ben Elijah was not exceptional in his positive attitude to the legends of Christian saints, and such attitudes were to become even more prevalent in the fifteenth century.

One of the Jewish scholars who presaged this shift was Profayt Duran. His broad knowledge of Church history went beyond a critical analysis of the New Testament and included the theological and historical literature of scholars like Peter Lombard and Vincent de Beauvais. Duran also used exempla from Church history to convey moral lessons. In the introduction to *Ma'aseh efod* (1403), he surveyed the major streams of Jewish spirituality and exposed their flaws, in particular the neglect of biblical study.[58] To promote the study of the Bible, he drew

[54] See R. D. Ray, 'Medieval Historiography', 35–8; on the *Golden Legend*, see Bietenholz, *Historia and Fabula*, 62–94.   [55] See Bremond, Le Goff, and Schmitt, *L'Exemplum*, 92.

[56] Cited in Lévy, 'La Traduction de *L'Historia de Praeliis* par Immanuel ben Jacob', 279.

[57] See Schmitt, 'La parola addomesticata'.

[58] See Baer, *A History of the Jews in Christian Spain*, ii. 474–5 n. 41; J. Cohen, 'Profiat Duran's "The Reproach of the Gentiles"'; Kozodoy, 'A Study of the Life and Works of Profiat Duran'; Rappel,

attention to its status in Christian society, especially the book of Psalms, which was central to both Jewish and Christian prayer. According to Duran, the neglect of biblical study and excessive involvement in other spiritual doctrines were responsible for all the troubles that befell the Jews in his time, including their expulsion from parts of France and Germany and the decrees of 1391 that led to the massacre of many Spanish Jews. He believed that the Jewish communities of Aragon were saved from the pogroms because they regularly recited verses from the Psalms.[59]

Profayt Duran provided the following exemplum:

A very wise and pious Christian said that when he began to study the books of philosophers, a man appeared to him in a dream, beating him cruelly. He asked him why he was beating him even though he had done no violence and there was no deceit in his mouth. The man replied that he had been commanded by the Creator to strike him and to beat him for having neglected to study the holy books and pursuing the study of books of philosophy. And he ordered him to beware, to take care not to turn his thoughts to any other study, but always to enquire into the sacred books, for that is the desire of the Almighty. Until here his speech. And he was the one who established for the Christians [lit.: Romans] the [custom] of constantly reciting the book of Psalms in their prayers and their supplications, and he made that book into a very great foundation.[60]

As Eleazar Gutwirth has shown, the dream is similar to one which Jerome related to Eustochium, in which a battle rages in Jerome's soul between classical culture, which seemed to him to be fine and superior, and Christian culture, namely the Bible, which seemed to him to be inferior.[61] He was filled with feelings of guilt, since classical culture was pagan. After a fierce struggle, Jerome swore he would eschew the classical books and persevere with his study of the Bible. It is easy to see why Duran used this dream. He wanted his readers to spend less time reading philosophy, the Talmud, and the mystical teachings of kabbalah and to concentrate on the Bible.

Duran recounted Jerome's dream without Judaizing it or adapting it to a Jewish audience. The same exemplum could have been heard in a Christian sermon, and it appears, for example, in a similar, but abridged, version in the *Golden Legend*.[62] Duran took the exemplum and achieved a twofold purpose: he praised

'Introduction to Duran's *Ma'aseh efod*' (Heb.), esp. 753–8; Talmage, 'Introduction' (Heb.) to Profayt Duran, *Polemical Writings*, 10–17.

[59] Profayt Duran, *Ma'aseh efod*, 14; Talmage, 'Keep your Sons from Scripture', 91–2.

[60] Profayt Duran, *Ma'aseh efod*, 14.

[61] See Jerome, *Letter* 22; see also Gutwirth, 'Actitudes judías hacia los cristianos en la España del siglo XV', 191–2; id., 'Religion and Social Criticism in Late Medieval Rousillon', 146–7.

[62] See Jacobus de Voragine, *Legenda aurea* (New York edn., 587–8); see also Ryan and Ripperger, Foreword to Jacobus de Voragine, *The Golden Legend*, p. vii.

an important aspect of Christian intellectual culture, bibliocentrism, and noted its popular contexts (prayer and supplication); and he criticized Jewish scholars for failing to adopt the positive approach of the Christians, using the method *a minori ad majus*—if Christians were placing so much emphasis on studying the Old Testament, how much more so should Jews? By inserting the exemplum immediately after his discussion of the decrees of 1391, Duran stressed Christian piety—particularly that of the monastic orders, for whom the reading of Psalms was an important part of their routine—and called upon Jews to emulate it. The piety of the friars was a prominent motif in Jewish–Christian polemic, and Christian disputants frequently made use of the friars' and monks' morality as proof of their religion's superiority.[63]

Jerome was well known to medieval Jews because of the centrality of his Latin translation of the Bible, known as the Vulgate, to the frequent religious polemics. Jews had to address the differences between the Hebrew scriptures and Jerome's translation, and both Profayt Duran and Isaac Nathan studied the Vulgate for purposes of interreligious debate. The differences between the two versions led Nathan to produce a Hebrew concordance, rather than simply translating the existing Latin one, and Profayt Duran devoted an entire chapter of *Shame of the Gentiles* to criticism of Jerome's translation. A different opinion however can be found in the Castilian translation of the Old Testament, the Alba Bible (1422–33): there the translator, Moses Arragel, praised Jerome's decision to use Jewish knowledge in producing the Vulgate.[64]

Drawing a parallel with Christian society in order to criticize Jewish society was a literary device frequently used by Jewish preachers and moralists in Spain and southern France. Similar positive perceptions of Christian institutions and customs can be found in Jacob Anatoli, Menahem Me'iri, Solomon Alami ibn Lahmish, Isaac Nathan, Joel ibn Shuaib, Isaac Arama, and Joseph Jabez.[65] It is unclear to what extent preachers and writers identified with the contents of the exempla and their images of Christianity and how much their intentions were simply to criticize Jewish society, but, even if this is just a literary convention, its significance should not be overlooked. Profayt Duran added a positive image of Christian biblical scholarship and religious piety to a long list of positive images of Christian culture in other areas, and the number of positive examples from Christian society and culture would have a cumulative effect on the image of Christianity in the Jewish collective memory.

---

[63] See e.g. Jacob b. Reuben, *Milḥamot hashem*, 10; Joseph Kimhi, *Sefer haberit*, 26.

[64] Isaac Nathan, *Me'ir nativ*, 1; Profayt Duran, *Kelimat hagoyim*, 12 (ed. Talmage, 64); see R. Ben-Shalom, '*Me'ir Nativ*'; Fellous, *Histoire de la Bible de Moïse Arragel*, 132–3.

[65] See R. Ben-Shalom, '*Me'ir Nativ*'; Saperstein, 'Christians and Jews'.

Abraham Zacut noted that historical knowledge about non-Jewish nations was beneficial to Jewish polemicists. He did not, however, illustrate this with a subject that was common to both religions or one that often came up in disputations between them, such as the life of Jesus. Instead, he chose to use the lives of Christian saints.

Therefore I mention some people of alien faith, who otherwise would not deserve to be mentioned, for instance, their 'saints'. Holy Scripture also mentions evildoers and heathens although they deserve no mention. This was, however, necessary because it is to our great advantage.[66]

It might be argued from the 'Introduction to the Author' that Zacut was compelled to deal with Christian saints because of the disputations. However, a very different picture emerges from the rest of *Sefer yuḥasin*. He began with Peter the Apostle—who came from Galilee, ruled as the first pope in Antioch, and was killed by order of the emperor—and Simon Magus the Samaritan, citing the Christian tradition about Simon Magus's death, which first appears in the apocryphal *Acts of Peter*. According to the tradition, Simon Magus used his magical powers to fly, so that everyone would acknowledge his divinity, but Peter's prayers caused him to fall to his death. Zacut also explained the term 'simony', the purchase of sacred things, after the magician Simon the Samaritan, who appears in the New Testament, and mentioned that Simon was later identified with Simon Magus, Peter's rival.[67]

Zacut mentioned Augustine's conversion to Christianity under Ambrose's influence several times, which may have been an indirect correction of Shimon ben Tsemah Duran's version in which Augustine was a disciple of Gregory I.[68] He also mentioned that Jerome translated the Old Testament into Latin—having learnt Hebrew from a Jew in Jerusalem at night, since at the time the Jews had bound themselves not to teach Hebrew to non-Jews—died at the age of 98 (actually 78) and was buried in Bethlehem, and that he wrote other books. Jerome himself mentioned his nocturnal studies in Jerusalem and the fears of Bar Hanina, the Jew who taught him. In *Shame of the Gentiles* Profayt Duran also mentioned Jews helping Jerome, adding that they were boors, who together with Jerome filled the Latin translation with errors. Zacut also noted Jerome's views on synchronizing secular and Christian history several times.[69]

[66] Zacut, *Sefer yuḥasin* (ed. Filipowski, 231a).

[67] Ibid. 244a–b; for the story in the New Testament, see Acts 8: 18–19; see also Figueras, 'Simon Magus' (Heb.); Roberts, 'Simon Magus'.

[68] Shimon b. Tsemah Duran, *Keshet umagen*, 40; Zacut, *Sefer yuḥasin* (ed. Filipowski, 248a; see also 232a–b, 234a, 248a).

[69] Zacut, *Sefer yuḥasin* (ed. Filipowski, 246b–247a, 236a; see also 232a); Jerome, *Letter* 84, 123.

Zacut also mentioned the Christianization of Egypt by monks and wrote about Joachim of Fiore, Saints Francis and Dominic, and the establishment of the mendicant orders.[70] He briefly commented on Vincent Ferrer's sermons against the Jews and noted the date on which he was canonized.[71] He mentioned Christian theologians, writers, and philosophers, such as Boethius, Gregory I, Albert the Great, Thomas Aquinas, Nicholas of Lyre, and Petrarch,[72] and took a special interest in Isidore of Seville, whom he greatly admired for his works in diverse fields (astrology, theology, cosmography, historiography), but primarily because of his astrological predictions, which came true more than 900 years later. A lot of the historical information in *Sefer yuḥasin* is taken from Isidore. Zacut also described some miracles that occurred to Christians and the feast days associated with them, such as the feast of the archangel Michael celebrated on 29 September to mark his appearance on a mountain in Apulia.[73] Along with his interest in Christian saints, Zacut was also curious about the veneration of relics. He described the discoveries of the clothing Mary prepared for Jesus, the spear with which the Roman soldier stabbed Jesus on the cross, and John the Baptist's ashes.[74]

All these references to Christian saints, Christian feasts, the veneration of relics, popes, and the history of the Church confute Zacut's claim that he dealt with these subjects solely for polemical purposes: not one of them is connected to interreligious dispute. As mentioned in Chapter 1, this claim should be understood as a justification to Jews with negative views of historiography. The parallel that Zacut drew between the 'evil men' mentioned in the Torah and the Christian saints mentioned in his book is not maintained as he did not depict the Christian saints as evil. He described what happened to them just as any Christian historiographer would have. He used the expression 'the Christians said' several times, but that was what was expected of a Jewish historiographer. It would have done his book no harm if he had omitted all those events, and it seems the only reason he included them was that they were part of general history. The only conclusion is that, in most cases, Zacut discussed the history of Christianity out of personal interest.

[70] 'Moosis, a monk in Egypt in the year 76 brought many Egyptians to Christianity' (Zacut, *Sefer yuḥasin* (ed. Filipowski, 246*b*)). On 'Moosis', the abbot mentioned by John Cassian in his *Conferences*, see Markus, *The End of Ancient Christianity*, 183. 'Then, the monk Joachim wrote *Foklis Apokalypse*, an abbreviated book of visions of John the Evangelist' (Zacut, *Sefer yuḥasin* (ed. Freiman, p. xlvi)). The reference is probably to Joachim of Fiore's *On Revelation* (see Reeves, *Joachim of Fiore*, 17). 'In 405 saints Francis of Italy and Dominic of Spain established Christian monasteries' (Zacut, *Sefer yuḥasin* (ed. Filipowski, 248*b*)).

[71] Zacut, *Sefer yuḥasin* (ed. Freiman, p. xlvi).

[72] Ibid. (ed. Filipowski, 247*a*; ed. Freiman, pp. xxxix, xlv–xlvi).

[73] Ibid. (ed. Filipowski, 249*a*; ed. Freiman, p. xli); see Jacobus de Voragine, *Legenda aurea* (New York edn., 578–80).   [74] Zacut, *Sefer yuḥasin* (ed. Freiman, pp. xxxiv–xliii).

THE PAPACY

One of the Jews' major interests in the Church was the institution of the papacy. They were particularly interested in periods of tension in the Church, such as the Western Schism.[75] Historical and political sensitivity was at its height, and Jews often took advantage of the split in the Christian world for polemical and ideological purposes. This tendency is evident, for example, in the polemical works of Profayt Duran and Hasdai Crescas, as well as those of Abraham Zacut.[76]

Isaac Nathan discussed the Western Schism in *Me'amets koah* and extracted moral lessons from the dramatic political and religious events that occurred. He claimed that Gerónimo de Santa Fe and Vincent Ferrer failed in their attempts to instil faith in the Christian messiah into the hearts of Jews and Conversos because of their treachery.[77] In order to do so, he explained the schism as the historical background to events in Aragon during and after the Disputation of Tortosa.

After the death of the antipope Clement VII in 1394, the Council of Cardinals decided not to elect a new pope until they had all sworn that the one elected would make every effort to bring about the unification of the Church. In the oath, they undertook not to oppose any solution to the schism proposed by the council. It was explicitly stated that the pope had to accept any decision of the council, even if it required him to relinquish the papacy. However, the elected pope, Pedro de Luna (antipope Benedict XIII), did not attach much importance to his commitment or his oath as a cardinal, and when the Council of Cardinals demanded that he abdicate, he refused but had to flee to Aragon. He continued to argue that he was the true pope even after another Avignon pope was elected at the Council of Pisa in 1409 and after the reunification of the Avignon and Roman papacies at the Council of Constance in 1417. As a result, during the Disputation of Tortosa in 1413–14, the pope, the leader of the Christian world, was in Aragon.[78] Isaac Nathan explained all this and the reasons why Benedict had fled:

Here is what my ears have heard and my eyes have seen, in the year 5165, the sixth millennium after the Creation, a new king arose in Aragon and Catalonia and Roussillon and Spain, and the 'pope of the moon' [Pedro de Luna] was there. He fled there because all or most of the kings of the land did not believe in him, for he despised his oath and broke the covenant that he had entered into with the council, swearing he would leave

---

[75] From 1378 to 1417 there were two 'popes', one in Rome and one in Avignon in France. The Avignon popes were considered illegitimate and referred to as 'antipopes'.

[76] See Profayt Duran, *Kelimat hagoyim*, 5, 8, 4 (ed. Talmage, 30, 45, 26); Talmage, notes (Heb.) to Profayt Duran, *Polemical Writings*, 26 n. 8; Crescas, *Sefer bitul ikarei hanotserim*, 8 (ed. Lasker, 76).

[77] See R. Ben-Shalom, 'The Social Context of Apostasy among Fifteenth-Century Spanish Jewry', 187–91; id., 'The Tortosa Disputation' (Heb.), 22–3, 45.

[78] See R. Ben-Shalom, 'The Tortosa Disputation', 23.

the papacy, so long as it transpired that the election of the pope who preceded him was not legal and not in keeping with the written customs.[79]

The details of the later stages of the schism and the proposals for unifying the Church were well known outside the universities, the Church, and the government. Supposedly, Jews were not involved, but they were cognizant of the social and religious crisis in the Christian world.

Isaac Nathan connected the kings' withdrawal of their support from Benedict with the circumstances of his election. He described the commitment that the cardinals had undertaken and Benedict's violation of it and explained that the cardinals decided to depose Benedict because of doubts about whether the election of his predecessor, Clement VII, was legitimate, since Urban VI had been elected pope in Rome a few months earlier. However, he was mistaken: in 1395 the University of Paris and the cardinals of France demanded that Benedict abdicate without making any reference to the legitimacy or otherwise of Clement, the university suggesting that both Benedict and Urban should resign. The Council of Pisa also denied Benedict's legitimacy without referring to his predecessor: it decided that Benedict was guilty of heresy. Despite this, Isaac Nathan's understanding of events was correct. The main point of the controversy was the legitimacy of Clement VII, but political motives precluded its being placed at the centre of the conciliar discussion. The connections that Nathan made between Benedict's standing in the Christian world, the changes in the monarchy in Aragon, and the Disputation of Tortosa attest to a correct historical understanding of the events. The disputation was an attempt by Benedict to regain support.[80]

Isaac Nathan also discussed the reasons that lead to treachery. The first he noted was the aspiration for 'authority and government, wealth and honour',[81] which he illustrated with an additional exemplum:

We have also seen one of the deputies elected pope over all his peers, for he abstained for twenty-five years from wine and all human pleasures and led a life of abstinence and extreme asceticism: none was like him. And the day after his election, one of his admirers purchased a large fish, known as a lamprey for 30 florins, one of the most valued, to celebrate his election and ordered that it be prepared in the best manner. And he brought it before him, and [the pope] ate from it to the full and imbibed the spiced wine like all men who enjoy pleasure. And his confessor saw it and ordered his servant to take it away, and [the servant] tried to take it, but [the pope] did not let him. And after [the pope] ate and drank, his confessor rebuked him and said: 'For twenty-five years I have

---

[79] See R. Ben-Shalom, 'The Tortosa Disputation', 43.

[80] See ibid. 21–3; on views of the pope in conciliar circles, see Tierney, *Foundations of the Conciliar Theory*, esp. 1–20, 157–247.

[81] MS Guenzburg 113/1 (Russian State Library, Moscow—Institute of Microfilmed Hebrew Manuscripts, no. 6793), fo. 77*b*.

been in your house, I have served you, I have grown accustomed to all your ways, your chastity and abstinence, and you always had less than enough. And now you have sunk into the deep mire of the pleasure from this fish, and you have eaten and been satisfied like one of the gluttonous vulgar men. You ought to have forbidden yourself [this fish] for it fills you with much blood.[82] But perhaps the man who acquired it for you was to blame; perhaps he was compelled by your honour and his desire to serve and to find favour in your eyes.' And his reply was: 'For twenty-five years I have tried to catch that fish, and now it has come into my hands. How I have yearned for it. How could I leave it before I had filled my belly with its delicate taste and satisfied all the cravings of my heart and soul for the long time I abstained from it?' And the confessor was a blameless, upright, and truly God-fearing man, and he understood the way [of the pope], so he left him and went away from him.[83]

In the Christian tradition the fish is a symbol of Jesus,[84] and in this exemplum the expensive, tasty lamprey is a metaphor for the position of pope. The story criticizes the hypocrisy of men in positions of authority in Christian society. Criticism of monks was not unusual in medieval Christian literature,[85] and the motif of devouring a fish as a parable for monastic hypocrisy was well known. It appeared, for example, in the song of one of the wandering minstrels of the twelfth century.

> Now the monk has come to the bishop's palace
> pale and thin from fasting
> but soon, with hardworking screech of teeth,
> is devouring six large pieces of fish
> consuming at dinner a huge pike.[86]

Although the pope and his confessor are not named in Isaac Nathan's story, placing this exemplum immediately after the one about Benedict XIII makes it likely that he is the one meant: Pedro de Luna was highly esteemed by Pope Gregory XI for his wisdom and strict, moral lifestyle, which was why he made him a cardinal.[87] Vincent Ferrer, who was Pedro de Luna's confessor after he became antipope Benedict, left him and went on a preaching mission in November 1399, twenty-five years after Pedro de Luna became a cardinal.[88]

---

[82] Gluttony is one of the seven deadly sins.

[83] MS Guenzburg 113/1, fos. 77*b*–78*a*.

[84] See 'Poisson', in Chevalier and Gheerbrant, *Dictionnaire des Symboles*, 774; Whittick, *Symbols, Signs, and Their Meaning*, 183–5. The initials of Iesus Christus Theou Uios Soter (Jesus Christ, son of God, saviour) form the Greek word *ichthus*, 'fish'.

[85] See e.g. Boutet and Struble, *Littérature, politique et société dans la France du Moyen Âge*, 200–3; Lawrence, *The Friars*, 152–65; Szittya, *The Antifraternal Tradition in Medieval Literature*.

[86] 'Or est venuz li monies ad episcopium / pallidus et macer propter ieiunium / sed mox assiduo stridore dentium / sex frustra devorans magnorum piscium / in cena consumens ingentem lucium' (see Dobiache-Rojdestvensky, *Les Poésies des goliards*, 114; Erasmus, *In Praise of Folly*, 79).

[87] See Flick, *The Decline of the Medieval Church*, i. 273, 274.

[88] See R. Ben-Shalom, 'The Tortosa Disputation' (Heb.), 36.

Contemporary readers, endlessly fed propaganda by both opponents and supporters of the pope, knew very well how many years after Pedro de Luna's appointment as cardinal Vincent Ferrer left,[89] and—unlike readers of later periods—would have realized at once who was meant. Ferrer's charisma and the respect he enjoyed throughout Europe provided valuable political support for Benedict, who tried to prevent him leaving. Although Ferrer claimed that he left Avignon because of a revelation in which God told him to go on a preaching tour,[90] the fact that he left shortly after the king of France withdrew his support (July 1398) must also have made a strong impression on the public. Even if Ferrer personally continued to support Benedict, the opposition party probably exploited his departure and circulated their own interpretation of it.

However, the assumption that this was a piece of propaganda aimed at Benedict XIII raises certain difficulties: no Christian source for this has been found; Vincent Ferrer and Pedro de Luna met in 1377, when Ferrer went to study in Toulouse, two years after de Luna was appointed cardinal, and they parted ways in 1394, six years after Benedict was elected pope, so de Luna and Ferrer were closely associated for less than twenty-five years. Nevertheless, the purpose of the story is not accuracy in every historical detail: its moral and political lessons are much more important. In any case, even if the exemplum dealt with other characters, it would still provide evidence of Isaac Nathan's interest in the institution of the papacy and his know-ledge of the close relationship between the pope and his confessor and of the life-style of the popes. His residence in Arles, near the papal palace at Avignon, certainly made it easy for him to obtain historical information, propaganda, and gossip.

Another story in *Me'amets koah* describes a pietist movement that swept western Europe led by a Christian monk whom the masses regarded as a saint and who was burned at the stake in Rome by order of Pope Martin V. The story includes historical details such as the countries through which the monk passed, and, although his name is not mentioned, he can be identified as the Carmelite friar, Thomas Connecte, Vincent Ferrer's 'successor', who conducted preaching tours of France, Flanders, and Italy.[91]

---

[89] See R. Ben-Shalom, 'The Tortosa Disputation' (Heb.), 24; Sabine, *A History of Political Theory*, 294–8. There is a parallel example in the counter-propaganda organized by Benedict's party. In 1411 Boniface Ferrer, Vincent's brother, wrote a denunciation that contained an exemplum describing the relationships between Pope Clement VII and a priest holding a high office in the Church. As in the exemplum in *Me'amets koah*, the high-ranking priest strongly censured the pope for his ambition, hypocrisy, and greed. Ferrer deliberately left out the name of the priest, but it was clear to everyone that he was referring to Pierre d'Ailly, who after the Council of Pisa decided to leave Benedict XIII and join the other side (see Guenée, *Entre l'église et l'état*, 212–13 and the exemplum there, 226–9, 270–3).   [90] See Montagnes, 'Saint Vincent Ferrier devant le schisme'.
[91] R. Ben-Shalom, 'A Minority Looks at the Mendicants'. Connecte was actually burned on the orders of Eugenius IV.

History of the Church 171

Me'amets koaḥ reveals that Isaac Nathan followed events in Christian society closely and understood the historical and political processes behind them. In this he was part of a broader phenomenon—one which is not reflected in the major genres like halakhah (including legal codes and responsa literature), philosophy, or kabbalah, which had no room for mundane matters or historical discussions— but which appears in, for example, books of ethics and sermons. Isaac Nathan, a Jewish leader in Provence, active in education and religious polemic, believed that Jews should know the history of the Christians and thought that it would be of interest to a large Jewish readership.

As we saw earlier, Abraham Zacut also took an interest in the history of the Church, and *Sefer yuḥasin* contains discussions of the various schisms and information about the popes involved.[92] Although Zacut's claim that he was dealing with the subject for polemical reasons is not credible, he did include negative and ludicrous images of the papacy. One is a story about a hideous bear-like child resulting from a relationship between a pope and his niece:

A boy with hair and claws as large as a bear's was born. And the woman who gave birth to him from the pope was the daughter of the brother of the pope, and because of this disgrace, he cut out and erased all the images of bears that were in his home and on his family's coat of arms.[93]

Zacut was probably alluding to Nicholas III, a member of the Orsini family, who was pope from 1277 to 1280. There were two bears on the Orsini coat of arms, but there was none on Nicholas's.[94] Although the original source of this story appears to be lost, it may have been part of the propaganda against Nicholas (and the Orsinis) circulated by their long-time rivals, the Colonna family or by the pro-French party that contended with the Orsinis to elect the new pope after Nicholas's death.[95] Zacut did not draw out the implications of the story, but left it to the reader's own judgement; however, as far as he was concerned, the story was historically true in every detail.

Zacut also repeated the famous legend of the female pope:

In 858 of the Christian era, there was a woman from England who studied philosophy in Athens. She came to Rome disguised as a man and became pope for two years and five months. She became pregnant by her major-domo, gave birth in the marketplace as she

[92] Zacut, *Sefer yuḥasin* (ed. Filipowski, 244a, 244b, 246a; ed. Freiman, pp. xlv, xlvi, xlvii, xlix).
[93] Ibid. (ed. Freiman, p. xlv). [94] See Bertucci, 'Orsini', 929–30; Weber, 'Nicholas III'.
[95] See Kirsch, 'Orsini', esp. 325–6. The story may have referred to two cardinals of the Orsini family who were opposed to the pro-France party, Matteo Rosso and Giordano Orsini. They were arrested at the Council of Cardinals and held in custody.

walked away from home, and then died. Hence they have the law of grasping the testicles of a [newly elected] pope to see if he is a man. ⟨Her name was Joan.⟩[96]

Zacut's story is the first Hebrew version of the legend of Pope Joan. The polemical nature of this story seems to be clearer than the previous one. Joan's disguise and the discovery of the deception (after she conceived, gave birth, and died) make the papacy look ludicrous. In particular, the reader might be amused by the custom supposedly adopted by the Christians to examine the manhood of each new pope.

The legend of Pope Joan was accepted as historical fact by Christians. It was first written down in the middle of the thirteenth century by the Dominicans Jean de Mailly and Stephen de Bourbon.[97] Another version was very widely disseminated, as it was interpolated into Martin of Opava's *Chronicle of Popes and Emperors*, written at the request of Clement IV, who was pope from 1265 to 1268. It was translated into many languages and used to instruct novices.[98] In the Middle Ages historical truth was not only judged on content or plausibility, but also on the authority of the writer. When the writer was commissioned by the papacy, no one doubted the accuracy of the work.[99]

The legend of Pope Joan appears in the *Chronicle of Popes and Emperors* between Leo IV, pope from 847 to 855, and Benedict III, pope from 855 to 857. A comparison of the legend in the *Chronicle of Popes and Emperors*[100] and *Sefer yuḥasin* reveals many similarities: her name (Joan),[101] her country of origin (England),[102] where she studied (Athens), the length of her time in the papal

[96] Zacut, *Sefer yuḥasin* (ed. Freiman, pp. xl–xli). The words in angle brackets are from the version in *Sefer yuḥasin* (ed. Filipowski, 249a).

[97] See Boureau, *La Pappesse Jeanne*; Pardoe and Pardoe, *The Female Pope*, 16; Von Dollinger, *Fables Respecting the Popes of the Middle Ages*, 13–14. Some scholars assume that the mendicants invented and spread the story in reaction to what they regarded as deliberate harassment by several popes (including Innocent IV) (see Pardoe and Pardoe, *The Female Pope*, 59; Von Dollinger, *Fables Respecting the Popes of the Middle Ages*, 29–30).

[98] About thirty years after Martin of Opava's death, the interpolation was found in most of the manuscripts of the chronicle. A few initial doubts about the story's authenticity were heard in the second half of the fifteenth century (see Von Dollinger, *Fables Respecting the Popes of the Middle Ages*, 64; Guenée, *Histoire et culture historique dans l'Occident médiéval*, 35, 56, 249, 282, 292, and bibliographical references, 433, 1276–9).

[99] Ibid. 133–6; Pardoe and Pardoe, *The Female Pope*, 22; Von Dollinger, *Fables Respecting the Popes of the Middle Ages*, 19–20.   [100] Martin of Opava, *Chronicle of Popes and Emperors*, 428–9.

[101] Martin of Opava called her John. Apparently Boccaccio was the first to give her a feminine name, but it was Giliberta. The name Joan was used only towards the end of the fifteenth century and first appeared in manuscripts of the *Chronicle of Popes and Emperors* at that time (see Pardoe and Pardoe, *The Female Pope*, 23–6).

[102] Many believed that the epithet *Anglicus* denoted Joan's English origin, although Martin of Opava wrote 'John English, who was born in Mainz' (see Pardoe and Pardoe, *The Female Pope*, 19–21, 34–5).

office (two years and five months), the identity of the man who made her pregnant (her major-domo),[103] where she gave birth (the marketplace),[104] and her death in childbirth. Although the *Chronicle of Popes and Emperors* was probably not the direct source for *Sefer yuḥasin*,[105] it is clear that Zacut condensed a similar version.

The main difference is the test of manhood that every newly elected pope had to undergo according to *Sefer yuḥasin*. Although this might seem to have a polemical purpose, it is not the case. The addition originated in a tradition about a hollow-bottomed porphyry chair, used to examine the pope's genitalia, which was part of many Christian traditions about Pope Joan circulating in the second half of the fifteenth century.[106] It is mentioned by Bartolomeo Platina, who was in charge of the Vatican library from 1471 to 1484, Felix Haemmerlein in around 1490, and Hartmannus Schedel in 1493.[107] Zacut's description is faithful to the Christian tradition in nearly every detail, and he made no attempt to use the story to denigrate the papacy, as later Protestant writers did, or to embellish it, as some other Christian writers did.[108]

As well as the stories of the adulterous pope and the female pope, there is also polemical potential in the legend of the discovery of the holy cross. I discussed Zacut's version of this in Chapter 3 and showed how he subtly changed his sources to disparage Christianity.[109] Although there are images in *Sefer yuḥasin* whose purpose is to undermine Christianity's self-image, Zacut mostly remains faithful to his Christian sources. Compared with other Jewish polemical literature, these

---

[103] The first version reads: 'Sed in papatu per suum familiarem impregnatur'; the second: 'Tandem tamen fragilitate feminea devicta a quodam dyacono secretario suo impregnata est' (Martin of Opava, *Chronicle of Popes and Emperors*, 428). *Secretario* could be interpreted as 'major-domo'. Some have interpreted *familiaris* as a reference to an old lover of Joan's (see Pardoe and Pardoe, *The Female Pope*, 26).

[104] In Martin of Opava, *Chronicle of Popes and Emperors*, 428, the exact location is given—on the way from St Peter's to the Lateran between the Colosseum and the Church of St Clemens. However, both of these were busy public spaces.

[105] For example, the date found in Zacut, 858 CE, is not in *Chronicle of Popes and Emperors*.

[106] See Bietenholz, *Historia and Fabula*, 101; Boureau, *La Pappesse Jeanne*, 16–82; Pardoe and Pardoe, *The Female Pope*, 31–3; Von Dollinger, *Fables Respecting the Popes of the Middle Ages*, 47–53. The source of the legend about the use of the hollow-bottomed porphyry chair (which the pope did in fact possess) is the 'visions' of the Dominican Robert d'Usez (*c.*1291).

[107] Bietenholz, *Historia and Fabula*, 101; Pardoe and Pardoe, *The Female Pope*, 31–3.

[108] See Pardoe and Pardoe, *The Female Pope*, 64–71. Felix Haemmerlein, for example, described in his *De nobilitate et rusticitate dialogus* (around 1490) how the junior cleric who ascertained that the new pope was a man yelled loudly, 'He has testicles!', and all of the priests in the audience replied, 'Bless the Lord!' (cited ibid. 33).

[109] Zacut, *Sefer yuḥasin* (ed. Filipowski, 246*a*); see also Funkenstein, *Perceptions of Jewish History*, 32–40.

images are very mild and lack any sharp invective or malicious distortion.[110] The mildness of Zacut's polemic is striking in his comments about the theological debates between the Catholic Church and the Greek Orthodox Church, such as whether the communion wafer should be leavened (the Greek position) or unleavened (the Catholic position);[111] or the source of the Holy Spirit: 'that the Greeks said emanated from the Father, not the Son, while the Catholics said he was from both'. Zacut added: 'Blessed are we, Israel, as we have only one God, who created us.'[112] The stories about the adulterous pope and the discovery of the holy cross are, then, exceptions that prove the rule. Zacut did not deal with the history of the Church for polemical purposes, but out of cultural and historical interest. His book does have a polemical purpose, but it was not his sole or even his main motive for writing.

Scholars not only discussed popes and events connected with them out of historical or cultural interest or for polemical purposes. Some were motivated by apocalyptical or messianic beliefs. For example, Isaac Abravanel discussed the papacy from its beginning, when Peter, the first pope, was engaged in teaching the Christian population in Rome after the destruction of the Temple.[113] Until the reign of Constantine, Roman emperors persecuted Christians: many were killed, and popes were forced to hide in grottos and caves. Only after Constantine donated the city to Sylvester was the papacy established in Rome.[114] Abravanel called the papal palace a 'palace of strangers' (Isa. 25: 2), because the pope was usually not from Rome, and most of the cardinals came from elsewhere in the Christian world.[115] He wrote disparagingly about the idea that the pope was infallible and noted that the pope determined the rules of behaviour for all Christians through the threat of excommunication and indulgences. According to Abravanel, the pope fulfilled the prophecy from the book of Daniel of the little horn whose eyes were like the eyes of man and whose mouth spoke arrogantly (Dan. 7: 8),[116] and he anticipated the imminent coming of the messiah and the destruction of Rome because it was the seat of the pope and the cardinals.[117]

---

[110] See e.g. A. S. Abulafia, 'Invectives against Christianity in the Hebrew Chronicles of the First Crusade'; Official, *Sefer yosef hamekane*; Rosenthal, Introduction, ibid. 28; Mülhausen, *Sefer nitsahon*.

[111] Zacut, *Sefer yuhasin* (ed. Freiman, p. xlvii).

[112] Ibid. This debate led to the schism between the Catholic Church and the Greek Orthodox Church.

[113] Abravanel, *Ma'ayenei hayeshuah*, 8: 5 (Jerusalem edn., 336).

[114] See ibid. (Jerusalem edn., 337); on the Donation of Constantine, see Chapter 3 above.

[115] Abravanel, *Mashmia yeshuah*, 3: 5 (Jerusalem edn., 453).

[116] Abravanel, *Ma'ayenei hayeshuah*, 8: 5 (Jerusalem edn., 338).

[117] Abravanel on Isa. 34: 6–14 (*Perush al nevi'im aharonim*, 167–8).

Another tradition about the pope was included in a Jewish sermon written around 1425.[118] The anonymous author described a miracle which led to a simple, humble Christian being elected pope instead of another, who had already been appointed but was less worthy.[119] The exact source of the story is unknown, but according to Marc Saperstein it is connected to the legend of the election of Pope Gregory I in the *Gesta Romanorum*.[120] In the sermon, the preacher contrasted Moses' modesty with the arrogance of Pharaoh: Moses' good traits were the cause of his ascent; Pharaoh's arrogance the cause of his downfall.[121] He also used Christian humility, which the pope often cited, as a model to teach the Jews of the diaspora how they should live and which, if adopted, would lead to the downfall of Rome.

Isaac Nathan also used exempla about popes to provide moral lessons. He stressed humility and modesty as the supreme values in Christian society and demonstrated the dangers of treachery and hypocrisy. In *Me'amets koaḥ*, Benedict XIII is depicted as a treacherous pope who broke his oath and, hence, was deprived of political support and forced to flee Avignon. There is no explicit criticism of the institution of the papacy itself; on the contrary, it seems that Isaac Nathan's depiction of Benedict's poor behaviour was meant to contrast with an overall positive perception of the papacy. Such a positive view appears in the story about the wandering preacher, Thomas Connecte: the pope was the only one who perceived Connecte's corruption. Connecte's death at the stake symbolized the victory of reason, morality, public order, and responsibility over charismatic, popular outbursts, which were often accompanied by a breakdown of the social framework. The pope's appearance in such examples reflects his important place in Jewish historical consciousness, since there would be no point in writing an exemplum about someone its readers had no respect for.

Many historical traditions about popes—legendary and authentic—were introduced into Jewish sermons, ethical treatises, polemics, and chronicles. The various discussions of the papacy were closely tied to its image in Jewish historical consciousness during the Middle Ages. The papacy was generally perceived as a protective institution that countered many of the destructive forces in Christian society, such as the masses of common people and the monastic orders. For many,

[118] See Saperstein, *Jewish Preaching*, 97–8; MS 1022.1/3 (Cambridge University Library—Institute of Microfilmed Hebrew Manuscripts, no. 17029), fos. 57*b*, 73, 87*b*.

[119] MS 1022.1/3, fos. 171*b*–172*a*.

[120] See Saperstein, *Jewish Preaching*, 98 n. 16; id., 'Stories in Jewish Sermons', 103.

[121] Pharaoh's downfall also served as a prefiguration of the downfall of Edom in the future messianic era (see Saperstein, *Jewish Preaching*, 98 n. 16; id., 'Stories in Jewish Sermons', 103).

the pope symbolized social order in western Europe, a social order which included Jews and protected their lives and property.[122]

[122] See Stow, *The '1007 Anonymous' and Papal Sovereignty*, 21–4; see also id., 'The Attitude of the Jews to the Papacy' (Heb.). From the regulations of the conference of Jewish communities in Barcelona, in 1354, it appears that in the kingdom of Aragon, the pope was regarded as the person who could best protect the Jews from outbreaks of mob violence (see Baer, *A History of the Jews in Christian Spain*, ii. 27). On the Sephardi version of the Ashkenazi legend of the Jewish Pope and its roots in the theme of the Jewish convert as subversive, see R. Ben-Shalom, 'The Converso as Subversive'.

CHAPTER FIVE

History of the Iberian Monarchies

T HE KINGDOMS OF the Iberian peninsula, Castile and Aragon in particular, loomed large in Jewish historical consciousness. In *Megilat hamegaleh*,
Abraham bar Hiyya devoted a major part of his astrological-political analysis of
human history to the rise of Islam and its struggles against Christianity including
the Crusades and the Reconquest of Iberia. Abraham bar Hiyya was the first Jew
in Christian Spain to write about any events in the history of Spain. He began by
describing the decline of the Umayyad empire following the Abbasid revolt (750
CE) which reduced Ummayad territory to Al-Andalus and noted a series of events
that occurred in Spain: the establishment of the caliphate of Cordova by the surviving Umayyads; the liquidation of the Umayyad dynasty (the poisoning of Abd
al-Malik by his brother Abd a-Rahman in 1008 and the execution of Abd a-
Rahman in 1009); the rise of the principalities (*taifa*s) (1031); the emergence of the
Almoravid dynasty (1094); and the wars in the early twelfth century between the
Christian kingdoms and the Almoravids (the conquests of Alfonso I the Battler
of Aragon, who took Tudela in 1115 and Saragossa in 1118).[1]

According to Abraham bar Hiyya, Iberia had no major role to play at the End
of Days, but he linked the local tension between Christianity and Islam with
events in the more important arena of the Land of Israel, which he interpreted as
part of a process directed by God that would transform the entire world into the
'Land of Israel' and allow the Jews of the diaspora to inherit the lands of non-
Jews.[2]

Abraham ibn Daud was one of the first Spanish Jews to take much interest in
local history, and Salo Baron acknowledged his important contribution to Jewish
historiography. Baron stressed in particular Ibn Daud's *History of Rome*, in which
he wrote about the invasion of Spain by barbarian tribes during the reign of
Emperor Honorius and noted that the country, which was previously called
Hispania, was given the name Andalus by the Vandals. He also mentioned the

---

[1] Abraham bar Hiyya, *Megilat hamegaleh*, 5: 142–3; see also 4: 97–100.

[2] Abraham bar Hiyya thought the End of Days would begin with a war in the Land of Israel in
1129 (ibid. 5: 144, 146); see also Abraham ibn Ezra, 'Visions of Rabbi Abraham ibn Ezra' (Heb.),
116–17.

great men of the Spanish Church, Isidore and Leander, as well as Pope Gregory I, 'the great philosopher', in his discussion of Muhammad.[3]

In the *History of Rome*, Ibn Daud tried to explain how Christianity spread to the Iberian peninsula and to elucidate the historical process that induced the barbarian tribes to accept the new religion. He surveyed the history of Rome from its foundation to the period of the Christian emperors: the last chapter deals entirely with Spain.

And Emperor Andres [Honorius] reigned in his place for six years and died, and during his reign the sons of Uz who are the Goths entered Spain. There were three groups: the Vandals, the Alans, and the Suevi, and Spain was called Andalus after the Vandals. And they seized the whole land of Spain from a people known as Hispan: the land was called Hispania after them. They were the descendants of Tubal, son of Japheth, and the sons of Uz defeated and killed them and settled in their place, but did not defeat the inhabitants of the land of Navarra, who are called Basques, and who to this very day have refuge in their own land. And then Roderic, the king of the Suevi [*recte* Uz, the Goths], grew stronger and slew all the kings of the Vandals and the Alans, and seized Barcelona and Saragossa from them, up to Lerida and Cordova and Seville and Toledo and Merida and Astorga. Up to the River Rhone, he conquered everything while he was still an idol worshipper. And Andres, the king of Rome, died and was succeeded by Todos [Theodosius II], who reigned for ten years and married [a daughter of] the king of Uz. And war ceased between them, for the king of Uz was stronger, and he conquered all of the land of Rome from the Romans until he married [a daughter of] King Todos. . . . And none of the kings of Uz followed the doctrine of Edom, until the reign of Reccared. He upheld that religion and killed whoever did not obey it, until everyone, great and small, had converted to the doctrine of Edom. And the doctrine of Edom held sway throughout the land of Spain as it did in the land of Rome and Italy and the rest of the lands of the sons of Japheth.[4]

Although this historical survey contains a number of errors, it provides a general picture of the history of the barbarian peoples in Spain.[5] However, the ideological and literary motif that links the events in Spain is the barbarians' acceptance of Christianity. Ibn Daud knew nothing about the Arian period in Visigothic history. He wrote that the great conqueror Roderic (probably Theodoric I, 471–526 CE) was a pagan, and that the kings who followed him were pagans until the reign of Reccared, who converted to Catholicism.

According to Gerson Cohen, this survey reflects Ibn Daud's historical and philosophical approach. For Ibn Daud, the inheritance of the Roman empire by

---

[3] Baron, *A Social and Religious History of the Jews*, vi. 206–10.

[4] Ibn Daud, *Zikhron divrei romi* (Mantua edn., 22; ed. Vehlow, 124–31).

[5] On the errors, see Klein and Molner, 'Rabbi Abraham ben David' (Heb.), *Hatsofeh lehokhmat yisra'el*, 8 (1924), 34–5.

the Visigoths and the spread of Christianity in Spain marked the end of a lengthy historical process, intended to install Christianity in its natural soil—the kingdom of Edom. Ibn Daud, following Abraham ibn Ezra, rejected the identification of Edom with Rome; however, contrary to Ibn Ezra, who argued that Spanish Jews did not live in the Edomite exile, Ibn Daud showed that the opposite was true, that the Jews of Spain were living in the very heart of the Edomite exile. The Visigoths, unlike the Romans, were 'the sons of Uz', descendants of the biblical Edom and, in Cohen's words, one can speak of a 'rediscovery of Edom'. Although Cohen's messianic interpretation of the structure of *Sefer hakabalah* has been challenged recently,[6] Ibn Daud's historical system in the *History of Rome* might have had some apocalyptic connotations. In his view, the Iberian peninsula might be the centre of eschatological events, and the entire process of redemption might take place in Spain. Furthermore, even if we discard Cohen's apocalyptic explanation, his Hispanocentric explanation is still valid. Cohen argued that Ibn Daud's approach was consistent with contemporary neo-Gothic nationalist trends. At the time, Spanish theoreticians argued that Spain ought no longer to be subject to the authority of Rome, and certain trends within the monarchy, expressed in the assumption of the title *imperator*, were of a piece with the Church's demands in Compostela for religious hegemony.[7]

The basis of twelfth-century Gothic historiography was Isidore of Seville's *History of the Goths, Vandals, and Suevi*. In it King Sisebut's reign is represented as the peak of the sixth and final stage of history, which began with the Incarnation. The transfer of power from the emperors of Rome to the Christian kings of Spain was part of the divine plan, and the forced conversion of Jews to Christianity following Sisebut's edict of 616 was the first step in the completion of human history, uniting Jews and non-Jews in the sacrifice of the Mass.[8] If Gerson Cohen is right,

---

[6] See Krakowski, 'On the Literary Character of Abraham ibn Da'ud's Sefer Ha-Qabbalah'.

[7] G. D. Cohen (following Yitzhak Baer) points to a similar trend among Ibn Daud's contemporaries, Judah Halevi, Yohanan ibn Daud (Johannes Avedahut of Toledo), and Abraham bar Hiyya (Introduction and notes to Ibn Daud, *Sefer hakabalah*, 250–9). Ibn Daud's emphasis on the barbarian peoples in Spain can be compared to the revised Gothic myth about Pelagius in the cave of Covadonga in, for example, *Historia Silense* written by a clergyman from Leon–Castile around 1115 (see Barkai, *Cristianos y Musulmanes en la España medieval*, 112–14; id., 'Images of Self and Enemy among Christians and Muslims in Spain' (Heb.), 127–8; id., *Science, Magic, and Mythology in the Middle Ages* (Heb.), 83–4; McCluskey, 'Malleable Accounts', 214–16). On the Hispanization of Jewish history in Ibn Daud's works, see Vehlow, Introduction to Ibn Daud, *Zikhron divrei romi*, 56–61. On thirteenth-century and subsequent neo-Gothic nationalist trends, see Deyermond, 'Written by the Victors'.

[8] See J. Cohen, 'Isidore of Seville's Anti-Jewish Polemic' (Heb.); id., *Living Letters of the Law*, 95–122. Cohen interpreted the anti-Jewish polemic in Isidore's *On the Catholic Faith against the Jews* according to this historiographical approach (see Reydellet, 'Les Intentions idéologiques et politiques dans la Chronique d'Isidore de Séville').

Ibn Daud adopted a similar historiographical approach, which allowed him to achieve the same messianic aims but from a Jewish perspective, although this might not have been obvious to all of his readers. For many readers, Ibn Daud was an important source of knowledge about the history of Jews and non-Jews, especially of the Spanish kingdoms. An interesting example of this is his praise of Alfonso VII, king of Castile from 1127 to 1157:

However, after [Nasi R. Joseph b. Ferrizuel's] death, the heretics [Karaites] erupted again until the reign of King Don Alfonso, son of Raymond, king of kings, the *imperator*.... The following are the circumstances under which the heretics were suppressed in Castile. This king, Don Alfonso, son of Raymond, was a king of kings and a righteous king. He prevailed over all the Ishmaelites living in Spain, and compelled them to pay tribute. His kingdom grew mighty and the 'Lord gave him rest from all his enemies around him' [see Josh. 21: 42]. Now the time that he reigned over Edom was thirty-eight [*recte* thirty] years. Inasmuch as the kingdom grew strong under his hand, he succeeded in taking from the Ishmaelites Calatrava, which lies on the main road from the Ishmaelite to the Christian part of the country.

[At about that time] the rebels against the Berber kingdom had crossed the sea to Spain, after having wiped out every remnant of the Jews from Tangiers to Al-Mahdiya. ... They tried to do the same in all the cities of the Ishmaelite kingdom in Spain. ... However, he who prepares the remedy before the affliction, exalted be his name ... anticipated [the calamity] by putting it into the heart of Alfonso, the *imperator*, to appoint our master and rabbi Judah Hanasi ben Ezra over Calatrava and to place all the royal provisions in his charge. ... He supervised the passage of the refugees, released those bound in chains and let the oppressed go free by breaking their yoke and undoing their bonds. ...

When all of the nation had finished passing over [the border] by means of his help, the king sent for him and appointed him lord of all his household and ruler over all his possessions. He [then] requested of the king to forbid the heretics to open their mouths throughout the land of Castile, and the king commanded that this be done.[9]

This enthusiastic and lengthy description is unusual for *Sefer hakabalah*, and Gerson Cohen argued that consequently it repays close reading. He emphasized the biblical terms with which Alfonso is described ('king of kings', 'a righteous king', 'king over Edom'), which call to mind King David. According to Cohen, Alfonso's heir would be Armilus, a figure from medieval Jewish apocalyptic literature, described as the last king of Edom, who would rule over ten kings and strike terror into all of humanity. 'King of kings' does not therefore mean only the ruler of the entire land of Spain but also symbolizes Alfonso's rule over the ten kings of the last empire. Furthermore, Alfonso reigned in Toledo, which was alle-

---

[9] Ibn Daud, *Sefer hakabalah*, ch. 7, lines 365–404 (ed. Cohen: Heb. section, 69–72; Eng. section, 95–9); see G. D. Cohen, Introduction and notes, ibid.

gorically identified with Rome. Cohen points out that Alfonso, unlike other Christian rulers, did not enact any laws to improve the situation of Spanish Jewry, and this fact could not have escaped Ibn Daud's notice. Therefore the only explanation for his lengthy and detailed encomium of Alfonso was his place in the apocalyptic scheme.[10]

The messianic approach to history might be one characteristic of Ibn Daud's writing, but it was certainly marginal. His depiction of Alfonso contains no allusions to the apocalyptic figure of Armilus and should be interpreted differently. Nowhere in the apocalyptic literature, the Aramaic translations of the Bible (Targums), or the legends and homilies in Midrash was Armilus described as ecstatically as Alfonso was by Ibn Daud. There Armilus is always the son of Satan, ruling over the land of Satan, and terrifying the entire world, particularly the Jews.[11] Even in the philosophical literature—represented, for example, by Sa'adiah Gaon—which interpreted Jewish apocalyptic thought rationally and rejected the demonic descriptions of Armilus, he was never depicted favourably. He was described, together with a king whose decrees are 'more terrible than those of Haman [in the book of Esther]', as defeating the messiah, son of Joseph, capturing and killing Jews, and bringing upon them a great catastrophe.[12] If Ibn Daud wanted to depict Alfonso as Armilus, he ought to have stressed not only his power, but also his wickedness and his negative attitude towards Jews.

Therefore, there must have been other reasons for Ibn Daud's extravagant praise of Alfonso. The main benefit Jews obtained from him, according to Ibn Daud, was his promotion of Jewish courtiers, especially Judah ben Ezra, to key positions. Owing to this, the Jews nearly succeeded in eradicating Karaism—a recurrent literary motif in stories about Alfonso and Judah ben Ezra. The ideal political system, according to Ibn Daud, was a strong Christian monarchy and a powerful Jewish leadership, as the king's support of the Jewish courtiers protected the Jews from the flourishing heresy. According to Haim Hillel Ben-Sasson:

The description of the recent past indicated an optimistic view of the future. The chronicle shows that in 1160 the high-ranking families of Christian Spain were convinced that the true path of rabbinic Judaism and the secure existence of communities and individuals had been regained as a result of the political functions of leading Jews and the firmer position of the victorious Castile monarchy.[13]

[10] G. D. Cohen, Introduction and notes, ibid. 259–62; Fernández Urbina and Targarona Borrás, 'La historia romana', 15–16.

[11] See *Sefer zerubavel*, 79; *Yemot hamashiah*, 96–7; see also Even Shmuel, Introduction (Heb.), ibid. 90–1.

[12] See Sa'adiah Gaon, *Sefer hanivhar be'emunot uvedeot*, 8 (ed. Kapah, 251–2); Schwartz, *The Messiah in Medieval Jewish Thought* (Heb.), 36–45.

[13] H. H. Ben-Sasson, 'On Medieval Trends in Jewish Chronography' (Heb.), 393; see also 391–2.

Yosef Yerushalmi discussed the generally positive approach of the Jews to the institution of monarchy in Spain and argued that it was a result of the hostile attitude of the common people to the Jews. The Jews understood that the king was the only one who could protect them, and hence the courtier class made alliance with the monarchy a key point of policy, a situation that continued from the reign of Alfonso VI, king of Castile from 1072 to 1109, until the Expulsion in 1492.[14] In addition, positive images of Spanish kings were part of a historiographical trend, which first appeared in *Sefer hakabalah* and recurred frequently in chronicles from the thirteenth to the fifteenth centuries. This trend also reflected an interest in the history of Spain and provided information about the political and cultural activities of the monarchies of the Iberian peninsula.

Judah ben Isaac Halevi ibn Shabbetai, who lived from the end of the twelfth to the early thirteenth century, wrote a book on Spanish history. It was burned by the Jews of Saragossa and apparently lost, depriving us of important historical information. However, some of Ibn Shabbetai's contemporaries managed to read it,[15] and, in another book, *Divrei ha'alah vehanidui*, Ibn Shabbetai included several details about the contents of the lost book, noting that it dealt with 'the pious, the wise, the charitable, and the poets, leaders, and notables, and those who help others in trouble, the upholders of the Torah, renowned men, and the princes, advisers and kings'.[16] He wrote elsewhere: 'How did the simple minded not fear or the scoundrels not tremble, and not one ass among them did tremble in awe of the five kings of Spain. . . . I have constructed books of their virtues, their deeds of might and heroism.'[17] Ibn Shabbetai was probably the first Spanish Jew to write a history of the kings of Spain.

Jacob ben Elijah also dealt with Spanish history, including the story of how Saint James of Compostela's bones reached the Iberian peninsula. He included it along with legends of other saints and martyrs; however, he dealt with this important Spanish myth first. He also began his sequence of secular events with events in Spain: the history of the Almohad caliphate and the decrees between 1130 and 1269 forcing Jews in north-western Africa and Spain to convert. He noted that these decrees led to the destruction of synagogues, the burning of books, and prohibitions against keeping the sabbath and celebrating Jewish festivals. According

---

[14] See Yerushalmi, *The Lisbon Massacre of 1506 and the Royal Image in the Shevet Yehudah*, 35–66. He concentrates especially on Solomon ibn Verga and the exiled Jews. See also Hacker, 'New Chronicles on the Expulsion of the Jews from Spain' (Heb.), 211–13.

[15] Vider, 'The Burned Book of Judah ibn Shabbetai' (Heb.), 122–5. Yonah bar Solomon ibn Bahalul's *Minḥat kenaot* contains evidence that he used Ibn Shabbetai's book.

[16] Dishon, 'The Lost Book of History by Judah ibn Shabbetai' (Heb.), 191; see id., 'New Light on Judah ibn Shabbetai as a Historian' (Heb.); Huss, 'Critical Editions of "Minḥat yehudah", "Ezrat hanashim", and "Ein mishpat"', i. 189–90.

[17] Dishon, 'The Lost Book of History by Judah ibn Shabbetai' (Heb.), 191.

to Jacob ben Elijah, Jews reacted to these decrees by choosing to live as Conversos and clandestinely following their religion.[18]

Jacob ben Elijah wrote during the last days of the Almohad caliphate and recorded its decline from the reign of Abd al-Mu'min (1130–63) to that of Abu Yusuf Yakub al-Mansur (1184–99). According to his account, the caliphate collapsed as a result of its rulers' mistreatment of Jews. The appeals of the forcibly converted Jews to God led to the liquidation of the Almohad dynasty.[19]

Jacob Mann noted the importance of Jacob ben Elijah as a source of information about the Jews under the Almohads, as there are very few references to these events in other Hebrew chronicles or writings.[20] Hayim Hirschberg compared the reactions of the Jews of northern Africa and those of Germany and France to the Crusades and asserted that, in contrast to Ashkenazi historiography, 'the Jews of the Maghrib did not have any writers and poets of their own who knew how to unfold the array of all the memories'.[21] Jacob ben Elijah's testimony indicates that, although the literary response of the Jews of Muslim Spain and northern Africa was meagre, nonetheless, the events reverberated in the historical consciousness of the Jews of western Europe.

Jacob ben Elijah linked the rise of the Almohad caliphate, the destruction of the Jewish communities, the forced conversions, the Conversos' ability to preserve their Jewish identity, and the collapse of the caliphate into one historiographical paradigm, a Judaeocentric understanding of world history. This understanding was also reflected in his description of the conquest of Majorca by King James I of Aragon between 1229 and 1232, which he regarded, like the fall of the Almohad caliphate, as an outcome of the Muslim king of Majorca's mistreatment of Jews.

Very little is known about the Jews of Majorca during the Muslim period. As I have noted, Mann mentioned the importance of Jacob ben Elijah's testimony, but very few other scholars have given it any attention.[22] According to Jacob ben

---

[18] Jacob b. Elijah, *Igeret ya'akov mivenetsiah*, 23; on Jews in the Almohad period, see Slouschz, 'Forced Conversions in Maimonides' Time' (Heb.); Korkus, 'On the Attitude of the Al-Muhadin Leaders to the Jews' (Heb.).

[19] Jacob b. Elijah, *Igeret ya'akov mivenetsiah*, 23. He was apparently referring to the deaths of Abu Muhammad Abdallah al-Adil in 1227 and his brother Abu al-Ala Idris al-Mamun in 1232 (see Mann, 'Une source de l'histoire juive au XIIIe siècle', 367–8; Dinur, *Israel in the Diaspora* (Heb.), Pt. II, vol. i, 389 n. 25).   [20] Mann, 'Une source de l'histoire juive au XIIIe siècle'.

[21] See M. Ben-Sasson, 'On the Jewish Identity of the *Anusim*' (Heb.), 19; Halkin, 'Forced Conversion in the Time of the Almohads' (Heb.), 102 n. 17; Hirschberg, 'On the Decrees of the Almohads and Trade with India' (Heb.), 137.

[22] Jacob b. Elijah, *Igeret ya'akov mivenetsiah*, 23–4; see Mann, 'Une source de l'histoire juive au XIIIe siècle', 368–71. Jacob ben Elijah's information on Majorca is not mentioned by Baer (*A History of the Jews in Christian Spain*) or Beinart ('Majorca'). See also Graetz, *The History of the Jews* (Heb.), v. 33; Pons, *Los judíos del reino de Mallorca durante los siglos XIII y XIV*, 9–16).

Elijah, the Jews of the island (or the city of Palma, which was then also called Majorca) were persecuted and sold into slavery by order of the Muslim king, probably Abu Yahya Muhammad al-Tinmalali. James I's conquest of the city of Majorca on 31 December 1229 is recorded in great detail. Jacob ben Elijah described a well-planned battle that ended with a large number of the city's inhabitants and Abu Yahya and his family slain (Abu Yahya was actually taken alive).[23] From the perspective of contemporary Jews—or at least of Jacob ben Elijah—James was a second Cyrus, an emissary of God. Jacob ben Elijah began his account with the words: 'And the Almighty awakened the heart of our lord the king who reigned over the land of Aragon' (see Ezra 1: 1). This is a continuation of the sympathetic historiographical approach to the kings of Spain found in Ibn Daud and Ibn Shabbetai. Modern historians would probably see James's favourable attitude to Jews as a case of realpolitik.[24]

Jewish interest in the history of Spain and its kings continued during the fourteenth century. According to one account, Don Joseph ibn Wakar of Toledo, a Jewish leader from Castile and physician to Enrique II, king of Castile from 1369 to 1379, was sent on a diplomatic mission to the Muslim kingdom of Granada and took with him a book for the Arabic scholar Lisan al-Din ibn al-Hatib. The book contained a summary of the history of the Iberian peninsula from the time of the mythical Visigothic hero Pelagius to Enrique's reign, including the royal dynasties of Leon, Castile, Navarre, Portugal, and Aragon, which Ibn Wakar had apparently excerpted from the *Crónica general de 1344* and translated into Arabic. Ibn al-Hatib used it as a source for his *History of Granada*.[25] Also in the fourteenth century several events from the history of the Spanish kingdoms up to 1300 were recorded in the anonymous chronicle from Provence and Languedoc that was added to Solomon ibn Verga's *Shevet yehudah* by his son Joseph ibn Verga.[26] Although the chronicle's major interest was the south of France, it records the conquest of several cities in Castile by the Almohads, including Calatrava and the area around Toledo in 1195 and mentions that Jews fought side by side with Christians in the defence of Toledo. It also refers to the death of Yakub al-Mansur in 1199, the taking of the mountain fastness of Salvatierra (Ciudad Real) by the Almohads in 1211, and the crushing defeat

---

[23] See Bisson, *The Medieval Crown of Aragon*, 64–5; see also the description of the massacre of Muslims in *Crònica general de Pere III el Cerimoniós* (120–1).

[24] See Baer, *A History of the Jews in Christian Spain*, i. 138–44.

[25] See Martínez Antuña, 'Una versión Árabe compendiada de la "Estoria de España"', esp. 114–16; see also Baer, *A History of the Jews in Christian Spain*, i. 367, 450 n. 53; Judah b. Asher, *She'elot uteshuvot zikhron yehudah*, no. 51 (471); Stearns, 'Two Passages in Ibn al-Khatib's Account of the Kings of Christian Iberia'.   [26] See Introduction, n. 20 above.

of the Almohads by the united kings of Spain at Las Navas de Tolosa in 1212.[27]

Interest in the history of Spanish kings was even more marked in the fifteenth century, as is clearly evinced in the work of Joseph ben Tsadik, Abraham Zacut, Isaac Abravanel, and Solomon ibn Verga. Joseph ben Tsadik's many references to general, as well as Spanish and Portuguese, history in *Kitsur zekher tsadik* almost disguise the fact that he was Jewish. In his brief 'Introduction to the Author', he mentioned, alongside the historiographical and didactic purpose of the Jewish chain of tradition, that he would discuss 'other great events that occurred in every time period, whether for the good or the bad, and the memory of the kings of Spain and the kings of Portugal and the destruction of Constantinople and Negroponte'.[28] These included El Cid in Saragossa and Valencia; the Reconquest in the eleventh century and the conquest of Toledo by Alfonso VI; the coronation of Alfonso VI as emperor of Castile; the marriage of Ferdinand III of Castile to the daughter of the Byzantine emperor and his great conquests in the thirteenth century; the death of Alfonso IX of Castile; the conquest of Tarifa by Sancho IV; the conquest of Jaén by Ferdinand IV; the wars Alfonso XI and his sons waged over Gibraltar and other places; the war of the brothers Pedro I the Cruel and Enrique II; the death of Juan I of Castile and the law he passed annulling the Spanish calendar and replacing it with one that began with the Incarnation of Jesus; the death of Álvaro de Luna; the marriage of Ferdinand II of Aragon to Isabella of Castile and the war between Castile and Portugal; and the Castilian victories in Granada up to 1487.[29]

Joseph ben Tsadik's focus on the kings of Spain and Portugal was consistent with Christian historiography, and he explicitly stated that he used Christian chronicles.[30] He was primarily interested in the Castilian dynasty: from King Ferdinand III to Queen Isabella—his own time—he did not leave out a single ruler and mentioned them in precise chronological order. He expanded in particular on Ferdinand IV, who reigned from 1295 to 1312. Beyond his interest in Ferdinand himself, Joseph ben Tsadik ascribed moral significance to events of his reign. This was, of course, an accepted historiographical approach among Jews and one of their justifications for engaging in historiography. In this case, the moral lesson is extracted from the conquest of Alcaudete (Jaén) by Ferdinand:

---

[27] Ibn Verga, *Shevet yehudah*, 146–7; see Graetz, *The History of the Jews* (Heb.), iv, app. 1, 417–18, 420.

[28] Joseph b. Tsadik, *Kitsur zekher tsadik* (ed. Neubauer, 85).

[29] Ibid. 92–100; see Baer, *A History of the Jews in Christian Spain*, i. 89, 396 n. 30; Cantera Burgos, *El Libro de la cabala de Abraham ben Salomon de Torrutiel*, 49–64; R. Menéndez Pidal, *La España del Cid*, 86–7; Joseph b. Tsadik, *Kitsur zekher tsadik* (ed. Moreno Koch, 42, 44, 49–52, 54–5, 57–65).

[30] Joseph b. Tsadik, *Kitsur zekher tsadik* (ed. Neubauer, 96): 'and the writers of the annals of the kings say . . .'.

King Don Ferdinand, son of King Don Sancho IV, reigned for eleven years [*recte* seventeen] , in 5062 [1302, *recte* 1312], and captured Alcaudete. And the writers of the annals of the kings say that he decreed that the high-ranking people be taken to a desolate place, a land of persecution, and thrown from the top of the tall rocks to the bottom of the mountain. And during the trial, they shouted and cried out and said: 'Hear all you nations, the king has decreed that we be unlawfully slain; he did not even agree to hear our claims. Hence we summon him to go and face a judgement with us within thirty days.' And it was testified that the king died within that same time. In truth, that is a very great matter.[31]

This story about the sudden death of Ferdinand IV was first written in 1340–5 by Ferrán Sánchez de Valladolid, chief notary of Castile and Chancellor of the Privy Seal in the time of King Alfonso XI (d. 1350). Ferrán Sánchez was most likely also the author of the *Chronicle of the Three Kings* (Alfonso X, Sancho IV, Ferdinand IV) and the *Chronicle of Alfonso XI* (1344). The story explains the strange unexpected death of the king in his bed three days after his victory in Alcaudete (4 Sept. 1312),[32] and thirty days after he unjustly put to death two brothers, who were later identified as Juan and Pedro Alfonso de Carvajal, knights of the Order of Calatrava. This episode led to Ferdinand being known as El Emplazado, 'the Summoned'.[33] Joseph ben Tsadik stresses its moral significance: 'In truth, that is a very great matter', most likely as a warning for high-ranking officials in both Christian and Jewish society.

    Joseph ben Tsadik was also interested in Alfonso X the Wise of Castile, who ruled from 1252 to 1284.

King Don Alfonso the Wise, son of King Don Ferdinand, mentioned above, reigned after him for seventy [*recte* thirty-two] years, in the year 5052, which is 1290 of the Caesar era and 1252 of the Christian era.[34] He married Dona Violante, daughter of the wise, excellent King James of Aragon, who received his wisdom from Nahmanides of blessed memory and fathered two sons, Don Ferdinand de la Cerda and Don Alonso de la Cerda, and conquered the kingdom of Murcia. In the fourth year of his reign, he commanded the scholar Judah ben Moses Hakohen, a constable in Toledo, to translate from the Arabic language into the vernacular [Castilian] the notable book, written by the scholar Abu Abdallah ibn Jabir al-Sabi, who taught about the constellations, the stars, and their forms as they are arranged in the heavens. And it also contained the astrological tables commissioned by the king. And I have seen this splendid, super-

---

[31] Joseph b. Tsadik, *Kitsur zekher tsadik* (ed. Neubauer, 96). Abraham ben Solomon Ardutiel tells of two high-ranking brothers who were killed by Ferdinand IV (see Moreno Koch (ed.), *Dos crónicas hispanohebreas del siglo XV*, 55 n. 200).   [32] See O'Callaghan, *The Gibraltar Crusade*, 136.

[33] *Crónica del Rey Don Fernando el IV*, 18 (ed. Benavides, i. 242–3); see *Crónica de D. Alfonso el Onceno*, 3 (ed. Cerdá y Rico, 10); Ximena Jurado (ed.), *Catálogo de los Obispos de las Iglesias Catedrales de Jaén y Anales eclesiásticos de este Obispado*, 202.

[34] The Caesar era in Spain, which was used until the fourteenth century, started in 38 BCE.

ior book with my own eyes, and it is written entirely in pure gold, and I say that he who has not seen this book has never seen such a glorious, ornate item in his whole life. And in his wisdom, the king, a man of all wisdom, enacted rules and legal codes relating to their laws, with which to judge all the people in his kingdom, and called them Las Siete Partidas [the Seven-Part Code], and commanded that all of these laws and codes be preserved and that all the judges rule according to them, and when these books, laws, and codes of his spread throughout the kingdom, all of the scholars and kings and all of the ministers and all of the people who came after him agreed to act in accordance with them to this very day.[35]

Joseph ben Tsadik showed great admiration for Alfonso's cultural initiatives and wrote about them at great length.[36] This is all the more striking given his usually terse style: he did not describe a single Jewish figure—not a king, a prophet, a scholar, nor a community leader—at such length. In chapter 50 of *Kitsur zekher tsadik*, he dealt, among other matters, with the literary history of the Jews, but did not describe any Jewish creative work with the same enthusiasm with which he described the translation of Al-Sabi's book of astronomy and the Alfonsine Tables, which provided data for the calculation of the position of the sun, moon, and planets.[37] He also praised Alfonso's legislative endeavours, which culminated in the legal code, Las Siete Partidas. The code took a long time to come into force in Castile and was only really in use from the middle of the fourteenth century. The laws relating to Jews and Judaism in Las Siete Partidas were not particularly repressive, and that probably explains Joseph ben Tsadik's favourable attitude towards it.[38]

Abraham Zacut also noted Alfonso X's legislative activity and stressed the fact that up to his time Las Siete Partidas served as the kingdom's lawbook. He also expressed admiration for Alfonso's other cultural achievements. In *Sefer yuḥasin*, he recorded the Jewish scholars up to his own time, and, after writing about Meir Halevi Abulafia of Burgos and Toledo and Nahmanides, he described Alfonso's projects:

In the year 5012 [1252], Don Alfonso the Wise was crowned king on the last day of May, and he loved the sciences, in particular astronomy, and then by order of the king, the scholar Isaac ben Sid, cantor of Toledo compiled tables of the hosts of the heavens, with great accuracy, and no one was comparable to them in the accuracy of the tables and the

---

[35] Joseph b. Tsadik, *Kitsur zekher tsadik* (ed. Neubauer, 95–6).

[36] See Márquez-Villanueva, 'The Alfonsine Cultural Concept'; O'Callaghan, *The Learned King*.

[37] See *The Alfonsine Tables of Toledo*, 135–42, 225–42; Díaz-Esteban, 'Jewish Literary Creation in Spanish' (Heb.); Gingerich, 'Alfonso the Tenth as a Patron of Astronomy'; Romano, 'The Jews' Contribution to Medicine, Science, and General Learning' (Heb.).

[38] For an analysis of these laws, see Carpenter, *Alfonso X and the Jews*, 64–5; see also Baer, *A History of the Jews in Christian Spain*, i. 116–17; Castro, *The Spaniards*, 66; O'Callaghan, *The Learned King*, 37.

books of astronomy . . . and they are called 'Zig Alfonso'. And from the lands where the sun rises to the lands where it sets, Germany, France, and England, and all of Italy and Spain, they all broke the earlier tables and make use of these tables to this very day. . . . In the fourth year of his reign, 5016, [the king] ordered Judah ben Moses Hakohen of Toledo to translate into the vernacular [Castilian] the distinguished book written by the Ishmaelite Abu al-Hasan [Ali ibn Abi Rijal] mentioning 1,022 large stars. . . . And he prepared a legal code [the Seven-Part Code], and all the scholars, kings, and ministers act in accordance with it to this day, and he also gathered all the scholars to compose a large book of history about all that happened from the days of Adam the first [man] to his own time, and that is a wondrous thing.[39]

Zacut, who was an astronomer, knew better than Joseph ben Tsadik how the Alfonsine Tables were created. Over time, Alfonso's name was linked to them, while the names of Isaac ben Sid and Judah ben Moses were forgotten. This was not entirely accidental. A prologue to the Alfonsine Tables contains a fanciful account of a grand meeting of astronomers from the three religions supposedly held in Toledo under the auspices of Alfonso X. They were ordered to discuss the movement of the stars and to produce the tables. In this fictionalized account the project is supervised by two Muslims. Thomas Glick emphasizes that this reflects two significant value judgements: first, Arab astronomy is the authoritative science; second, Jews do not lead.[40] However, Zacut's account shows that the Jews remembered and preserved in writing the fact that the project was directed by Jewish scholars and not by Muslims or Alfonso. In addition to Alfonso's astronomical and legal undertakings, Zacut also mentioned that he commissioned the *Primera crónica general de España*.

Joseph ben Tsadik's and Abraham Zacut's appreciation of the cultural accomplishments in Castile shows that they had internalized the cultural values of the Christian environment. Like Joseph ben Tsadik, Zacut ascribed great importance to Spanish history, and in *Sefer yuḥasin* he described political events in Spain and provided quite accurate information about the origin of the kings of Castile and Aragon. He reviewed Spanish history from the foundation of Hispania, Portugal, and Aragon by the biblical Tubal,[41] including the takeover of Spain by Carthage under Hannibal, the partition of the Iberian peninsula between Carthage and Rome and the wars against Scipio,[42] the wars of the Visigoths and their migration

[39] Zacut, *Sefer yuḥasin* (ed. Filipowski, 221*b*–222*a*).

[40] Glick, "'My Master, the Jew'", 170–2.

[41] Zacut, *Sefer yuḥasin* (ed. Filipowski, 232*b*–233*a*); see also *Crónica pseudo-Isidoriana*, 14: 'Ex Tubal Yspani venerunt'; Alfonso X, *Primera crónica general de España*, i. 6*b*, 14*a*.

[42] Zacut, *Sefer yuḥasin* (ed. Filipowski, 241*b*). Zacut often drew illuminating historical comparisons. He compared the Mongol ruler Tamburlaine to Hannibal, because of his great courage and skilful manoeuvres: 'Tamburlaine king of the Tartars crossed the Euphrates River with 400,000 cavalry and 600,000 foot soldiers and conquered large kingdoms in the Land of Israel and the Turks

through Europe from the sack of Rome in 410 to the conquest of Spain,[43] the Muslim conquest,[44] some erroneous information on the conquest of Muslim Saragossa by El Cid,[45] the conquest of Almeria in 1147 by the duke of Barcelona with help from the Genoan fleet,[46] the union of Castile and Leon at the beginning of the thirteenth century,[47] and the battles with the Almohads and the halting of their advance at Toledo.[48]

Zacut also included a lot of information about the Spanish kings of the fifteenth century:

And then came King Don Alfonso V [1396–1458], king of Aragon, for then the kingdom was divided, and he was the son of King Don Ferdinand I [1380–1416], king of Aragon. King Don Alfonso was the brother of King Don Juan II [1398–1479], king of Navarre and Aragon, father of Ferdinand the Catholic [II of Aragon and V of Castile, 1452–1516], king of Castile; he is the one who in [our] time expelled [the Jews] from Spain. . . . In 1434 Genoa expelled King Alfonso V of Aragon, who was the one who took Naples. . . . In 1440 Ferdinand I [of Antequera], king of Aragon, Sicily, and Sardinia died. He reigned for twenty-one [*recte* four] years; he was the son of King Don Juan I of Castile, who died after falling off his horse, and Ferdinand's brother was King Don Enrique III of Castile [1379–1406], who died prematurely. This king Ferdinand ruled Castile [as regent from the end of 1406] until the son of King Enrique III grew up [Juan II]. When the king of Aragon [Martin I, 1356–1410] died without sons, they sent for Ferdinand to reign in Aragon. In 1412 he began to reign over the Balearic Isles, which are Majorca and Minorca, and over Aragon and Lusitania. (This is not true, for Lusitania is Portugal.) . . . In 1455 [*recte* 1458] King Alfonso V, who captured Naples, died and bequeathed Aragon and Sicily to his brother, Don Juan II, and his son, Ferdinand [1423–94], by a mistress [Giraldona Carlino] he left in Naples. His name was Pitado [*sic*], after his grandfather [Ferdinand I]. King Don Juan of Aragon reigned for twenty-four [*recte* twenty-one] years and he escaped from Castile during the war in Olmedo. On 22 May 1445 he fled to Aragon. The Castilian admiral [Fadrique Enríquez] escaped with him. He gave his daughter [Juana Enríquez] in marriage to the king [Juan], who was a widower, and she gave birth to his son at noon on 10 March 1452. This son was Ferdinand [II of Aragon and V of Castile], who became king of Spain and Sicily, after the death of his brother Carlos IV of Navarre [1421–61], son of another wife [Blanca of Navarre, *c.*1391–1441] of the king. In 1454 the king of

fought him, and he killed 200,000 men in the camp [of the Turks] and also captured [Bayzid I] and delivered him in chains of gold, and in his power Tamburlaine was similar to Hannibal' (ibid. (ed. Freiman, p. xlvii)).

[43] Ibid. (ed. Filipowski, 246*b*).   [44] Ibid. (ed. Filipowski, 248*a*).

[45] Ibid. (ed. Filipowski, 212*a*); see also Freiman, Corrections and notes, ibid., p. xxv.

[46] Ibid. (ed. Freiman, p. xliii). It is interesting that the part played by Alfonso VII is not mentioned (see Alfonso X, *Primera crónica general de España*, i. 661*a*).

[47] Zacut, *Sefer yuḥasin* (ed. Freiman, p. xliv).   [48] Ibid. (ed. Freiman, pp. xliv–xlv).

Castile, Don Juan II died, and his son Don Enrique IV [1425–74] reigned for twenty years.[49]

Zacut apparently had access to a Spanish chronicle and perhaps others as well. He selected events and correlated them with those in other kingdoms in order to create a universal chronicle. Although he used Christian chronicles, sometimes verbatim, he occasionally added his own comments, such as that Ferdinand I of Antequera could not have ruled Lusitania as it was Portugal. His Jewish perspective is reflected in comments such as that it was Ferdinand 'the Catholic' who expelled the Jews from Spain. Zacut mentioned the details of Ferdinand's family tree several times, noting that his mother was the daughter of the Castilian admiral. As I will show below, these genealogical details played an important role in the historical consciousness of the exiles from Spain, who developed various myths around the figure of Ferdinand and his Jewish courtier Abraham Seneor.

Obviously, Zacut's chronicle cannot be compared to the diverse and sophisticated Spanish historiographies which covered the political history of the Iberian peninsula in great detail. The kings of Aragon, Castile, Navarre, and Portugal engaged court historians, whose function was to record and glorify their deeds. However, even without economic and political incentives, Jews took great interest in Iberian political history, and this interest manifested itself in chronicles and other literary works. It seems then that it would be better to compare Jewish historiography in Spain with Jewish historiography elsewhere. Jewish historiographers in Spain showed a much greater interest in the history of the surrounding society and focused on political events in Spain and on the dynasties of kings of Castile–Leon and Aragon.[50]

ISIDORE OF SEVILLE

Joseph ben Tsadik's *Kitsur zekher tsadik* is much smaller in scope than *Sefer yuḥasin*, and many subjects that Zacut dealt with are absent from it. For example, Joseph ben Tsadik scarcely mentions Christian saints and the cult of relics. Nonetheless, both men were clearly interested in the Spanish saint, Isidore of Seville, first mentioned in Ibn Daud's *History of Rome*. Zacut often attributed historical information to Isidore[51] and described his literary activity:

In the year 4414, which is 615 of the Christians, Isidore, the bishop of Seville, who is called Hispalensis and in Latin Sevilia, died. He was a disciple of Pope Gregory. He

[49] Zacut, *Sefer yuḥasin* (ed. Freiman, pp. xlvii–xlviii).

[50] Cf. 'Order of the Kings of Rome', where the emphasis is on the succession of Byzantine emperors (in Neubauer, *The Order of the Sages and Historical Events* (Heb.), doc. 9 (i. 185–6); see also Barkai, Introduction to Moreno Koch (ed.), *Dos crónicas hispanohebreas del siglo XV*, 15–16).

[51] See e.g. Zacut, *Sefer yuḥasin* (ed. Filipowski, 232b, 233a, 234a).

wrote books on astronomy, theology, cosmography, and history from the time of Adam until his own days. He knew in astronomy what would happen in more than 900 years. He lived in the days of Muhammad and died seventeen years before Muhammad.[52]

Zacut admired Isidore of Seville for his scientific, theological, and historical studies, as well as for his prowess as an astronomer. Despite what he said in his 'Introduction to the Author' about only mentioning Christian saints for polemical reasons, he offers no criticism of Isidore.[53]

A similar motive inspired Joseph ben Tsadik's description of the reinterment of Isidore's bones:

King Don Ferdinand reigned in the year 4775, the Christian year 1015, and in the thirty-fourth year of his reign, which was 1049 of the Christians, the king sent many ministers and notables to Ibn Habib, king of Seville, to remove the bones of the great scholar Saint Gidro [Isidore] and to bring them for burial to the city of Leon. And that is why we had to write in our book things that seem to be nonsense, for in our own time we have seen with our eyes a little of what Saint Gidro the great scholar wrote as a prophet who foresaw great things that would happen after 700 years.[54]

The real reason Ferdinand wanted Isidore's bones interred in Leon was because Isidore was a saint, not because of his scholarship or his wisdom. According to *Historia Silense*, the delegation to Seville intended to disinter the bones of another saint, Saint Justa, but they were unable to find her, and Isidore's spirit appeared to them and asked that his body be taken to Leon.[55] Joseph ben Tsadik's style is usually terse, but here he departed from it to explain why he had included the story of Isidore. He also called Isidore 'Saint Gidro', but without any derogatory intent.

However, it is strange that these two writers should emphasize Isidore's prophetic skills when his writings indicate that he did not engage in prophecy at all. Norman Roth suggested that they may have erroneously attributed Julian of Toledo's *Prognostics of the Future Age* to Isidore.[56] But this is probably not the reason. It was not the Jews who endowed Isidore with the attributes of a prophet: they merely adopted an image that was prevalent in the Spanish historical

---

[52] Ibid., 247*b*; on the errors in the dates, see N. Roth, *Jews, Visigoths and Muslims in Medieval Spain*, 16–18.

[53] See Zacut, *Sefer yuḥasin* (ed. Filipowski, 231*a*) (discussed in Ch 4 above); Cantera Burgos, *El Libro de la cabala de Abraham ben Salomon de Torrutiel*, 49 n. 5.

[54] Joseph b. Tsadik, *Kitsur zekher tsadik* (ed. Neubauer, 92).

[55] See Castro, *The Spaniards*, 184. The Muslim king is Ibn Abad, also called Almutadid (1042–69), not Ibn Habib. The bones were disinterred in 1063 (see Cantera Burgos, *El Libro de la cabala de Abraham ben Salomon de Torrutiel*, 31 nn. 2–3). Roth explained Joseph b. Tsadik's mistake about the time of Ferdinand I as originating in Ximenez de Rada's *De rebus Hispaniae* (see N. Roth, *Jews, Visigoths and Muslims in Medieval Spain*, 16–18).

[56] N. Roth, *Jews, Visigoths and Muslims in Medieval Spain*, 17, 25.

consciousness and which appeared in, for example, *Primera crónica general de España*.[57] Javier Castaño demonstrated that pseudo-Isidorian prophecies were a major element in the propaganda of Ferdinand and Isabella as they tried to intensify the war against the Muslim kingdom of Granada in 1485–7. These prophecies, publicized mainly in a letter disseminated (among Muslims and Jews as well) by the marqués of Cadiz, Rodrigo Ponce de Leon, foretold the conquest of the last Muslim stronghold in the Iberian peninsula and eschatological struggles against internal enemies, especially heretics and Jews. In them, Ferdinand was depicted as the eschatological 'hidden' messiah and the new King David who would lead Spain to victory. According to Castaño, Jews associated themselves with the messianic-eschatological atmosphere that swept Castile at the time and neutralized its anti-Jewish motifs.[58]

Unlike Zacut, Joseph ben Tsadik saw no need to apologize for combining Jewish and general history. Nor did he attach less value to historical stories whose purpose was—according to Zacut—to console, to instill fear of God, to gladden, or to amuse.[59] In his view, engaging in general history required no justification. Only in recounting the story of Isidore of Seville did he see fit to apologize to his readers. However, he may have meant to imply that it was not really 'nonsense'. It is interesting to compare his position with that of Abraham ben Solomon Ardutiel (known erroneously as *meteruti'el*, 'of Torrutiel'), who wrote a supplement to Ibn Daud's *Sefer hakabalah* in 1510.[60] He recounted Joseph ben Tsadik's story about Isidore but expanded upon it, attributing Isidore's success and the fulfilment of his prophecies to wisdom acquired from a Jewish sage:

And I have heard that this scholar studied with a great Jewish sage. They say that when Titus went [to conquer] Jerusalem, the father of Gidro who was in charge of the kingdom of Seville, went with him, and when Jerusalem was conquered by Titus all the commanders of the soldiers entered the city to loot it and take booty. And the father of Gidro went in, and found a large house, and when he wanted to go out of the house he looked at the wall and owing to his wisdom saw a kind of opening in the wall, and broke through the wall, and found there a large chamber full of books. And there he saw an old man, reading. He was amazed and said to him: 'What are you doing in this place?' And the sage said to him: 'For several years now I have known that Jerusalem would be destroyed, and I built this house and made this chamber and placed in it these books to

---

[57] 'Este sant Esidro fue muy noble de spirito pora dezir las coasas que quien de uenir' (Alfonso X, *Primera crónica general de España*, i. 277a).

[58] Castaño, 'Profetismo político pseudo-isidoriano y polémica religiosa'; see Mackay, 'Castile and Navarre', 618.   [59] See Zacut, *Sefer yuḥasin* (ed. Filipowski, 232a).

[60] Abraham b. Solomon Ardutiel, *Hashlamat sefer hakabalah*, 294; on the relationship between the two chronicles, see David (ed.), *Two Hebrew Chronicles from the Period of the Expulsion from Spain* (Heb.), 12–13.

read and brought with me all of my sustenance and said that perhaps I shall save my life.' And he took him forth from there and brought him to Seville, where he honoured and revered him. And he had a son whose name was Gidro, and he read with that sage and built a large house outside Seville, which stands until today, and he wrote down things that would occur in the world until the coming of our messiah, as he learned them from his master, the sage, and some of these things we have seen with our own eyes.[61]

As is usual in myths, time is fluid: hence Isidore's father, who lived in the sixth century, appears in a story set in the time of Titus, who lived in the first.[62] Isidore's father rescued the Jewish sage who had foreseen the destruction of Jerusalem, and the Jew repaid the favour by teaching his son ancient Jewish wisdom. All of Isidore's prophecies are, therefore, actually based on Jewish knowledge of astrology. Another version of the myth occurs in *Sefer hayashar* written in Spain or by one of the exiles from Spain.[63]

Castaño noted the political and literary contexts of the Jewish versions of the story. They were part of a broader mythographical and theological discourse, which included Christian myths as well as some Muslim ones. The Christian source of the story about the destruction of Jerusalem and the Jewish sage is the *Vindicta salvatoris*,[64] which in the fourteenth and fifteenth centuries found its way into Spanish renderings (*La estoria del noble Vaspasiano, enperador de Roma*, in Catalonian, Castilian, and Portuguese) from the French version (*La Venjance nostre Seigneur*). This distinctly anti-Jewish work presented the destruction of Jerusalem by Vespasian as divine punishment for the Crucifixion of Jesus. In it, the rescued sage is Joseph of Arimathea, who is released by Vespasian after being held in a Jewish prison for forty years. The story provided ideological support for the persecution, forced conversion, and expulsion of Jews. Abraham ben Solomon and *Sefer hayashar* neutralized the anti-Jewish elements and produced a counter-history which claimed a Jewish source for the pseudo-Isidorian prophecies[65] and made it possible for their readers to think of the famous Christian scholar as 'one

---

[61] Abraham b. Solomon Ardutiel, *Hashlamat sefer hakabalah*, 294–5. According to tradition, the 'large house outside Seville' is the monastery San Isidoro del Campo, which is about 8 km from the city (see Cantera Burgos, *El Libro de la cabala de Abraham ben Salomon de Torrutiel*, 32 n. 3).

[62] That a Spanish minister should be present at the fall of Jerusalem to Titus was suggested by the *Book of Josippon*, which mentions the nations that helped Titus, including some from western Europe, such as Britain and Burgundy (*Sefer yosipon*, 6: 88 (ed. Hominer, 343–4); see Abravanel on Deut. 28: 49 (*Perush al hatorah*, iii. 267). This was also part of the Christian historiographical tradition in Spain.

[63] In *Sefer hayashar*, it is Isidore himself who met the Jewish sage in Jerusalem (see Dan, Introduction (Heb.) to *Sefer hayashar*, 7–17; Flusser, *The Book of Josippon* (Heb.), ii. 17–18 nn. 49–51). The versions in Abraham b. Solomon Ardutiel's *Hashlamat sefer hakabalah* and *Sefer hayashar* contain a number of identical or very similar expressions, which shows that they influenced one another or had a common source.

[64] On the various versions of the 'vengeance of the Saviour', see Yuval, *Two Nations in Your Womb*, 47–9.   [65] Castaño, 'Profetismo político pseudo-isidoriano y polémica religiosa'.

of their own'. The story is a typical transfer legend, which explains how ancient wisdom or authority was transferred from one place to another. Such legends were widespread in the Middle Ages: among Jews—reflecting their respect for the important centres of Torah—and Christians—reflecting their attitude to the classical world.[66]

Isaac Abravanel also had a positive attitude to Isidore of Seville: 'For Isidore, an ancient illustrious sage, one of the great men of the Christians, has written this in the fifth chapter of the book *Etymologiarum*, a chapter worth remembering.'[67] Abravanel's, Zacut's, and Joseph ben Tsadik's esteem for Isidore of Seville may reflect the general Jewish attitude to him. Despite Isidore's anti-Jewish polemics and his involvement in anti-Jewish Church legislation, Jews in Spain, like the Christians around them, greatly admired him, and did not hesitate to express this sentiment in their writings.[68]

HERCULES

Until the end of the fifteenth century, Jewish scholars almost totally ignored Greek and Roman legends, which were important building blocks of Christian European culture. Abraham Zacut and Isaac Abravanel were the first to recognize the importance of these myths and to systematically introduce subjects from them into their writings.[69]

On a number of occasions, Abravanel described the exploits of Hercules, the hero of Greek mythology, and he clearly ascribed greater importance to him than to other mythical figures. In his commentary on Joshua, Abravanel compared the building of stone altars to the custom of ancient nations of erecting monuments in the countries they conquered to mark their rule over them and cited the monuments built by the Romans whose ruins could still be seen throughout Europe.[70] He emphasized—following *Primera crónica general de España*—that Hercules erected such monuments: 'Wherever the great giant Hercules, builder of cities and states, was, he did such a thing.'[71] Abravanel cited the example of Hercules and the Roman ruins to support his historical interpretation of the Bible. Moreover, he presented the two examples as historical stories in every sense—the tales of Hercules, mythical founder of cities, are part of universal history just as the remains of Rome are.

---

[66] See Zfatman, *Between Ashkenaz and Sepharad* (Heb.), 100 n. 70, 111 n. 95.

[67] Abravanel, *Mashmia yeshuah*, 3: 7 (Jerusalem edn., 462).

[68] See Albert, 'Isidore of Seville'; J. Cohen, 'Isidore of Seville's Anti-Jewish Polemic' (Heb.), bibliography, 88–9; id., *Living Letters of the Law*, 100–22.

[69] See R. Ben-Shalom, 'Graeco-Roman Myth and Mythology in the Historical Consciousness of Medieval Spanish Jewry' (Heb.).   [70] Abravanel on Josh. 8: 30 (*Perush linevi'im rishonim*, 44).

[71] Ibid.; see Alfonso X, *Primera crónica general de España*, i. 8b.

In *Sefer yuḥasin*, Zacut described the battle between the centaurs and the Lapiths, who lived in Thessaly: 'There was a great war between centaurs, who are half man and half horse, and the men of Thessaly in Yavan, which is Greece. Then all the centaurs were killed; none of these beasts survived.'[72] Abravanel wrote about Hercules fighting against the centaurs in connection with Joel 2: 4: 'The appearance of them is like the appearance of horses; and like horsemen they run':

And those ancients of the Greeks, the tellers of history, have already written about the men they called centaurs, who they said had the appearance of men from their waist up, and from their waist down were horses. And the verifiers among them wrote that the truth of this matter was that in those ancient times, men began to ride horses on a hill, and they did battle with them to loot and plunder, and the other people in the valley fled from them, and thought they were strange creatures, that the man and the horse were all one body, that the top half was a man and the bottom half was a horse. And the great Hercules came, fought with them, and killed them, and captured some of them alive, and then the truth became known that they were men riding on horses.[73]

The battle between the Lapiths and the centaurs was popular with Italian humanists. The centaurs symbolized humanity's bestial nature, and their defeat symbolized the victory of civilization over barbarism. At about the same time that Zacut and Abravanel were writing, Michelangelo was working on his *Battle of the Lapiths and the Centaurs*, with the encouragement of the humanist and member of the Academy of Florence, Angelo Poliziano, who told the artist the story in detail.[74]

Zacut related a simple version of the myth: the centaurs looked like strange creatures—half horse, half man—fought against humans and were defeated. In contrast, Abravanel's rational explanation based on classical historiography is of particular interest. He drew a distinction between the 'tellers of history', who imparted the myth literally, and the 'verifiers', who examined the myth critically and interpreted it rationally. These commentators, known from various periods in Greek history, searched for the original events behind the myths and, in doing so, often created new myths of their own.[75] According to Abravanel, the verifiers said that the true nature of the centaurs became widely known after Hercules captured some of them alive, and it turned out that they were ordinary people who had discovered how to ride horses. Palaephatus provides a historical explanation of how the tale about the centaurs arose, but many others, including Galen, denied

---

[72] Zacut, *Sefer yuḥasin* (ed. Filipowski, 235*b*).

[73] Abravanel on Joel 2: 4 (*Perush al nevi'im ukhetuvim*, 68); on the battle between the Lapiths and the centaurs and Hercules' war with them, see Graves, *The Greek Myths*, 360–2, 475–8. Ibn Verga cited the story, probably following Abravanel (Ibn Verga, *Shevet yehudah*, 44).

[74] Vasari, *The Life of the Painters, Sculptors and Architects*, iv. 112.

[75] See Veyne, *Did the Greeks Believe in Their Myths?*, 67–8.

their existence.[76] The verifiers' rational version enabled Abravanel to acknowledge the mythological text as an authentic historical source, and use it to interpret
the Bible. In doing so, he was following hermeneutic trends that were prevalent in
western Europe. The perception of the centaurs as armed horsemen was known
in Spain as far back as the thirteenth century. *Primera crónica general de España*
describes Hercules' victory over them, and *Grande e general estoria* contained the
idea that the name 'centaurs' was a combination of *ciento* (one hundred (people))
and *armadoas* (armed).[77] However, Abravanel was following Enrique de Villena's
popular *Los doze trabajos de Hércules*, which described Hercules' battle against the
centaurs and, under the heading 'The Truth', related how the discovery of horse
riding made it possible to defeat the Greeks and how Hercules turned the tables
on the 'centaurs'.[78] De Villena was greatly admired in Abravanel's social circles.[79]

Abravanel's focus on Hercules was not surprising in view of his importance in
west European culture: he was the patron of Florence, he was claimed to have
founded the dynasty of the dukes of Burgundy, and he appeared in the medallions
on the facade of the Colleoni chapel in Bergamo, in the tapestries of the Beauvais
cathedral, and in a painting by Albrecht Dürer.[80] But Abravanel's special interest
in Hercules may have stemmed primarily from his central place in Spanish historiography—he was regarded as the founder of the ancient Spanish monarchy.

Robert Tate has shown that the link between Hercules and the Iberian peninsula was first made in the thirteenth century by the archbishop of Toledo,
Rodrigo Ximenez de Rada. De Rada sought to connect ancient Spain to the classical world and wrote that Hercules conquered the Iberian peninsula and founded
many cities there. He also created a connection between Hercules and Hispanus,
the successor to the kingdom. In contrast, in Alfonso X's historiographical
works—*Primera crónica general de España* and *Grande e general estoria*—Hercules
is described as an astrologer, Hispanus is his nephew, and Pyrrhus, the legendary
ruler of Spain, succeeded him.[81] It seems certain that the *Primera crónica general
de España*, possibly in a version edited in Converso circles,[82] was the primary
source for Abravanel's tales of Hercules, including the detail that he was a 'great

[76] Veyne, *Did the Greeks Believe in Their Myths?*, 54–6, 67.

[77] Alfonso X, *Primera crónica general de España*, i. 8*a*; id., *Grande e general estoria*, i (ed. García
Solalinde, 329–30).

[78] De Villena, *Los doze trabajos de Hércules*, 15; see R. Ben-Shalom, 'The Myths of Troy and
Hercules as Reflected in the Writings of Some Jewish Exiles from Spain', 240.

[79] See Gutwirth, 'Don Ishaq Abravanel and Vernacular Humanism in Fifteenth Century Iberia',
esp. 646–7.   [80] See Seznec, *The Survival of the Pagan Gods*, 18, 24–5, 32, 186, 203.

[81] See Tate, 'Mythology in Spanish Historiography', 4–7. Tate does not discuss the earlier appear-
ances of Hispan in Muslim historiography. See also Fernández-Ordóñez, 'El taller de las "Estorias"',
68–70.

[82] Baer, 'Don Isaac Abravanel's Attitude to History and the State' (Heb.), 246 n. 13.

astronomer'.[83] Abravanel wrote that Pyrrhus, king of Spain, helped Nebuchad-nezzar, king of Babylon, to conquer Jerusalem in the days of the First Temple and that after the conquest he led the exiles to Spain. As far as we know, the link between Hercules (or members of his family) and the conquest of Jerusalem was first made in twelfth-century Spain.[84]

And you ought to know that with the king of Babylon in his [attack] on Jerusalem came kings and ministers from other kingdoms, and led Jews to their countries, and one of these was Pyrrhus, king of Spain. And the great Hercules from the land of Greece went forth throughout the world to conquer countries with his mighty wisdom and heroism, and he passed through the land of the west, and, after many heroic feats in conquering the countries, he came with many ships and a large army to Spain and settled there, and he reigned over the whole country of Spain. And since he yearned for his country and homeland, he went to the country of Italy, and from there to the country of Greece, and he was one of those who went to destroy the great city of Troy for the third time. And when Hercules journeyed from Spain, he gave his kingdom to the son of his sister who was called Hispan, and from his name the entire land of Spain is called Hispania in the vernacular language, and that Hispan had but one daughter and she married Pyrrhus who was also from Greece and he was at the destruction of the First Temple, and brought with him from there men of Judah, Benjamin, and Shimon and the Levites and the priests who were in Jerusalem, many people, who came with him willingly.[85]

The Jewish version of this myth first appeared in Abravanel's writings, but the tradition that Spanish Jewry originated from the exiles of the First Temple already existed among Jews in the tenth century, and there were other traditions that dated the arrival of the Jews to the time of King Solomon.[86] The myth served several purposes: it attested to the intellectual and cultural greatness of Spanish Jewry as descendants of the tribe of Judah; Jewish courtiers used it to prove their descent from the House of David in order to gain an advantage over others;[87] and

---

[83] Zacut, *Sefer yuḥasin* (ed. Filipowski, 235*a*); cf. Alfonso X, *Primera crónica general de España*, i. 8*a*: 'Hercules was so good a master of the art of the stars, that the sages would say that he held the sky on his shoulders.' Zacut ascribed the words of the sages in *Primera crónica general de España* to Atlas (*Sefer yuḥasin* (ed. Filipowski, 234*a*)).

[84] See J. Menéndez Pidal, 'Leyendas del último rey godo', 878–9.

[85] Abravanel on 2 Kings (*Perush linevi'im rishonim*, 680). He was the source for Capsali (*Seder eliyahu zuta*, 2: 40 (ed. Shmuelevitz, Simonsohn, and Benayahu, i. 143–5) and Joseph Sambari (*Sefer divrei yosef*, 93 (ed. Shtober, 259–60)).

[86] See Beinart, 'Cuándo llegaron los Judíos a España?', 13; id., 'When Did the Jews Arrive in Spain?' (Heb.), 21–2.

[87] See Abravanel on the Ibn Daud and Abravanel families (on Zech. 12: 7 (*Perush al nevi'im aharonim*, 239)); see also Beinart, 'The Image of the Jewish Courtier in Christian Spain' (Heb.), 63; H. H. Ben-Sasson, 'On Medieval Trends in Jewish Chronography' (Heb.), 388, 392–3.

converts used it to prove that their forefathers had not been involved in the Crucifixion of Jesus.[88]

From the Jewish perspective, this version was preferable to the one popular among Spanish Christians, according to which Jews came to Spain after the destruction of the Second Temple. The link established by Christians between the destruction of the Temple and the Jews' rejection of Jesus was liable to lead to the accusation that Spanish Jews were the descendants of those directly responsible for Jesus's death.[89] There is an edifying example of the link between Jesus's Crucifixion and the antiquity of the Jews in Spain in *Seder eliyahu zuta*. After giving Abravanel's version nearly verbatim, Elijah Capsali wrote:

And although all the inhabitants of Spain, young and old, paid the king 30 coins, like the 30 coins for which the Jews sold Jesus their God, according to the words of the Christians, the inhabitants of Toledo, the large city, were not obliged to pay this tax for they were not in Jerusalem at the time of Jesus, hence they were not obliged and paid nothing.[90]

Toledo, the city where exiles of the First Temple settled, is distinguished from all the other areas in Spain, which were populated by the descendants of other exiles. However, it was not true that the Jews of Toledo were exempt from the tax. From the thirteenth century, the Jews of Castile were obliged to pay the church a tax of 30 dinars, to recall Judas Iscariot's betrayal of Jesus, and the Jews of Toledo were the first to pay in 1219. The idea was probably passed down to Capsali by Spanish exiles. It appeared, for example, in *Refundición de la crónica de 1344*, probably written by a Converso from Toledo in the fifteenth century, which also contained letters claiming to be from the Jews of Toledo to the Jews of Jerusalem, warning them not to kill Jesus.[91]

At that time the Conversos had to respond to various Christian circles in Castile and Aragon who maligned them for their Jewish origin and impure blood. Toledo was the scene of anti-Converso activity, beginning with the uprising led

[88] See Baer, *A History of the Jews in Christian Spain*, i. 16; Beinart, 'Cuándo llegaron los Judíos a España?', 6–7; id., 'When Did the Jews Arrive in Spain?' (Heb.), 14; see R. Menéndez Pidal, *Crónicas generales de España*, 157–61, esp. 159.

[89] See Hook, 'Some Problems in Andrés Bernáldez's Account of the Spanish Jews', esp. 231–48; see also Nirenberg, 'Mass Conversion and Genealogical Mentalities', 29 n. 72.

[90] Capsali, *Seder eliyahu zuta*, 2: 40 (ed. Shmuelevitz, Simonsohn, and Benayahu, i. 144).

[91] Castaño, 'Una fiscalidad sagrada', esp. 191–8. Later, Capsali wrote that the exemption of the Toledo Jews was cancelled by Isabella of Castile (*Seder eliyahu zuta*, 2: 60 (ed. Shmuelevitz, Simonsohn, and Benayahu, i. 188); see also Matt. 26: 15; Baer, 'Don Isaac Abravanel's Attitude to History and the State' (Heb.), 403 n. 13; Beinart, 'Cuándo llegaron los Judíos a España?', 7, 10; id., 'When Did the Jews Arrive in Spain?' (Heb.), 14, 17; Levy, *Worlds Meet* (Heb.), 290–1; R. Menéndez Pidal, *Crónicas generales de España*, 159)).

by Pedro Sarmiento, the supreme judge, early in 1449, and the publication of his *Sentencia estatuto* against Conversos who held public office.[92] Since Toledo was at the centre of political events, it is not surprising that the myth draws a distinction between Toledo and the rest of the kingdom.

Abravanel distinguished—unlike some Jewish traditions—between the Spanish diaspora and other diasporas. Although he thought that exiles from the time of the First Temple also went to other countries[93] and that exiles expelled by Titus and Hadrian joined those who were already in Spain,[94] he stressed that, based on their lineage, the Jews of Spain were regarded as First Temple exiles, while the others were considered to have arrived after the destruction of the Second Temple.[95] Both Abravanel and Capsali mention cities settled by exiles of the First Temple and claim that their names have Hebrew origins: Toledo is derived from Tolitula, referring to the Jews' wandering (*tiltul*, but actually from its Arabic name Tolaytula) on their way from Jerusalem; Maqueda is named after Makkedah in the Land of Israel; Escalona is named after Ashkelon; and Lucena means 'to be like Luz in the Land of Israel, prepared for prophecy'.[96] Abravanel argued that the Jews of the Spanish diaspora enjoyed greater respect and material prosperity than those of other diasporas, because of its greater antiquity[97] and because they engaged in 'clean' occupations, in contrast to those in other places (particularly Germany).[98]

Arab historians also recounted the early history of Spain, and versions can be found in the writings of Al-Mas'udi (d. 956), Ibn al-Athir (1160–1234), and

[92] See Baer, *A History of the Jews in Christian Spain*, ii. 277–83; Beinart, 'Large-Scale Forced Conversion and the Fate of the *Anusim*' (Heb.); Orfali, 'Jews and Conversos in Fifteenth-Century Spain'; Nirenberg, 'Mass Conversion and Genealogical Mentalities'; id., 'Spanish "Judaism" and "Christianity" in an Age of Mass Conversion'; R. Ben-Shalom, 'The Social Context of Apostasy among Fifteenth-Century Spanish Jewry', 184–7.

[93] 'And there is no doubt that those Jews from the destruction of the First Temple also came to France and England and to Germany and to the other kingdoms of the sons of Edom' (Abravanel on 2 Kings (*Perush linevi'im rishonim*, 681)). Many Jewish communities, in western and eastern Europe, as well as in Asia, traced their foundations to the time of the destruction of the Second Temple.

[94] Abravanel on Kings, Introduction (*Perush linevi'im rishonim*, 425).

[95] Abravanel, *Mashmia yeshuah*, 9: 1 (Jerusalem edn., 556).

[96] Abravanel on 2 Kgs 25 (*Perush linevi'im rishonim*, 680); Beinart, 'Cuándo llegaron los Judíos a España?', 9, 11; id., 'When Did the Jews Arrive in Spain?' (Heb.), 17–18.

[97] Abravanel, *Ma'ayenei hayeshuah*, 12: 7 (Jerusalem edn., 413).

[98] Abravanel used the expression 'clean occupations' to distinguish those of Spanish Jews from those of Ashkenazi Jews, who engaged in usury as their sole occupation. He accepted Profayt Duran's version of the expulsion of the Jews from England on the charge of 'shaving coins' as true and an accepted Jewish tradition (Abravanel, *Sefer yeshuot meshiho*, 46a). In contrast, see Solomon ibn Verga and Samuel Usque, who rejected the accusation as a Christian libel (Dinur, *Israel in the Diaspora* (Heb.), Pt. II, vol. ii, 574–5). For a summary of the subject, see Shatzmiller, 'Solomon ibn Verga and the Expulsion of English Jewry' (Heb.).

Al-Marakshi (d. 1224).[99] According to the main Muslim tradition, Isban (Hispan) was the son of Titus 'of the barbarians of Rome', so Jews were unable to use this tradition to prove they were among the First Temple exiles.[100] Moses ibn Ezra was also only familiar with Muslim traditions, and hence he wrote that Hispan was 'the master [of Hispania] during the rule of the Romans before the Goths ... and the capital of his kingdom was Seville. Hispania was called after him, and by the earlier ones [was called] Ispamia.'[101]

Popular traditions often begin with a simple core and evolve over centuries.[102] The core of this myth was a Jewish tradition about the arrival of Jews in Spain after the destruction of the First Temple. Over time, as the cultural and social needs of Spanish Jewry changed, Muslim and Christian traditions about the participation of the king of Spain in Nebuchadnezzar's conquest of Jerusalem were added to it, as were the figures from classical mythology adopted by the Christians of Spain. The final version, which appears in Abravanel, is therefore a product of Spanish historiography and Christian myth—apparently in a Converso version. However, in order to understand how Abravanel shaped Hercules' image in his writings, we first have to look at the medieval Christian approach to Graeco-Roman mythology.

Early Christians had an euhemeristic approach to pagan gods, regarding them as ancient kings and eminent men who were honoured and admired whilst alive and more so after their deaths. Eventually people began to regard them as gods and established rituals in their honour. At first, Christian euhemerism had polemical aims; however, these were soon abandoned with the demise of paganism, and it became a tool for historical research. This trend existed as early as Eusebius's *Church History* and also appeared in the works of Jerome and Paulus Orosius, but its most complete expression is in the writings of Isidore of Seville, who stated that 'those who the pagans claim are gods were then ordinary men'.[103] Isidore placed heroic figures from mythology and pioneers of civilization, such as

---

[99] See Halkin, notes (Heb.) to Moses ibn Ezra, *Sefer ha'iyunim vehadiyunim*, 55, note to line 93.

[100] Al-Mas'udi reported a tradition that Isban was a descendant of Japheth son of Noah and another that claimed he was descended from Ispahan of Persia (see *Muruj adh-dhahab*, i. 359–60). A tradition cited by Ibn al-Athir claimed that Hispania was named after a man called Hispany, who was crucified there (see *Kitab al-kamil fi al-tarikh*, iv. 439–41). According to another version, Isban son of Titus invaded Iberia, defeated the Africans, and settled there, establishing his capital in Seville. Later Isban conquered Jerusalem and transferred the treasure, including booty from the Temple, to Spain. Many generations later, another people invaded Spain, and only later was it invaded by the Goths. Ahmad ibn Muhammad al-Maqari of Tlemcen summarized the various Muslim traditions. He wrote that Isban sailed to Jerusalem, destroyed the city, and killed 100,000 Jews. He also took with him to Iberia 100,000 Jewish prisoners (see Ahmad ibn Muhammad al-Maqqari, *Nafh al-tib*, 131–2).   [101] Moses ibn Ezra, *Sefer ha'iyunim vehadiyunim*, 55.

[102] See Zfatman, *Between Ashkenaz and Sefarad* (Heb.), 118.

[103] Isidore of Seville, *Etymologiarum*, 11: 1.

Prometheus, alongside biblical figures such as the patriarchs, the judges, and the prophets, thus creating a continuum of profane and sacred history. Although there were also differing views,[104] nearly all medieval chroniclers followed Isidore.[105] However, a physical-astrological understanding of mythology and a moral-allegorical understanding of pagan gods emerged alongside the euhemerist approach. One of the most important works that used these various approaches to mythology was Boccaccio's *Genealogy of the Pagan Gods*, written in the second half of the fourteenth century, which until the mid-sixteenth century was a major source of knowledge of pagan gods.[106]

Abraham Zacut and Isaac Abravanel's approach to the Graeco-Roman gods was similar to the euhemerist approach of the Christians. One particularly important influence on Abravanel was Alonso Tostado, bishop of Avila (*c*.1410–55), who was connected to the Mendosa family, in whose circles Abravanel was later active. Tostado, under Boccaccio's influence, wrote the most important work on the gods in Spanish literature, *Las questiones sobre los dioses de los gentiles*, which emphasized the euhemerist approach alongside the physical-astrological and the moral-allegorical.[107] Thus Abravanel viewed Hercules not as a god, but as a man who performed great feats, one of which was the founding of the kingdom of Spain. He described Hercules' heroism in the west (based on his tenth labour, stealing the cattle of Geryon) and his decision to then settle on the western edge of the world. Hercules came to Spain with a fleet of ships and an army, conquered the land, and reigned over it. After his longing for Greece became irresistible, he decided to return, and left Hispanus to succeed him, and the entire land is named Hispania after him. Pyrrhus, who reigned after him, married Hispanus's daughter.

In the fifteenth century the myth of Hercules was once again at the centre of the political and intellectual scene in Castile, with court historians attempting to harness history for ideological purposes. Mossen Diego de Valera (the son of a Converso), for example, used the myth in an attempt to prove the superiority of the Spanish kingdom (and Castile as its successor) over Rome, France, and the other kingdoms of Europe. He fixed the precise dates of Hercules and his conquests in Spain to the years between the third destruction of Troy, an event that Hercules took part in, and the fourth destruction of Troy by the Greeks (the

---

[104] See e.g. Gregory of Tours, *Suffering of the Seven Martyrs*, 37.

[105] See Seznec, *The Survival of the Pagan Gods*, 11–19.

[106] Ibid. 220–4. It was well known in Castile in the fifteenth century and was translated into Castilian by order of Iñigo López de Mendoza (see Gómez Moreno, *España y la Italia de los humanistas*, 158; id., *El Prohemio e carta del Marqués de Santillana y la teoría literaria del s XV*, 95–7; Piccus, 'El traductor español de "De genealogia Deorum"').

[107] See R. Ben-Shalom, 'Graeco-Roman Myth and Mythology in the Historical Consciousness of Medieval Spanish Jewry' (Heb.), 463–6; Saquero Suárez-Somonte and González Rolán, 'Las questiones sobre los dioses de los gentiles del Tostado'.

version in the *Iliad*). This enabled de Valera to prove that the Spanish kingdom was founded before Rome, which was founded by the Trojan Aeneas fleeing the fourth destruction of Troy, and the other kingdoms, which were founded by refugees from the same war.[108]

However, there were also attempts to minimize Spain's connection to the classical world during the fifteenth century, which included adopting a negative attitude to Hercules, maligning his origin and character and claiming that he was a pirate and a robber and even that he was not the Hercules of the twelve labours. This trend was part of a rejection of anything not Spanish.[109] Abravanel, a Jew whom society would have considered a non-Spanish 'Other', would have identified with the old version of the myth, which reflected a far more open attitude. However, Zacut related a myth of the origin of the name 'Hispania', according to which, the country was named after a local king, Hesperus, not Hispanus.[110] This version was adopted by those who rejected the myth of Hercules and Hispanus, who was regarded as a trespasser and the descendant of the infamous pirate. During the reign of Ferdinand and Isabella, the Herculean myth regained favour, as it provided support for Ferdinand in his attempt to form a united kingdom, and, as well as in the writings of Diego de Valera, it appeared in *Historia de los hechos de Don Rodrigo Ponce de León Marqués de Cádiz*.[111]

Joseph Shatzmiller discussed how Jews in western Europe used the foundation myths of the societies they lived in as a basis for political claims within the Jewish community.[112] Other scholars have shown that the myth of Jewish antiquity in Spain enabled Jews and Conversos to refute the accusation that they had played a part in Jesus's Crucifixion and to cope with threats of expulsion.[113]

---

[108] See Cirot, *Les Histoires générales d'Espagne*, 68 n. 4. On the role of the court historian in Castile in shaping national identity, see Bermejo Cabrero, 'Orígenes del oficio de cronista real'; Tate, 'El cronista real castellano durante el siglo XV'.

[109] Tate, 'Mythology in Spanish Historiography', 10–11. This is particularly striking in Fabricio de Vagad (see Cirot, *Les Histoires générales d'Espagne*, 58).

[110] Zacut, *Sefer yuḥasin* (ed. Filipowski, 234b). According to *Primera crónica general de España*, the country conquered by Hercules was called Esperia, but during the reign of Hispanus the name was changed to España (Alfonso X, *Primera crónica general de España*, i. 9b, 11a). This is also how Spanish history was described in *Crònica general de Pere III el Cerimoniós* (19–20) and by Ximenez de Rada (see Cirot, *Les Histoires générales d'Espagne*, 32–4; Ibn Daud, *Zikhron divrei romi* (Mantua edn., 24; ed. Vehlow, 124–7)).

[111] *Historia de los hechos de Don Rodrigo Ponce de León*, 147–8; see Tate, 'Mythology in Spanish Historiography', 9–13. It also appears in a Spanish Jewish tradition that found its way into *Seder eliyahu zuta*: 'And the king of Aragon ruled over all of Spain. And since the day that Hispan ruled over Hispania, Spain has never been ruled by a single king but by a great number [of kings]. But now, this king [Ferdinand] ruled over all' (Capsali, *Seder eliyahu zuta*, 2: 59 (ed. Shmuelevitz, Simonsohn, and Benayahu, i. 187)). [112] Shatzmiller, 'Politics and the Myth of Origins'.

[113] See Baer, *A History of the Jews in Christian Spain*, i. 16; Beinart, 'Cuándo llegaron los Judíos a España?', 6–7; id., 'When Did the Jews Arrive in Spain?' (Heb.), 14–15; Castaño, 'Una fiscalidad

The myth also created a link between the founding of the Spanish diaspora and the founding of Spain itself, since Pyrrhus, the son-in-law of Hispan, the nephew of Hercules, brought the Jews there. Thus Jews and non-Jews were linked through a shared origin and a shared fate.[114] This was further emphasized by the story of the Jewish sage who was brought to the Iberian peninsula and associated with the mythologized figure of Isidore of Seville recounted by Abraham ben Solomon and in *Sefer hayashar*.

Abravanel's story of Hercules fits nicely with the Christian Spanish myths that shaped Hispanic consciousness. Ron Barkai has shown how Christian chroniclers tried to use the myths—like that of Pelagius in the cave at Covadonga and Saint James of Compostela—to construct a Hispanic self-image, centred around the perception of a unified Spanish territory and a clear distinction between Spain and the other countries of the world. In some Christian chronicles this unity also included the Muslim population.[115]

Barkai also discussed the patriotic views of Spanish Jews, pointing out that they had a sense of belonging in Spain expressed, for example, in the Judaization of the names of the cities. However, unlike Christians, for whom Spain was their home, past, present, and future; for Jews, it was their home at the present, but the Land of Israel was their original one. In Barkai's view, although the Jews loved Spain, their spiritual link to the Land of Israel was stronger than their earthly link to the soil of Spain.[116]

The myth of the origins of the Jewish diaspora in Spain should be read in the context of the Spanish myths and the sense of belonging to Spain. Just as the Christians stressed the uniqueness of Spain among all the countries of the world, so the Jews stressed the uniqueness of the Spanish diaspora among all the others. Christians placed an emphasis on ancient mythological founders, and Jews saw

sagrada', 191–4. As early as the twelfth century the convert Petrus Alfonsi claimed, in *Dialogi Petri et Moysi Judaei*, that the Jews living outside of Palestine were guilty of the Crucifixion (see J. Cohen, 'The Jews as the Killers of Christ'; id., *Living Letters of the Law*, 214 n. 40; Merhavia, *The Talmud in Christian Eyes* (Heb.), 96).

[114] See Genot-Bismuth, 'L'Argument de l'histoire dans la tradition espagnole de polémique judéo-chrétienne', 204–6; Weinryb, 'The Beginnings of East-European Jewry in Legend and Historiography'. *Refundición de la crónica de 1344* tells how the Jews came to Spain willingly in the time of King Solomon (Beinart, 'Cuándo llegaron los Judíos a España?', 6–7; id., 'When Did the Jews Arrive in Spain?' (Heb.), 14). Other Jewish traditions hold that the Jews came in the time of Amaziah, king of Judah, and that King Solomon sent a delegation to Spain headed by Adoniram (ibid. 15–16; Shatzmiller, 'Politics and the Myth of Origins', 59).

[115] Barkai, *Cristianos y Musulmanes en la España medieval*, 293–7; id., 'Images of Self and Enemy among Christians and Muslims in Spain' (Heb.), 341–2.

[116] See Barkai, 'The Patriotism of Spanish Jews in the Middle Ages' (Heb.); on the Muslim period, see Aloni, 'Zion and Jerusalem in the Poetry of Spain' (Heb.), esp. 257; Hacker, 'Invitation to an Intellectual Duel' (Heb.), esp. 355–6 nn. 29–30.

themselves as an integral part of that same myth. The Christians based their self-image on, among other things, the racial purity of the royal house as direct descend-ants of Visigothic kings,[117] and Jews tried to use this myth to prove that they were descended from the House of David.

Solomon ibn Verga noted the relationship between the Jewish and Spanish myths in chapter 7 of *Shevet yehudah*, which contains a famous fictitious dialogue between a symbolic 'King Alfonso' and a typological Christian sage 'Thomas'. He cited the Jewish myth of the antiquity of Spanish Jewry in a version similar to Abravanel's and added several interesting details. Thomas told the king about how Nebuchadnezzar divided the Jewish prisoners: two thirds, including the tradesmen, scholars, and merchants, he took with him to Babylon, and the remaining third, which included the members of the House of David and the priests of the Temple, he gave to Pyrrhus and Hispanus in gratitude for their help in conquering the city.[118] Hence, Thomas remarked, the king need not be amazed to find members of the House of David—like the Abravanel family—among the Jews in Spain.

In King Alfonso's answer to Thomas, the Jewish and the Christian myths are presented side by side:

And it became known throughout the world that among all the peoples, there is no one who, like these poor Jews, can tell of his origin, descent, and pure roots. And we see that our forefathers, great kings, delighted in their descent from the Godos [Goths]. And some of the tellers related that the Godos were descended from the seed of Gad, the son of Jacob the patriarch. And someone came from this seed to Rome and converted to the faith of Jesus and achieved greatness and succeeded in becoming the head of all the advisers called consuls. Afterwards he became king, and from him came the family of Godos. And when you examine all the other peoples [of the world] you will not discover from which root they come . . . neither about these nor those do we know the truth of their origin . . . and this means but to say that there are no renowned roots for the fami-lies, while for these poor Jews, their roots have stood.[119]

Alfonso claimed that the royal house of Spain belonged to the Visigothic royal dynasty, Godos, which was the biblical tribe Gad,[120] and hence the kings of

[117] See Barkai, *Cristianos y Musulmanes en la España medieval*, 293–7; id., 'Images of Self and Enemy among Christians and Muslims in Spain' (Heb.), 44–7, 53, 128, 274, 340.

[118] Ibn Verga, *Shevet yehudah*, 33. Unlike Abravanel's story, in which only Pyrrhus took part in the battle for Jerusalem, according to Ibn Verga, Hispanus also participated (see Beinart, 'Cuándo llegaron los Judíos a España?', 12–13; id., 'When Did the Jews Arrive in Spain?' (Heb.), 19).

[119] Ibn Verga, *Shevet yehudah*, 34–5.

[120] Ibid. 44–5; on the neo-Gothic myth in Spain, see Maravall, *El concepto de España en la Edad Media*, 326–37. The Goths were generally regarded as the descendants of the biblical Gog and Magog (see Albo, *Sefer ha'ikarim*, ii. 42, 862), a tradition which also appeared in a number of Christian sources (*Crónica pseudo-Isidoriana*, 14; Alfonso X, *Primera crónica general de España*, i. 4b, 5b; Pero Niño, *El victorial*, 32) and in Zacut's *Sefer yuḥasin* (ed. Filipowski, 232b; ed. Freiman, p. xl).

Spain surpassed all the other peoples, who lacked a clear historical tradition about their precise origin.[121] The myth of unbroken Visigothic succession emerged in the ninth century and became official historiography from the time of Lucas de Tuy and Rodrigo Ximenez de Rada in the thirteenth. During the fifteenth century the myth underwent a revival due to the new need to legitimize the novel and illegitimate dynasty of the Trastámara. It appeared, for example, in the *Historiae hispanica* written in 1470 by Ruy Sánchez, bishop of Palencia; in *Crónica de Juan II de Castilla* by Álvar García de Santa María; in the work of Alonso de Cartagena, who claimed that Juan II of Castile was descended from King Alaric who sacked Rome in 410; and in the work of Fernan Perez de Guzman, who asserted that Enrique III was a descendant of Reccared, the Visigothic king who embraced Catholic Christianity.[122] The myth was also accepted by the Jews, as expressed in *Seder eliyahu zuta*: 'He, King Don Juan II, who came from the race of ancient Spanish Kings.'[123] At the same time, the Jewish myth in *Shevet yehudah* emphasized the superior lineage of the Jews of Spain as direct descendants of King David, and hence King Alfonso was faced with the fact that among the Jewish families in Spain there were some of greater nobility than his own. Even the convert Pablo de Santa María was reputed to have said that if nobility meant antiquity then the Jews had stronger claims than anyone.[124]

Although it is a fictional narrative, it is deeply rooted in the Christian perception of the Jews in Spain. The acceptance of the Jewish myth as a fact by Thomas is confirmed by statements made by other Christians in fifteenth-century Spain. From the second half of the fifteenth century, the issue of Jewish lineage and nobility was at the heart of a raging polemic between the opponents of the Conversos and their supporters. The racist claims against the Conversos,

[121] To contradict the claims of the 'other peoples', Ibn Verga, like Abravanel, relied on Isidore of Seville's discussion of the foundation of Rome (Ibn Verga, *Shevet yehudah*, 34; see Chapter 2 above; see also Abravanel, *Mashmia yeshuah*, 3: 7 (Jerusalem edn., 461–3); on Isa. 35: 10 (*Perush al nevi'im aḥaronim*, 169–73); Beinart, 'Cuándo llegaron los Judíos a España?', 13 n. 29; id., 'When Did the Jews Arrive in Spain?' (Heb.), 19 n. 29).

[122] See Cacho Blecua, 'Los historiadores de la Crónica sarracina', esp. 44–5; Cantera Burgos, *Álvar García de Santa María y su familia de conversos*, 460–2; Maravall, *El concepto de España en la Edad Media*, 304; Netanyahu, *The Origins of the Inquisition in Fifteenth Century Spain*, 517–77; Deyermond, 'Written by the Victors', 61; Shepard, *Lost Lexicon*, 26. In the chronicle of Juan II of Castile, the kings of Leon and Castile are said to be the descendants of Pelagius (see Álvar García de Santa María, *Crónica de Juan II de Castilla*, 2–3).

[123] Capsali, *Seder eliyahu zuta*, 1: 56 (ed. Shmulevitz, Simonsohn, and Benayahu, i. 180).

[124] Gutwirth mentions Santa María, Diego de Valera, and Fernan Perez de Guzman ('Lineage in Fifteenth-Century Hispano-Jewish Thought', 87). They were all linked to the Conversos (see Netanyahu, *The Origins of the Inquisition in Fifteenth Century Spain*, 517, 578, 1265–6 n. 1; Nirenberg, 'Mass Conversion and Genealogical Mentalities', esp. 31–2; Shepard, *Lost Lexicon*, 140). The information about Santa María is from Juan de Lucena, *De vita beata*, 147–8.

regarding their lowly Jewish origin and the need to oust them from their high positions in Spanish society, were countered by a number of intellectuals from the Converso camp, who emphasized the ancient nobility of the Jews and their descent from the House of David. Some even asserted that the Jewish nobility was superior in its attributes to Spanish nobility.[125] That was in fact one of the conclusions drawn from the version of the myth by Ibn Verga, who was apparently closely associated with the Conversos and actively supported them.[126]

The foundation myth of the Spanish diaspora cited by Isaac Abravanel and Solomon ibn Verga is similar to the foundation myths of other European peoples. The Jewish myth asserted that the Jews came to Spain with Pyrrhus, a Greek hero from the royal family of Hercules, who therefore was no less important than the Trojan heroes who appeared in other national stories. In the Middle Ages, it was common knowledge that the Jews of the Iberian peninsula had come from far away. According to the myth, however, they were not the progeny of exiled or expelled people who came to Spain against their will but descendants of a group who willingly migrated to the west, after the disaster which, by divine command, befell Jerusalem, as the Trojan followers of Aeneas and Frankion did after the fall of Troy. Like the people of Italy, France, Germany, and England, they sought to establish a new settlement in western Europe. Through this myth, the Spanish Jews were able to share in the same patriotic Hispanic trends that developed in the Iberian peninsula throughout the Middle Ages. These trends, as I noted, generally emphasized the national Hispanic aspects, sometimes at the expense of religious ones. They could, therefore, be the basis for patriotic identification for Jews.

From the end of the fourteenth century, the Jews of Spain underwent a series of crises (the massacres of 1391, the preaching of Vincent Ferrer, the Valladolid laws of 1412, the Disputation of Tortosa), and from the second half of the fifteenth century the issue of Jewish lineage and nobility were at the centre of a stormy polemic between the opponents of the Conversos and their supporters. The claims that Conversos were of lowly Jewish origin and should be removed from positions of authority were countered by Converso intellectuals, who stressed the ancient nobility of the Jews and their descent from King David. The Jewish communities had to redefine their religious and social boundaries in response to the rise in the number of converts, the growing extremism of the mendi-

---

[125] See Netanyahu, *The Origins of the Inquisition in Fifteenth Century Spain*, 554–69, 578–83; Edwards, 'Conversos, Judaism and the Language of Monarchy'; Nirenberg, 'Mass Conversion and Genealogical Mentalities', esp. 29–30.

[126] See Benayahu, 'A Source on the Expellees in Portugal and Their Departure for Thessalonica' (Heb.), 250; on Ibn Verga's familiarity with the royal house in Castile, see *Shevet yehudah*, 52; Baer, *A History of the Jews in Christian Spain*, i. 325–7.

cant friars, and the new ideological trends that advocated the expulsion of the Jews from Spain, as had happened in England and France. A striking expression of these trends is contained in *Fortalitium fidei* (*c.*1464), by Alfonso de Espina, confessor to King Enrique IV of Castile. De Espina disputed when the Jews had arrived in the Iberian peninsula and whether or not they came freely.[127] The merging of the Hispanic and Jewish foundation myths was a response to these new trends. It helped Jews redefine their identity in Spain and in particular to enhance its Hispanic elements.

ORAL TRADITIONS

According to Ramón Menéndez Pidal, romances first appeared in the Iberian peninsula at the end of the thirteenth century, when *jongleurs* began to reconstruct excerpts from the medieval Spanish *cantares de gesta* and turn them into narrative songs with short dramatic plots. Romances quickly became popular among all classes of society: the courts of the nobility, the military leadership, the educated clergy, and the common people. They were treasure houses of historical information and popular traditions and reflected the customs of the feudal period and its values. Added to local topics such as tales of knights, episodes about Christian and Moorish kings, and the Reconquest, were tales from neighbouring countries, primarily France, such as those about Charlemagne. In addition, many regional styles developed: Asturian, Andalusian, Castilian, Aragonese, Catalonian, and Portuguese.

The Jews of Spain also embraced romances, and after the Expulsion they preserved them as part of their cultural heritage. For more than 500 years the exiles and their descendants, particularly the women, sang romances in Ladino, which differed from the language of the places where they settled and rebuilt their lives. The romances preserved by Jews contain a core from the various areas of Iberia they left, which over time absorbed local additions (Turkish, Greek, Slav, Moroccan).[128]

Scholars have studied the place of these romances in the life of Spanish Jews by looking at such aspects of them as intrigues, wars, issues of social status, family relations, taboos, and so on. Their social role helped to preserve them over hundreds of years of oral transmission in the two branches of the Spanish diaspora: northern Africa under the Spanish protectorate and the Ottoman empire. The historical information they contain was also documented in the Spanish

---

[127] See Baer, *A History of the Jews in Christian Spain*, i. 306–78; ii. 1–292; R. Ben-Shalom, 'The Blood Libel in Arles' (Heb.), 400–2; Meyuhas Ginio, 'The Expulsion of the Jews from France' (Heb.); id., '"The Fortress of the Faith" at "the End of the West"' (Heb.), i. 186.

[128] Attias, *Spanish Romancero* (Heb.), 3–20.

chronicles, and scholars have discussed the historical aspects of the romances insofar as they are connected to the history of Spain.[129] However, until now the historical traditions in the Jewish romances have not been studied.

A romance from Tetuán, *Urraca salva a su hermano de prisión*, tells how Alfonso, who would become King Alfonso VI of Castile, was rescued by his sister Urraca after he had been imprisoned by their brother, King Sancho II. Some of the names are wrong, but in essence the story is historically accurate. The events are documented in various chronicles and in a parallel romance printed in Saragossa in 1550.[130] While the Jews were still in Spain, the names of the heroes of the romances were recalled with greater exactitude, and their content was closer to the historical events. The romance *Las almenas de Toro* tells the same story and contains historical events and literary motifs (although most are distorted) from the epic of El Cid, such as Sancho II's siege of Toro, Urraca's love for El Cid, and possibly a hint of incest between Alfonso and Urraca.[131] A romance from Tangier (*Búcar sobre Valencia* or *El moro que reta a Valencia*) preserves a dialogue that occurred after the conquest of Valencia between El Cid and the Muslim emir of the Almoravids, which is also described in several Spanish chronicles and in *Poema de mio Cid*. Other stories of El Cid, such as the wedding between him and Jimena at the king's command after El Cid had killed her father and the execution of Count Ordóñez, also appear in romances.[132] Another romance from Tetuán, *El sueño de Doña Alda*, preserved the dream of the wife of the Carolingian hero Roland in which she is informed of his imminent death at the battle of Roncevaux. Some excerpts from the *Chanson de Roland* were preserved in other romances,[133] and *Jorelencio, Jorelencio* preserved the story of the abduction of Doña Leonor Téllez, the wife of Juan Lorenzo, from Acuñia by Ferdinand I of Portugal.[134]

---

[129] See Mackay, 'The Ballad and the Frontier in Late Medieval Spain'.

[130] See Weich-Shahak, *Romancero Sefardí de Marruecos*, no. 2.

[131] See Armistead and Silverman, *The Judeo-Spanish Ballad Chapbooks of Yacob Abraham Yoná*, 37–44; Attias, *Spanish Romancero* (Heb.), no. 2 (62–4); see also Barkai, *Sephardi Mythology* (Heb.), 199–244.

[132] Arce, 'Cinco nuevos romances del Cid'; Armistead and Silverman, 'Sobre unos romances del Cid recogidos en Tetuán'; Attias, *Spanish Romancero* (Heb), no. 2 (62–4), no. 28 (108–9); Weich-Shahak, *Romancero Sefardí de Marruecos*, no. 3.

[133] Armistead and Silverman, *The Judeo-Spanish Ballad Chapbooks of Yacob Abraham Yoná*, nos. 2–3 (56–73); Weich-Shahak, *Romancero Sefardí de Marruecos*, no. 4; see Barkai, *Sephardi Mythology* (Heb.), 187–92.

[134] See Alonso García, *Literatura oral del ladino*, 68–70; Attias, *Spanish Romancero* (Heb.), no. 3 (64–6); Weich-Shahak, *Romancero Sefardí de Marruecos*, no. 8. On the legend of Flores and Blancaflor which entered Spanish historiography from Morocco and other areas and appeared in the Judaeo-Spanish romances *The Moorish Queen Xerifa*, *Count Flor*, and *The Two Sisters, Queen and Captive*, see Grieve, *Floire and Blancheflor and the European Romance*, 23–36, 193–8.

Oral historical traditions were not only transmitted through romances. On several occasions, Ibn Daud related traditions passed down over generations in his family and among his acquaintances.[135] Nahmanides also recorded the oral transmission of historical details from generation to generation, including family histories and communal and urban facts, such as when a certain tower was constructed.[136] Solomon ibn Verga collected many oral traditions in *Shevet yehudah*,[137] and Elijah Capsali's *Seder eliyahu zuta* contains the stories of those expelled from Spain in 1492.[138] In several instances, Capsali mentioned the names of the storytellers. For example, he heard the 'stories of Andalusia . . . from the lips of a wise, clever man, one of the notables and sages of Andalusia, Rabbi Joseph Halevi Hakim, whose distinguished forefathers were among those who sat at the king's gate',[139] and about the marriage of Ferdinand and Isabella from Rabbi Jacob: 'a very sharp, clever man, we met face to face. He was one of the exiles and he ate at our table. He spoke to me and what he said I wrote in ink in the book.'[140] *Seder eliyahu zuta* is important not only because of the historical traditions it contains but because it attests to the oral heritage of Spanish Jewry. The collective memory of Spanish Jews contained a great deal of historical information, which can now only be found in Christian and Muslim chronicles. Capsali managed to gather a few scraps of it. Although he edited the testimonies—in 1517 and 1523—he stated that he recorded many of them in 1492, and the traditions about Spain contained in *Seder eliyahu zuta* were an authentic part of the historical consciousness of Spanish Jewry on the eve of the Expulsion.[141]

THE FALL OF VISIGOTHIC SPAIN

The long story of the conquest of Visigothic Spain by the Muslims is recounted in *Seder eliyahu zuta* in several chapters, enlivened with many sub-plots.[142] The main line of the story is how Count Julian, the military commander of Roderic, the last Visigothic king, conspired with the Muslims after the king raped his

---

[135] Ibn Daud, *Sefer hakabalah*, ch. 7, lines 201–2; see also lines 289, 317 (ed. Cohen: Heb. section, 59, 64, 66; Eng. section, 79, 86, 88–9); Ashtor, *History of the Jews in Muslim Spain* (Heb.), i. p. ii.

[136] Nahmanides, *Torat hashem temimah*, 144.

[137] Ibn Verga, *Shevet yehudah*, 72; see Ankori, *An Encounter in History* (Heb.), 114–16; see also 56.

[138] Many of the Jews expelled from Spain passed through Crete where Elijah Capsali lived, and he recorded their stories of Christian and Muslim Spain: 'The poor were always welcome in our home, and the expelled ones gathered under our roof, and the pleasant Spanish [Jews], who were dispersed, always passed through here. . . . And when they came they would stop here and tell me everything about the Expulsion from Spain' (*Seder eliyahu zuta*, Introduction (ed. Shmuelevitz, Simonsohn, and Benayahu, i. 11)).   [139] Ibid.; see Benayahu, Introduction (Heb.), ibid., iii. 13, 25.

[140] Capsali, *Seder eliyahu zuta*, 2: 58 (ed. Shmuelevitz, Simonsohn, and Benayahu, i. 185).

[141] See also Bonfil, 'Between the Land of Israel and Babylonia' (Heb.), 6.

[142] Capsali, *Seder eliyahu zuta*, 2: 41–5 (ed. Shmuelevitz, Simonsohn, and Benayahu, i. 145–55).

daughter, Florinda. Although the story contains many legendary additions, its basic outline is the same as that which appears in a number of Spanish chronicles attempting to explain the Visigothic defeat.[143] The historical background for this legend was a division among the Visigoths, which led to the followers of Wittiza, Roderic's predecessor, joining the invading Muslims.

Christians from both sides of the division—for and against Roderic—as well as Arab writers have left their mark on the story. The descendants of the Visigoths who had supported Wittiza came to occupy important positions in the new Muslim society and claimed that the disorder in the Visigothic kingdom from the time of Roderic's coronation was to blame for the defeat. The story of Julian's betrayal developed among the Christians under Muslim rule, and the rape of his daughter as the main cause of the Visigoth defeat first appeared in the mid-eleventh century in *Chronica pseudo-Isidoriana*, written by a Mozarab from Toledo. Later the various versions were adapted in *De rebus Hispanie*, written by Rodrigo Ximenez de Rada in 1243, and in *Crónica general de España de 1344*. Later versions tend to exonerate Roderic and blame Julian or Florinda (who is nicknamed *la cava*, 'the whore'). In *Crónica del Pedro I*, for example, the royal chancellor Pedro López de Ayala (d. 1407) places all the responsibility on Julian and states that the rape may have been invented to justify the betrayal. Similar interpretations appear in other fifteenth-century chronicles, such as *El victorial*, *Estoria de los Godos*, and Pedro de Corral's *Crónica del Rey Don Rodrigo*. They all minimize the king's offence as far as possible and blame the loss of Spain on Julian's betrayal, on his daughter, or on the nature of women—in keeping with the medieval perception of women and as an analogy to the sin of Eve.[144] Even in the early versions, it was difficult to distinguish history from fiction: by the end of the fifteenth century, most of the historical facts were totally obscured, and the story had became a legend.[145] Capsali's version has several motifs that differ from those in the Spanish works; however, most of the elements had appeared in earlier Christian and Arab chronicles, and Capsali, who heard these things from the exiles, gave them his own literary treatment.[146]

[143] See Barkai, *Cristianos y Musulmanes en la España medieval*, 39–40; id., 'Images of Self and Enemy among Christians and Muslims in Spain' (Heb.), 45–6. In *La crónica de Alfonso III*, the defeat is blamed on the adulteries and evil behaviour of the last kings, Wittiza and Roderic.

[144] See Fogelquist, Introduction to Pedro de Corral, *Crónica del Rey Don Rodrigo*, i. 41, 48–52, 55–8. There is a contradiction between the deeds of King Roderic and the moral interpretation given to them. For example, the rape of Julian's daughter is blamed on the nature of women, who arouse men's sexual appetites. This contradiction does not exist in Capsali's version. Without the addition of the tendentious Christian interpretation, the acts described there speak for themselves and incline the reader to identify with Julian. See Grieve, *The Eve of Spain*, 53–7.

[145] See Fogelquist, Introduction to Pedro de Corral, *Crónica del Rey Don Rodrigo*, 7–18.

[146] See Simonsohn, 'The Jews of Christian Europe according to *Seder eliyahu zuta*' (Heb.), 67–8; id., '*Seder eliyahu zuta*: "Chronicles" and "Stories of Spain"' (Heb.), 77–8. Simonsohn also showed

Although the traditions passed on to Capsali were historically inaccurate, *Seder eliyahu zuta* provides important evidence that Jews had access to Spanish chronicles. According to Shlomo Simonsohn, the story about the conquest of Visigothic Spain helped Jews refute the Christian accusation that they had handed the country over to the Muslims, and several elements are, in his view, of Jewish origin. The polemic between Jews and Christians in fifteenth-century Spain contributed to 'historical discussions' of this kind.[147] The Jews' betrayal of Toledo and their delivery of the city to the Muslims are described in various Spanish chronicles,[148] suggesting that in Spanish historical consciousness a link was made between Julian's betrayal that led to the fall of Spain and the Jewish betrayal that led to the fall of Toledo.

Although one cannot discount the possibility that Spanish Jews used the story of King Roderic and Count Julian for polemical purposes, it might have been an integral part of their historical consciousness. It would appear that, in their stories, the Jewish exiles from Spain forgot the forced conversions under Visigothic rule, which were ended by the Muslim conquest, and attributed them to the time of Constantine (who as the first Christian emperor was regarded as one of the greatest enemies of the Jews).[149] Instead they perceived the beginning of Muslim rule as a period of harsh decrees and forced conversion.[150] In this instance, Christian historical consciousness influenced the collective memory of the Jews and engendered their 'national' identification with one of the most significant and grievous events in Hispanic Christian history.

The exiles' oral traditions show no traces of the interpretative additions of the fourteenth and fifteenth centuries.[151] In their version King Roderic died an

---

that several elements in the story are drawn from ancient historiographical sources, such as the cannibalism of the Muslims, who cooked their prisoners in cauldrons to frighten the enemy. This information first appeared in a ninth-century Egyptian chronicle by Ibn Abd al-Hakim.

[147] Simonsohn, '*Seder eliyahu zuta*: "Chronicles" and "Stories of Spain"' (Heb.), 80; on the accusations of betrayal levelled at the Jews, see Ashtor, *The Jews of Moslem Spain*, i. 18, 407–8 n. 5; Baer, *A History of the Jews in Christian Spain*, i. 23.

[148] Fogelquist, Introduction to Pedro de Corral, *Crónica del Rey Don Rodrigo*, i. 65, 75; *Crónica general de España de 1344*, 2: 92 (ed. Catalán and Soledad de Andrés, 141–2).

[149] See Chapter 3 above.

[150] Capsali, *Seder eliyahu zuta*, 2: 47 (ed. Shmuelevitz, Simonsohn, and Benayahu, i. 157); see R. Ben-Shalom, 'Jewish Martyrdom and Martyrology in Aragon and Castile in 1391' (Heb.), 271–2.

[151] The oral traditions of the exiles have remained faithful to the ancient textual basis of the story, which probably appeared in the lost Arab chronicle of the historian of Andalusia, Ahmed ibn Muhammed Abu Musa al-Razi, as well as in the Christian version of the *Crónica general de España de 1344*, which was based on Gil Peres' Portuguese translation of Al-Razi's chronicle (see *Crónica general de España de 1344*, 2: 75–99 (ed. Catalán and Soledad de Andrés, 91–199)). In this context, special attention should be paid to the depiction of Julian's daughter's character and beauty: 'Avia nonbre don Jullano, e avia huna hija muy fermosa e muy buena donzella e que avia muy gran sabor de seer

ignominious death in battle with the Muslims and was never buried. Thus, Roderic received his own personal punishment, along with the Christian loss of territory. This differs from the Christian versions, which claim that he survived the battle and even note where he is buried.[152] Furthermore, in the Jewish versions, no accusations are levelled at Count Julian or his daughter.

The reason for the success of the Muslim conquest of Iberia was also briefly and accurately recorded by Isaac Abravanel, who discussed it in connection with King David's affair with Bathsheba, a motif which also appears in the Christian chronicles:

The events in Spain during the reign of King Don Roderic happened because he lay with the daughter of Count Julian, who resided in Ceuta, [and he] brought all the Ishmaelites from across the sea, and they captured all of Spain to take his vengeance upon the king who lay with his daughter.[153]

THE RECONQUEST

After relating the fall of Spain to the Muslims, Capsali dealt with the beginning of the Reconquest and the establishment of the Christian kingdoms. The Spanish exiles preserved a tradition according to which the Christians held on to a mountainous strip on the border between Spain and France (the Cantabrian and Pyrenean mountains), secluded themselves in fortified cities, and succeeded in keeping their independence under a descendant of the Visigothic kings (probably Pelagius). The exiles also told Capsali that most of the Christians converted to Islam, and only a small number remained true to their ancestral faith.[154]

Capsali's knowledge of Muslim Spain and the reasons for its fall was not very precise, and apparently the exiles only provided him with general information on the subject. He explained Spain's separation from the Abbasid caliphate not as a result of the establishment of independent Ummayad emirates and their break

---

muy buena muger' (ibid. 2: 77 (ed. Catalán and Soledad de Andrés, 97)); cf.: 'And the girl was in the house of the king and he found her more pleasing and graceful than all the other maidens . . . and her beauty aroused passion in his heart. . . . And the girl was blessed with a fine mind and replied wisely' (Capsali, *Seder eliyahu zuta*, 2: 41 (ed. Shmuelevitz, Simonsohn, and Benayahu, i. 146–7)). On the queen's attitude to Julian's daughter, see *Crónica general de España de 1344*, 2: 78–9 (ed. Catalán and Soledad de Andrés, 101–2); cf. Capsali, *Seder eliyahu zuta*, 2: 41 (ed. Shmuelevitz, Simonsohn, and Benayahu, i. 146–7).

[152] Capsali, *Seder eliyahu zuta*, 2: 46 (ed. Shmuelevitz, Simonsohn, and Benayahu, i. 156). Roderic's burial place in Viseu was first mentioned in the eleventh-century *Crónica del Alfonso III* but was not mentioned in *Crónica general de España de 1344* (see Fogelquist, Introduction to Pedro de Corral, *Crónica del Rey Don Rodrigo*, i. 71).

[153] Abravanel on 2 Sam. 11: 14–26 (*Perush linevi'im rishonim*, 342).

[154] Capsali, *Seder eliyahu zuta*, 2: 46 (ed. Shmuelevitz, Simonsohn, and Benayahu, i. 156).

with the Abbasids but rather as the result of the king of Morocco leaving his kingdom to his two sons: one inheriting Morocco and the other Al-Andalus. This weakened Muslim Spain and enabled Christian expansion.

His knowledge of the Christian kingdoms was more accurate: the French helped the Spanish at the beginning; the Christian kingdoms were along the northern edge of the peninsula; they entered into alliances with one another in order to withstand the Muslims; they experienced defeats and victories, and one Christian kingdom grew strong while another grew weak; and they succeeded in expanding their territories and conquering several Muslim cities, although at first only in northern Spain.[155]

Capsali explained how Muslim power in Spain was further diminished, when the king of Al-Andalus divided his territory between his two sons. Apparently, as in the case of the separation of Al-Andalus from the Abbasid caliphate, he thought the Muslims behaved in the same way as Christians. Christian kings traditionally divided their inheritance between their sons: a custom which obstructed Christian expansion. In fact, Al-Andalus was divided into many principalities (*taifa*s), and Christians tended to attack one of them at a time, often in alliance with other Muslims. According to Capsali, the Christians thus repelled the Muslims step by step, although Granada held out for a long time.[156]

THE FALL OF GRANADA

King Ferdinand's war with the Muslim kingdom of Granada from 1481 to the surrender of the city in 1492 which marked the end of the Reconquest is discussed at length in *Seder eliyahu zuta*. The exiles depicted Granada as a strong kingdom, which resisted the Christians for many years and which would send out bands of soldiers to attack and loot Christian cities. Capsali laid special emphasis on the size and strength of Ferdinand's army as well as his decision to take the city of Alhama—in 1486 according to Capsali, although it actually fell in 1482—which he described as a particularly strong fortress and correctly estimated its strategic importance as 'the key to the kingdom of Granada'. The conquest of Alhama forced a wedge between the cities of Granada and Malaga and was an important base for the continued Christian conquests, as other contemporary sources attest.[157]

---

[155] Ibid. 2: 53 (ed. Shmuelevitz, Simonsohn, and Benayahu, i. 170).

[156] Ibid. (ed. Shmuelevitz, Simonsohn, and Benayahu, i. 170–1).

[157] Ibid. 2: 61 (ed. Shmuelevitz, Simonsohn, and Benayahu, i. 189–90); see *Historia de los hechos de Don Rodrigo Ponce de León*, 15–17, 199–214; Ladero Quesada, *Castilla y la conquista del Reino de Granada*, 19–25.

Other contemporary Jewish works contain similarly accurate historical details. Abraham Zacut, for example, characterized the conquest of Alhama and later of Malaga as key events in the Reconquest before the final defeat of the kingdom of Granada.[158] Others, such as *Minḥat zikhron mazkeret avon*, sometimes have the events in the wrong order, so that the conquest of Malaga appears before the conquest of Alhama.[159] *Seder eliyahu zuta* differs from many contemporary Jewish discussions of these events, because it devotes so much space to the military campaigns and the political struggle in Spain, without linking them to the Expulsion. The material collected in *Seder eliyahu zuta* attests to the Spanish exiles' political and historical understanding of the final stages of the Reconquest. Compared with another important source of fifteenth-century oral history, the *romances fronterizos*, or frontier ballads, some of which dealt with the conquest of Granada, the descriptions by the exiles contain a plenitude of accurate historical details.[160]

According to *Seder eliyahu zuta* the kingdom of Granada withstood the armies of Spain, France, and other kingdoms for a very long time.[161] In its final years it was ruled by the Nasrids: Ali Abu al-Hasan (called Muley Hacén by the Spanish chroniclers), 'a brave warrior from the Ibn al-Hamar family, a noble family of high rank with a great lineage to the ancient kings of Damascus',[162] and his three sons.[163] The last of these, 'Boabdil', was received with great honour in Fez after the fall of Granada:

For the kings of Granada occupied an extremely noble, high-ranking status among the Ishmaelites, from the ancient kings of Damascus who were always men of great repute, and the religion of the Ishmaelites preserved and greatly honoured their lineage and roots. . . . And the seed of the monarchy and the family of rulers of Granada were called Ibn al-Hamar. And there is no finer lineage among all the kings of Ishmael, both near and far, than that.[164]

---

[158] 'And in the year 1482 they took Alhama in the kingdom of Granada and from then on began the war between Ishmael and Edom [for] ten years. On 18 August 1487 Malaga was captured. On 1 January 1492 Granada was captured and by the end of that July the Jews were expelled from Castile and Aragon and Sicily and Sardinia' (Zacut, *Sefer yuḥasin* (ed. Freiman, p. xlix)).

[159] Hacker, 'New Chronicles on the Expulsion of the Jews from Spain' (Heb.), 220; see also nn. 97–8.

[160] Cf. Carrasco Urgoiti, *El moro de Granada en la literatura*, 30–46; Mackay, 'The Ballad and the Frontier in Late Medieval Spain'; on the romance about Boabdil's surrender at Lucena, see Cirot, 'Le Romance sur la capture de Boabdil'.

[161] Capsali, *Seder eliyahu zuta*, 2: 61 (ed. Shmuelevitz, Simonsohn, and Benayahu, i. 192).

[162] Ibid. 62 (ed. Shmuelevitz, Simonsohn, and Benayahu, i. 193).

[163] See Moreno Koch, 'La conquista de Granada y la expulsión de Sefarad según las crónicas hispanohebreas', 331 n. 11.

[164] Capsali, *Seder eliyahu zuta*, 2: 66 (ed. Shmuelevitz, Simonsohn, and Benayahu, i. 203–4).

This seems to echo Nasrid propaganda, which emphasized the family's distinguished genealogy and connection to the prophet Muhammad, in contrast to other Spanish historiographical works, such as *Primera crónica general de España* which stressed the lowly origin of the first Nasrid, Muhammad ibn Naṣr (1237–73).[165]

Ali Abu al-Hasan fell in love with a beautiful Christian captive, who, after her conversion to Islam, was called Zoraya. The old king preferred Zoraya to his wife and this angered his wife, his daughter, and his sons. According to the exiles, this affair marked the beginning of Granada's downfall. The queen and her sons left for a 'small city', Boabdil rebelled against him, and Al-Hasan was forced to leave the city of Granada and find refuge in Malaga. Boabdil was received in Granada as the new king, Muhammad XII.

Although the love affair between Al-Hasan and Zoraya did cause a scandal in the royal court, it cannot be regarded as the main reason for the fall of Granada. Granada fell because it had been economically and demographically weakened by the depredations of the Christians, and the Muslim kingdoms in northern Africa were in no position to come to its aid. Nonetheless, that is how the events were perceived in the historical consciousness of contemporary Christians, Muslims, and Jews. The Spanish chronicles presented the love affair as the major cause of the fall of Granada and as a foil to the rape of Count Julian's daughter, which precipitated the Muslim conquest of Spain in the eighth century, or the rape of Pelagius's sister by a Muslim governor, which began the Reconquest. In all three myths a sexual transgression led to the loss of a kingdom. Contemporary Muslim chroniclers, such as the anonymous author of *Nubdhat al-'aṣr*, also believed that Zoraya was the cause of Granada's downfall.[166]

Al-Hasan won many battles against the Spaniards while he was in Malaga. He conquered and destroyed 'one of the cities of the king of Spain which is on the border', which may have been Cañete or, more likely, Ajarquia in 1483,[167] which helped him regain the sympathy and support of the inhabitants of Granada. In response to Al-Hasan's successes, Boabdil mustered an army to attack the Christian city of Lucena. The Christians set a trap for him, roundly defeated him, and took him prisoner. According to Capsali, the battle took place within the city, but in fact the Christians attacked Boabdil's army on its way back to the border town of Loja.[168] Capsali's record of the vast number of Muslim casualties is consistent with accounts in Christian and Muslim chronicles. Boabdil was

---

[165] Harvey, *Islamic Spain*, 275–6.

[166] Capsali, *Seder eliyahu zuta*, 2: 62–3 (ed. Shmuelevitz, Simonsohn, and Benayahu, i. 192–5); Harvey, *Islamic Spain*, 266–7; López de Coca, 'The Making of Isabel de Solis', 227.

[167] Capsali, *Seder eliyahu zuta*, 2: 63 (ed. Shmuelevitz, Simonsohn, and Benayahu, i. 195); Harvey, *Islamic Spain*, 275–6.

[168] Capsali, *Seder eliyahu zuta*, 2: 63 (ed. Shmuelevitz, Simonsohn, and Benayahu, i. 195–6).

brought before Ferdinand, who ordered him thrown into prison. This conforms with the *Crónica de los Reyes Católicos*, written by Ferdinand and Isabella's chancellor, Fernando del Pulgar, and is probably closer to the truth than *Nubdhat al-'aṣr*, according to which Boabdil was received immediately after the battle with princely honours by Ferdinand, who understood Boabdil's strategic importance and plotted to use him to conquer Granada.[169]

The sharp distinction Capsali drew between Al-Hasan, the old king, and Boabdil, the young one, which recurs throughout the chronicle, was no mere literary motif but an integral part of the political and strategic discourse of the Reconquest. Fernando del Pulgar described a meeting of Ferdinand's council in 1483 which deliberated over whether to release Boabdil from prison and give him a Christian army so he could fight his father. Those advocating his release argued that Boabdil should be used to fuel the civil war in Granada. Those opposed argued that Ferdinand was waging a war against an old, infirm king, whose people had grown weary of him and who, due to his physical disabilities, would be unable to conduct the fighting against them properly. By releasing Boabdil they might allow a vigorous new enemy to arise.[170]

The people of Granada appealed to Al-Hasan to return as king, whereupon the queen fled with her two sons and daughter, and one son died during the flight. The king, fearing a new rebellion by his sons and the queen, sent an army after them. They were initially received in Almeria, but then the inhabitants decided to hand them over to the king. Al-Hasan sent his brother, Muhammad al-Zagal, to recover them, telling him not to harm Yusuf, the remaining son. The city was placed under siege, and the queen and her two children came out and gave themselves up, after being promised that no harm would come to them. On the way back to Granada, Al-Zagal had Yusuf killed, so that he could seize the throne for himself should the opportunity arise.

The siege of Almeria is described in other contemporary sources, for example, by the chronicler, Hernando de Baeza, who based his record on information he received directly from Boabdil. In Baeza's version, greater emphasis is placed on Al-Hasan's role in the siege, and the murder of Yusuf was not instigated by Al-Zagal but was part of a plot by Zoraya to enable one of her sons to ascend the throne.[171] According to the exiles, Al-Hasan was inconsolable after the death of Yusuf—

[169] Capsali, *Seder eliyahu zuta*, 2: 63 (ed. Shmuelevitz, Simonsohn, and Benayahu, i. 196); Harvey, *Islamic Spain*, 278–9.

[170] Bernáldez, *Historia de los Reyes Católicos*, 70 (ed. Rosell, 607); Capsali, *Seder eliyahu zuta*, 2: 62–4 (ed. Shmuelevitz, Simonsohn, and Benayahu, i. 103, 195–7); Del Pulgar, *Crónica de los Reyes Católicos*, 39; see Harvey, *Islamic Spain*, 279–81.

[171] Hernando de Baeza, *Las cosas que pasaron entre los reyes de Granada desde el tiempo del rrey don Juan de Castilla, segundo de este nombre*, cited in López de Coca, 'The Making of Isabel de Solís', 229.

like King David after the death of Absalom. He brought the queen to his home and installed her there alongside Zoraya. Afterwards, he fell seriously ill and was bedridden until his death. According to *Nubdhat al-'aṣr*, he had epilepsy and lost his eyesight and all sensation in parts of his body. Since Boabdil was still being held prisoner by the Christians, he was succeeded by Al-Zagal. Ferdinand saw his chance to take Granada. He released Boabdil and provided him with weapons, soldiers, and a promise to help him overthrow his uncle and regain the throne of Granada.

After describing the agreement in detail, Capsali wrote that Ferdinand kissed him and blessed him and sent him on his way escorted by Christian knights. This would seem to be a minor detail, perhaps even a literary convention; however, it is clear from Del Pulgar's chronicle that the Spaniards took great care to avoid humiliating Boabdil during his detention and that, even before his release, discussions were held in Castile about whether he should be permitted to kiss Ferdinand's hand. For Ferdinand this was a matter of principle: he would allow Boabdil to kiss his hand if he were a free man but could not permit it as long as he was his prisoner.[172]

According to Capsali, Boabdil was taken in by Ferdinand and agreed to his proposal, and they attacked the kingdom of Granada. Although Boabdil was forced to flee from his uncle Al-Zagal at Almeria, Ferdinand took several cities in 1485, including Ronda and Marbella, as well as some border fortresses. In the meantime, the people of Granada once more gave their support to Boabdil and rose up against Al-Zagal, who was forced to flee.

Capsali omitted many details of the struggle between Boabdil and Al-Zagal, including fighting in the streets of Granada near the Alhambra palace; the peace treaty between them and Boabdil's acknowledgement of Al-Zagal as king; Boabdil's fight against Ferdinand's forces in Loja and his capture—for the third time—after the surrender of the city; Boabdil's release and his renewed war against Al-Zagal in Granada; and Boabdil's final victory. In fact, it was only after Ferdinand's siege of Baza (1489) and Al-Zagal's humiliating surrender to Ferdinand, which included his handover of Almeria and Guadix, that the various factions in Granada united and supported Boabdil.

The internal intrigues and struggles in Granada have not yet been thoroughly studied. However, the end of the story in its abridged form in *Seder eliyahu zuta* is consistent with what is known from other historical sources: Muhammad al-Zagal was ousted from Granada and went to Almeria, and Boabdil took control of the city until it fell to Ferdinand.[173]

---

[172] Harvey, *Islamic Spain*, 281.

[173] Ibid. 285–306; Ladero Quesada, *Castilla y la conquista del Reino de Granada*, 37–49.

Ferdinand's siege of Malaga lasted a long time. It was a strong, well-fortified city on the coast, and, according to Capsali, it held out for more than six months: in fact it held out for more than two years, from 1485 to 1487, despite the Christians breaking down the walls. However, the city was short of food, and its inhabitants were forced to eat their horses, donkeys, camels, and other animals.[174] A delegation was sent to Ferdinand to negotiate a surrender, but their request was denied. Finally, when the hunger became intolerable, the Muslims handed over the city to Ferdinand without a treaty of surrender and were taken into slavery. Capsali is quite accurate here. The fall of Malaga is also mentioned in *Sefer yuḥasin* and is the last historical event mentioned in *Kitsur zekher tsadik*. A comparison of these three sources shows that the version in *Seder eliyahu zuta* is preferable: it is full of historical details and well narrated. Zacut and Joseph ben Tsadik, unlike Capsali, gave the date. However, Joseph ben Tsadik did not stress the significance of the fall of the city, the brutality of the siege, or the heroism of the Muslim fighters, nor did he mention that the inhabitants were taken into slavery.[175] Zacut included the additional detail that a Muslim infiltrated the Christian camp and killed a courtier and a woman who happened to be in the king's tent, believing they were Ferdinand and Isabella. Zacut also noted the number of Christians who were killed and the number of Muslim inhabitants of Malaga who starved to death during the siege. Apparently, Zacut ascribed as much importance to the fall of Malaga as the exiles did.[176]

Among the numerous prisoners taken by the Christians in Malaga were many Jews. The courtier Abraham Seneor was at the centre of the enormous efforts by the Castilian communities to ransom them. This event is also briefly mentioned in *Kitsur zekher tsadik* and *Sefer yuḥasin*.[177] The exiles' stories, however, shed light on Abraham Seneor's efforts, and the ransoming of the Jews becomes a historical tale with a tragic opening, an intriguing plot, a wise hero, a trick, and a happy ending.[178]

In 1490 Ferdinand broke his alliance with Boabdil and attacked the kingdom of Granada with a large army and captured many Muslim cities. A year later he laid siege to the city of Granada itself. The Muslims fought bravely, so he established a fortified city of his own called Santa Fe two miles from Granada to block-

[174] Also mentioned in *Nubdhat al-'aṣr* (see Harvey, *Islamic Spain*, 299–300).

[175] Joseph b. Tsadik, *Kitsur zekher tsadik* (ed. Neubauer, 100; ed. Moreno Koch, 65); Zacut, *Sefer yuḥasin* (ed. Freiman, p. xlix); Capsali, *Seder eliyahu zuta*, 2: 65 (ed. Shmuelevitz, Simonsohn, and Benayahu, i. 201); see Harvey, *Islamic Spain*, 294–300; Ladero Quesada, *Castilla y la conquista del Reino de Granada*, 50–4.

[176] Zacut, *Sefer yuḥasin* (MS Hunt. 504 (Neubauer 2202) (Bodleian Library, Oxford), fos. 497a–b.

[177] Joseph b. Tsadik, *Kitsur zekher tsadik* (ed. Neubauer, 100); Zacut, *Sefer yuḥasin* (ed. Freiman, p. xlix).

[178] Capsali, *Seder eliyahu zuta*, 2: 65 (ed. Shmuelevitz, Simonsohn, and Benayahu, i. 201–2).

ade it—a method he had used at Malaga.[179] The Muslims were still divided between Boabdil and Al-Zagal, and neither side was prepared to give up the throne. That, according to Capsali, was the main reason for their downfall.

After a nine-month siege and with the Christians in control of all the cities and villages in the area, Granada surrendered. All the inhabitants, nobles and commoners, were allowed to leave Spain, and Christian ships were made available to take them to northern Africa. Boabdil received 100,000 florins from Ferdinand and permission to take all his property. He left with his mother, his sister, his retinue, and the nobles of the kingdom. Al-Zagal also left Spain with much property, and both were received with great honour in Fez. Those Muslims who wanted to remain, mainly the commoners, were promised an exemption from taxes for ten years. However, Ferdinand broke his promises very quickly and forced them to convert to Christianity.

Capsali's description of Granada's surrender is quite accurate. Boabdil was treated very generously; the rights of the Muslims who wanted to stay were guaranteed, including certain exemptions from taxes, although not an overall exemption as Capsali reported; the Muslims were provided with ships, at the expense of the Spaniards, to take any of them who wanted to leave to northern Africa. However, the Spaniards honoured their commitments for eight years, before, in 1499, they forced the Muslims of Granada to convert. The fact that Boabdil arrived in Fez and stayed there with the king is confirmed in a number of sixteenth- and seventeenth-century Muslim and Christian sources, although it is contradicted by another claim that he arrived in Tlemcen. Al-Zagal left for northern Africa before the siege of Granada, so the description of his reception in Fez is fallacious.[180]

An interesting aspect of Capsali's account is the character of Queen Isabella of Castile. The exiles depict her as exerting an enormous influence on Ferdinand and being in favour of expelling the Jews from Spain. They were more ambivalent towards Ferdinand: he also signed the Edict of Expulsion but was greatly admired for the conquest of Granada. Capsali omitted all reference to Isabella's role in the wars and political manoeuvring and linked her to the Reconquest only in relation to the persecution and expulsion of the Jews. For Capsali, Isabella was the main enemy of the Jews. She took a vow during the siege of Granada—under the influence of an antisemitic priest—to expel them if God allowed the city to fall. Ferdinand, on the other hand, was much praised in the chapters dealing with the

---

[179] The establishment of Santa Fe is also mentioned in *Minḥat zikhron mazkeret avon* (Hacker, 'New Chronicles on the Expulsion of the Jews from Spain' (Heb.), 220).

[180] Harvey, *Islamic Spain*, 307–27; Ladero Quesada, *Castilla y la conquista del Reino de Granada*, 65.

wars and politics and was denigrated only for his inability to stand up to Isabella in her determination to expel the Jews.

Joseph Hacker has discussed the contradictory images of the 'Catholic monarchs' in the historical consciousness of the exiles and concludes that the generally favourable attitude of Spanish Jews to the institution of monarchy did not prevent them from criticizing specific rulers, including Ferdinand and Isabella.[181] The differing attitudes in the oral traditions are linked to the fame of the Catholic monarchs as the heroes of the Reconquest. The exiles had absorbed the Hispanic ideal of the Reconquest, which made it difficult for them to denigrate anything Ferdinand did: hence they remained ambivalent towards him.

The disparity between the oral traditions of the exiles and the state chronicles is also interesting. The writers of the chronicles dealt mainly with military and political events on the Christian side and usually related events in Muslim Granada very briefly, often omitting significant historical details. In contrast, the exiles' traditions reveal their greater interest in Muslim Granada. They focused on the internal struggles of the Nasrids, the intrigues, and the civil war, and devoted less attention to the battles and the discussions of Ferdinand's council.

JAMES I OF ARAGON AND AN ASHKENAZI SAGE

Seder eliyahu zuta also contains a story about James I of Aragon and an Ashkenazi sage, which reflects the special relationship between Jews and Christians in Spain known as *convivencia*. The term *convivencia* was introduced into Hispanic historiography by Américo Castro, who borrowed it from Ramón Menéndez Pidal and is sometimes understood as 'living together' and sometimes as merely 'existing together'. *Convivencia* was a product of the complex social dynamics between the three religions in the Iberian peninsula, reflecting the Christian or Muslim majority's attitude to the minorities and the integration of the minority groups into the daily social life and culture of the majority. *Convivencia* was a particular feature of the thirteenth century and James's reign. He maintained close personal connections with Jews—who held important posts in his administration, such as financiers, treasurers, physicians, and interpreters—and adopted favourable policies towards them.[182] Although this period saw its share of religious fanaticism and socio-economic hostility, there were also many 'ideal elements' in Jewish life.[183]

[181] Hacker, 'New Chronicles on the Expulsion of the Jews from Spain' (Heb.), 211–13.

[182] See Assis, 'The Jews in the Kingdom of Aragon' (Heb.), 42–3, 76; Baer, *A History of the Jews in Christian Spain*, i. 138–44; id., 'On Criticism of the Disputations of Yehiel of Paris and Nahmanides' (Heb.), 137; H. H. Ben-Sasson, 'Moses ben Nahman' (Heb.), 316; Glick, 'Convivencia'.

[183] Baer, *A History of the Jews in Christian Spain*, i. 180–1; see Carrete Parrondo, 'Fraternization between Jews and Christians in Spain', esp. 20 n. 18; J. Ray, 'Beyond Tolerance and Persecution'; on expressions of *convivencia* in criminal life in Aragon, see Luria, 'Complicidad criminal'.

In the Jewish tradition, James is often depicted as being especially friendly towards Nahmanides, the relationship being like that between a rabbi and his student.[184] The historian Hyam Maccoby dramatized the relationship in a play on the Disputation of Barcelona, which was also made into a film;[185] however, the historical documents contain very little relevant information, except that Nahmanides received a sum of money from the king and was permitted to respond to a sermon given by him in the synagogue of Barcelona.[186]

The close relationship between a king and a Jewish sage was a well-known literary topos in Spain. In Capsali's version, the sage is an Ashkenazi kabbalist, who had persuaded Nahmanides to turn to mysticism,[187] and there is no hint of a friendship between James and Nahmanides. At the end of the story, the king realizes that 'there is no God in the whole land other than the God of the people of Israel', and 'the Gentiles in the land of Spain, upon hearing of [the wondrous deeds based on kabbalah], believed in the God of Israel, and worshipped him in secret but not openly'.[188] The Ashkenazi sage may reflect the belief, part of the historical consciousness of Spanish Jewry, that kabbalah came to Spain from Ashkenaz.[189] It is also possible, however, that a historical episode involving an actual Ashkenazi sage, Abraham ben Alexander Axelrad, became intertwined with the legend of Nahmanides. As far as is known, Axelrad, a pupil of Eleazar ben Judah of Worms, went from Cologne to Aragon and from there to Castile, where he was received by Alfonso X.[190] Solomon ben Abraham Adret, who was born around 1235, apparently met Axelrad when Adret was a young man living with his parents.[191] At that time Nahmanides may still have been in Spain, and

[184] See Joseph b. Tsadik, *Kitsur zekher tsadik* (ed. Neubauer, 95).

[185] Maccoby, *Judaism on Trial*; Sax (dir.), *The Disputation*.

[186] See Baer, 'On Criticism of the Disputations of Yehiel of Paris and Nahmanides' (Heb.), 137; Assis, 'The Jews in the Kingdom of Aragon' (Heb.), 76.

[187] Capsali, *Seder eliyahu zuta*, 2: 51–2 (ed. Shmuelevitz, Simonsohn, and Benayahu, i. 168); see Idel, 'Studies in the Method of the Author of *Sefer hameshiv*' (Heb.), 230–1, n. 228.

[188] Capsali, *Seder eliyahu zuta*, 2: 51–2 (ed. Shmuelevitz, Simonsohn, and Benayahu, i. 166–9); cf. Simonsohn, '*Seder eliyahu zuta*: "Chronicles" and "Stories of Spain"' (Heb.), 78, 168.

[189] See Idel, 'Kabbalah and Ancient Philosophy in the Works of R. Isaac and Judah Abravanel' (Heb.).

[190] See J. Dan, *The Esoteric Doctrine of Ashkenazi Hasidism* (Heb.), 259; Scholem, 'Abraham ben Alexander'. In 1295, in the context of the messianic prophecies in Avila, Solomon ben Abraham Adret wrote: 'And I saw a man from Ashkenaz whose name was Abraham of Cologne, and he passed us by and went as high as the king of Castile, the father of the king who is now reigning [Sancho IV]' (*Teshuvot harashba*, 34 (ed. Dimitrovsky, i. 105–6); see Baer, 'The Historical Background of the *Ra'aya mehemna*' (Heb.), 345–9; id., *A History of the Jews in Christian Spain*, i. 120; see also Shimon b. Tsemah Duran, *Sefer magen avot*, 3.4.76*b*; Zacut, *Sefer yuhasin* (ed. Filipowski, 87*a*–88*b*)).

[191] Adret, *Teshuvot harashba*, 34 (ed. Dimitrovsky, i. 105–6).

Axelrad and Nahmanides may have met in Barcelona.[192] Axelrad, a mystic well versed in magic, was involved in a number of supernatural phenomena in Cologne, including fortune telling.[193] He also demonstrated his prophetic mode of preaching for the rabbis of Catalonia and impressed them enormously.[194] Alfonso had an interest in magic and kabbalah and probably had Axelrad brought to his court.[195]

THE CORONATION OF THE EMPEROR AND ALFONSO X THE WISE

A close relationship between a Spanish king and a Jew is also portrayed in a story about Alfonso X's bid to become Holy Roman Emperor:

In those days the pope wished to install an emperor in keeping with the custom, and all of the kings gathered from the ends of the world in Alessandria della Paglia to take the crown. The kings arrived and paraded together, each carrying in his hand a crown of gold, silver, and precious gems, and the more ornate the crown, the better. The king of Spain also wanted to walk before the pope—perhaps he would see fit to crown him— but his crown was not as precious as those of the other kings, for he was poor. Hence he was ashamed to walk before the pope lest they all, seeing his crown, jeer at him: for the poor man is of no more worth than a dead man. And one of the leaders of the Jews came to the king and saw him and said to him: 'Why is your face so sad today?' And the king told him what was grieving his heart, leaving nothing out. And the Jew extended his help to the king and said: 'I will advise you as to what you should do, make yourself a lovely crown of white flour, unlike all of those kings who have made their crowns of gold and silver and precious gems, and take that crown, place it before the pope, and say to him: "I did not go the way of grandeur and pride in making my crown, nor did I make it out of gold and silver and royal treasure and lands, but out of modesty and fear of God."' And the king found the Jew's advice to his liking and decided to follow it and hurried to his tent and said to his servants: 'Hasten to take semolina flour, do as I say, and make me a lovely crown after sifting it thirteen times.' And his servants did as he commanded and engraved upon it all manner of fowl and beasts. . . . And on that day the pope sat on his throne as was the custom, and the kings came, bowed before him, and paid him homage, and one said: 'I deserve to be emperor; it is all mine', and another said: 'It is mine.' And

---

[192] The image of Nahmanides as a miracle worker was part of the historical consciousness of the Jews of Spain in the fifteenth century (see Ibn Musa, *Magen varomaḥ*, 109).

[193] Adret, *Teshuvot harashba*, 34 (ed. Dimitrovsky, i. 105–6); according to Axelrad, it was the 'revelation of Elijah' (see Scholem, *The Origin of the Kabbalah and Sefer habahir* (Heb.), 67–8).

[194] Ibid.; see Idel, 'Between Ashkenaz and Castile in the Thirteenth Century' (Heb.), 496–8.

[195] See Márquez-Villanueva, 'The Alfonsine Cultural Concept', 89–90; see also: 'Otrosi fizo trasladar toda [la] ley de los judios et aun el su Talmud et otra sciencia que an los judios muy escondida a que llaman Cabala' (*Libro de la caza*, cited ibid. 107 n. 84; see Barkai, *Science, Magic, and Mythology in the Middle Ages* (Heb.), 16 n. 25).

each took his crown and placed it before the pope, thinking that he who had a crown greater than that of his [fellow] king would be emperor and [enjoy] wealth and honour. Then the king of Spain spoke and said: 'I did not go the way of grandeur and pride, for a man's pride shall bring him low. Here, my lord pope, is my crown, the humble in spirit shall attain honour.' And the pope saw the crown, and it found favour in his eyes, and in his heart he felt contempt for all the kings who thought they would become emperor by the size of their crown and its richness. And he raised that crown with his two hands and placed it on the head of the king of Spain. And all of the people hailed him, saying: 'Long live the king!' And although the custom is that the pope does not crown the emperor except with his feet, he did not wish to shame that crown which was made of bread, so he seized it with his hand and that was a great thing. And the kings saw this and bowed their heads. And such were the lofty, immensely wise things that the Jews did, and their voices were decisive in all cases of dispute and assault.[196]

At the end of the Middle Ages, the Holy Roman Emperor, ruler of an area roughly equivalent to Belgium, Holland, Germany, Switzerland, Austria, the Czech Republic, Slovenia, and northern Italy, was believed to be the heir of the Roman emperors.[197] In the Iberian peninsula some kings similarly used the title emperor as a symbol of their aspirations to control the other kings, Christian and Muslim, and to restore the unity of Spain as it was under the Visigoths (reflected, for example, in the writings of Isidore of Seville). However, Alfonso X was the first Spanish king to claim a right to the crown of the Holy Roman Empire. He spent vast sums of money trying to obtain it and was elected emperor in 1257, on the death of Friedrich II. However, he was forced to relinquish the throne shortly thereafter. Alfonso's imperial ambition was a lifetime obsession and contributed much to his demise as a statesman, as well as to the economic disintegration of his kingdom. News of the failure of his visit to the pope in Beaucaire in 1275 circulated in Spain and the rest of Europe and made the wisest king the object of ridicule.[198] This last stage of the political saga is not mentioned at all in the Jewish myth. On the contrary, the myth reflects Jewish identification with the imperial ambitions of the kings of the Iberian peninsula.

As is often the case, the account is exaggerated, but in the thirteenth century the king of Aragon had many Jewish advisers, and the kingdom of Valencia,

[196] Capsali, *Seder eliyahu zuta*, 2: 53 (ed. Shmuelevitz, Simonsohn, and Benayahu, i. 173).

[197] See Zacut, *Sefer yuḥasin* (ed. Filipowski, 249a); see also Yuval, 'Towards 1240' (Heb.), 117; id., *Two Nations in Your Womb*, 281.

[198] See Folz, *The Concept of Empire in Western Europe*, 40–1, 122–3; Herrmann, *Alfons X. von Kastilien als römischer König*; Maravall, *El concepto de España en la Edad Media*, 412–62; Merriman, *The Rise of the Spanish Empire*, i. 110–12; Post, '"Blessed Lady Spain"'; Salvador Martínez, *Alfonso X, the Learned*, 121–212. On Isidore of Seville's 'Laus spaniae' in his *History of the Goths, Vandals, and Suevi*, where he states that Spain has the most sublime Christian monarchy and deserves to succeed Rome, see J. Cohen, *Living Letters of the Law*, 113 n. 70.

which was a separate Christian domain within Aragon and had a Muslim majority, was almost entirely run by Jews. In Castile, Alfonso X brought more Jewish sages into his close circle than any of the other kings of the time. Moreover, Jews who served as physicians to kings had a real influence on politics in Castile and Aragon.[199] The Jew in the story may well be drawn from Todros ben Joseph Halevi Abulafia, who held a special position at Alfonso's court and enjoyed his complete confidence and in 1275 accompanied him on his visit to Pope Gregory X in Beaucaire in Provence.[200] There is even a historical background to the king's poverty. Alfonso had passed laws intended to curb waste in the kingdom, partly out of religious motives. Todros ben Judah Halevi Abulafia mentioned the event in a poem: 'And the king and his deputies wore rags like wretched paupers, and the lords found no food to eat, not two turtledoves nor two baby pigeons.'[201] In the myth the king's humility and modesty, attributes for which Alfonso was widely known, are the main reason for his election as emperor, and it is the Jewish adviser who urged the king to behave humbly in order to win the pope's favour. Similar stories of Alfonso (without the Jewish element) are found in late fifteenth-century Castilian historiography. In *Historia de los hechos de Don Rodrigo Ponce de León*, Alfonso's greatness is borne out by the fact that he was elected emperor, although no mention is made there that he had to relinquish the long-sought title shortly afterwards.[202]

SAMUEL BEN MEIR HALEVI ABULAFIA AND KING PEDRO OF CASTILE

The good relationship between Pedro the Cruel, king of Castile from 1350 to 1369, and his courtier, chief agent, and treasurer, Samuel Halevi Abulafia, is described in great detail and with many legendary embellishments in *Seder eliyahu zuta*. Pedro's reign is depicted as an ideal period in which 'the Jews were raised very high; he lifted them up, and carried them all the days of old. And he gave them ten times as much status and greatness than did the kings of

---

[199] See Amador de los Rios, *Historia social, política y religiosa de los Judíos de España y Portugal*, ii. 47–55; Assis, 'The Jews in the Kingdom of Aragon' (Heb.), 43; Baer, *A History of the Jews in Christian Spain*, i. 120–4; Romano, 'Alfonso X y los judíos', esp. 163–7; id., 'Cortesanos judíos en la corona de Aragón'; id., *Judíos al servicio de Pedro el Grande de Aragón*; id., 'Judíos escríbanos y trujamanes de árabe en la corona de Aragón.

[200] See Baer, *A History of the Jews in Christian Spain*, i. 119, 127; id., 'Todros ben Judah Halevi' (Heb.), 279–80. On this journey, Alfonso relinquished his claim to the throne of the Holy Roman Empire.

[201] Todros b. Judah Abulafia, *Gan hameshalim vehaḥidot*, 393 (57) (ed. Yellin, Pt. 1, vol. i. 82); see Baer, 'Todros ben Judah Halevi' (Heb.), 274.

[202] *Historia de los hechos de Don Rodrigo Ponce de León*, 149.

Spain before him, and most of the emissaries that he sent to the kings were Jews.'[203]

In a fanciful tale, Capsali described one of Samuel Halevi's missions to Flanders. He showed his 'Jewish' wisdom when he managed to escape from a Christian mob who had never seen a Jew before and wanted to get a glimpse of the 'killer of God'. Samuel Halevi turned the Christians' prejudicial image of Jews against them. He wrapped his prayer shawl around the head of a goat with a large beard and hung his phylacteries between its eyes. The Christians stoned the goat to death and erected a monument over it.[204] This story contrasted the tolerant attitudes of the Christians of Spain with those of the northern 'barbarians' and mocked the image of the demonic Jew that developed in western Europe.[205]

Another story tells of Samuel Halevi's mission to the king of 'Pishkaya' (probably Portugal), where he was sent in 1358 by Pedro to complete a treaty between the two kingdoms.[206] Samuel Halevi's involvement in Castile's foreign relations is also memorialized in the magnificent synagogue of El Transito, which he had built in Toledo:

Since the day of Ariel's exile, none like unto him has arisen in Israel. . . . He appears before kings to stand in the breach. . . . Unto him people came from the ends of the earth [see Jer. 16: 19]. . . . The king exalted him and set him on high, above all his princes. Into his hands he entrusted all that he had . . . and since the day of our exile no son of Israel has attained to such exalted estate.[207]

Samuel Halevi was considered to have attained the highest political position of any Jew since the fall of the Second Temple, a perception that unquestionably influenced the traditions that were given expression in *Seder eliyahu zuta*. The exiles described him as 'second to the king in his wealth, wisdom, and capability' and conducting 'the affairs of the entire kingdom of Spain'.[208]

Idealized depictions of the high status of Jews, especially Jewish courtiers and emissaries, during Pedro's reign were certainly influenced by the real figure of

---

[203] Capsali, *Seder eliyahu zuta*, 2: 54 (ed. Shmuelevitz, Simonsohn, and Benayahu, i. 174); see Simonsohn and Benayahu, notes (Heb.), ibid. 174 n. 1, 177 n. 17; H. H. Ben-Sasson, 'The Spanish Exiles Speak of Themselves' (Heb.), 206–7.

[204] Capsali, *Seder eliyahu zuta*, 2: 54 (ed. Shmuelevitz, Simonsohn, and Benayahu, i. 174–5).

[205] Ibid. 2: 55 (ed. Shmuelevitz, Simonsohn, and Benayahu, i. 176–8); on demonic images of Jews in Spain, see Gutwirth, 'The Jews in 15th Century Castilian Chronicles', 388 n. 33.

[206] Capsali, *Seder eliyahu zuta*, 2: 54 (ed. Shmuelevitz, Simonsohn, and Benayahu, i. 174); see Baer, *A History of the Jews in Christian Spain*, i. 363; Netanyahu, *The Origins of the Inquisition in Fifteenth Century Spain*, 1197 n. 56; Suárez Fernández, 'Castilla', 59. The treaty included a commitment to a joint fleet and a marriage between Ferdinand, heir to the Portuguese throne, and Pedro's daughter, Beatrice. [207] See Baer, *A History of the Jews in Christian Spain*, i. 363.

[208] Capsali, *Seder eliyahu zuta*, 2: 54 (ed. Shmuelevitz, Simonsohn, and Benayahu, i. 176).

Samuel Halevi.[209] Nonetheless, they may also be a response to the propaganda disseminated by Pedro's stepbrother and rival for the throne, Enrique de Trastámara. Enrique exploited Pedro's attitude to the Jews of Castile, calling him 'king of the Jews' and claiming that he 'loved' Jews, served as their 'tool', and even that he was of Jewish descent.[210] Enrique described Samuel Halevi as the real ruler of Castile, much as he is described in *Seder eliyahu zuta*. Enrique's propaganda penetrated deep into the Castilian collective consciousness and influenced Jews' perception of themselves and their place in Castile. In this way, the historical image of ideal life during Pedro's reign and the central role played by Jews in Castile's internal and external politics became part of the exiles' historical consciousness.

Capsali devoted an entire chapter to Samuel Halevi's downfall, but he mistakenly set the events in 1391. Samuel Halevi was arrested in 1360 and executed by order of the king in 1361. According to *Seder eliyahu zuta*, the Castilian nobles had been envious of Samuel Halevi's lofty position for a long time and had tried in vain to defame him. An opportunity presented itself when one of Samuel Halevi's associates disclosed that Samuel Halevi had hidden a large fortune in three pits under the marble pillars of the synagogue. When they learned of this, the nobles offered the king one-tenth of each of their private fortunes for the war against the Muslims, if all the eminent men of the kingdom declared how great their fortunes were on pain of death. The king agreed, and Samuel Halevi, not knowing that his secret had been revealed, made a false declaration. The nobles then revealed Samuel Halevi's secret to the king, who had him executed.[211]

Contemporary Spanish documents record Samuel Halevi's attempts to strengthen the Crown of Castile against the rebellious nobility,[212] and, in the light of this, the exiles' claim that the nobles had a hand in Samuel Halevi's undoing cannot be simply dismissed. However, Pedro's court historian, Pedro López de Ayala, made no mention of a plot against Samuel Halevi and claimed that he was

[209] Netanyahu, *The Origins of the Inquisition in Fifteenth Century Spain*, 96–110. Pedro's physician, Abraham ibn Çarça, was discussed by the Muslim historian Abd al-Rahman ibn Chaldun (see Sánchez-Albornoz, *La España musulmana según los autores islamitas y cristianos medievales*, 418). Pedro López de Ayala mentioned Samuel Halevi alongside Abraham ibn Verga and other Jewish courtiers from the Ibn Verga and 'Aben-Caçi' families in his poem 'Rimado del Palacio' (see Amador de los Rios, *Historia social, política y religiosa de los Judíos de España y Portugal*, ii. 231–2 n. 2).

[210] See Graetz, *The History of the Jews* (Heb.), v. 343. Enrique's propaganda made a strong impact in France, and many accepted his claims about Pedro the Cruel's Jewish blood (see Amador de los Rios, *Historia social, política y religiosa de los Judíos de España y Portugal*, ii, 207–10; Valdeón Baruque, *El chivo expiatorio*, 37).

[211] Capsali, *Seder eliyahu zuta*, 2: 55 (ed. Shmuelevitz, Simonsohn, and Benayahu, i. 176–8).

[212] Baer, *A History of the Jews in Christian Spain*, i. 363.

arrested on the king's initiative.[213] Amador de los Rios suggested several reasons for the change in Pedro's attitude: perhaps Samuel Halevi's fortune aroused his greed; perhaps Pedro wanted to rid himself of the stigma of favouring Jews; perhaps he was trying to appease the Christian clergy; perhaps he hoped to win the support of the cities, which had been subject to a harsh fiscal policy enforced by Samuel Halevi.[214] Benzion Netanyahu attempted to link Samuel Halevi's arrest to the humiliating treaty that Pedro was forced to enter into with Aragon in 1361, after Samuel Halevi, the treasurer at the time, was unable to provide funds to continue the war.[215] The Spanish exiles' attempt to exonerate Pedro from any blame in the affair can be interpreted as part of the pro-monarchic trend in Jewish historiography then prevalent in Spain.

The story of Samuel Halevi's downfall is also recorded in a number of Spanish chronicles, including *Continuación de la crónica de España* by Gonzalo de Hinojosa and his successors and an anonymous supplement to Juan Rodriguez de Cuenca's *Sumario de los reyes de España*, apparently dating from the second half of the fifteenth century. A group of Jewish courtiers from Toledo devised a plot against Samuel Halevi, whom they thought had been robbing the kingdom for more than twenty years and must now be the richest man in the world. They suggested to Pedro that he test Samuel Halevi's loyalty by asking him to return the money, and, if he refused, to extract it from him by torture. The king accepted their proposal and asked Halevi for a loan to pay for his children's weddings. When Samuel Halevi refused, he was arrested and executed. Later Pedro very much regretted Samuel Halevi's death.[216]

There was a great deal of envy, avarice, and malicious gossip in court circles, and the Christian version cannot simply be discounted. In 1415 Solomon Alami ibn Lahmish stated that, as a result of the Jewish courtiers' intrigues, scheming, and bad advice, they were banned from the court.[217] However, this does not support Netanyahu's claim that in the fourteenth century a change took place in the behaviour of Jewish courtiers, and they became more cruel, conniving, and

[213] Pedro López de Ayala, *Crónica del Rey Don Pedro y del Rey Don Enrique*, ii. p. xxii.

[214] Amador de los Rios, *Historia social, política y religiosa de los Judíos de España y Portugal*, ii. 247; see Valdeón Baruque, *El chivo expiatorio*, 31 n. 34.

[215] Netanyahu, *The Origins of the Inquisition in Fifteenth Century Spain*, 102–9.

[216] See *Sumario de los reyes de España*, 72b–73a; see also Amador de los Rios, *Historia social, política y religiosa de los Judíos de España y Portugal*, ii. 244–5; Netanyahu, *The Origins of the Inquisition in Fifteenth Century Spain*, 107, 1197 n. 67; for the date of the anonymous supplement, see De Llaguno Amirola, notes to *Sumario de los reyes de España*, 95b.

[217] Alami ibn Lahmish, *Igeret musar*, 44–5; on social criticism in *Igeret musar*, see Gutwirth, 'Social Tensions within XVth Century Hispano-Jewish Communities', 1–57; on the intrigues within the circles of courtiers during the reign of Enrique de Trastámera, see Netanyahu, 'The Conversion of Don Samuel Abravanel'.

vicious.[218] The Christian version must be read against the background of the intensive anti-Jewish propaganda that was revived in Castile at the time.

Jewish treachery was a popular literary motif in Castile, and during the civil war from 1355 to 1369 they were often accused of betraying their country. The story of Judas Iscariot, who betrayed Jesus, was a popular theme for twelfth- and thirteenth-century Spanish poets, such as Gonzalo de Berceo, who described 'the Jew' as 'a false, disloyal man'.[219] Priests and chroniclers invented Jewish conspiracies and revived the claim that Jews handed over the Christian Visigothic cities (particularly Toledo) to the Muslims in the eighth century.[220] In these circumstances, it is not surprising that Jews attempted to cast off the traitor stereotype and to place the blame on the Castilian nobles.

It is also possible that the exiles' version of Samuel Halevi's fate was a reaction to a historiographical trend developed in the fifteenth century by Pablo de Santa María. In his *Scrutinium scripturarum*, he presented Samuel Halevi's arrest and death, as well as the 1391 pogroms and the Valladolid discriminatory laws of 1412, as events of apocalyptic significance, presaging the destruction of Judaism and the final, eschatological victory of Christianity. Santa María wrote in response to Jewish claims that 'the sceptre will not pass from Judah' (Gen. 49: 10) was verified by the high positions Jews held in Spanish courts, particularly in Castile and Leon. He asserted that Jews believed that the courtiers' success testified to the rightness of their ways and justified their misguided adherence to their faith. According to him, the death of Samuel Halevi, 'the highest among the Jews and very high-ranking in the royal court', heralded the beginning of their fall from positions of power. He dated Samuel Halevi's death to 1358—the End of Days according to Nahmanides' and Gersonides' calculations (1,290 years (see Dan. 12: 11) after 68 CE, the year of the destruction of the Second Temple). According to Santa María the redemptive process was accelerated by the pogroms of 1391 and by the conversion of thousands of Jews in the fifteenth century.[221]

---

[218] See Assis, *The Golden Age of Aragonese Jewry*, 293–5; H. H. Ben-Sasson, 'The Spanish Exiles Speak of Themselves' (Heb.), 204; Netanyahu, *The Origins of the Inquisition in Fifteenth Century Spain*, 107.

[219] Gonzalo de Berceo, *Milagros de nuestra Señora*, cited in Gutwirth, 'The Jews in 15th Century Castilian Chronicles', 382 n. 11.

[220] See Alfonso X, *Primera crónica general de España*, i. 316a–b; Pedro López de Ayala repeated the story about the Jewish betrayal of the Christians in Toledo in the eighth century. He also devoted an entire chapter to the story of Samuel Halevi's arrest, the confiscation of his property, his torture and death (*Crónica del Rey Don Pedro y del Rey Don Enrique*, 28 (ed. Orduna, i. 58–9); see Netanyahu, *The Origins of the Inquisition in Fifteenth Century Spain*, 108; see also Ashtor, *The Jews of Moslem Spain*, i. 18, esp. 407–8 n. 5; N. Roth, *Jews, Visigoths and Muslims in Medieval Spain*, 73–4).

[221] Pablo de Santa María, *Scrutinium scripturarum*, 2.4.10 (Burgos edn., 523); see Amador de los Rios, *Historia social, política y religiosa de los Judíos de España y Portugal*, ii. 210–11 n. 1; Glatzer, 'Pablo

Samuel Halevi was perceived in the same way in the memorial inscription in the El Transito synagogue, in *Seder eliyahu zuta*, and in the work of the former Jew Santa María as 'the highest among the Jews'. Santa María's anti-Jewish historiography had serious implications for Jews, and, owing to his status and influence in Castile, he was able to make sure they were realized. He railed against Jews holding high positions in Spain, regarded their wealth as a social injustice, and called on the Spaniards to humiliate and isolate them. In response, Jews developed a counter-history. The fact that Samuel Halevi was killed by order of the king was not open to question, but by placing most of the blame on the nobles and clearing the king of any complicity in the plot—while placing part of the guilt on Samuel Halevi himself for lying to the king about his wealth—Jews were able to hold fast to their traditional image of the relationship between king and courtier. This version, which sees Samuel Halevi as a flawed man, who was punished for his excessive greed, counters Santa María's interpretation, which viewed the affair as an apocalyptic event. This solution also enabled Jews to stand by their polemical interpretation of Genesis 49: 10. Thus, other Jewish courtiers, such as Abraham Seneor, who rose to a high position in Castile in the fifteenth century, could replace Samuel Halevi, and again give credence to the claim that 'the sceptre will not pass from Judah'.[222]

Santa María linked Samuel Halevi's fall to the pogroms of 1391, and saw it as part of the eschatological process. The Jewish traditions recorded in *Seder eliyahu zuta* also linked these two historical events. However, Santa María lived at the time and knew that Samuel Halevi was killed about thirty years before the pogroms. *Seder eliyahu zuta* mistakenly dated Samuel Halevi's death to the same time as the pogroms, which created an artificial link between them: in the wake of his Jewish courtier's treachery, the king wanted all the Jews in his kingdom to convert, and this led to the killing of Jews and forced conversions. According to Santa María the Jews converted voluntarily after the pogroms had died down; according to *Seder eliyahu zuta*, the Jews converted 'against their will and not to their good'.[223] Both versions regarded Samuel Halevi's fall as a key event in the

de Santa María' (Heb.), esp. 149–54; Gersonides on Dan. 12: 11, 16; Nahmanides, *Sefer hage'ulah*, 3 (ed. Chavel, 294).

[222] A letter sent from Castile to Italy in 1487 (apparently about Abraham Seneor) reads: 'and bless our God who in his great mercy and goodness does not turn aside from us, nor will the sceptre turn aside from Judah, he is our exilarch, who is [responsible] for us, who holds the seal of the communities' (Baer, *Die Juden im christlichen Spanien*, doc. 360 (ii. 385); see H. H. Ben-Sasson, 'The Spanish Exiles Speak of Themselves' (Heb.), 205–6; see also Abravanel on Gen. 49: 12 (*Perush al hatorah*, i. 435); R. Ben-Shalom, 'The Courtier as the "Sceptre of Judah"' (Heb.)).

[223] Capsali, *Seder eliyahu zuta*, 2: 55 (ed. Shmuelevitz, Simonsohn, and Benayahu, i. 178); see R. Ben-Shalom, 'Jewish Martyrdom and Martyrology in Aragon and Castile in 1391' (Heb.), esp. 276–7; Glatzer, 'Pablo de Santa María' (Heb.), 152–3. The traditions cited by Capsali did not

history of the Jews in Spain, which led to the pogroms of 1391 and created the Converso phenomenon, the greatest crisis of Spanish Jewry before the Expulsion of 1492. Catastrophe was avoided by Isaac ben Jacob Canpanton, the 'reviver of the yeshivas', and his pupils Isaac Aboab, Isaac de Leon, Joseph ben Abraham Hayyun, and Simon Mimi, who together generated a Jewish spiritual renaissance during the second half of the fifteenth century.

The historical narratives of Castilian Jews and Christians show how vital historical reflection was in the consciousness of members of those communities. Seemingly ingenuous stories that appear to contain a superficial mixture of historical fact and legend take on a totally different meaning when they are presented in the political and ideological context of their time. Events in Castile connected with the intrigues of the court and the relationship between the king and his Jewish courtiers became a tool in the hands of the different factions of Iberian society. On the one hand, this points to the importance of Spanish history in the eyes of the Jews and, on the other, to the prominent role played by Jews, particularly courtiers like Samuel Halevi, in the historiography and mythography of Christian Spain, although the Christian chronicles generally attempted to minimize favourable descriptions of Jewish involvement in the service of the Crown.[224] Neither Christian nor Jewish chronography was a simple, straightforward relating of historical facts. They were intricate ideological systems with clear messages. Jewish historical traditions depicted the excellent relations between Jewish courtiers and the king and the good advice the courtiers gave. In contrast, in Christian chronicles the opposite image emerged, an image that appeared again and again in the fourteenth century and even more so in the fifteenth. The court rabbi of Castile, Abraham Benveniste, for example, who provided much assistance to the royal court, is described in *Crónica de Juan II de Castilla* as giving a lot of bad advice to the nobleman Juan Hurtado de Mendoza. Hurtado de Mendoza followed that advice and, together with Benveniste, acted dishonestly in his handling of the affairs of the kingdom.[225] In *El victorial*, Hurtado de

conceal that conversions took place after 1391, and the reference is probably to conversions in the time of the Valladolid statutes and Vincent Ferrer's preaching from 1412 to 1415. Although the converts are called *anusim* (forced converts), there is an implicit criticism that their conversions were undertaken too lightly.

[224] See Gutwirth, 'The Jews in 15th Century Castilian Chronicles'. Pedro López de Ayala dealt at length with Samuel Halevi's financial and political involvement in the service of Pedro the Cruel, and, in contrast to the trends that prevailed in the Castilian chronicles, he did not cast aspersions on his activities. Another exception in this regard was Abraham Seneor, who was described by the chronicler Alonso de Palencia in *Décadas Latinas* (8.2.10) as an excellent, loyal, and very experienced adviser (see Gutwirth, 'Abraham Seneor', 180–2, n. 53; see also *Crónica anónima de Enrique IV de Castilla*, i. 427).

[225] See Gutwirth, 'The Jews in 15th Century Castilian Chronicles', 382–4, 387.

Mendoza is similarly described as a well-intentioned knight who supported the king but acted under the harmful influence of Jews, and hence the affairs of the Castilian kingdom deteriorated.[226] *El victorial* also contains a disparaging description of Samuel Halevi's actions and bad advice, particularly his disrespectful attitude towards the nobility. Among other things, it says that Samuel Halevi taught Pedro the art of fortune-telling by the stars and invocations—the work of Satan, which leads to death—and thus Samuel Halevi was indirectly blamed for Pedro's death.[227]

There is another historical tradition about the deaths of Pedro and Samuel Halevi in Abraham Zacut's *Sefer yuḥasin*. Zacut, unlike Capsali, held Pedro fully responsible for Halevi's death. However, from a perspective that saw history as reflecting a moral purpose directed by the divine will, he wrote that the king's death at the hand of his brother Enrique at the battle of Montiel in 1369 was retribution for Samuel Halevi's murder.[228] According to this view of history, the death of Samuel Halevi—the greatest Jewish courtier in Castile—called for an explanation, and Enrique's victory in the long civil war in Castile was perceived in Jewish historical consciousness as Pedro's deserved fate for having betrayed his treasurer.

Pero Niño, who wrote *El victorial*, and Abraham Zacut both regarded Samuel Halevi as the cause of Pedro's death. Pero Niño accused Samuel Halevi of exerting a negative magical influence on the king, while Zacut believed that Pedro brought about his own death by killing his Jewish courtier. Many of the oral traditions in *Seder eliyahu zuta* about Jewish courtiers and their accomplishments grappled in one way or another—often through counter-history—with historical traditions that were current in Christian society. Those traditions depicted Jewish courtiers as pursuing their own personal interests and giving the king poor counsel. Most of these traditions probably originated among the Spanish nobility, who were extremely hostile towards the Jewish courtiers who supported the Crown's centralizing policy.

---

[226] Pero Niño, *El victorial*, 320.

[227] Ibid. 48–9; see Gutwirth, 'The Jews in 15th Century Castilian Chronicles', 386–7.

[228] Zacut, *Sefer yuḥasin* (ed. Filipowski, 224*a*). Zacut dated Pedro's death to 1390, which is a similar chronological error to the one made by the exiles recorded in *Seder eliyahu zuta* in dating the Samuel Halevi affair to 1391. King Pedro was depicted realistically in Samuel Çarça's account of the civil war in Castile and the damage it caused to many Jewish communities. When the king of Granada came to help Pedro and punish the rebellious towns, Pedro indeed ordered that 'they should not raise their hands against the Jews for they were not guilty', but at the same time he let the Muslims take Jews into slavery (Çarça, *Mekor ḥayim*, 201; see Gutwirth, 'History and Intertextuality in Late Medieval Spain', esp. 167).

ABRAHAM SENEOR AND
FERDINAND II THE CATHOLIC

The story of the Jewish courtier Abraham Seneor, which Capsali recounts at length in *Seder eliyahu zuta,* is also used to make an ideological point. According to the tradition, Seneor was instrumental in Ferdinand II of Aragon's marriage to Isabella after the Jews decided that he was preferable to all the other kings competing for Isabella's hand. The story is, of course, a legend with no basis in the historical reality of 1468–9, when the match was arranged. Ferdinand was the heir apparent, not the king, and, as Eleazar Gutwirth has shown, Seneor—described as 'highly respected by the entire kingdom' and the 'Jew whom the king placed in charge of all the Jews to do unto them as he saw fit'[229]—was appointed as the court rabbi much later, in around 1477. It seems that this anachronistic story was informed by Abraham Seneor's important role in the service of Ferdinand and Isabella from 1473 until the Expulsion and his support in formulating the agreement between them and King Enrique IV (1425–74).[230] Alongside errors in historical detail and folkloric elements, the myth contains many details based on the political reality of fifteenth-century Castile.

The Jews who moved in the court circles of Castile were well acquainted with the details of the Hispanic royal dynasties. Abraham Zacut, for example, included in *Sefer yuḥasin* a detailed description of the lineage of the kings of Aragon and Castile and placed special emphasis on the fact that Ferdinand was the son of Juan II of Aragon and Juana Enríquez (1425–68), daughter of the admiral of Castile, Fadrique Enríquez (1390–1473), who had fought alongside Juan II at Olmedo against the king of Castile.[231] In the oral traditions of the exiles, the details of the royal dynasty are used to prove Ferdinand's Jewish origin. According to this story, the admiral of Castile raped a married Jewish woman named Paloma. The admiral is not mentioned by name, but the reference is to Fadrique Alfonso (1334–58), illegitimate son of King Alfonso XI and brother of King Enrique de Trastámara. The son—also not mentioned by name, but he was Alonso Enríquez (1354–1429)—was raised by his father and inherited the position of admiral of Castile. He was the father (actually grandfather) of Juana Enríquez. Later, after Juana poisoned Carlos, the heir apparent, Ferdinand took his place as heir and

---

[229] Capsali, *Seder eliyahu zuta,* 2: 56 (ed. Shmuelevitz, Simonsohn, and Benayahu, i. 185).

[230] Ibid. 2: 56 (ed. Shmuelevitz, Simonsohn, and Benayahu, i. 184–5); see Baer, *A History of the Jews in Christian Spain,* ii. 315; Beinart, *The Expulsion from Spain* (Heb.), 367–8; Gutwirth, 'Abraham Seneor', esp. 178–81.

[231] See Zacut, *Sefer yuḥasin* (ed. Freiman, pp. xlvii–xlviii). On the co-operation between Fadrique Enríquez and Juan II, see *Continuación de la crónica de España,* 121–34.

later king of Aragon. Ferdinand's Jewish descent was, then, the main reason the Jews of Castile, led by Abraham Seneor, decided to support his marriage to Isabella and to prefer him over other candidates. The myth also described at length how the Jews achieved their aim.[232]

The details of Ferdinand's dynasty and his connection to the Enríquez family are quite accurate. Speculations about the Enríquez family's Jewish blood were not invented by the exiles but were part of court gossip and political rumour. They were mentioned in various writings, such as the statement defending the Conversos, *Instrucción del relator para el Obispo de Cuenca (Lope Barrientos), a favor de la nación hebrea* written in 1449 by the Converso Fernán Díaz de Toledo. These rumours also came up in Inquisition trials at the end of the fifteenth century and still surrounded the Enríquez family in the sixteenth.[233] Nicolás López Martínez has suggested that the story was circulated by hostile Jews or perhaps Conversos.[234] It may also have been disseminated by the supporters of Juana la Beltraneja (1462–1530) in her attempt to claim the throne of Castile.[235] Amador de los Rios asserted that the story was spread as far back as the fourteenth century by opponents of the Enríquez family,[236] and David Romano has shown that the story was also known in Portugal in the first half of the fifteenth century, as it appears in Fernão Lopes' *Crónica del Rei dom Joham I* in connection with the visit of Alonso Enríquez to Oporto in 1384.[237] According to Maurice Kriegel, the story was brought there to impugn the new royal dynasty of Enrique de Trastámara in

[232] Capsali, *Seder eliyahu zuta*, 2: 57 (ed. Shmuelevitz, Simonsohn, and Benayahu, i. 182–5).

[233] See Romano, 'Ascendencia judía de Ferdinand el Católico?' According to *Seder eliyahu zuta*, Isabella reminded Ferdinand of his Jewish descent when he refused to expel the Jews for her, and Ferdinand 'who was infuriated, took his sandal off his foot and threw it at the queen's head and it struck her . . . and the animosity between the two increased' (Capsali, *Seder eliyahu zuta*, 2: 67 (ed. Shmuelevitz, Simonsohn, and Benayahu, i. 205)). The story appears again, in a nearly identical form (the thrown sandal is replaced with a slap) in 1485 at the trial of Marie Sanchez, a resident of Guadalupe: 'y el rey oviera enojo, y le diera una bofetada, e que la reyna jurara de vengar aquella bofetada' (protocol of Inquisition trial of Marie Sanchez, in Baer, *Die Juden im christlichen Spanien*, doc. 393 (ii. 444); cited in Romano, 'Ascendencia judía de Ferdinand el Católico?', 166–7).

[234] See López Martínez, *Los judaizantes castellanos y la Inquisición*, 105 n. 68.

[235] The struggle between Isabella and Juana is described at length in *Seder eliyahu zuta*, with an emphasis on the war between King Afonso V of Portugal and Juana, on one side, and Isabella of Castile and Ferdinand of Aragon, on the other. Although the exiles knew the sad end of the 'romance' between Ferdinand and the Jews, nonetheless they identified with Isabella and Ferdinand's party, which accused Juana, daughter of Enrique IV of Castile, of being illegitimate. According to the exiles, Juana made use of Ferdinand's alleged Jewish descent, and in reply she was impugned for her illegitimate birth (Capsali, *Seder eliyahu zuta*, 2: 56, 59 (ed. Shmuelevitz, Simonsohn, and Benayahu, i. 180, 187)).

[236] See Amador de los Rios, *Historia social, política y religiosa de los Judíos de España y Portugal*, ii. 207 n. 1. The note is based on an apparently unpublished article.

[237] See Romano, 'Ascendencia judía de Ferdinand el Católico?', 168–9. According to the sources cited by Romano, Dona Paloma was from Guadalcanal.

Castile.[238] It may also have served as the Portuguese response to Enrique's propaganda about Pedro the Cruel's Jewish origin: at the time Portugal was very displeased by Castile's turn towards Aragon.

Rumours of the Enríquez family's and Ferdinand's Jewish blood were not, then, a Jewish invention, but rather part of fifteenth-century Iberian politics, and it is not at all surprising that Jews used the story for their own purposes. In a brief chronicle written between 1527 and 1529, Isaac ben Jacob ibn Faraj, an exile from Iberia, noted that in aristocratic circles in Spain it was common knowledge that Ferdinand was descended from Dona Paloma.[239] In *Seder eliyahu zuta* Ferdinand's descent from a Jewish bastard is not emphasized, but his strong ties to the Jews are. An account is included of how Spain's Jews reacted to the news that Ferdinand and Isabella had defeated Juana and united Aragon and Castile:

> In every province and in every city wherever the word of the king and his law reaches, the king will reign over Aragon and Castile, joy and gladness for the Jews for they say to one another: 'He is one of our brethren, of Jewish blood is he, may the works of our hands be blessed.'[240]

The Jewish myth may have been constructed around the Christian story of Ferdinand's Jewish ancestry in an attempt to explain why so many of the leaders of Castilian Jewry, particularly Abraham Seneor, supported the 'Catholic monarchs'. Jews did prefer a united, centralized kingdom and supported Ferdinand and Isabella. In the end, however, Ferdinand and Isabella turned their backs on the Jews, established the Spanish Inquisition, clashed with the Conversos, and expelled all the Jews from Spain. The emphasis on Ferdinand's Jewish descent may have provided an explanation for the Jews' mistaken decision to back Ferdinand and Isabella and to prefer them over Juana la Beltraneja, who, if she had been victorious, would have united Castile and Portugal, which might have changed the fate of Spanish Jewry.[241] The myth probably evolved even before the Expulsion,

---

[238]   See Kriegel, 'Histoire sociale et ragots', esp. 97.

[239]   See Marx, 'The Expulsion of the Jews from Spain', 100.

[240]   Capsali, *Seder eliyahu zuta*, 2: 59 (ed. Shmuelevitz, Simonsohn, and Benayahu, i. 187–8).

[241]   I am not dealing in this context with the real reasons why Abraham Seneor and others gave their support to Ferdinand and Isabella. As Gutwirth noted, even if Castile had united with Portugal after Juana and Afonso had emerged victorious from the civil war, a centralized, authoritarian kingdom would have been established (see Gutwirth, 'Abraham Seneor', 184; cf. Vicens Vives, *Historia crítica de Fernando II de Aragón*, 387–9). Gutwirth ascribed Seneor's support for Ferdinand and Isabella to his social connections in Segovia. In any case, throughout his entire career, Seneor served as an effective instrument in the implementation of the kingdom's centralizing policy. Kriegel cautiously suggested another reason for the story: Ferdinand's Jewish roots were a stain on his lineage, and hence the Expulsion was perceived as the act of a non-legitimate king, in marked contrast to the positive attitude towards the Jews of Juan II, who had pure Visigothic blood (see 'Histoire sociale et ragots', 94).

when it became clear that Ferdinand and Isabella's centralizing policy was also unfavourable to Jews. It is worth noting that in the stories of the exiles, the Spanish Inquisition's persecutions of Conversos were perceived as directed against Jews as well, since they were accused of being in collusion with them.

THE RELATIONSHIP BETWEEN JEWS AND CHRISTIANS IN JEWISH HISTORICAL CONSCIOUSNESS

According to the exiles from Spain, during the reign of Juan II, king of Castile from 1406 to 1454, 'Israel dwelt safely, every man under his vine and under his fig tree [see Mic. 4: 4], and the Jews lorded it over the people of nations and did as they wished and magnified themselves.'[242] Jews also took pride in the accomplishments of the Conversos, who became the economic, social, and intellectual backbone of the Spanish elite and continued to practise Judaism, while the king, the nobles, and the people turned a blind eye.[243] They described Juan II's son, Enrique IV, who reigned from 1454 to 1474, as 'a man of integrity, of uprightness, who loves restfulness, is modest and very humble in spirit', and his reign is also glowingly depicted as a time of peace and tranquility.[244]

Alongside these idealized descriptions, Haim Hillel Ben-Sasson has presented other Jewish positions which indicate that in the years prior to the Expulsion, the situation of Jews was constantly worsening. He states that the exiles generally pointed to the 1480s as the turning point. But some oral traditions in *Seder eliyahu zuta* indicate that the anti-Jewish decrees went as far back as the thirteenth century.

And after the Edomites had captured Spain from the hands of the Ishmaelites, the Jews who lived in the kingdom of Spain came under the reign of the nations. . . . They troubled and oppressed the people of Israel and decreed against them several forced conversions and several expulsions . . . and the later decrees caused them to forget the earlier ones, and they would have constrained the Jews from being part of several lands, if it had not been the Lord who was on their side. . . . For not one or two kings ruled over all of Spain but seven kings, and when one king expelled them, they would go to another

[242] Capsali, *Seder eliyahu zuta*, 2: 56 (ed. Shmuelevitz, Simonsohn, and Benayahu, i. 180).

[243] Ibid. See H. H. Ben-Sasson, 'The Spanish Exiles Speak of Themselves' (Heb.), 207; on the Jews' negative perceptions of Conversos, see Netanyahu, *The Marranos of Spain*. Among the many criticisms raised by scholars, see G. D. Cohen, Review of B. Netanyahu, *The Marranos of Spain*; see also Netanyahu's response, 'On the Historical Meaning of the Hebrew Sources Related to the Marranos', esp. 87–91; R. Ben-Shalom, 'The Social Context of Apostasy among Fifteenth-Century Spanish Jewry', 176–84.

[244] Capsali, *Seder eliyahu zuta*, 2: 56 (ed. Shmuelevitz, Simonsohn, and Benayahu, i. 180).

king who seemed right to them, and after some time the king who had expelled them annulled his vow and allowed them to come back, so they returned to their cities. This is what the people of the nations and the Jews did all the days, and in this manner there was never an overall expulsion from one end of Spain to the other.[245]

Jewish historical memory skewed Iberian historical reality. During the Reconquest, Jewish life was in fact renewed in many of the places that the Christians took from the Muslims. Capsali explicitly noted that there was some confusion in the historical consciousness: 'the later decrees caused them to forget the earlier ones'. The decrees against the Jews of Spain from 1391 and throughout the fifteenth century did in fact cause the memory of the rescue of Conversos from Muslim rule and the social and cultural revival the Reconquest initiated among the Jews of Spain to fade. The claim that Jews were expelled from one Christian kingdom after another has no historical foundation and was probably inspired by the fact that individual Jews or groups of Jews moved between Christian kingdoms in an attempt to exploit the political divisions in Spain. For example, the Jews of Aragon and Castile threatened James I and Ferdinand III that they would leave their kingdoms if they enforced the decision of the Fourth Lateran Council of 1215 obliging Jews to wear a distinguishing mark.[246] Against the background of the unification of Castile and Aragon, which led to the Expulsion, a mistaken perception of the past developed. Possibly, under the influence of the expulsions from France in the fourteenth century, expulsions from the various kingdoms were imagined, although these were described as small-scale and causing no considerable hardship. Ben-Sasson believed that, despite these perceptions of the past, the exiles did not disagree in their assessments of life in Spain. One emphasized the prosperity, another, the troubles, but 'they all agreed that despite the persecutions, the Jews of Spain nonetheless possessed great wealth. Their lives, particularly of the upper classes, were relatively comfortable; in any event they felt integrated into their country.'[247]

The historical information that Capsali received from the exiles covered all spheres of life in Spain—politics, war, and the founding of countries; gossip from the royal court and the estates of the nobility; the conditions in Jewish communities, yeshivas, forced conversions, and anti-Jewish decrees; tales of Jewish leaders and courtiers; Conversos; and the Expulsion. The relationships between the Christian majority society and the Jewish minority, including the sufferings of

[245] Capsali, *Seder eliyahu zuta*, 2: 53 (ed. Shmuelevitz, Simonsohn, and Benayahu, i. 171).

[246] See Beinart, '"The Jewish Sign"' (Heb.), 29, 33; Limor, *Between Jews and Christians* (Heb.), ii. 227.

[247] H. H. Ben-Sasson, 'The Spanish Exiles Speak of Themselves' (Heb.), 201; see also 200; Monsalvo Antón, 'Mentalidad antijudía en la Castilla medieval'.

Jews, are often descibed.[248] There were also many legends mixed in with the facts, and the Spanish exiles misled Capsali about many things, especially chronology, but that is typical of oral history.[249] The historical information preserved in *Seder eliyahu zuta* probably represents just the tip of the iceberg. Many traditions— from general and Jewish history—were passed down orally, and some of them simply disappeared. However, if they fell into the hands of people with a special interest in the past, such as Elijah Capsali, their chances of preservation were improved.[250]

For the exiles, the stories they told Capsali may have functioned as historical explanations of an idyllic past, explanations they gave themselves in the light of the terrible crisis they faced in the present and which might answer the question of why they failed to foresee what was coming and were so complacent before the Expulsion. I agree that these accounts were not idealized after the Expulsion to heighten the horror or to intensify the impression it left, since in the very same year when the Jews were expelled from Spain, they wrote of their ties with the Christian kingdom.[251] Jewish scholars expressed a high regard for Christian intellectual culture before (for example, Isaac Arama) and after (for example, Joseph Jabez) the Expulsion, and this attitude is also affirmed in works translated from Latin by Jews in the fifteenth century.[252]

These oral traditions had a social aspect that was representative and forma-tive.[253] The representative side was manifested in *convivencia*. These traditions, however, were preserved until the Expulsion and even after it because of their formative function. They shaped Jews' perceptions of Christians and thus con-trolled the relationship between Jews and Christians and kept it on a solid foot-ing. The historical traditions made it possible to moderate hate and restrain the development of undesirable images. In addition, they enabled Jews among the

---

[248] Dobrovolski, 'Traditional Peasant Culture' (Heb.), 38; on how the exiles expressed their experi-ences of conversion, discriminatory decrees, and expulsion, see H. H. Ben-Sasson, 'Exile and Redemption in the Eyes of the Spanish Exiles' (Heb.).

[249] See Henige, *The Chronology of Oral Tradition*.

[250] See Bonfil, 'Can Medieval Storytelling Help Understanding Midrash?', esp. 239–40; Dobrovolski, 'Traditional Peasant Culture' (Heb.), 40; Goody, *The Domestication of the Savage Mind*; Prins, 'Oral History', esp. 120–5; Vansina, *Oral Tradition as History*.

[251] H. H. Ben-Sasson, 'The Spanish Exiles Speak of Themselves' (Heb.), 201. One example is the celebrations held by the Jews when Granada fell to the Christians.

[252] Ibid. 222–3; R. Ben-Shalom, 'Between Official and Private Dispute', 68–71; Gutwirth, 'Actitudes judías hacia los cristianos en la España del siglo XV', esp. 194–5. See the admiration expressed by the translator Abraham ibn Nahmias for the wisdom of the Christians, particularly Thomas Aquinas, in 1490, about two years before the Expulsion (ibid.); Zonta, 'Latin Scholastic Influences on Late Medieval Hebrew Physics'.

[253] See Malinowski, 'Myth in Primitive Psychology', esp. 101, 146; Turner, *Dramas, Fields and Metaphors*.

upper classes to retain their positions of power and pass them on to their heirs. If the expression of tranquil life, 'every man under his vine and under his fig tree', reflected the reality of 'the Jews lord[ing] it over the people of the nations' and if the beneficial counsel of Jews to the king enhanced the security of Jews in Spain, then the simple Jewish masses ought to have continued supporting the upper class and identifying with their aspirations. Indeed, in *Seder eliyahu zuta*, the divine response to the harsh anti-Jewish edicts in Spain was the political power of the Jewish courtiers, which enabled them to direct the course of Hispanic politics and to rule over the broad strata of Christian society.[254]

It seems that these historical traditions were even capable of moderating internal Jewish criticism of the courtiers, which was voiced in censorial or ethical works, such as Solomon Alami ibn Lahmish's *Igeret musar*. He attacked the courtiers for their pride, their manipulations in the royal court, their ostentatiousness, their neglect of the Torah and failure to observe the commandments, and the fact that, under the socio-economic pressure of the Valladolid laws of 1412, they chose to convert to Christianity in order to maintain their high social status.[255] The fact that these oral traditions survived the Expulsion from Spain attests to their vitality and their central place in Spanish historical consciousness. Nor did Alami disapprove of the system by which the courtiers rose in the royal court or their lobbying in favour of the Jews, but he believed that the courtiers' corruption had caused them to be ousted from the king's court in the past and once Jewish lobbyists no longer played a role there, it was only a short step to the enactment of harsh edicts against Jews.[256] However, the activity of men like Abraham Seneor and Isaac Abravanel during the fifteenth century apparently tempered criticism of the courtiers, which erupted during the crisis of 1412–15. Ben-Sasson pointed out that the Jews of Spain maintained their favourable attitude towards the courtiers from the fourteenth century until after the Expulsion and took pride in their services to the Crown.[257]

The oral historical traditions of the Jewish courtiers also express the fusion of Jewish and general history in the historical consciousness of Spanish Jews. There does not seem to have been a clear division between the two. The Jews of Spain dealt with both Jewish and Spanish history, and the images of the past of the Iberian peninsula created a single history in their consciousness.

[254] Capsali, *Seder eliyahu zuta*, 2: 53 (ed. Shmuelevitz, Simonsohn, and Benayahu, i. 173).

[255] Alami ibn Lahmish, *Igeret musar*, 39, 44–6; see Baer, *A History of the Jews in Christian Spain*, ii. 241–3.   [256] Alami ibn Lahmish, *Igeret musar*, 45.

[257] H. H. Ben-Sasson, 'The Spanish Exiles Speak of Themselves' (Heb.), 203–8.

Conclusion

THROUGHOUT THIS STUDY I have emphasized the positive aspects of the Jews' perception of the Spanish kingdom and its history; they also had feelings of hatred, anger, and loathing aroused by the recurring abuses by the Spanish Crown and its institutions, as well as by the common people. The suffering of the Jews in the diaspora was a central theme of books of historiography and chronicles such as Ibn Verga's *Shevet yehudah* and Profayt Duran's *Ma'amar zikhron hashemadot*, as well as of the stories of the exiles that were included in *Seder eliyahu zuta*. In all these, feelings of admiration and abhorrence, attraction and repulsion, towards the Spanish kingdom in all its cultural and social senses existed side by side.

Attraction to and repulsion from Christian culture played an important role in Jewish historical consciousness. The image of Rome was constructed on a congeries of contradictory emotions and perceptions. Previous studies have emphasized the manifestations of hatred for the historical Rome—which represented the medieval Christian world—and the hopes for its destruction. But there was also admiration for Roman culture and appreciation of its accomplishments. The polarity of these positions ought not to surprise us, for in historical consciousness, as in other mental domains, we do not always find cognitive logic or systematic order, and complexity, contradiction, and chaos often dominate. In relation to ancient Christianity and in particular to Jesus, ambivalent attitudes were also found. On the one hand, there was the perception of early Christianity as part of Second Temple Judaism and as a deviation that stemmed from good but mistaken intentions. On the other, there was the growing historical knowledge that contemporary Christianity was essentially different from Jesus's original intentions, and later Christianity was held responsible for the deviation. Jesus was regarded as the crux that, at one and same time, belonged yet did not belong to Jewish history. Although the contemporary Church was perceived as an institution that had deviated from its original values, Jews did not disregard its glorious history and cultural achievements. The exempla and hagiography of the Church served as moral and polemical raw material, and Jews became cognizant of the moral and intellectual power of distinctly Christian values and institutions, especially the papacy. Although Jews resented the papacy as the main symbol of the Church, they acknowledged its tolerance, especially compared with other elements in Christian society, and its ability to maintain the status quo, in which some role was also assigned to the Jews.

The attraction and repulsion can be explained by the Jews' status during the Middle Ages as a minority in a mainly Christian society. Often, Jews were relegated to the margins, and their reaction was to reject social, cultural, and, of course, religious elements of the majority. On the other hand, mechanisms of integration and co-operation functioned in Spain and southern France, a situation unique to these countries during the Middle Ages. This led to adoption, acceptance, and approval, which furthered acceptance by the majority. Consequently, it is not always possible to distinguish cause and effect, whether it was the co-operation of Christian and Jewish societies that led to the acceptance of elements of Christian culture, or whether sympathetic Jewish responses led to co-operation.

Cultural images and how they are represented cannot be separated from the discourse between the minority and the majority, and they should be explained against the backdrop of the balance of power between Christians and Jews. In Christian historical consciousness, the history of the Jews was limited to the period from Abraham to the coming of Jesus. After the destruction of the Temple, there was no longer any real place for Jews in history—they were dispossessed, and their historical memories, culture, and image were distorted. The historical image of Jews became part of the negative stereotype of real Jews in the diaspora. In the face of the Christian perception of the Jew as the 'Other', it was natural for Jews to develop a similar attitude to Christians. One might have expected, then, to find among Jews an extreme ethnocentric approach to Christianity. However, as studies in social psychology have shown, stereotypical images and ethnocentric approaches are influenced by a myriad of elements, including the degree of affinity between the groups, geography, history, economics and class, the social and political cohesiveness of the groups, the amount of social contact and interaction between them, the knowledge each group possessed of the other, and so on. One cannot determine absolutely whether close affinity between groups—as was the case of the Jewish communities in Spain and southern France—will ameliorate the negative images and create less stereotypical, more precise perceptions or will arouse hostility and lead to the formation of more negative, stereotypical perceptions.

This study has shown that an extreme ethnocentric approach did not develop in the historical consciousness of the Jews of Spain and southern France as a reaction to the negative stereotypical image of Jews in Christian literature. Jewish historical consciousness was influenced not only by Christian historiography and theology but also, and perhaps particularly, by the local discourse with Christian culture. It is true that among the modes of representation of Christians, there were distortions and disparaging images, the result of a religious polemic that led to the creation of counter-histories. However, as a rule, Jews did not hold a monolithic, stereotypical perception of Christians, and in many cases the absolute disparity between the categories of Jewish culture and Christian culture as autonomous objective systems was obliterated.

Bibliography

ABNER OF BURGOS, 'The First Letter' (Heb.), ed. Judah M. Rosenthal, in Meir Ben Horin, Bernard D. Weinryb, and Solomon Zeitlin (eds.), *Studies and Essays in Honour of Abraham A. Neuman* [Meḥkarim umasot likhevod avraham a. neuman] (Leiden, 1962), Heb. section, 6–11.

—— 'Polemical Letters' (Heb.), in Judah M. Rosenthal, *Studies and Sources* [Meḥkarim umekorot], vol. i (Jerusalem, 1967), 326–61.

—— 'The Second Letter' (Heb.), ed. Judah M. Rosenthal, in S. Belkin et al. (eds.), *Festschrift in Honour of Rabbi Dr Abraham Weiss* [Sefer yovel likhevod harav dr avraham vais] (New York, 1964), 483–510.

—— 'The Third Letter' (Heb.), ed. Judah M. Rosenthal, *Studies in Bibliography and Booklore*, 5 (1961), 42–51.

ABOAB, IMMANUEL, *Nomología, o, discursos legales de Imanuel Aboab*, ed. Moisés Orfali (Salamanca, 2007).

ABRAHAM BAR HIYYA, *Hegyon hanefesh ha'atsuvah*, ed. Geoffrey Wigoder (Jerusalem, 1972).

—— *Megilat hamegaleh lerabi avraham bar ḥiya hanasi*, ed. Abraham Poznanski, introd. Julius Guttmann (Berlin, 1904).

—— *Sefer ha'ibur*, ed. Herschell [Tsevi] Filipowski (London, 1851).

ABRAHAM B. SOLOMON ARDUTIEL, *Hashlamat sefer hakabalah*, in Abraham E. Harkavy (ed.), *Both New and Old: Sources and Studies in Jewish History and Literature* [Ḥadashim gam yeshanim: mekorot umeḥkarim betoledot yisra'el uvesifruto] (Jerusalem, 1970), 285–304; Yolanda Moreno Koch (ed.), *Dos crónicas hispanohebreas del siglo XV* (Barcelona, 1994), 67–112.

ABRAVANEL, ISAAC, *Ma'ayenei hayeshuah*, in id., *Perush al nevi'im ukhetuvim*, 267–421.

—— *Mashmia yeshuah*, in id., *Perush al nevi'im ukhetuvim*, 423–606.

—— *Perush al hatorah*, 3 vols. (Jerusalem, 1964).

—— *Perush al nevi'im aḥaronim* (Jerusalem, 1979).

—— *Perush al nevi'im ukhetuvim* (Jerusalem, 1960).

—— *Perush linevi'im rishonim* (Jerusalem, 1955).

—— *Sefer yeshuot meshiḥo* (Königsberg, 1861).

ABULAFIA, ANNA SAPIR, 'Invectives against Christianity in the Hebrew Chronicles of the First Crusade', in Peter W. Edbury (ed.), *Crusade and Settlement* (Cardiff, 1985), 66–72.

ABULAFIA, TODROS B. JUDAH, *Gan hameshalim vehaḥidot*, 3 vols., ed. David Yellin (Jerusalem, 1932).

ADRET, SOLOMON B. ABRAHAM, *Teshuvot harashba*, 2 vols., ed. Haim Z. Dimitrovsky (Jerusalem, 1990).

AESCOLY, AARON Z. (ed.), *Jewish Messianic Movements* [Hatenuot hameshiḥiyot beyisra'el], 2nd edn. (Jerusalem, 1988).

AHMAD IBN MUHAMMAD AL-MAQQARI, *Nafḥ al-tib* (Beirut, 1949).

AL-BIRUNI, ABU RAYHAN, *The Chronology of Ancient Nations*, trans. C. E. Sachau (London, 1879).

AL-MAS'UDI, *Muruj adh-dhahab*, 2 vols., ed. C. Barbier de Meynard (Paris, 1861).

AL-QIRQISANI, *The Book of Lights and Watch-Towers*, in Leon Nemoy (ed.), 'Al-Qirqisani's Account of the Jewish Sects and Christianity', *Hebrew Union College Annual*, 7 (1930), 317–97.

ALAMI IBN LAHMISH, SOLOMON, *Igeret musar o igeret hatokhaḥah veha'emunah*, ed. Abraham Meir Habermann (Jerusalem, 1946).

ALBA CECELIA, AMPARO, and CARLOS SAÍNZ DE LA MAZA, 'La primera epístola de Alfonso de Valladolid', *Sefarad*, 53 (1993), 157–70.

—— and ——'La segunda epístola de Alfonso de Valladolid', *Sefarad*, 51 (1991), 391–416.

ALBERT, BAT-SHEVA, 'Isidore of Seville: His Attitude towards Judaism and His Impact on Early Medieval Canon', *Jewish Quarterly Review*, 80 (1990), 207–20.

ALBO, JOSEPH, *Sefer ha'ikarim*, 2 vols. (Tel Aviv, 1964).

The Alfonsine Tables of Toledo, ed. José Chabás and Bernard R. Goldstein (Dordrecht, 2003).

ALFONSO DE BAENA, JUAN, *Cancionero*, 3 vols., ed. José María Azaceta (Madrid, 1966).

ALFONSO X, *Grande e general estoria, primera parte*, ed. Antonio García Solalinde (Madrid, 1930); *General estoria*, 10 vols., ed. Pedro Sánchez-Prieto Borja et al. (Madrid, 2009).

—— *Primera crónica general de España que mandó componer Alfonso el Sabio y se continuaba bajo Sancho IV en* 1289, 2 vols., ed. Ramón Menéndez Pidal (Madrid, 1955).

ALHARIZI, JUDAH, *Taḥkemoni: o maḥberot heman ha'ezraḥi*, ed. Yosef Yahalom and Naoya Katsumata (Jerusalem, 2010); Eng. trans.: *The Book of Taḥkemoni: Jewish Tales from Medieval Spain*, trans. David Simha Segal (Oxford, 2001).

ALMAZAN, VINCENT (WAYNE), 'L'Exemplum chez Vincent Ferrier', *Romanische Forschungen*, 79 (1977), 288–332.

ALON, GEDALIAH, 'The Attitude of the Pharisees to Roman Rule and the House of Herod' (Heb.), *Zion*, 3 (1935), 300–22.

—— *The Jews in the Land of Israel during the Mishnaic and Talmudic Periods* [Toledot hayehudim be'erets-yisra'el bitekufat hamishnah vehatalmud], 2 vols. (Tel Aviv, 1956); Eng. trans.: *The Jews in Their Land in the Talmudic Age*, 2 vols. in 1, ed. and trans. Gershon Levi (Cambridge, Mass., 1989).

ALONI, NEHEMIA, 'Zion and Jerusalem in the Poetry of Spain' (Heb.), in Issachar Ben-Ami (ed.), *The Legacy of Spanish and Eastern Jews: Studies* [Moreshet yehudei sefarad vehamizraḥ: meḥkarim] (Jerusalem, 1982), 235–59.

ALONSO DE PALENCIA, *Décadas Latinas*, ed. Antonio Paz y Melia, Biblioteca de autores españoles, 258 (Madrid, 1975).

ALONSO GARCÍA, DAMIÁN, *Literatura oral del ladino entre los Sefardíes de oriente a través del romancero* (Madrid, 1970).

ALPHANDÉRY, PAUL, 'Sur les Passagiens: À propos d'un livre récent', *Revue des Études Juives*, 82 (1926), 353–61.

ÁLVAR GARCÍA DE SANTA MARÍA, *Crónica de Juan II de Castilla*, ed. Juan de Mata Carriazo y Arroquia (Madrid, 1982).

AMADOR DE LOS RIOS, JOSÉ, *Études historiques, politiques et littéraires sur les juifs d'Espagne* (Paris, 1861).

—— *Historia social, política y religiosa de los Judíos de España y Portugal*, 2 vols. (Madrid, 1876).

ANKAR, AVISHAI, 'Rabbi Judah ben Ilai: The Man and His Time' [R. yehudah ben ilai: ha'ish utekufato] (Ph.D. thesis, Bar-Ilan University, 1987).

ANKORI, ZVI, *An Encounter in History: The Relations of Jews and Christian Greeks through the Ages* [Yahadut veyavnut notserit: mifgash ve'imut bimerutsat hadorot] (Tel Aviv, 1984).

ARAMA, ISAAC B. MOSES, *Akedat yitshak*, 6 vols. (Pressburg, 1849).

—— *Hazut kashah*, in id., *Akedat yitshak*, vol. vi.

ARCE, AUGUSTÍN, 'Cinco nuevos romances del Cid', *Sefarad*, 21 (1961), 69–75.

ARENDT, HANNAH, 'What Was Authority?', *Nomos*, 1 (1958), 81–112.

ARIELI, YEHOSHUA, 'New Horizons in Eighteenth- and Nineteenth-Century Historiography' (Heb.), in Mosche Zimmermann, Menahem Stern, and Joseph Salmon (eds.), *Studies in Historiography* [Iyunim behistoryografyah] (Jerusalem, 1998), 145–68.

ARMISTEAD, SAMUEL G., and JOSEPH H. SILVERMAN, *The Judeo-Spanish Ballad Chapbooks of Yacob Abraham Yoná* (Berkeley, Calif., 1971).

—— and —— 'Sobre unos romances del Cid recogidos en Tetuán', *Sefarad*, 22 (1962), 385–96.

ASHTOR, ELIYAHU, *History of the Jews in Muslim Spain* [Korot hayehudim bisefarad hamuslemit], 2 vols. (Jerusalem, 1966); Eng. trans.: *The Jews of Moslem Spain*, 3 vols., trans. Aaron Klein and Jenny Machlowitz Klein (Philadelphia, Pa., 1973).

ASMUSSEN, JES PETER, 'Manichaean Literature', in E. Yarshater (ed.), *Persian Literature* (Albany, NY, 1988), 51–71.

ASSIS, YOM TOV, *The Golden Age of Aragonese Jewry: Community and Society in the Crown of Aragon, 1213–1327* (London, 1997).

—— 'The Jews in the Kingdom of Aragon and Its Protectorates' (Heb.), in Haim Beinart (ed.), *The Sephardi Legacy* [Moreshet sefarad] (Jerusalem, 1992), 36–80.

ATTIAS, MOSHE, *Spanish Romancero: Romances and Folk Songs in Judaeo-Spanish* [Romansero sefaradi: romansot veshirei am biyehudit-sefaradit] (Jerusalem, 1956).

AUGUSTINE, *On the Literal Interpetation of Genesis* (*De Genesi ad litteram*, ed. Joseph Zycha, Corpus scriptorum ecclesiasticorum Latinorum, 28 (Vienna, 1894)).

AVI-YONAH, MICHAEL, *In the Days of Rome and Byzantium* [Biyemei roma ubizanti-yon] (Jerusalem, 1970).

Avot derabi natan, ed. Solomon Schechter (Vienna, 1887).

BABINGER, FRANZ, *Laudivius Zacchia, Erdichter der 'Epistolae Magni Turci' (Neapel 1473 u. ö)*, Bayerische Akademie der Wissenschaften, Philosophische–Historische Klasse, Sitzungsberichte, 13 (Munich, 1960).

BAER, YITZHAK, 'Don Isaac Abravanel's Attitude to History and the State' (Heb.), in id., *Studies and Essays in Jewish History* [Meḥkarim umasot betoledot am yisra'el], ii. 397–416.

—— *Galut*, trans. Robert Warshaw (New York, 1947).

—— 'The Hebrew *Sefer yosipon*' (Heb.), in id., *Studies and Essays in Jewish History* [Meḥkarim umasot betoledot am yisra'el], ii. 27–101.

—— 'The Historical Background of the *Ra'aya mehemna*' (Heb.), in id., *Studies and Essays in Jewish History* [Meḥkarim umasot betoledot am yisra'el], ii. 306–49.

—— *A History of the Jews in Christian Spain*, 2nd edn., 2 vols. (Philadelphia, Pa., 1971).

—— *Die Juden im christlichen Spanien*, 2 vols. (Berlin, 1929–36).

—— 'Eine jüdische Messiasprophetie auf das Jahr 1186 und der dritte Kreuzzug', *Monatsschrift für Geschichte und Wissenschaft des Judentums*, 70 (1926), 113–22.

—— 'The Messianic Movement in Spain at the Time of the Expulsion' (Heb.), in id., *Studies and Essays in Jewish History* [Meḥkarim umasot betoledot am yisra'el], ii. 381–97.

—— 'New Comments on *Shevet yehudah*' (Heb.), in id., *Studies and Essays in Jewish History* [Meḥkarim umasot betoledot am yisra'el], ii. 417–44.

—— 'On Criticism of the Disputations of Yehiel of Paris and Nahmanides' (Heb.), in id., *Studies and Essays in Jewish History* [Meḥkarim umasot betoledot am yisra'el], ii. 128–87.

—— 'The Political Situation of Spanish Jewry in the Time of R. Judah Halevi' (Heb.), in id., *Studies and Essays in Jewish History* [Meḥkarim umasot betoledot am yisra'el], ii. 251–68.

—— 'R. Abraham ben Samuel Zacut' (Heb.), in *Hebrew Encyclopedia* [Ha'entsiklopedyah ha'ivrit] (Tel Aviv, 1949–80), i, cols. 318–21.

—— *Studies and Essays in Jewish History* [Meḥkarim umasot betoledot am yisra'el], 2 vols. (Jerusalem, 1986).

—— 'Todros ben Judah Halevi and His Time' (Heb.), in id., *Studies and Essays in Jewish History* [Meḥkarim umasot betoledot am yisra'el], ii. 269–305.

BALDRIC OF DOL, *History of Jerusalem* (*Historia Jerosolimitana*, Recueil des Historiens des Croisades: Historiens Occidentaux, 4 (Paris, 1879), 1–111).

BAR-KOCHVA, BEZALEL, 'Jewishness and Greekness: Between Science and Publicism' (Heb.), *Tarbiz*, 63 (1993/4), 451–80.

BARKAI, RON, *Cristianos y Musulmanes en la España medieval (el enemigo en el espejo)* (Madrid, 1984).

—— 'Images of Self and Enemy among Christians and Muslims in Spain during the Reconquista (Eighth to Thirteenth Centuries)' [Dimui atsmi vedimuyei oyev etsel hanotserim ve'etsel hamuslemim bisefarad bitekufat harekonkistah] (Ph.D. thesis, Hebrew University of Jerusalem, 1979).

—— 'The Patriotism of Spanish Jews in the Middle Ages and the Patriotism of Christians and Muslims' (Heb.), *Proceedings of the Eighth World Congress on Jewish Studies* [Divrei hakongres ha'olami hashemini lemada'ei hayahadut], vol. ii (Jerusalem, 1972), 39–46.

—— *Science, Magic and Mythology in the Middle Ages* [Mada, magyah, umitologyah biyemei-habeinayim] (Jerusalem, 1987).

—— *Sephardi Mythology* [Hamitologyah hasefaradit] (Tel Aviv, 2003).

BARNES, TIMOTHY D., *Constantine and Eusebius* (Cambridge, 1981).

—— 'Emperor and Bishops, A.D. 324–344: Some Problems', *Journal of Ancient History*, 3 (1978), 53–75.

BARON, SALO W., 'The Historical Outlook of Maimonides', *Proceedings of the American Academy for Jewish Research*, 6 (1934–5), 5–113.

—— *A Social and Religious History of the Jews*, 2nd edn., 18 vols. (New York, 1958).

BEAUNE, COLETTE, *Naissance de la nation France* (Paris, 1985).

BEINART, HAIM, 'Cuándo llegaron los Judíos a España?', *Estudios*, 3 (1962), 5–32; published as 'When Did the Jews Arrive in Spain?' (Heb.), in id., *Essays on Spain* [Pirkei sefarad], vol. i (Jerusalem, 1998), 13–35.

—— *The Expulsion from Spain* [Gerush sefarad] (Jerusalem, 1995); published in English as *The Expulsion of the Jews from Spain*, trans. Jeffrey M. Green (Oxford, 2002).

—— 'The Image of the Jewish Courtier in Christian Spain' (Heb.), in *Elite Groups and Leadership in the Histories of the Jews and the Nations: The Tenth Conference on the Study of History, Hanukah 1965* [Kevutsot ilit veshikhvot manhigut betoledot yisra'el uvetoledot ha'amim: hakenes ha'asiri le'iyun behistoryah, ḥanukah 1965] (Jerusalem, 1967), 55–71.

—— '"The Jewish Sign" and Enforcement of the "Order of the Sign" during the Reign of the Catholic Monarchs' (Heb.), in Shmuel Almog et al. (ed.), *A Collection of Articles Presented to Shmuel Ettinger* [Kovets ma'amarim shai lishemu'el etinger] (Jerusalem, 1988), 29–41.

—— 'Large-Scale Forced Conversion and the Fate of the *Anusim*' (Heb.), in id. (ed.), *The Sephardi Legacy* [Moreshet sefarad] (Jerusalem, 1992), 280–308.

—— 'Majorca', in *Encyclopaedia Judaica* (Jerusalem, 1971), xi, cols. 795–804.

BEN-SASSON, HAIM HILLEL, *Continuity and Change* [Retsef utemurah], ed. Joseph Hacker (Tel Aviv, 1984).

—— *Essays on Medieval Jewish History* [Perakim betoledot hayehudim biyemei-habein-ayim], ed. Joseph Hacker (Tel Aviv, 1977).

—— 'Exile and Redemption in the Eyes of the Spanish Exiles' (Heb.), in Shmuel Ettinger et al. (eds.), *Yitzhak Baer Festschrift* [Sefer yovel leyitsḥak baer] (Jerusalem, 1961), 216–27.

—— 'Moses ben Nahman: A Man in the Complexities of His Time' (Heb.), in id., *Continuity and Change* [Retsef utemurah], 316–27.

—— 'On Medieval Trends in Jewish Chronography and Its Problems' (Heb.), in id., *Continuity and Change* [Retsef utemurah], 379–401.

—— 'The Spanish Exiles Speak of Themselves' (Heb.), in id., *Continuity and Change* [Retsef utemurah], 138–298.

BEN-SASSON, MENAHEM, 'On the Jewish Identity of the *Anusim*: A Study of Voluntary Conversion during the Almohad Period' (Heb.), *Pe'amim*, 52 (1990), 16–37.

BEN-SASSON, YONAH, *Jewish Thought: Study and Research* [Hagut yehudit: iyun veheker] (Jerusalem, 1987).

—— 'R. Joseph Albo's Idea of History' (Heb.), in Menahem Ben-Sasson, Robert [Reuven] Bonfil, and Joseph Hacker (eds.), *Culture and Society in Medieval Jewish History: Studies Dedicated to the Memory of Haim Hillel Ben-Sasson* [Tarbut vehevrah betoledot yisra'el biyemei-habeinayim: kovets ma'amarim lezikhro shel hayim hilel ben-sason] (Jerusalem, 1989), 493–516.

BEN-SHALOM, ISRAEL, *The House of Shammai and the Zealots' Struggle against Rome* [Beit shamai uma'avak hakana'im neged romi] (Jerusalem, 1993).

—— 'Rabbi Judah bar Ilai and His Attitude to Rome' (Heb.), *Zion*, 49 (1984), 9–24.

BEN-SHALOM, RAM, 'The Authorship of the *Me'ir nativ* Concordance' (Heb.), *Kiryat sefer*, 64 (1993), 754–60.

—— 'Between Official and Private Dispute: The Case of Christian Spain and Provence in the Late Middle Ages', *AJS Review*, 27 (2003), 23–72.

—— 'The Blood Libel in Arles and the Franciscan Mission in Avignon in 1453' (Heb.), *Zion*, 63 (1998), 391–408.

—— 'Christian Art in the Intellectual World of Jewish Scholars: The Case of Isaac Nathan from Arles' (forthcoming).

—— 'The Converso as Subversive: Jewish Traditions or Christian Libel?', *Journal of Jewish Studies*, 50 (1999), 259–83.

—— 'The Courtier as the "Sceptre of Judah": The Letters and Panegyrics to Courtiers of Yom Tov ben Hana, Scribe of the Jewish Community of Montalbán' (Heb.), in Eli Yassif et al. (eds.), *Ot Letovah: Essays in Honor of Professor Tova Rosen*, El Prezente: Studies in Sephardic Culture, 6 (Be'er Sheva, 2012), 196–224.

—— 'Exempla and Historical Consciousness in the Middle Ages: The Case of Philip, Alexander the Great and the Conquest of Athens' (Heb.), in Amir Horowitz et al. (eds.), *The Past and Beyond: Studies in History and Philosophy Presented to Elazar Weinryb* [He'avar ume'ever lo: iyunim bahistoryah uvafilosofyah shai le'elazar veinrib] (Raanana, 2006), 99–116.

—— *Facing Christian Culture: Historical Consciousness and Images of the Past among the Jews of Spain and Southern France during the Middle Ages* [Mul tarbut notsrit: toda'ah historit vedimuyei avar bekerev yehudei sefarad uprovans biyemei habeinayim] (Jerusalem, 2006).

—— 'The Foundation of Christianity in the Historical Perceptions of Medieval Jews and according to the Anonymous "Various Elements on the Topic of Christian Faith" (MS London, British Library Add. 27129, 88b–92a [Italy, 15th–16th century])', in Israel J. Yuval and Ram Ben-Shalom (eds.), *Conflict and Religious Conversation in Latin Christendom: Studies in Honour of Ora Limor* (Turnhout, 2014), 221–52.

—— 'Graeco-Roman Myth and Mythology in the Historical Consciousness of Medieval Spanish Jewry' (Heb.), *Zion*, 66 (2001), 451–94.

—— 'How to Remember a Leader? Hasdai Crescas in the Eyes of his Contemporaries and the Generation of the Expulsion' (Heb.) (forthcoming).

—— 'Isaac Nathan, "The Light of Our Exile": Leadership, Polemics and Intellectual Creation in Provençal Jewry in the Fifteenth Century' [Yitshak natan, meor galutenu: hanhagah, pulmus viyetsirah intelektualit bemerkaz ḥayeiha shel yahadut provans bame'ah ha-15] (MA thesis, Tel Aviv University, 1989).

—— 'Jewish Martyrdom and Martyrology in Aragon and Castile in 1391: Between Spain and Ashkenaz' (Heb.), *Tarbiz*, 70 (2000/1), 227–82.

—— '*Me'ir Nativ*: The First Hebrew Concordance of the Bible and Jewish Bible Study in the Fifteenth Century, in the Context of Jewish–Christian Polemics', *Aleph*, 12 (2011), 201–76.

—— 'A Minority Looks at the Mendicants: Isaac Nathan the Jew and Thomas Connecte the Carmelite', *Journal of Medieval History*, 30 (2004), 213–43.

—— 'The Myths of Troy and Hercules as Reflected in the Writings of Some Jewish Exiles from Spain', in Harvey J. Hames (ed.), *Jews, Muslims and Christians in and around the Crown of Aragon* (Leiden, 2004), 229–54.

—— 'Polemic Historiography in *Sefer yuḥasin*' (Heb.), in *Proceedings of the Eleventh World Congress on Jewish Studies* [Divrei hakongres ha'olami ha'aḥad-asar lemada'ei hayahadut], vol. ii/1 (Jerusalem, 1994), 121–8.

—— 'The Social Context of Apostasy among Fifteenth-Century Spanish Jewry: Dynamics of a New Religious Borderland', in J. Cohen and M. Rosman (eds.), *Rethinking European Jewish History* (Oxford, 2009), 173–98.

—— 'The Tortosa Disputation: Vincent Ferrer and the Problem of the Forced Converts according to Isaac Nathan' (Heb.), *Zion*, 56 (1991), 21–45.

—— 'The Unwritten Travel Journal to the East of Joseph ibn Caspi: Images and Orientalism' (Heb.), *Pe'amim*, 124 (2010), 7–52.

BEN-YEHUDA, ELIEZER, *Dictionary of the Hebrew Language, Old and New* [Milon halashon ha'ivrit hayeshanah vehaḥadashah], 17 vols. (Tel Aviv, 1948–9).

BENAYAHU, MEIR, 'Rabbi David Benveniste and His Letter to Rabbi Abraham ibn Yaish' (Heb.), *Sefunot*, 11 (1971–8), 269–97.

—— 'A Source on the Expellees in Portugal and Their Departure for Thessalonica' (Heb.), *Sefunot*, 11 (1971–8), 233–65.

BENIN, STEPHEN D., *The Footprints of God: Divine Accommodation in Jewish and Christian Thought* (Albany, NY, 1993).

BENJAMIN OF TUDELA, *Sefer masaot shel rabi binyamin mitudelah*, ed. Marcus N. Adler (New York, repr. 1964); Spanish trans.: *Libro de viajes*, ed. J. R. Magdalena Nom de Deu (Barcelona, 1989).

BENSON, C. DAVID, *The History of Troy in Middle English Literature* (Totawa, NJ, 1980).

BENSON, ROBERT L., 'Political Renovatio: Two Models from Roman Antiquity', in Robert L. Benson and Giles Constable (eds.), *Renaissance and Renewal in the Twelfth Century* (Cambridge, Mass., 1982), 339–86.

—— and GILES CONSTABLE (eds.), *Renaissance and Renewal in the Twelfth Century* (Oxford, 1982).

BEQUETTE, JOHN, *The Eloquence of Sanctity: Rhetoric in Thomas of Celano's 'Vita Prima Sancti Francis'* (Quincy, Ill., 2003).

BERGER, DAVID, 'Christian Heresy and Jewish Polemic in the Twelfth and Thirteenth Centuries', *Harvard Theological Review*, 48 (1975), 287–303.

BERGER, DAVID, 'Gilbert Crispin, Alan of Lille, and Jacob ben Reuben: A Study in the Transmission of Medieval Polemic', *Speculum*, 49 (1974), 34–47.

—— 'On the Image and Destiny of Gentiles in Ashkenazi Polemical Literature' (Heb.), in Yom Tov Assis et al. (eds.), *Facing the Cross: The Persecutions of 1096 in History and Historiography* [Yehudim mul hatselav: gezerot tatnu [856/1096] bahistoryah uvahistoryografyah] (Jerusalem, 2000), 74–91.

—— 'On the Uses of History in Medieval Jewish Polemic against Christianity: The Search for the Historical Jesus', in Elisheva Carlebach, John M. Efron, and David N. Myers (eds.), *Jewish History and Jewish Memory: Essays in Honour of Yosef Hayim Yerushalmi* (Hanover, NH, 1998), 25–39.

BERGUA CAVERO, JORJE, 'El Príncipe de Viana, traductor de un tratado atribuido a Plutarco', in Manuela García Valdés (ed.), *Estudios sobre Plutarco: Ideas religiosas. Actas del III simposio internacional sobre Plutarco, Oviedo 30 de abril a 2 de Mayo 1992* (Madrid, 1994), 397–405.

BERLIOZ, JACQUES, and MARIE ANNE POLO DE BEAULIEU (eds.), *Les 'Exempla' médiévaux: Introduction à la recherche, suivie des tables critiques de l'"Index exemplorum" de Fredric C. Tubach* (Carcassonne, 1992).

BERMEJO CABRERO, JOSÉ LUIS, 'Orígenes del oficio de cronista real', *Hispania*, 40 (1980), 395–409.

BERNÁLDEZ, ANDRÉS, *Historia de los Reyes Católicos Don Fernando y Doña Isabel*, ed. Cayetano Rosell, Crónicas de los reyes de Castilla, 3, Biblioteca de autores españoles, 70 (Madrid, 1846).

BERNSTEIN, SIMON, *By the Rivers of Spain: Lamentations over the Destruction of Jerusalem and the 1391 Pogroms as a Spanish Jewish Custom, according to a Unique Manuscript in the Royal Library in Lisbon* [Al neharot sefarad: kinot keminhag sefarad al ḥurban yerushalayim ve'al hapuranuyot ad gezerot 1391 lefi ketav-yad yaḥid ba'olam basifriyah hamamlakhtit belisbon] (Tel Aviv, 1957).

BERTUCCI, TEMISTOCLE, 'Orsini', in Vittorio Spreti (ed.), *Enciclopedia storiconobiliare italiana* (Bologna, 1928–32), iv. 929–40.

BIDEZ, JOSEPH, *La Vie de l'empereur Julien* (Paris, 1930).

BIETENHOLZ, PETER G., *Historia and Fabula: Myths and Legends in Historical Thought from Antiquity to the Modern Age* (Leiden, 1994).

BISSON, THOMAS N., *The Medieval Crown of Aragon: A Short History* (New York, 1991).

BLOCH, HERBERT, 'The New Fascination with Ancient Rome', in Robert L. Benson and Giles Constable (eds.), *Renaissance and Renewal in the Twelfth Century* (Cambridge, Mass., 1982), 615–36.

BLOCH, MARC, *Feudal Society*, trans. L. A. Manyon (London, 1961).

BLUMENFELD-KOSINSKY, RENATE, *Reading Myth: Classical Mythology and Its Interpretation in Medieval French Literature* (Stanford, Calif., 1997).

BOCCACCIO, GIOVANNI, *Concerning Famous Women*, ed. Guido A. Guarino (London, 1964).

BOETHIUS, *The Consolation of Philosophy*, trans. Patrick Gerard Walsh (Oxford, 1999).

BONAVENTURE, *Life of St. Francis*, in *The Little Flowers of St. Francis*, trans. E. Gurney-Salter, introd. Hugh McKay (London, 1966), 303–97.

BONFIL, ROBERT (REUVEN), 'Between the Land of Israel and Babylonia: Trends in the Study of the History of Jewish Culture in Southern Italy and Christian Europe in the Early Middle Ages' (Heb.), *Shalem*, 5 (1987), 1–30.

—— 'Can Medieval Storytelling Help Understanding Midrash? The Story of Paltiel: A Preliminary Study on History and Midrash', in Michael Fishbane (ed.), *The Midrashic Imagination: Jewish Exegesis, Thought, and History* (Albany, NY, 1993), 228–54.

—— 'How Golden was the Age of the Renaissance in Jewish Historiography?', *History and Theory*, 27 (1988), 78–102.

—— 'The Legacy of Spanish Jewry in Historical Writings' (Heb.), in Haim Beinart (ed.), *The Sephardi Legacy* [Moreshet sefarad] (Jerusalem, 1992), 746–58.

BONFILS, IMMANUEL B. JACOB, *The Book of the Gests of Alexander of Macedon: Sefer Toledot Alexandros ha-Makdoni. A Mediaeval Hebrew Version of the Alexander Romance by Immanuel ben Jacob Bonfils*, ed. and trans. I. J. Kasis (Cambridge, Mass., 1962).

BORCHARDT, PAUL, 'The Sculpture in Front of the Lateran as Described by Benjamin of Tudela and Magister Gregorius', *Journal of Roman Studies*, 26 (1936), 68–70.

BORGEHAMMAR, STEPHAN, *How the Holy Cross Was Found: From Event to Medieval Legend* (Stockholm, 1991).

BORN, LESTER K., 'Ovid and Allegory', *Speculum*, 9 (1934), 362–79.

BOSSUAT, ANDRÉ, 'Les Origines troyennes: Leur rôle dans la littérature historique du XVe siècle', *Annales de Normandie*, 8 (1958), 187–97.

BOUREAU, ALAIN, *La Légende dorée* (Paris, 1984).

—— *La Papesse Jeanne* (Paris, 1988).

BOURNE, ELLA, 'Classical Elements in the Gesta Romanorum', in Christabel Forsyth Fiske (ed.), *Vassar Medieval Studies* (New Haven, Conn., 1923), 345–76.

BOUTET, DOMINIQUE, and ARMAND STRUBLE, *Littérature, politique et société dans la France du Moyen Âge* (Paris, 1979).

BOWMAN, STEVEN B., *The Jews of Byzantium, 1204–1453* (Tuscaloosa, Ala., 1985).

—— 'Sefer Yosippon: History and Midrash', in Michael Fishbane (ed.), *The Midrashic Imagination: Jewish Exegesis, Thought, and History* (Albany, NY, 1993), 280–94.

BOYLE, JOHN A., 'The Dynastic and Political History of the Il-Khans', in id. (ed.), *Cambridge History of Iran*, vol. v: *The Saljuq and Mongol Periods* (Cambridge, 1968), 340–50.

BREISACH, ERNST, *Historiography: Ancient, Medieval and Modern* (Chicago, 1983).

BREMOND, CLAUDE, JACQUES LE GOFF, and JEAN-CLAUDE SCHMITT, *L'Exemplum*, Typologie des sources du Moyen Âge Occidental, 40 (Turnhout, 1982).

BREZZI, PAOLO, 'Chroniques universelles du Moyen Âge et histoire du salut', in Jean-Philippe Genet (ed.), *L'Historiographie médiévale en Europe: Actes du colloque organisé par la Fondation Européenne de la Science au Centre de Recherches Historiques et Juridiques de l'Université Paris I du 29 mars au 13 avril 1989* (Paris, 1991), 235–45.

BROWNING, ROBERT, *The Emperor Julian* (London, 1975).

CACHO BLECUA, JUAN MANUEL, 'Los historiadores de la Crónica sarracina', in Rafael Beltrán et al. (eds.), *Historias y ficciones: Coloquio sobre la literatura del siglo XV* (Valencia, 1992), 37–55.

CAHN, WALTER, 'Moses ben Abraham's Chroniques de la Bible', *Artibus et Historiae*, 8 (1987), 55–66.

CANTERA BURGOS, FRANCISCO, *Abraham Zacut: Siglo XV* (Madrid, 1935).

—— *Álvar García de Santa María y su familia de conversos: Historia de la Judería de Burgos y de sus conversos más egregios* (Madrid, 1952).

—— *El Judío Salamantino Abraham Zacut: Notas para la historia de la astronomía en la España medieval* (Madrid, 1931).

—— *El Libro de la cabala de Abraham ben Salomon de Torrutiel y un fragmento histórico de José ben Zaddic de Arévalo* (Salamanca, 1928).

CAPSALI, ELIJAH B. ELKANAH, *Seder eliyahu zuta: toledot ha'otomanim uvenetsiah vekorot am yisra'el bemamlekhot turkiyah, sefarad uvenetsiah*, 3 vols., ed. Aryeh Shmuelevitz, Shlomo Simonsohn, and Meir Benayahu (Jerusalem, 1976–83).

ÇARÇA, SAMUEL, *Mekor ḥayim*, in Yitzhak Baer, *Die Juden im christlichen Spanien* (Berlin, 1929–36), doc. 209 (ii. 200–1).

CARPENTER, DWAYNE E., *Alfonso X and the Jews: An Edition of and Commentary on Siete Partidas 7.24 'De los Judíos'* (Berkeley, Calif., 1986).

CARRASCO URGOITI, MARÍA SOLEDAD, *El moro de Granada en la literatura (del siglo XV al XIX)* (Granada, 1989).

CARRETE PARRONDO, CARLOS, 'Fraternization between Jews and Christians in Spain before 1492', *American Sephardi*, 9 (1978), 15–21.

CARY, GEORGE, *The Medieval Alexander* (Cambridge, 1967).

CASTAÑO, JAVIER, 'Una fiscalidad sagrada: Los "treinta dineros" y los judíos de Castilla', *Studi Medievali*, 42 (2001), 165–204.

—— 'Profetismo político pseudo-isidoriano y polémica religiosa en autores judíos de Castilla y Fez', in Mercedes García-Arenal (ed.), *Judíos en tierras del Islam*, vol. ii (Madrid, 2003), 1–25.

CASTRO, AMÉRICO, *Santiago de España* (Buenos Aires, 1958).

—— *The Spaniards: An Introduction to Their History* (Berkeley, Calif., 1985).

CÁTEDRA GARCÍA, PEDRO MANUEL, *Sermón, sociedad y literatura en la Edad Media: San Vicente Ferrer en Castilla (1411–1412). Estudio bibliográfico-literario y edición de los textos inéditos* (Valladolid, 1994).

CAVADINI, JOHN C., *The Last Christology of the West: Adoptionism in Spain and Gaul, 785–820* (Philadelphia, Pa., 1993).

CHAZAN, ROBERT, 'Anti-Usury Efforts in Thirteenth-Century Narbonne and the Jewish Response', *Proceedings of the American Academy for Jewish Research*, 41–2 (1973–4), 45–67.

—— *Barcelona and Beyond: The Disputation of 1263 and Its Aftermath* (Berkeley, Calif., 1992).

—— *Daggers of Faith: Thirteenth-Century Christian Missionizing and the Jewish Response* (Berkeley, Calif., 1989).

—— 'The Letter of R. Jacob ben Elijah to Friar Paul', *Jewish History*, 6 (1992), 51–63.

—— 'A Medieval Hebrew Polemical Mélange', *Hebrew Union College Annual*, 51 (1980), 89–110.

—— 'Polemical Themes in the Milhemet Mizvah', in Gilbert Dahan (ed.), *Les Juifs au regard de l'histoire: Mélanges en l'honneur de Bernard Blumenkranz* (Paris, 1985), 169–84.

—— 'The Timebound and the Timeless: Medieval Jewish Narration of Events', *History and Memory*, 6 (1994), 5–34.

CHÉHAB, MAURICE H., *Tyr à l'époque des croisades*, 2 vols. (Paris, 1979).

CHELINI, JEAN, and HENRY BRANTHOMME, *Les Chemins de Dieu: Histoire des pèlerinages chrétiens des origines à nos jours* (Paris, 1982).

CHESNUT, GLENN F., 'Eusebius, Augustine, Orosius, and the Later Patristic and Medieval Christian Historians', in Harold W. Attridge and Gohei Hata (eds.), *Eusebius, Christianity, and Judaism* (Detroit, 1992), 687–713.

CHEVALIER, JEAN, and ALAIN GHEERBRANT, *Dictionnaire des symboles: Mythes, rêves, coutumes, gestes, formes, figures, couleurs, nombres* (Paris, 1982).

CIROT, GEORGIUS, *Les Histoires générales d'Espagne entre Alphonse X et Philippe II (1284–1556)* (Bordeaux, 1904).

—— 'Le Romance sur la capture de Boabdil', *Bulletin hispanique*, 31 (1929), 268–9.

COBOS BUENO, JOSÉ MARÍA, *Un astrónomo en la academia renacentista del maestre de Alcántara Fray Juan de Zúñiga y Pimentel* (Badajoz, 2001).

COHEN, GERSON DAVID, 'Esau as Symbol in Early Medieval Thought', in id., *Studies in the Variety of Rabbinic Cultures*, 243–69.

—— 'Messianic Postures of Ashkenazim and Sephardim (prior to Sabbethai Zevi)', Leo Baeck Memorial Lecture 9, in Max Kreutzberger (ed.), *Studies of the Leo Baeck Institute* (New York, 1967), 117–58.

—— Review of B. Netanyahu, *The Marranos of Spain*, *Jewish Social Studies*, 29 (1967), 178–84.

—— 'The Story of the Four Captives', in id., *Studies in the Variety of Rabbinic Cultures*, 157–208.

—— *Studies in the Variety of Rabbinic Cultures* (Philadelphia, Pa., 1991).

COHEN, JEREMY, 'The Blood Libel in Solomon ibn Verga's *Shevet Yehudah*', in Mitchell Hart (ed.), *Jewish Blood: Reality and Metaphor in Jewish History, Religion, and Culture* (London, 2009), 116–35.

—— *The Friars and the Jews: The Evolution of Medieval Anti-Judaism* (Ithaca, NY, 1986).

—— 'Isidore of Seville's Anti-Jewish Polemic: A Revised Evaluation' (Heb.), in *Proceedings of the Eleventh World Congress on Jewish Studies* [Divrei hakongres ha'olami ha'ahad-asar lemada'ei hayahadut], vol. ii/1 (Jerusalem, 1994), 83–9.

—— 'The Jews as the Killers of Christ in the Latin Tradition, from Augustine to the Friars', *Traditio*, 39 (1983), 1–27.

—— *Living Letters of the Law: Ideas of the Jew in Medieval Christianity* (Berkeley, Calif., 1999).

—— 'The Mentality of the Medieval Jewish Apostate: Peter Alfonsi, Hermann of Cologne, and Pablo Christiani', in T. M. Endelman (ed.), *Jewish Apostasy in the Modern World* (New York, 1987), 20–47.

COHEN, JEREMY, 'Polemic and Pluralism: The Jewish–Christian Debate in Solomon ibn Verga's *Shevet Yehudah*', in Israel J. Yuval and Ram Ben-Shalom (eds.), *Conflict and Religious Conversation in Latin Christendom* (Turnhout, 2014), 167–90.

—— 'Profiat Duran's "The Reproach of the Gentiles" and the Development of Jewish Anti-Christian Polemic', in Daniel Carpi et al. (eds.), *Shlomo Simonsohn Jubilee Volume* (Tel Aviv, 1993), 71–84.

—— 'Roman Imperial Policy toward the Jews from Constantine until the End of the Palestinian Patriarchate (ca. 429)', *Byzantine Studies*, 3 (1976), 1–29.

—— 'Towards a Functional Classification of Jewish Anti-Christian Polemic in the High Middle Ages', in Bernard Lewis and Friedrich Niewohner (eds.), *Religionsgespräche im Mittelalter* (Wiesbaden, 1992), 93–114.

COHEN, YEHEZKEL, 'The Image of the Non-Jew in the Tannaitic Period' (Heb.), *Eshel be'er sheva*, 2 (1980), 39–62.

COHN, NORMAN, 'Medieval Millenarianism: Its Bearing on the Comparative Study of Millenarian Movements', in Sylvia L. Thrupp (ed.), *Millennial Dreams in Action: Studies in Revolutionary Religious Movements* (New York, 1970), 31–43.

COLBERT, EDWARD P., *The Martyrs of Córdoba (850–859): A Study of the Sources* (Washington DC, 1962).

COLEMAN, JANET, *Ancient and Medieval Memories: Studies in the Reconstruction of the Past* (Cambridge, 1992).

Continuación de la crónica de España del arzobispo Don Rodrigo Jiménez de Rada por el obispo Don Gonzalo de la Hinojosa, Colección de documentos inéditos para la historia de España por el Marqués de la Fuensanta del Valle, 106 (Madrid, 1893).

CRESCAS, HASDAI, *Sefer bitul ikarei hanotserim*, ed. Daniel J. Lasker, trans. Joseph Ben Shem Tov (Jerusalem, 1990).

Crónica anónima de Enrique IV de Castilla, 1454–1474: Crónica castellana, 2 vols., ed. María Pilar Sánchez-Parra (Madrid, 1991).

Crónica de 1404, in *Crónica general de España de 1344*, ed. Diego Catalán and María Soledad de Andrés (Madrid, 1971), 239–86.

Crónica de D. Alfonso el Onceno, ed. Francisco Cerdá y Rico (Madrid, 1788).

Crónica del Rey Don Fernando el IV, in *Memorias de Don Fernando IV de Castilla*, vol. i, ed. Antonio Benavides (Madrid, 1860).

Crónica general de España de 1344: Edición crítica del texto español de la Crónica de 1344 que ordenó el Conde de Barcelos Don Pedro Alfonso, ed. Diego Catalán and María Soledad de Andrés, Fuentes cronísticas de la historia de España, 2 (Madrid, 1971).

Crònica general de Pere III el Cerimoniós: Dita comunament Crònica de Sant Joan de la Penya, ed. Amadeu-Jesús Soberanas Lleó (Barcelona, 1961).

Crónica pseudo-Isidoriana, ed. Antonio Benito Vidal, Textos Medievales, 5 (Valencia, 1961).

DA PIERA, MESHULLAM, *Shir ge'ulah*, in Aaron Ze'ev Aescoly (ed.), *Jewish Messianic Movements* [Hatenuot hameshihiyot beyisra'el], 2nd edn. (Jerusalem, 1988), 214.

DAN, JOSEPH, *The Esoteric Doctrine of Ashkenazi Hasidism* [Torat hasod shel hasidut ashkenaz] (Jerusalem, 1968).

DAN, YARON, 'Josephus and Justus of Tiberias' (Heb.), in Uriel Rappaport (ed.), *Josephus: Historian of Palestine in the Hellenistic and Roman Period* [Yosef ben matityahu: historyon shel erets yisra'el batekufah hahelenistit veharomit] (Jerusalem, 1983), 57–78.

DANTE, *De Monarchia*, ed. Karl Witte (Vienna, 1874); Eng. trans.: *Monarchy*, ed. and trans. Prue Shaw (Cambridge, 1966).

DAVID, ABRAHAM, 'A Fragment of a Hebrew Chronicle' (Heb.), *Alei sefer*, 6–7 (1979), 198–200.

—— 'The Historiographical Work of Gedaliah ibn Yahya, Author of Shalshelet hakabalah' [Mifalo hahistoryografi shel gedalyah ibn yaḥya, ba'al shalshelet hakabalah] (Ph.D. thesis, Hebrew University of Jerusalem, 1976).

—— 'On the History of the Sages in Jerusalem in the Sixteenth Century in Light of Documents from the Cairo Genizah' (Heb.), *Shalem*, 5 (1987), 229–49.

—— (ed.), *Two Hebrew Chronicles from the Period of the Expulsion from Spain* [Shetei khronikot ivriyot midor gerush sefarad], 2nd edn. (Jerusalem, 1991).

D'AVRAY, DAVID L., *The Preaching of the Friars: Sermons Diffused from Paris Before 1300* (Oxford, 1985).

DE LANGE, NICHOLAS, 'Jewish Attitudes to the Roman Empire', in Peter D. A. Garnsey and Charles R. Whittaker (eds.), *Imperialism in the Ancient World* (Cambridge, 1978), 255–81.

DE VILLENA, ENRIQUE, *Los doze trabajos de Hércules*, in *Obras completas*, vol. i, ed. Manuel Arroyo Stephens (Madrid, 1994).

DEL PULGAR, FERNANDO, *Crónica de los Reyes Católicos*, ed. Juan de Mata Carriazo (Madrid, 1943).

DEL VALLE, CARLOS, 'La tercera carta apologética de Abner de Burgos', *Miscelánea de Estudios Árabes y Hebraicos*, 37–8 (1988–9), 353–71.

DELLING, GERHARD, 'Philons Enkomion auf Augustus', *Klio*, 54 (1972), 171–92.

DELUMEAU, JEAN, *La Peur en occident (XIVe–XVIIIe siècles)* (Paris, 1978).

DEYERMOND, ALAN D., 'El "Auto de los reyes magos" y el renacimiento del siglo XII', in S. Neumeister (ed.), *Actas del IX Congreso de la Asociación Internacional de Hispanistas*, vol. i (Frankfurt am Main, 1989), 187–94.

—— *A Literary History of Spain: The Middle Ages* (London, 1971).

—— 'Written by the Victors: Technique and Ideology in Official Historiography in Verse in Late-Medieval Spain', *Medieval Chronicle*, 6 (2009), 59–90.

DÍAZ-ESTEBAN, FERNANDO, 'Jewish Literary Creation in Spanish' (Heb.), in Haim Beinart (ed.), *The Sephardi Legacy* [Moreshet sefarad] (Jerusalem, 1992), 330–63.

DINBURG, BEN-ZION, 'The House of Study and Prayer for Jews on the Temple Mount in the Arab Period' (Heb.), *Zion*, 3 (1909), 54–87.

DINUR, BEN-ZION, *Israel in the Diaspora* [Yisra'el bagolah], Pt I, 4 vols.; Pt II, 6 vols. (Tel Aviv, 1958–73).

DISHON, JUDITH, 'The Lost Book of History by Judah ibn Shabbetai' (Heb.), *Zion*, 37 (1971), 191–9.

—— 'New Light on Judah ibn Shabbetai as a Historian' (Heb.), *Bitsaron*, 63 (1972), 56–65.

DOBIACHE-ROJDESTVENSKY, OLGA, *Les Poésies des goliards* (Paris, 1931).

DOBROVOLSKI, KAZIMIERZ, 'Traditional Peasant Culture' (Heb.), in Abraham Shtal (ed.), *From the Literature of Education: A Collection of Translated Articles*, vol. vii: *A Knowledge of Reading and Writing and the Transition to a Modern Culture* [Misifrut haḥinukh: kovtsei ma'amarim meturgamim, 7: yediat kero-ukhetov vehama'avar letarbut modernit] (Jerusalem, 1973), 28–41.

DÖNITZ, SASKIA, 'Historiography among Byzantine Jews: The Case of Sefer Yosippon', in Robert [Reuven] Bonfil et al. (eds.), *Jews in Byzantium: Dialectics of Minority and Majority Cultures* (Leiden, 2012), 951–68.

—— *Überlieferung und Rezeption des Sefer Yosippon* (Tübingen, 2013).

DORMAN, MENAHEM, *Marsilius of Padua, or On the Sovereignty of the People* [Marsilyus ish padovah, o al ribonut ha'am] (Ramat Gan, 1972).

DOSSAT, YVES, 'Le Culte de Saint Dominique à Fanjeaux en 1325', *Annales du Midi*, 88 (1976), 199–206.

—— 'La Répression de l'hérésie par les évêques', *Cahiers de Fanjeaux*, 6 (1971), 217–51.

DRIJVERS, JAN WILLEM, *Helena Augusta: The Mother of Constantine the Great and the Legend of Her Finding of the True Cross* (Leiden, 1992).

DURAN, PROFAYT, *Atsat aḥitofel veḥushai ha'arki*, in id., *Ma'aseh efod*, 206–9.

—— *Polemical Writings: Shame of the Gentiles and Be Not Like Thy Fathers* [Kitvei pulmus liprofayt duran: kelimat hagoyim ve'igeret al tehi ka'avoteikha], ed. [Frank] Ephraim Talmage (Jerusalem, 1981).

—— *Kelimat hagoyim*, in id., *Polemical Writings*, 1–69.

—— *Ma'aseh efod* (Vienna, 1865).

—— *Teshuvot be'anshei aven* (*Cinco cuestiones debatidas de polémica*, ed. José Vicente Niclós Albarracín, annotated by Carlos del Valle Rodríguez (Madrid, 1999)).

DURAN, SHIMON B. TSEMAH, *Keshet umagen*, in Prosper Murciano, 'Simon Ben Zemah Duran "Keshet u-Magen": A Critical Edition' (Ph.D. thesis, New York University, 1975).

—— *Sefer hatashbets* (Lemberg, 1891).

—— *Sefer magen avot: Philosophical Section. Facsimile of the Unique Edition of Leghorn, 1785* (Jerusalem, 1970).

DUVERNOY, JEAN, *Le Catharisme*, vol. i: *La Religion des cathares* (Toulouse, 1989).

EDWARDS, JOHN, 'Conversos, Judaism and the Language of Monarchy in Fifteenth-Century Castile', in Isaac Benabu (ed.), *Circa 1492. Proceedings of the Jerusalem Colloquium: Litterae Judaeorum in Terra Hispanica* (Jerusalem, 1992), 207–23.

EHRLICH, DROR, *The Thought of R. Joseph Albo: Esoteric Writing in the Late Middle Ages* [Haguto shel r. yosef albo: ketivah ezoterit beshilhei yemei habeinayim] (Ramat Gan, 2009).

EINBINDER, SUSAN L., *No Place of Rest: Jewish Literature, Expulsion, and the Memory of Medieval France* (Philadelphia, Pa., 2009).

EISENBERG, SAADIA R., 'Reading Medieval Religious Disputation: The 1240 "Debate" Between Rabbi Yeḥiel of Paris and Friar Nicholas Donin' (Ph.D. thesis, University of Michigan, 2008).

ERASMUS, *In Praise of Folly*, trans. Roger Clarke (London, 2008).

EVEN SHMUEL, YEHUDA (ed.), *Midrashim of Salvation: Jewish Apocalyptic from the End of the Babylonian Talmud to the Beginning of the Sixth Millennium* [Midreshei ge'ulah: pirkei ha'apokalipsah hayehudit meḥatimat hatalmud habavli ve'ad reshit ha'elef hashishi] (Tel Aviv, 1943).

FALBEL, NACHMAN, 'On a Heretic Argument in Levi ben Abraham ben Chaim's Critique on Christianity', in Israel Gutman (ed.), *Proceedings of the Seventh World Congress of Jewish Studies* [Divrei hakongres ha'olami hashevi'i lemada'ei hayahadut], vol. iv (Jerusalem, 1981), 29–45.

FELDMAN, LOUIS H., 'The Jewish Sources of Peter Comestor's Commentary on Genesis in his Historia Scholastica', in Dietrich-Alex Koch and Hermann Lichtenberger (eds.), *Begegnungen zwischen Christentum und Judentum in Antike und Mittelalter: Festschrift für Heinz Schreckenberg* (Göttingen, 1993), 93–122.

FELLOUS, SONIA, *Histoire de la Bible de Moïse Arragel: Quand un rabbin interprète la Bible pour les chrétiens* (Paris, 2001).

FERNÁNDEZ CONDE, FRANCISCO JAVIER, 'Religiosidad popular y piedad culta', in Ricardo García-Villoslada (ed.), *Historia de la Iglesia en España*, vol. ii (Madrid, 1982), 289–357.

FERNÁNDEZ-ORDÓÑEZ, INÉS (ed.), *Alfonso X el Sabio y las crónicas de España* (Valladolid, 2000).

—— *Las 'Estorias' de Alfonso el Sabio* (Madrid 1992).

—— 'El taller de las "Estorias"', in id. (ed.), *Alfonso X el Sabio y las crónicas de España*, 61–82.

FERNÁNDEZ URBINA, JOSÉ MIGUEL, and JUDIT TARGARONA BORRÁS, 'La historia romana de Abraham ibn Daud', *Helmántica: revista de filolgía clásica y hebrea*, 124/5 (1990), 297–342.

FIGUERAS, PAU, 'Simon Magus' (Heb.), in *Hebrew Encyclopedia* [Ha'entsiklopedyah ha'ivrit] (Tel Aviv, 1949–80), vol. xxxii, cols. 115–16.

FINKELSTEIN, ELIEZER E. (LOUIS), *Introduction to Tractates* Avot *and* Avot de-rabi natan [Mavo lemasekhtot avot ve'avot derabi natan] (New York, 1951).

FIRST, MITCHELL, *Jewish History in Conflict: A Study of the Major Discrepancy Between Rabbinic and Conventional Chronology* (Northvale, NJ, 1997).

FLICK, ALEXANDER CLARENCE, *The Decline of the Medieval Church*, 2 vols. (New York, 1967).

FLUSSER, DAVID, *Judaism and the Origins of Christianity* [Yahadut umekorot ha-natsrut] (Tel Aviv, 1979).

—— 'Rome in the Eyes of the Hasmoneans and the Essenes' (Heb.), *Zion*, 48 (1983), 149–75.

—— *The Book of Josippon* [Sefer yosipon], vol. ii [commentary] (Jerusalem, 1981).

FOLZ, ROBERT, *The Concept of Empire in Western Europe from the Fifth to the Fourteenth Century* (Frome, Som. 1969).

FRAKER, CHARLES F., 'Abraham in the "General Estoria"', in Francisco Márquez-Villanueva and Carlos Alberto Vega (eds.), *Alfonso X of Castile, the Learned King: An International Symposium, Harvard University, 17 November 1984* (Boston, Mass., 1990), 17–26.

FRAZER, JAMES GEORGE, *The Golden Bough: A Study in Magic and Religion*, 2 vols. (New York, 1929).

FRIMER, NORMAN, and DOV SCHWARTZ, *Philosophy in the Shadow of Terror: The Character, Writings, and Thought of R. Shem Tov ibn Shaprut* [Hagut betsel ha'eimah: demuto, ketavav vehaguto shel rabi shem tov ibn shaprut] (Jerusalem, 1992).

FUCHS, HARALD, *Der geistige Widerstand gegen Rom in der antiken Welt* (Berlin, 1964).

FULCHER OF CHARTRES, *A History of the Expedition to Jerusalem (1095–1127)* (*Historia Hierosolymitana*, Recueil des Historiens des Croisades: Historiens Occidentaux, 3 (Paris, 1866), 319–437).

FUNKENSTEIN, AMOS, 'Collective Memory and Historical Consciousness' (Heb.), in id., *Image and Historical Consciousness in Judaism and Its Cultural Environment* [Tadmit vetoda'ah historit beyahadut uvisevivatah hatarbutit], 13–30; first published in *History and Memory*, 1 (1989), 5–26.

—— *Image and Historical Consciousness in Judaism and Its Cultural Environment* [Tadmit vetoda'ah historit beyahadut uvisevivatah hatarbutit] (Tel Aviv, 1991).

—— 'The Image of the Ruler in Jewish Thought in the Late Middle Ages' (Heb.), in id., *Image and Historical Consciousness in Judaism and Its Cultural Environment* [Tadmit vetoda'ah historit beyahadut uvisevivatah hatarbutit], 180–8.

—— *Nature, History and Messianism in Maimonides* (Tel Aviv, 1983).

—— *Perceptions of Jewish History* (Berkeley, Calif., 1993).

—— *Theology and the Scientific Imagination from the Middle Ages to the Seventeenth Century* (Princeton, NJ, 1986).

GANS, DAVID, *Sefer tsemaḥ david*, ed. Mordechai Breuer (Jerusalem, 1973).

GAON, SOLOMON, *The Influence of the Catholic Theologian Alfonso Tostado on the Pentateuch Commentary of Isaac Abravanel* (New York, 1993).

GARCÍA-BALLESTER, LUIS, LOLA FERRE, and EDUARD FELIU, 'Jewish Appreciation of Fourteenth-Century Scholastic Medicine', *Osiris*, 6 (1990), 117–85.

GAVISON, ABRAHAM B. JACOB, *Omer hashikheḥah* (Livorno, 1748).

GEIGER, JOSEPH, 'The Revolt in the Time of Gallus and the Construction of the Temple in the Time of Julian' (Heb.), in Zvi Baras et al. (eds.), *The Land of Israel from the Destruction of the Second Temple until the Muslim Conquest*, vol. i: *Political, Cultural, and Social History* [Erets-yisra'el meḥurban bayit sheni ve'ad hakibush hamuslemi, 1: historyah medinit, ḥevratit vetarbutit] (Jerusalem, 1982), 202–17.

Genesis Rabbah [Midrash bereshit raba], ed. Chanoch Albeck, 3 vols. (Jerusalem, 1985–7).

Genesis Rabbati [Midrash bereshit rabati], ed. Chanoch Albeck (Jerusalem, 1940).

GENOT-BISMUTH, JACQUELINE, 'L'Argument de l'histoire dans la tradition espagnole de polémique judéo-chrétienne d'Isidore de Seville à Isaac Abravanel et Abraham Zacuto', in Yedida K. Stillman and Norman A. Stillman (eds.), *From Iberia to Diaspora: Studies in Sephardic History and Culture* (Leiden, 1999), 197–213.

GEOFFREY OF MONMOUTH, *History of the Kings of Britain* (*Historia regum Britannie*: Bern, Burgerbibliothek, MS, ed. Neil Wright (Cambridge, 1984)).

GERNENTZ, WILHELM, *Laudes Romae* (Rostock, 1918).

GERO, STEPHEN, 'The Legend of the Fourth Son of Noah', *Harvard Theological Review*, 73 (1980), 321–30.

GERSONIDES (LEVI B. GERSHOM), *Perush al daniyel*, in *Mikra'ot gedolot* (Tel Aviv, 1959).

—— *Perush al ester*, in id., *Perush al ḥamesh megilot* (Königsberg, 1860).

Gesta Romanorum: Or Entertaining Moral Stories, ed. Charles Swan and Wynnard Hooper (London, 1959); *Gesta Romanorum*, vol. 2: *Texte, Verzeichnisse*, ed. Brigitte Weiske (Tübingen, 1992).

GIBBON, EDWARD, *The Decline and Fall of the Roman Empire*, 3 vols. (New York, n.d.).

GIL, MOSHE, *The Kingdom of Ishmael during the Period of the Geonim*, vol. 1: *Studies in Jewish History in Islamic Lands in the Early Middle Ages* [Bemalkhut yishma'el bitekufat hageonim, 1: meḥkarim betoledot hayehudim be'artsot ha'islam biyemei-habeinayim hamukdamim] (Jerusalem, 1997).

—— *The Land of Israel during the First Muslim Period (634–1099)* [Erets yisra'el batekufah hamuslemit harishonah], 3 vols. (Tel Aviv, 1983).

GINGERICH, OWEN, 'Alfonso the Tenth as a Patron of Astronomy', in Francisco Márquez-Villanueva and Carlos Alberto Vega (eds.), *Alfonso X of Castile, the Learned King: An International Symposium, Harvard University, 17 November 1984* (Boston, Mass., 1990), 30–45.

GIUSTINIANI, VITO R., 'Sulle traduzioni latine delle Vite di Plutarco nell Quattrocento', *Rinascimento*, 1 (1961), 3–62.

GLATZER, MICHAEL, 'Pablo de Santa María (Solomon Halevi) and His Attitude towards the 1391 Pogroms' (Heb.), in Shmuel Almog (ed.), *History of Antisemitism* [Sinat-yisra'el bedoroteiha] (Jerusalem, 1940), 147–57.

GLICK, THOMAS F., 'Convivencia: An Introductory Note', in Vivian B. Mann et al. (eds.), *Convivencia: Jews, Muslims and Christians in Medieval Spain* (New York, 1992), 1–9.

—— ' "My Master, the Jew": Observations on Interfaith Scholarly Interaction in the Middle Ages', in Harvey J. Hames (ed.), *Jews, Muslims and Christians in and around the Crown of Aragon* (Leiden, 2004), 157–82.

GOLDIN, SIMHA, *Uniqueness and Togetherness: The Riddle of the Survival of Jewish Groups in the Middle Ages* [Hayiḥud vehayaḥad: ḥidat hisardutan shel hakevutsot hayehudiyot biyemei-habeinayim] (Tel Aviv, 1997).

GOLDSTEIN, BERNARD R., 'The Hebrew Astronomical Tradition: New Sources', *Isis*, 72 (1981), 237–51.

GOLDSTEIN, MORRIS, *Jesus in the Jewish Tradition* (New York, 1950).

GÓMEZ MORENO, ÁNGEL, *España y la Italia de los humanistas: Primeros ecos* (Madrid, 1994).

—— *El Prohemio e carta del Marqués de Santillana y la teoría literaria del s. XV* (Barcelona, 1990).

GÓMEZ REDONDO, FERNANDO, 'Don Álvar García de Santa María: Un nuevo modelo de pensamiento cronístico', *La Crónica: A Journal of Medieval Hispanic Languages, and Cultures*, 32 (2004), 91–108.

GONZALEZ-LOPEZ, EMILIO, 'The Myth of Saint James and Its Functional Reality', in José Rubia Barcia and Selma Margaretten (eds.), *Americo Castro and the Meaning of Spanish Civilization* (Berkeley, Calif., 1976), 91–111.

GOODY, JACK, *The Domestication of the Savage Mind* (Cambridge, 1977).

GORCE, MATTHIEU MAXIME, *St. Vincent Ferrier (1350–1419)* (Paris, 1935).

GRAETZ, HEINRICH, *History of the Jews: From When They Became a Nation to Recent Times* [Divrei yemei yisra'el: miyom heyot yisra'el le'am ad yemei hador ha'aharon], 9 vols., trans. Shaul P. Rabinowitz (Warsaw, 1891–1900); Eng. trans. James Gutheim (New York, 1873).

GRANDAZZI, ALEXANDRE, *The Foundation of Rome: Myth and History* (Ithaca, NY, 1997).

GRANT, MICHAEL, and JOHN HAZEL, *Gods and Mortals in Classical Mythology: A Dictionary* (New York, 1979).

GRAVES, ROBERT, *The Greek Myths: Combined Edition* (London, 1992).

GRAYZEL, SOLOMON, 'The Avignon Popes and the Jews', *Historia Judaica*, 2 (1940), 1–12.

GREEN, OTIS H., *Spain and the Western Tradition: The Castilian Mind in Literature from 'El Cid' to Calderón*, 4 vols. (Madison, Wis., 1963–6).

GREENHALGH, MICHAEL, *The Survival of Roman Antiquities in the Middle Ages* (London, 1989).

GREGORY OF TOURS, *Sufferings of the Seven Martyrs* (*Passio sanctorum martyrum septem dormientium apud Ephesum*, ed. Bruno Krusch, Monumenta Germaniae historica: scriptores rerum Merovingicarum, I/2 (Hanover, 1885), 397–403).

GRIEVE, PATRICIA E., *The Eve of Spain: Myths of Origins in the History of Christian, Muslim, and Jewish Conflict* (Baltimore, 2009).

—— *Floire and Blancheflor and the European Romance* (Cambridge, 1997).

GRIFFIN, NIGEL, 'Spanish Incunabula in the John Rylands University Library of Manchester', *Bulletin of the John Rylands University Library of Manchester*, 70/2 (1988), 17–20.

GROSSMAN, AVRAHAM, 'Saladin's Victory and the Aliyah of the Jews of Europe to the Land of Israel' (Heb.), in Yehoshua Ben-Arieh and Elchanan Reiner (eds.), *Studies in the History of Erets Yisra'el Presented to Yehuda Ben Porat* [Mehkarim betoledot erets yisra'el mugashim liyehudah ben porat] (Jerusalem 2003), 361–81.

GRUEN, ERICH S., *The Image of Rome* (Englewood Cliffs, NJ, 1969).

GUENÉE, BERNARD, *Entre l'église et l'état: Quatre vies de prélats français à la fin du Moyen Âge (XIIIe–XVe siècle)* (Paris, 1987).

—— *Histoire et culture historique dans l'Occident médiéval* (Paris, 1980).

—— *Le Métier d'historien au Moyen Âge: Études sur l'historiographie médiévale* (Paris, 1977).

—— *L'Occident aux XIVe et XVe siècles: Les États* (Paris, 1971).

GUIBERT OF NOGENT, *Deeds of God through the Franks* (*Gesta Dei per Francos*, Recueil des Historiens des Croisades: Historiens Occidentaux, 4 (Paris, 1879), 117–263).

GUREVICH, ARON, *Categories of Medieval Culture* (London, 1985).

GUTHMÜLLER, BODO, *Ovidio Metamorphoseos vulgare: Formen und Funktion der volkssprachlichen Wiedergabe klassischer Dichtung in der italienischen Renaissance* (Boppard, 1981).

GUTMAN, YEHOSHUA, *Hellenistic Jewish Literature: Judaism and Hellenism before the Hasmonean Period* [Hasifrut hayehudit–hahelenistit: hayahadut vehaheleniyut lifnei tekufat haḥashmona'im] (Jerusalem, 1958).

GUTTMANN, JULIUS, *Die Philosophie des Judentums* (Munich, 1933).

GUTWIRTH, ELEAZAR, 'Abraham Seneor: Social Tensions and the Court-Jew', *Mikha'el*, 11 (1989), 169–229.

—— 'Actitudes judías hacia los cristianos en la España del siglo XV: Ideario de los traductores del latín', *Actas del II Congreso Internacional Encuentro de las Tres Culturas, 3–6 Octubre 1983* (Toledo, 1985), 189–96.

—— 'Don Ishaq Abravanel and Vernacular Humanism in Fifteenth Century Iberia', *Bibliothèque d'Humanisme et Renaissance*, 60 (1998), 641–71.

—— 'Duran on Ahitophel: The Practice of Jewish History in Late Medieval Spain', *Jewish History*, 4 (1989), 59–74.

—— 'The Expulsion from Spain and Jewish Historiography', in Ada Rapoport-Albert and Steven J. Zipperstein (eds.), *Essays in Honor of Chimen Abramsky* (London, 1988), 141–61.

—— 'Hercules Furens and War: On Abravanel's Courtly Context', *Jewish History*, 23 (2009), 293–312.

—— 'History and Apologetics in XVth Century Hispano-Jewish Thought', *Helmantica*, 35 (1984), 231–42.

—— 'History and Intertextuality in Late Medieval Spain', in Mark D. Meyerson and Edward D. English (eds.), *Christians, Muslims, and Jews in Medieval and Early Modern Spain* (Notre Dame, Ind., 2000), 161–78.

—— 'The Jews in 15th Century Castilian Chronicles', *Jewish Quarterly Review*, 64 (1984), 379–96.

—— 'Lineage in Fifteenth Century Hispano-Jewish Thought', *Miscelánea de Estudios Árabes y Hebraicos*, 34 (1985), 85–91.

—— 'Religion and Social Criticism in Late Medieval Rousillon: An Aspect of Profyat Duran's Activities', *Mikha'el*, 12 (1991), 135–56.

—— 'Social Tensions within XVth Century Hispano-Jewish Communities' (Ph.D. thesis, University College London, 1978).

HACKER, JOSEPH, 'Invitation to an Intellectual Duel: Between Serres and Adrianople' (Heb.), in Ezra Fleischer et al. (eds.), *A Hundred Gates: Studies in Medieval Jewish Spiritual Life in Memory of Isadore Twersky* [Me'ah she'arim: iyunim be'olamam haruḥani shel yisra'el biyemei-habeinayim lezekher yitsḥak tverski] (Jerusalem, 2001), 349–69.

—— 'New Chronicles on the Expulsion of the Jews from Spain' (Heb.), *Zion*, 44 (1979), 201–28.

HALKIN, ABRAHAM S., 'Forced Conversion in the Time of the Almohads' (Heb.), *Jewish Social Studies*, 5 (Joshua Starr memorial issue) (1953), 101–10.

—— 'Rabbi Nissim of Marseilles: A Fourteenth-Century Philosopher' (Heb.), in Pinchas Peli (ed.), *Proceedings of the Fifth World Congress on Jewish Studies* [Divrei hakongres ha'olami haḥamishi lemada'ei hayahadut], vol. iii (Jerusalem, 1969), 143–9.

HALKIN, ABRAHAM S., 'Why was Levi b. Hayyim Hounded?', *Proceedings of the American Academy for Jewish Research*, 34 (1966), 65–76.

HALLEWY, ELIMELECH E., *Biographical-Historical Legends in the Light of Greek and Latin Sources* [Ha'agadah hahistorit–biyografit le'or mekorot yevanim velatiniyim] (Tel Aviv, 1972).

HARTMAN, DAVID, *Leadership in Times of Distress: On Maimonides' Epistles* [Manhigut be'itot metsukah: al igerot harambam] (Tel Aviv, 1985).

HARVEY, LEONARD P., *Islamic Spain 1250 to 1500* (Chicago, 1990).

HASAN-ROKEM, GALIT, 'Within Limits and Beyond: History and Body in Midrashic Texts', *International Folklore Review*, 9 (1993), 5–10.

HASKINS, CHARLES H., *The Renaissance of the Twelfth Century* (Cambridge, Mass., 1927).

HEATH, MICHAEL J., 'Renaissance Scholars and the Origins of the Turks', *Bibliothèque d'Humanisme et Renaissance*, 41 (1979), 453–71.

A Hebrew Alexander Romance according to MS London, Jews' College no. 145, ed. Wout J. Van Bekkum (Leuven 1992).

HELLER, BERNARD, 'Éléments parallèles et origine de la légende des sept dormants', *Revue des Études Juives*, 49 (1904), 190–218.

HELLER-WILENSKY, SARAH, *Rabbi Isaac Arama and His Teaching* [Rabi yitshak arama umishnato] (Jerusalem, 1956).

HENIGE, DAVID P., *The Chronology of Oral Tradition: Quest for a Chimera* (Oxford, 1974).

HERR, MOSHE DAVID, 'The Historical Significance of the Dialogues between Jewish Sages and Roman Dignitaries', *Scripta Hierosolymitana*, 22 (1971), 123–50.

—— 'Rome in Rabbinic Literature' (Heb.), in *Hebrew Encyclopedia* [Ha'entsiklopedyah ha'ivrit] (Tel Aviv, 1949–80), vol. xxx, cols. 773–5.

—— 'The Sages' Concept of History' (Heb.), in Avigdor Shinan (ed.), *Proceedings of the Sixth World Congress on Jewish Studies* [Divrei hakongres ha'olami hashishi lemada'ei hayahadut], vol. iii (Jerusalem, 1977), 129–42.

—— 'Titus Flavius Vespasian' (Heb.), in *Hebrew Encyclopedia* [Ha'entsiklopedyah ha'ivrit] (Tel Aviv, 1949–80), vol. xviii, col. 603.

HERRMANN, WILLY, *Alfons X. von Kastilien als römischer König* (Berlin, 1897).

HIRSCHBERG, HAYIM Z., 'On the Decrees of the Almohads and Trade with India' (Heb.), in Shmuel Ettinger et al. (eds.), *Yitzhak F. Baer Jubilee Volume* [Sefer yovel leyitshak baer] (Jerusalem, 1961), 134–53.

Historia de los hechos de Don Rodrigo Ponce de León Marqués de Cádiz (1443–1488), Colección de documentos inéditos para la historia de España por el Marqués de la Fuensanta del Valle, 106 (Madrid, 1893).

HOOK, DAVID, 'Some Problems in Andrés Bernáldez's Account of the Spanish Jews', *Mikha'el*, 11 (1989), 231–55.

HORBURY, WILLIAM, 'A Critical Examination of the Toledoth Jeshu' (Ph.D. thesis, Cambridge University, 1972).

HUNT, JAMES M., 'Constantius II in the Ecclesiastical Historians' (Ph.D. thesis, Fordham University, 2010).

HUPPERT, GEORGE, 'The Trojan Franks and Their Critics', *Studies in the Renaissance*, 12 (1965), 227–41.

HUSS, MATTI, 'Critical Editions of "Minḥat yehudah", "Ezrat hanashim", and "Ein mishpat" with Prefaces, Variants, Sources and Annotations' ['Minḥat yehudah', 'ezrat hanashim', 've'ein mishpat': mahadurot mada'iyot belivyat mavo, ḥilufei girsaot, mekorot uferushim], 2 vols. (Ph.D. thesis, Hebrew University of Jerusalem, 1991).

IBN AL-ATHIR, *Kitab al-kamil fi al-tarikh*, 12 vols. (Leiden, 1899).

IBN DAUD, ABRAHAM, *Divrei malkhei yisra'el bevayit sheni*, in id., *Ḥiburei hakhronografyah shel hara'avad harishon*, 24–63; *Abraham ibn Daud's Dorot 'Olam (Generations of the Ages): A Critical Edition and Translation of Zikhron Divrey Romi, Divrey Malkhey Yisra'el, and the Midrash on Zechariah*, ed. Katja Vehlow (Leiden, 2013), 132–347.

—— *Ḥiburei hakhronografyah shel hara'avad harishon* (Mantua, 1513; repr. Jerusalem, 1964).

—— *Sefer hakabalah*, ed. Gerson David Cohen (Philadelphia, Pa., 1967).

—— *Zikhron divrei romi miyom hibanutah ad teḥilat malkhut yishma'el*, in id., *Ḥiburei hakhronografyah shel hara'avad harishon*, 1–24; *Abraham ibn Daud's Dorot 'Olam (Generations of the Ages): A Critical Edition and Translation of Zikhron Divrey Romi, Divrey Malkhey Yisra'el, and the Midrash on Zechariah*, ed. Katja Vehlow (Leiden, 2013), 98–131.

IBN EZRA, ABRAHAM, *Haperush hakatsar al daniyel*, in Henry J. Mathews (ed.), *Miscellany of Hebrew Literature* (London, 1877), ii, Heb. section, 1–15.

—— *Perush al daniyel*, in *Mikra'ot gedolot* (Tel Aviv, 1959).

—— *Perush le'ovadyah*, in *Mikra'ot gedolot* (Tel Aviv, 1959).

—— 'Visions of Rabbi Abraham ibn Ezra Concerning the Year 1154 of the Creation' (Heb.), in David Cahana, *A Compilation of the Wisdom of Rabbi Abraham ibn Ezra* [Rabi avraham ibn ezra: kovets ḥokhmat hareva], vol. ii (Warsaw, 1894), 115–18.

IBN EZRA, MOSES, *Sefer ha'iyunim vehadiyunim*, ed. Abraham S. Halkin (Jerusalem, 1975).

IBN GAON, SHEM TOV B. ABRAHAM, *Migdal oz*, in Maimonides, *Mishneh torah* (Jerusalem, 1970).

IBN MUSA, HAYIM, *Magen varomaḥ ve'igeret liveno*, Hebrew University of Jerusalem Students' Workbooks (Jerusalem, 1970).

IBN SAHULA, ISAAC B. SOLOMON, *Meshal hakadmoni* (Tel Aviv, 1953); Eng. trans.: *Meshal haqadmoni: Fables from a Distant Past*, ed. Raphael Loewe (Oxford, 2003).

IBN SHAPRUT, SHEM TOV, *Even boḥan*, in *'La Piedra de Toque' (Eben Bohan): Una obra de controversia judeo-cristiana, libro I*, ed. J. V. Niclós (Madrid, 1977).

IBN SHUAIB, JOEL, *Nora tehilot* (Salonika, 1569).

IBN TIBBON, MOSES, *Sefer pe'ah*, in *The Writings of R. Moses ibn Tibbon*, 81–222.

—— *The Writings of R. Moses ibn Tibbon* [Kitvei r. mosheh ibn tibon], ed. Howard Kreisel, Colette Sirat, and Avraham Israel (Be'er Sheva, 2010).

IBN TIBBON, SAMUEL, *Perush hamilot hazarot*, in Moses Maimonides, *Moreh nevukhim*, ed. Yehuda Even Shmuel (Jerusalem, 1987), 11–92.

IBN VERGA, SOLOMON, *Shevet yehudah*, ed. Azriel Shohat, introd. Yitzhak Baer (Jerusalem, 1947).

IBN YAHYA, GEDALIAH, *Shalshelet hakabalah* (Venice, 1587).

IDEL, MOSHE, 'Between Ashkenaz and Castile in the Thirteenth Century: Incantations, Lists, and "Gates of Sermons" from Rabbi Nehemiah ben Solomon the Prophet's Circle and Their Influences' (Heb.), *Tarbiz*, 77 (2007/8), 475–554.

—— 'Kabbalah and Ancient Philosophy in the Works of R. Isaac and Judah Abravanel' (Heb.), in Menahem Dorman and Ze'ev Levy (eds.), *Judah Abravanel's Philosophy of Love: Four Lectures in a Haifa University Symposium* [Filosofyat-ha'ahavah shel yehudah abravanel: arba hartsaot beyom iyun shel universitat ḥeifah] (Tel Aviv, 1985), 73–112.

—— *Kabbalah: New Perspectives* (New Haven, Conn., 1988); Heb. trans.: *Kabalah: heibetim ḥadashim*, trans. Avriel Bar-Levav (Jerusalem, 1993).

—— 'On the Land of Israel in Medieval Jewish Mystic Thought' (Heb.), in Moshe Halamish and Aviezer Ravitzky (eds.), *The Land of Israel in Medieval Jewish Thought* [Erets-yisra'el bahagut hayehudit biyemei-habeinayim] (Jerusalem, 1991), 193–214.

—— 'Studies in the Method of the Author of *Sefer hameshiv*' (Heb.), *Sefunot*, 17 (1983), 185–266.

IR-SHAI, ODED, 'Constantine the Great's Prohibition of the Entry of Jews into Jerusalem: Between History and Hagiography' (Heb.), *Zion*, 60 (1995), 129–78.

ISAAC NATHAN, *Me'ir nativ, hanikra konkordansiyas* (Venice, 1524).

ISHAY, HAVIVA, 'On the Oedipal Rebellion of Todros Abulafia: An Intellectual Revisionist in Thirteenth-Century Spain' (Heb.), in Eli Yassif et al. (eds.), *Ot letovah: Essays in Honor of Professor Tova Rosen* [*Ot letovah: pirkei meḥkar mugashim leprofesor tovah rozen*], El Prezente: Studies in Sephardic Culture, 6 (Be'er Sheva, 2012), 176–95.

ISIDORE OF SEVILLE, *Etymologiarum sive originum libri XX*, ed. Wallace M. Lindsay (Oxford, 1911).

JACOB B. ELIJAH, *Igeret ya'akov mivenetsiah*, ed. Joseph I. Kobak, *Yeshurun*, 6 (1868), 1–34.

JACOB B. REUBEN, *Milḥamot hashem*, ed. Judah M. Rosenthal (Jerusalem, 1963).

JACOBUS DE VORAGINE, *Legenda aurea* (Leipzig, 1850); Eng. trans.: *The Golden Legend*, trans G. Ryan and H. Ripperger (New York, 1969).

JEROME, *Letter 22* (*Epistula 22 ad Eustochium*, Corpus scriptorum ecclesiasticorum Latinorum, 54, ed. Isidorus Hilberg (Vienna, 1910), 143–211).

—— *Letter 84* (*Epistula 84 ad Pammachium et Oceanum*, Corpus scriptorum ecclesiasticorum Latinorum, 55, ed. Isidorus Hilberg (Vienna, 1912), 121–34).

—— *Life of Paulus the First Hermit* (*Vita S. Pauli primi eremitae*, ed. Jacques-Paul Migne, Patrologia Latina, 23 (Paris, 1845), cols. 17–28).

JOHN MOSCHUS, *Life of Abbot Gerasimus* (*Pratum spirituale*, 107, ed. Jacques-Paul Migne, Patrologia Graeca, 87/3 (Paris, 1865), cols. 2965–70).

JOHN OF SALISBURY, *Policraticus* (ed. Jacques-Paul Migne, Patrologia Latina, 199 (Paris, 1855), cols. 385–823).

JONES, ARNOLD H. M., *The Later Roman Empire, 284–602: A Social, Economic and Administrative Survey*, 2 vols. (Baltimore, 1986).

JONES, CHRISTOPHER P., *Plutarch and Rome* (Oxford, 1971).

JOSEPH B. DAVID, *Perush al hatorah lerabenu yosef ben david misaragosah talmid rabenu nisim ben re'uven (haran)*, ed. Leon A. Feldman (Jerusalem, 1973).

JOSEPH HAKOHEN, *Emek habakha*, ed. Meir Letteris (Kraków, 1895).

JOSEPH SHALOM, 'Parma MS No. 553 (Reply to Abner)' (Heb.), in Judah Rosenthal, 'From "Alfonso's Book"' (Heb.), in Meir Ben Horin, Bernard D. Weinryb, and Solomon Zeitlin (eds.), *Studies and Essays in Honour of Abraham A. Neuman* [Meḥkarim umasot likhevod avraham a. neuman] (Leiden, 1962), Heb. section, 11–34.

JOSEPH B. TSADIK, *Kitsur zekher tsadik*, in Adolf Neubauer (ed.), *The Order of Sages and Historical Events* [Seder haḥakhamim vekorot hayamim], vol. i (Oxford, 1888), 85–100; Yolanda Moreno Koch (ed.), *Dos crónicas hispanohebreas del siglo XV* (Barcelona, 1994), 21–65.

JOSEPHUS, *Jewish Antiquities*, 9 vols., trans. Henry St John Thackeray (Cambridge, Mass., 1950); Heb. trans.: [Kadmoniyot hayehudim], 2 vols., trans. Abraham Schalit (Jerusalem, 1992).

JUAN DE LUCENA, *De vita beata*, in Antonio Paz y Melia (ed.), *Opúsculos literarios de los siglos XIV–XVI* (Madrid, 1892).

JUDAH B. ASHER, *She'elot uteshuvot zikhron yehudah* (Jerusalem, 1972).

JUDAH B. BARZILLAI AL-BARGELONI, *Perush sefer yetsirah* (Berlin 1885).

JUDAH HALEVI, *The Book of the Kuzari*, trans. Hartwig Hirschfeld (London, 1905).

JUDAH LOEW B. BEZALEL (MAHARAL OF PRAGUE), *Sefer netsaḥ yisra'el* (Tel Aviv, 1956).

JUSTIN MARTYR, *Dialogue with Trypho*, trans. Thomas B. Falls (Washington DC, 2003).

KAPLAN, YOSEF, *From Christianity to Judaism: The Story of Isaac Orobio de Castro*, trans. Raphael Loewe (Oxford, 1989).

KASHER, ARIEH, 'The Causal and Circumstantial Background to the Jews' War against the Romans' (Heb.), in id. (ed.), *The Great Jewish Revolt: Its Causes and Circumstances* [Hamered hagadol: hasibot vehanesibot liferitsato] (Jerusalem, 1983), 9–92.

—— *The Jews of Hellenistic and Roman Egypt* [Yehudei mitsrayim hahelenistit veharomit] (Tel Aviv, 1979).

KATZ, JACOB, *Between Jews and Gentiles: The Attitude of the Jews to Their Neighbours in the Middle Ages and the Early Modern Age* [Bein yehudim legoyim: yaḥas hayehudim lishekheneihem biyemei-habeinayim uviteḥilat hazeman heḥadash] (Jerusalem, 1977).

—— *Exclusiveness and Tolerance: Studies in Jewish–Gentile Relations in Medieval and Modern Times* (Oxford, 1961).

KELLY, JOHN N. D., *Jerome: His Life, Writings, and Controversies* (London, 1975).

KENAAN-KEDAR, NURIT, 'Symbolic Significance in Crusader Architecture: The Twelfth-Century Dome of the Church of the Holy Sepulchre' (Heb.), in Benjamin Z. Kedar (ed.), *The Crusaders in Their Kingdom: Studies in the History of the Land of Israel, 1099–1291* [Hatsalbanim bemamlakhtam: meḥkarim betoledot erets-yisra'el, 1099–1291] (Jerusalem, 1988), 169–79.

KIMELMAN, REUVEN, *The Mystical Meaning of* Lekhah dodi *and* Kabalat shabat [Lekhah dodi vekabalat shabat: hamashma'ut hamistit] (Jerusalem, 2003).

KIMHI, DAVID, *Perush leyo'el*, in *Mikra'ot gedolot* (Tel Aviv, 1959).

—— *Perush lizekharyah*, in *Mikra'ot gedolot* (Tel Aviv, 1959).

KIMHI, JOSEPH, *Sefer haberit*, in *Sefer haberit and David Kimhi's Disputations with Christianity* [Sefer haberit uvikuḥei radak im hanatsrut], ed. [Frank] Ephraim Talmage (Jerusalem, 1974), 21–68.

KIRSCH, JOHANN PETER, 'Orsini', in *Catholic Encyclopedia* (New York, 1913), 325–8.

KLAUSNER, JOSEPH, *Jesus: His Time, Life and Teachings* [Yeshu hanotseri: zemano, ḥayav, vetorato] (Tel Aviv, 1945).

KLEIN, MORDECAI, and ELCHANAN MOLNAR, 'Rabbi Abraham ben David as a Scholar of Jewish History' (Heb.), *Hatsofeh leḥokhmat yisra'el*, 5 (1921), 93–108, 165–75; 8 (1924), 24–35; 9 (1925), 85–8.

KLEINBERG, AVIAD M., *Flesh Made Word: Saints' Stories and the Western Imagination*, trans. Jane Marie Todd (Cambridge, Mass, 2008).

KOCHAN, LIONEL, *The Jew and His History* (New York, 1977).

KORKUS, DAVID, 'On the Attitude of the Al-Muhadin Leaders to Jews' (Heb.), *Zion*, 32 (1967), 137–60.

KOZODOY, MAUD, 'The Hebrew Bible as Weapon of Faith in Late Medieval Iberia: Irony, Satire, and Scriptural Allusion in Profiat Duran's *Al Tehi ka-Avotekha*', *Jewish Studies Quarterly*, 18 (2011), 185–201.

—— 'A Study of the Life and Works of Profiat Duran (Spain)' (Ph.D. thesis, Jewish Theological Seminary, 2006).

KRAKOWSKI, EVA, 'On the Literary Character of Abraham ibn Da'ud's Sefer Ha-Qabbalah', *European Journal of Jewish Studies*, 1 (2008), 219–48.

KRAUSS, SAMUEL, 'Eine judische Legende von der Auffindung des Kreuzes', *Jewish Quarterly Review*, 12 (1900), 718–31.

—— *Persia and Rome in the Talmud and the Midrash* [Paras veromi batalmud uvamidrashim] (Jerusalem, 1948).

KREY, PHILIP, 'The Apocalypse Commentary of 1329: Problems in Church History', in Philip Krey and Lesley Smith (eds.), *Nicholas of Lyra: The Senses of Scripture* (Leiden, 2000), 267–88.

KRIEGEL, MAURICE, 'Histoire sociale et ragots: Sur l'"ascendance juive" de Ferdinand le Catholique', in Fermín Miranda García (ed.), *Movimientos migratorios y expulsiones en la diáspora occidental*, Terceros encuentros judaicos en Tudela, 14–17 de julio de 1998 (Pamplona, 2000), 95–100.

LACAVE, JOSÉ LUIS, 'Las fuentes Cristianas del Sefer Yuhasin', in Pinchas Peli (ed.), *Proceedings of the Fifth World Congress on Jewish Studies* [Divrei hakongres ha'olami haḥamishi lemada'ei hayahadut], vol. ii (Jerusalem, 1969), 92–8.

—— 'El "Sefer Yuhasin" de Abraham Zacut' (Ph.D. thesis, University of Madrid, 1970).

LADERO QUESADA, MIGUEL ÁNGEL, *Castilla y la conquista del Reino de Granada* (Granada, 1987).

—— *Las fiestas en la cultura medieval* (Barcelona, 2004).

LANDES, RICHARD, 'The Massacres of 1010: On the Origins of Popular Violence in Western Europe', in Jeremy Cohen (ed.), *From Witness to Witchcraft: Jews and Judaism in Medieval Christian Thought*, Wolfenbütteler Mittelalter-Studien, 11 (Wiesbaden, 1996), 79–112.

LASKER, DANIEL J., 'The Impact of the Crusades on the Jewish–Christian Debate', *Jewish History*, 13 (1999), 23–36.

—— 'Jewish–Christian Polemic and Its Origins in the Lands of Islam' (Heb.), *Pe'amim*, 57 (1994), 4–16.

—— 'Karaism and the Jewish–Christian Debate', in Barry Wolfish (ed.), *Frank Talmage Memorial Volume*, vol. i (Haifa, 1993), 323–32.

LATINI, BRUNETTO, *The Book of the Treasure (Li Livres dou Tresor)*, trans. Paul Barrette and Spurgeon Baldwin (New York, 1993).

LAWEE, ERIC, *Isaac Abarbanel's Stance towards Tradition: Defense, Dissent, and Dialogue* (Albany, NY, 2001).

—— 'On the Threshold of the Renaissance: New Methods and Sensibilities in the Biblical Commentaries of Isaac Abarbanel', *Viator*, 26 (1995), 283–319.

LAWRANCE, JEREMY N. H., 'On Fifteenth-Century Spanish Vernacular Humanism', in Ian Michael and Richard A. Cardwell (eds.), *Medieval and Renaissance Studies in Honour of Robert Brian Tate* (Oxford, 1986), 63–79.

LAWRENCE, CLIFFORD HUGH, *The Friars: The Impact of the Early Mendicant Movement on Western Society* (London, 1994).

LAZARUS-YAFEH, HAVA, *Intertwined Worlds: Muslim Biblical Criticism in the Middle Ages* [Olamot shezurim: bikoret hamikra hamuslemit biyemei-habeinayim] (Jerusalem, 1999; Eng. edn.: Princeton, NJ, 1992).

LEIBOWITZ, YESHAYAHU, *On a World* [Al olam umelo'o: siḥot im mikha'el shashar] (Jerusalem, 1987).

LEIMAN, SHNAYER Z., 'Abarbanel and the Censor', *Journal of Jewish Studies*, 19 (1968), 49–61.

LEVI B. ABRAHAM B. HAYIM, *Livyat ḥen: hahakdamah vehaḥelek harishon min hama'amar hashishi: ekhut hanevuah vesodot hatorah*, ed. Howard Kreisel (Be'er Sheva, 2007).

LÉVY, ISRAEL, 'La Traduction de *L'Historia de Praeliis* par Immanuel ben Jacob', *Revue des Études Juives*, 6 (1882), 279–80.

LEVY, YOCHANAN, *Worlds Meet: Studies on the Status of Judaism in the Graeco-Roman World* [Olamot nifgashim: meḥkarim al ma'amadah shel hayahadut ba'olam hayevani–haroma'i] (Jerusalem, 1969).

LEVZION, NEHEMYA, 'Islamic Sects' (Heb.), in Hava Lazarus-Yafeh (ed.), *Essays on the History of Arabs and Islam* [Perakim betoledot ha'aravim veha'islam] (Tel Aviv, 1967), 176–98.

LEWIN, ADOLF, 'Eine Notiz zur Geschichte der Juden im Byzantinischen Reiche', *Monastschrift für Geschichte und Wissenschaft des Judentums*, 19 (1870), 117–22.

Libro de las generaciones, in *Crónica general de España de 1344*, ed. Diego Catalán and María Soledad de Andrés (Madrid, 1971), 218–334.

LIEBERMAN, SAUL, *Greek and Hellenism in the Land of Israel* [Yevanit veyavnut be'erets yisra'el: meḥkarim be'orḥot ḥayim be'erets yisra'el bitekufat hamishnah vehatalmud] (Jerusalem, 1984).

LIFSCHITZ, ABRAHAM, 'The Interpretation of Prophecy according to Abraham ibn Ezra and Isaac Abravanel' (Heb.), in Avigdor Shinan (ed.), *Proceedings of the Sixth World Congress of Jewish Studies* [Divrei hakongres ha'olami hashishi lemada'ei hayahadut], vol. i (Jerusalem, 1977), 133–9.

LIMOR, ORA, *Between Jews and Christians: Jews and Christians in Western Europe until the Beginning of the Modern Era* [Bein yehudim lenotserim: yehudim venotserim bema'arav eiropah ad reshit ha'et haḥadashah], 5 vols. (Tel Aviv, 1993–8).

—— 'Christian Sacred Space and the Jews', in Jeremy Cohen (ed.), *From Witness to Witchcraft: Jews and Judaism in Medieval Christian Thought*, Wolfenbütteler Mittelalter-Studien, 11 (Wiesbaden, 1996), 55–77.

—— 'Christian Sanctity, Jewish Authority' (Heb.), *Cathedra*, 80 (1996), 31–62.

—— *Die Disputationen zu Ceuta (1179) und Mallorca (1286): Zwei antijüdische Schriften aus dem Mittelalterlichen Genua* (Munich, 1994).

LINDER, AMNON, 'Ecclesia and Synagoga in the Medieval Myth of Constantine the Great', *Revue Belge de Philologie et d'Histoire*, 54 (1976), 1019–60.

—— 'Ex mala parentela bona sequi seu oriri non potest: The Troyan Ancestry of the Kings of France and the Opus Davidicum of Johannes Angelus de Legonissa', *Bibliothèque d'Humanisme et Renaissance*, 40 (1978), 497–512.

—— 'Jerusalem as a Focus of Conflict between Judaism and Christianity: Anti-Jewish Aspects of the Jerusalem Church from the Fourth Century' (Heb.), in Benjamin Z. Kedar and Zvi Baras (eds.), *Essays on the History of Jerusalem in the Middle Ages* [Perakim betoledot yerushalayim biyemei-habeinayim] (Jerusalem, 1979), 5–26.

—— 'The Myth of Constantine the Great in the West', *Studi Medievali*, 16 (1975), 43–95.

—— 'Roman Rule and the Jews in the Time of Constantine' (Heb.), *Tarbiz*, 44 (1974/5), 95–143.

LINEHAN, PETER, *History and the Historians of Medieval Spain* (Oxford, 1993).

The Little Flowers of St. Francis, trans. E. Gurney-Salter, introd. Hugh McKay (London, 1966).

Livro das linhagens, in *Crónica general de España de 1344*, ed. Diego Catalán and María Soledad de Andrés (Madrid, 1971), 215–335.

LIVY, *History of Rome*, trans. Benjamin O. Foster (Cambridge, Mass., 1967).

LÓPEZ DE COCA, JOSÉ ENRIQUE, 'The Making of Isabel de Solis', in Roger Collins and Anthony Goodman (eds.), *Medieval Spain: Culture, Conflict and Coexistence, Studies in Honour of Agnus Mackoy* (New York, 2002), 225–41.

LÓPEZ FÉREZ, JUAN ANTONIO, 'La traducción castellana de las "Vidas" realizada por Alfonso de Palencia', in Manuela García Valdés (ed.), *Estudios sobre Plutarco: Ideas religiosas. Actas del III Simposio Internacional sobre Plutarco, Oviedo 30 de abril a 2 de mayo 1992* (Madrid, 1994), 359–69.

LÓPEZ MARTÍNEZ, NICOLÁS, *Los judaizantes castellanos y la Inquisición en tiempo de Isabel la Católica* (Burgos, 1954).

LÓPEZ TORRIJOS, ROSA, *La mitología en la pintura española del Siglo de Oro* (Madrid, 1985).

LUNEAU, AUGUSTE, *L'Histoire de salut chez les pères de l'église: La Doctrine des âges du monde* (Paris, 1964).

LURIA, ILANA, 'Complicidad criminal: Un aspecto insólito de convivencia Judeo-Cristiana', in Carlos Carrete Parrondo (ed.), *Actas del III Congreso internacional encuentro de las tres culturas: Toledo, 15–17 octubre 1984* (Toledo, 1988), 93–108.

LUTTRELL, ANTHONY, 'Greek Histories Translated and Compiled for Juan Fernández de Heredia, Master of Rhodes, 1377–1396', *Speculum*, 35 (1960), 401–7.

MCCLUSKEY, RAYMOND, 'Malleable Accounts: Views of the Past in Twelfth Century Iberia', in Paul Magdalino (ed.), *The Perception of the Past in Twelfth-Century Europe* (London, 1992), 211–25.

MACCOBY, HYAM, *Judaism on Trial: Jewish–Christian Disputations in the Middle Ages* (London, 1982).

MCGINN, BERNARD, *Visions of the End: Apocalyptic Traditions in the Middle Ages* (New York, 1979).

MACHIAVELLI, NICCOLO, *The Discourses*, ed. Bernard Crick, trans. Leslie J. Walker (Harmondsworth, 1974).

—— *The Prince*, trans. Robert M. Adams (New York, 1977).

MACK, HANANEL, *Job and the Book of Job in Rabbinic Literature: Ela Mashal Hayah* ['Ela mashal hayah': iyov besifrut habayit hasheni uveinei ḥazal] (Ramat Gan, 2004).

MACKAY, ANGUS, 'The Ballad and the Frontier in Late Medieval Spain', *Bulletin of Hispanic Studies*, 60 (1983), 15–33.

—— 'Castile and Navarre', in Christopher Allmand (ed.), *New Cambridge Medieval History*, vol. vii: *c.1415–c.1500* (Cambridge, 1998), 606–26.

MAGISTER GREGORIUS, *On the Marvels of the City of Rome* ('Magister Gregorius, *De Mirabilibus Urbis Romae*: A New Description of Rome in the Twelfth Century', ed. Gordon McNeil Rushforth, *Journal of Roman Studies*, 9 (1919), 14–58).

MAIMONIDES (MOSES B. MAIMON), *Epistle to Yemen: The Arabic Source and the Three Hebrew Translations*, ed. Abraham S. Halkin, Eng. trans. Boaz Cohen (New York, 1952).

—— *Mishnah im perush mosheh ben maimon: nezikin*, ed. Yoseph Kapah (Jerusalem, 1965).

—— *Mishneh torah* (Jerusalem, 1970).

MALINOWSKI, BRONISLAW, 'Myth in Primitive Psychology', in id., *Magic, Science and Religion* (New York, 1954), 93–148.

MANN, JACOB, 'An Early Theologico-Polemical Work', *Hebrew Union College Annual*, 12–13 (1937–8), 411–59.

—— 'The Office of the Exilarch in Babylonia and Its Expansion at the End of the Geonic Period' (Heb.), in David Simonson, Abraham Freiman, and Moshe Schor (eds.), *S. A. Poznanski Memorial Volume* [Sefer zikaron likhevod s. a. poznanski] (Warsaw, 1907), 18–32.

—— 'Une source de l'histoire juive au XIIIe siècle: La Lettre polémique de Jacob B. Elie à Pablo Christiani', *Revue des Études Juives*, 82 (1926), 363–77.

MARAVALL, JOSÉ ANTONIO, *El concepto de España en la Edad Media* (Madrid, 1964).

MARCUS, IVAN G., *Rituals of Childhood: Jewish Acculturation in Medieval Europe* (New Haven, Conn. 1996).

MARKUS, ROBERT A., *The End of Ancient Christianity* (Cambridge, 1990).

MÁRQUEZ-VILLANUEVA, FRANCISCO, 'The Alfonsine Cultural Concept', in Francisco Márquez-Villanueva and Carlos Alberto Vega (eds.), *Alfonso X of Castile, the Learned King: An International Symposium, Harvard University, 17 November 1984* (Boston, Mass., 1990), 76–109.

MARTIN OF OPAVA, *Chronicle of Popes and Emperors* (*Chronicon pontificum et imperatorum*, ed. Ludwig Weiland, Monumenta Germaniae historica: scriptorum, 22 (Stuttgart, 1963), 377–475).

MARTÍNEZ ANTUÑA, MELCHOR, 'Una versión Árabe compendiada de la "Estoria de España" de Alfonso el Sabio', *Al-Andalus*, 1 (1933), 105–54.

MARTINI, RAYMUNDUS, *Dagger of Faith* (*Pugio fidei adversus Mauros et Judaeos* (Leipzig, 1687; repr. Farnborough, Hants, 1967)).

MARX, ALEXANDER, 'The Expulsion of the Jews from Spain: Two New Accounts', in id., *Studies in Jewish Bibliography and Booklore* (New York, 1944), 77–106.

MATTHEW PARIS, *Chronica majora*, 7 vols., ed. Henry Richards Luard (London, 1872–83).

MEIR B. SHIMON HAME'ILI, *Milḥemet mitsvah* ['Milḥemet mitsvah of R. Meir ben Shimon Hame'ili of Narbonne (fo. 214 of the Manuscript)' (Heb.)], in id., *Shitat hakadmonim: sefer milḥemet mitsvah lerabenu me'ir bar shimon meḥaber sefer hame'orot*, ed. Moshe Yehuda Hakohen Blau (New York, 1974), 305–57; William K. Herskowitz, 'Judeo-Christian Dialogue in Provence as Reflected in "Milhemet Mitzva" of R. Meir Hameili' (Ph.D. thesis, Yeshiva University, 1974).

MEIR, OFRA, *The Poetics of Rabbinic Stories* [Sugyot bapo'etikah shel sipurei ḥazal] (Tel Aviv 1993).

ME'IRI, MENAHEM, *Beit habeḥirah al masekhet avot* (Jerusalem, 1968).

—— *Ḥibur hateshuvah*, ed. Abraham Schreiber (New York, 1950).

MELAMED, ABRAHAM, 'The Myth of Venice in Italian Renaissance Jewish Thought', *Italia Judaica: Atti del I Convegno internazionale, Bari 18–22 maggio 1981* (Rome, 1983), 401–13.

—— 'The Perception of Jewish History in Italian Jewish Thought of the Sixteenth and Seventeenth Centuries: A Re-Examination', in *Italia Judaica II: Gli ebrei in Italia tra Rinascimento ed età barocca, atti del II convegno internazionale, Genova 10–15 giugno 1984* (Rome, 1986), 139–70.

—— *Wisdom's Little Sister: Studies in Medieval and Renaissance Jewish Political Thought* (Brighton, Mass., 2011).

—— 'Wisdom's Little Sister: The Political Thought of Jewish Thinkers in the Italian Renaissance' [Aḥotan haketanah shel haḥokhmot: hamaḥshavah hamedinit hayehudit biyemei habeinayim] (Ph.D. thesis, Tel Aviv University, 1976).

MENÉNDEZ PIDAL, JUAN, 'Leyendas del último rey godo (notas é investigaciones)', *Revista de Archivos, Bibliotecas y Museos* (1901), 858–95.

MENÉNDEZ PIDAL, RAMÓN, *Crónicas generales de España* (Madrid, 1918).

—— *La España del Cid* (Buenos Aires, 1943).

MERHAVIA, HEN-MELECH, 'Dante and His Political Essay' (Heb.), in Dante Alighieri, *Monarchy* [Al hamonarkhiyah], ed. and trans. Hen-Melech Merhavia (Jerusalem, 1962), 11–61.

—— *The Talmud in Christian Eyes* [Hatalmud bire'i hanatsrut hayaḥas lesifrut yisra'el shele'aḥar hamikra ba'olam hanotsri biyemei habeinayim [500–1248]] (Jerusalem, 1971).

MERRIMAN, ROGER BIGELOW, *The Rise of the Spanish Empire in the Old World and in the New*, 4 vols. (New York, 1962).

MEYUHAS GINIO, ALISA, 'The Expulsion of the Jews from France in the Fourteenth Century and Its Lesson in the Eyes of Alfonso de Espina, Author of *Metsudat ha'emunah*' (Heb.), *Mikha'el*, 12 (1991), 67–72.

—— ' "The Fortress of the Faith" at "the End of the West": Alfonso de Espina's *Metsudat ha'emunah* and Its Place in Medieval Polemical Literature' [' "Metsudat ha'emunah" "besof ma'arav": ḥiburo shel alfonso deh espinah, "metsudat ha'emunah" umekomo basifrut hapulmusit shel yemei habeinayim'], 3 vols. (Ph.D. thesis, Tel Aviv University, 1988).

Midrash tehilim, ed. Solomon Buber (Vilna, 1891).

MILIKOWSKI, CHAYIM, '*Seder olam* and Jewish Chronology during the Hellenistic-Roman Period' (Heb.), in Mosche Zimmermann, Menahem Stern, and Joseph Salmon (eds.), *Studies in Historiography* [Iyunim behistoryografyah] (Jerusalem, 1988), 59–71.

The Mirror of Perfection, in *The Little Flowers of St. Francis*, trans. E. Gurney-Salter, introd. Hugh McKay (London, 1966), 83–300.

MOMIGLIANO, ARNALDO, 'Pagan and Christian Historiography in the Fourth Century A.D.', in id. (ed.), *The Conflict between Paganism and Christianity in the Fourth Century A.D.* (Oxford, 1963), 79–99.

MONSALVO ANTÓN, JOSÉ MARÍA, 'Mentalidad antijudía en la Castilla medieval (ss. XII–XV)', in Carlos Barros (ed.), *Xudeus e conversos na historia: Actas do congreso internacional Ribadavia, 14–17 de octubre de 1991*, vol. i (Santiago de Compostela, 1994), 21–57.

MONTAGNES, BERNARD, 'Saint Vincent Ferrier devant le schisme', in Jean Favier et al. (eds.), *Genèse et débuts du grand schisme d'occident: Colloques internationaux du C.N.R.S., 586, Avignon, 1978* (Paris, 1980), 607–13.

MOORE, ROBERT IAN, *The Foundation of a Persecuting Society* (Oxford, 1990).

—— 'When did the Good Men of the Languedoc become Heretics?', paper delivered at international symposium 'Examining the Heretical Thought', Berkeley, Feb. 2006, <http://rimoore.net/GoodMen.html> (accessed 3 May 2014).

MORALEJO, SERAFIN, and FERNADO LÓPEZ ALSINA (eds.), *Santiago de Europa: Culto y cultura en la peregrinación a Compostela* (Santiago de Compostela, 1993).

MORENO KOCH, YOLANDA, 'La conquista de Granada y la expulsión de Sefarad según las crónicas hispanohebreas', in Emilia Cabrero Muñoz (ed.), *Andalucia medieval: Actas del I congreso de historia de Andalucia, diciembre de 1976*, vol. ii (Cordoba, 1978), 329–37.

MORENO KOCH, YOLANDA, (ed.), *Dos crónicas hispanohebreas del siglo XV*, introd. Ron Barkai (Barcelona, 1994).

MORREALE, MARGHERITA, 'Vernacular Scriptures in Spain', in Geoffrey W. H. Lampe (ed.), *Cambridge History of the Bible*, vol ii: *The West from the Fathers to the Reformation* (New York, 1994), 465–91.

MORTLEY, RAOUL, *The Idea of Universal History from Hellenistic Philosophy to Early Christian Historiography* (Lewiston, NY, 1996).

MOSES HAKOHEN OF TORDESILLAS, *Ezer ha'emunah*, 2 vols., ed. Yehuda Shamir (Coconut Grove, Fla., 1972).

MOSSHAMMER, ALDEN A., *The Chronicle of Eusebius and Greek Chronographic Tradition* (Lewisburg, Pa., 1979).

MOYA GARCÍA, CRISTINA, 'El *Doctrinal de príncipes* y la *Valeriana*: Didactismo y ejemplaridad en la obra de mosén Diego de Valera', *Memorabilia*, 13 (2011), 231–43.

MÜLHAUSEN, YOM TOV LIPMANN, *Sefer nitsaḥon*, facs. edn. (Jerusalem, 1984).

MURCIA, THIERRY, 'Ben Stada (ou Ben Stara) n'est pas Jésus: Une réponse à David Rokéah', *Revue des Études Juives*, 172 (2013), 189–99.

MYERS, DAVID N., 'Of Marranos and Memory: Yosef Hayim Yerushalmi and the Writing of Jewish History', in E. Carlebach et al. (eds.), *Jewish History and Jewish Memory* (London, 1998), 1–21.

NADLER, HELEN, *The Mendoza Family in the Spanish Renaissance, 1350 to 1550* (New Brunswick, NJ, 1979).

NAHMANIDES (MOSES B. NAHMAN), *Writings* [Kitvei rabenu mosheh ben naḥman], 2 vols., ed. Haim D. Chavel (Jerusalem, 1963).

—— *Perushei hatorah lerabenu mosheh ben naḥman (ramban)*, 2 vols., ed. Haim D. Chavel (Jerusalem, 1959–60).

—— *Sefer hage'ulah*, in id., *Writings*, i. 253–95.

—— *Torat hashem temimah*, in id., *Writings*, i. 141–75.

—— *Vikuaḥ haramban*, in id., *Writings*, i. 302–20.

NE'EMAN, SHLOMO, *The Birth of Civilization: A Thousand Years of Latin Europe* [Ledatah shel tsivilizatsyah: elef shenot eiropah halatinit] (Tel Aviv, 1975).

NENNIUS, *History of the Britons* (*Historia Brittonum*, ed. Joseph Stevenson (London, 1838)).

NETANYAHU, BENZION, 'The Conversion of Don Samuel Abravanel', in id., *Toward the Inquisition: Essays on Jewish and Converso History in Late Medieval Spain* (Ithaca, NY, 1997), 99–125.

—— *Don Isaac Abravanel: Statesman and Philosopher* (Philadelphia, Pa., 1972).

—— *The Marranos of Spain from the Late 14th to the Early 16th Century according to Contemporary Hebrew Sources* (Ithaca, NY, 1999).

—— 'On the Historical Meaning of the Hebrew Sources Related to the Marranos (A Reply to Critics)', in Josep M. Sola-Solé, Samuel G. Armistead, and Joseph H. Silverman (eds.), *Hispania Judaica: Studies on the History, Language and Literature of the Jews in the Hispanic World*, vol. i: *History* (Barcelona, 1980), 79–102.

—— *The Origins of the Inquisition in Fifteenth Century Spain* (New York, 1995).

NEUBAUER, ADOLF, *The Order of Sages and Historical Events* [Seder haḥakhamim vekorot hayamim], 2 vols. (Oxford, 1888–93).

NEUMAN, ABRAHAM A., 'Abraham Zacut, Historiographer', in Saul Lieberman (ed.), *Harry Austryn Wolfson Jubilee Volume on the Occasion of His Seventy-Fifth Birthday*, vol. ii (Jerusalem, 1965), Eng. section, 597–629.

—— 'Josippon: History and Pietism', in *Alexander Marx Jubilee Volume on the Occasion of his Seventieth Birthday*, vol. ii (New York, 1950), 637–67.

—— 'The Shebet Yehudah and Sixteenth-Century Historiography', in id., *Landmarks and Goals* (Philadelphia, Pa., 1953), 82–104.

NEWMAN, LOUIS I., *Jewish Influence on Christian Reform Movements* (New York, 1925).

NIRENBERG, DAVID, *Communities of Violence: Persecution of Minorities in the Middle Ages* (Princeton, NJ, 1996).

—— 'Mass Conversion and Genealogical Mentalities: Jews and Christians in Fifteenth-Century Spain', *Past and Present*, 174 (2002), 3–41.

—— 'Spanish "Judaism" and "Christianity" in an Age of Mass Conversion', in Jeremy Cohen and Moshe Rosman (eds.), *Rethinking European Jewish History* (Oxford, 2009), 149–72.

NISSIM B. MOSES OF MARSEILLES, *Ma'aseh nisim: perush latorah lerabi nisim ben rabi mosheh mimarsei*, ed. Howard Kreisel (Jerusalem, 2000).

Nizzahon vetus: Jewish–Christian Debate in the High Middle Ages. A Critical Edition of the Nizzahon Vetus with an Introduction, Translation, and Commentary, ed. David Berger (Philadelphia, Pa., 1979).

O'CALLAGHAN, JOSEPH F., *The Gibraltar Crusade: Castile and the Battle for the Strait* (Philadelphia, Pa., 2011).

—— *The Learned King: The Reign of Alfonso X of Castile* (Philadelphia, Pa., 1993).

OFFICIAL, JOSEPH B. NATAN, *Sefer yosef hamekane*, ed. Judah M. Rosenthal (Jerusalem, 1970).

OGILVIE, ROBERT M., *A Commentary on Livy, Books 1–5* (Oxford, 1965).

OPPENHEIMER, AHARON, 'The Bar Kokhba Revolt: Its Significance and Study' (Heb.), in id. (ed.), *The Bar Kokhba Revolt* [Mered bar kokhba] (Jerusalem, 1980), 9–21.

ORFALI, MOISÉS, 'Jews and Conversos in Fifteenth-Century Spain: Christian Apologia and Polemic', in Jeremy Cohen (ed.), *From Witness to Witchcraft: Jews and Judaism in Medieval Christian Thought*, Wolfenbütteler Mittelalter-Studien, 11 (Wiesbaden, 1996), 337–60.

—— 'La retribución divina en la historiografía sefardí (siglos XVI–XVII)', in Elena Romero (ed.), *Judaismo hispano: Estudios en memoria de Jósé Luis Lacave Riaño* (Madrid, 2002), 799–808.

OROSIUS, PAULUS, *Seven Books of History against the Pagans* (*Historiarum adversum paganos libri VII. Accedit eiusdem apologeticus* (Hildesheim, 1967)).

ORT, LODEWIJK J. R., *Mani: A Religio-Historical Description of His Personality* (Leiden, 1967).

PABLO DE SANTA MARÍA, *Scrutinium scripturarum* (Burgos, 1591).

PACHTER, MORDECHAI, 'The Homiletic and Ethical Literature of the Safed Sages in the Sixteenth Century and Its Main Ideas' [Sifrut haderush vehamusar shel ḥakhmei tsefat bame'ah ha-16 uma'arekhet ra'ayonoteiha ha'ikariyim] (Ph.D. thesis, Hebrew University of Jerusalem, 1976).

PACIOS LÓPEZ, ANTONIO, *La disputa de Tortosa*, 2 vols. (Madrid, 1957).

PADE, MARIANNE, 'The Latin Translations of Plutarch's *Lives* in Fifteenth-Century Italy and their Manuscript Diffusion', in Claudio Leonardi and Birger Munk Olsen (eds.), *The Classical Tradition in the Middle Ages and the Renaissance: Proceedings of the First European Science Foundation Workshop on 'The Reception of Classical Texts' (Florence, 26–27 June 1992)* (Spoleto, 1995), 169–83.

PAGIS, DAN, 'Lamentations over the Persecutions of 1391 in Spain' (Heb.), *Tarbiz*, 37 (1967/8), 355–73.

PAPAIOANNOU, SOPHIA, 'Founder, Civilizer and Leader: Virgil's Evander and his Role in the Origins of Rome', *Mnemosyne*, 56 (2003), 680–702.

PAPPAS, NICKOLAS, 'Plato's Aesthetics', in Edward N. Zalta (ed.), in *Stanford Encyclopedia of Philosophy* (Summer 2012 edn.), <http://plato.stanford.edu/archives/sum2012/entries/plato-aesthetics/> (accessed 3 May 2014).

PARDOE, ROSEMARY, and DARROLL PARDOE, *The Female Pope: The Mystery of Pope Joan: The First Complete Documentation of the Facts Behind the Legend* (Wellingborough, Northants, 1988).

Pasionario Hispánico, ed. Ángel Fábrega Grau, Monumenta Hispaniae sacra, liturgica, 6/2 (Madrid, 1955), 260–6.

PEDRO DE CORRAL, *Crónica del Rey Don Rodrigo (Crónica sarracina)*, ed. James Donald Fogelquist (Madrid, 2001).

PEDRO LÓPEZ DE AYALA, *Crónica del Rey Don Pedro y del Rey Don Enrique, su hermano, hijos del Rey Don Alfonso Onceno*, 2 vols., ed. Germán Orduna (Buenos Aires, 1994–7).

PEGG, MARK GREGORY, *The Corruption of Angels: The Great Inquisition of 1245–1246* (Princeton, NJ, 2001).

PERI, HIRAM, 'A Historical Poem in Old Castilian on the *Edades del mundo*' (Heb.), *Otsar yehudei sefarad*, 5 (1962), 55–61.

PERLMANN, MOSHE, 'The Medieval Polemics between Islam and Judaism', in Shelomo Dov Goitein (ed.), *Religion in a Religious Age* (Cambridge, Mass., 1974), 103–29.

PERO NIÑO, *El victorial: Crónica de Don Pero Niño, conde de Buelna*, ed. Juan de Mata Carriazo (Madrid, 1940).

PETER COMESTOR, *Scholastic History* (*Historia Scholastica*, ed. Jacques-Paul Migne, Patrologia Latina, 198 (Paris, 1855), cols. 1049–1722).

PICCUS, JULES, 'El traductor español de "De genealogia Deorum"', in *Homenaje a Rodríguez Moñino: Estudios de erudición que le ofrecen sus amigos o discipulos hispanistas norteamericanos*, vol. ii (Madrid, 1966), 59–75.

The Pilgrim's Guide to Santiago de Compostela: A Critical Edition, ed. Alison Stones et al., vol. i: *The Manuscripts: Their Creation, Production and Reception*; vol. ii: *The Text: Annotated English Translation; Latin Text Collated, Edited and Annotated* (London, 1998).

PLUTARCH, *Lives*, trans. Aubrey Stewart (London, 1880).

PONS, ANTONIO, *Los judíos del reino de Mallorca durante los siglos XIII y XIV* (Madrid, 1958).

POST, GAINES, "'Blessed Lady Spain': Vincentius Hispanus and Spanish National Imperialism in the Thirteenth Century', *Speculum*, 29 (1954), 198–209.

PRAWER, JOSHUA, 'Christian Perceptions of Jerusalem in the Early Middle Ages' (Heb.), in id., *Jerusalem: The Early Muslim Period, 638–1099* [Sefer yerushalayim: hatekufah hamuslemit hakedumah, 638–1099] (Jerusalem, 1987), 249–82.

—— *The Crusaders: A Portrait of a Colonial Society* [Hatsalbanim: deyoknah shel ḥevrah kolonialit] (Jerusalem, 1976).

—— *Histoire du Royaume Latin de Jérusalem*, 2 vols., trans. Gérard Nahon (Paris, 1975).

—— *The History of the Crusader Kingdom in the Land of Israel* [Toledot mamlekhet hatsalbanim be'erets yisra'el], 2 vols. (Jerusalem, 1984).

—— *The History of the Jews in the Latin Kingdom of Jerusalem* (Oxford, 1988).

PRINS, GWYN, 'Oral History', in Peter Burke (ed.), *New Perspectives on Historical Writing* (University Park, Pa., 1992), 114–39.

PUECH, HENRI-CHARLES, *Le Manichéisme: Son fondateur, sa doctrine* (Paris, 1949).

QUAIN, EDWIN A., 'The Medieval "Accessus ad auctores"', *Traditio*, 3 (1945), 215–64.

RAPPEL, DOV, 'Introduction to Profiat Duran's *Ma'aseh efod*' (Heb.), *Sinai*, 100 (1977), 749–95.

—— *The Seven Wisdoms: The Controversy over Secular Studies in Jewish Educational Literature before the Haskalah* [Sheva haḥokhmot: havikuaḥ al limudei ḥol besifrut haḥinukh hayehudit ad reshit hahaskalah] (Jerusalem, 1990).

RASHI, *Perush*, in *Mikra'ot gedolot* (Tel Aviv, 1959).

RAVITZKY, AVIEZER, 'On Kings and Statutes in Jewish Thought in the Middle Ages: From R. Nissim Gerondi to R. Isaac Abravanel' (Heb.), in Menahem Ben-Sasson, Robert [Reuven] Bonfil, and Joseph Hacker (eds.), *Culture and Society in Medieval Jewish History: Studies Dedicated to the Memory of Haim Hillel Ben-Sasson* [Tarbut veḥevrah betoledot yisra'el biyemei-habeinayim: kovets ma'amarim lezikhro shel ḥayim hilel ben-sason] (Jerusalem, 1989), 469–92.

—— 'The Teachings of Zeraḥiah ben She'altiel Hen and Maimonidean-Tibbonnide Philosophy in the 13th Century' [Mishnato shel r. zeraḥyah ben yitsḥak ben she'alti'el ḥen vehehagut hamaimonit–tibonit bame'ah ha-13] (Ph.D. thesis, Hebrew University of Jerusalem, 1978).

RAY, JONATHAN, 'Beyond Tolerance and Persecution: Reassessing Our Approach to Medieval Convivencia', *Jewish Social Studies*, NS 11/2 (2005), 1–18.

RAY, ROGER D., 'Medieval Historiography through the Twelfth Century: Problems and Progress of Research', *Viator*, 5 (1974), 33–59.

REAMES, SHERRY L., *The Legenda Aurea: A Re-Examination of Its Paradoxical History* (Madison, Wis., 1985).

REEVES, MARJORIE, *Joachim of Fiore and the Prophetic Future* (London, 1976).

REMBAUM, JOEL E., 'The Influence of "Sefer Nestor HaKomer" on Medieval Jewish Polemics', *Proceedings of the American Academy for Jewish Research*, 45 (1978), 155–85.

REMBAUM, JOEL E., 'The New Testament in Medieval Jewish Anti-Christian Polemics' (Ph.D. thesis, University of California, 1975).

RENAN, ERNEST, *Les Écrivains juifs français du XIVe siècle* (Paris, 1893).

REYDELLET, MARC, 'Les Intentions idéologiques et politiques dans la Chronique d'Isidore de Séville', *Mélanges d'archéologie et d'histoire de l'École Française de Rome*, 82 (1970), 363–400.

RIEGER, PAUL, 'The Foundation of Rome in the Talmud: A Contribution of the Folklore of Antiquity', *Jewish Quarterly Review*, NS 16 (1925–6), 227–35.

RILEY-SMITH, JONATHAN, *The First Crusade and the Idea of Crusading* (London, 1986).

RINCÓN GONZÁLEZ, MARÍA DOLORES, 'Los Reyes Católicos y sus modelos plutarquistas en un drama humanístico del s. XV', in Manuela García Valdés (ed.), *Estudios sobre Plutarco: Ideas religiosas. Actas del III Simposio internacional sobre Plutarco, oviedo 30 de abril a 2 de mayo 1992* (Madrid, 1994), 351–8.

ROBERTS, JOHN EDWARD, 'Simon Magus', in James Hastings (ed.), *Dictionary of the Apostolic Church* (New York, 1926), ii. 493–8.

ROKEAH, DAVID, 'Ben Stara is Ben Pantera: Towards the Clarification of a Philological-Historical Problem' (Heb.), *Tarbiz*, 39 (1969/70), 9–18.

—— *Jews, Pagans and Christians in Conflict* (Jerusalem, 1982).

—— *Judaism and Christianity in the Light of Pagan Polemic* [Hayahadut vehanatsrut bire'i hapulmus hapagani] (Jerusalem, 1991).

—— 'On Rabbi Judah bar Ilai and His Attitude to Rome' (Heb.), *Zion*, 52 (1987), 107–10.

ROMANO, DAVID, 'Alfonso X y los judíos: Problemática y propuestas de trabajo', in id., *De historia judía hispánica*, 373–99.

—— 'Ascendencia judía de Fernando el Católico?', *Sefarad*, 55 (1995), 163–71.

—— 'Cortesanos judíos en la corona de Aragon', in id., *De historia judía hispánica*, 401–13.

—— *De historia judía hispánica* (Barcelona, 1991).

—— 'The Jews' Contribution to Medicine, Science, and General Learning' (Heb.), in Haim Beinart (ed.), *The Sephardi Legacy* [Moreshet sefarad] (Jerusalem, 1992), 240–60.

—— *Judíos al servicio de Pedro el Grande de Aragón (1276–1285)* (Barcelona, 1983).

—— 'Judíos escríbanos y trujamanes de árabe en la corona de Aragón (Reinados de Jaime I a Jaime II)', in id., *De historia judía hispánica*, 239–73.

ROSENTHAL, JUDAH M., 'Interest from the Foreigner' (Heb.), in id., *Studies and Sources* [Mehkarim umekorot], i. 253–323.

—— 'A Religious Disputation between a Scholar Named Menahem the Apostate and the Dominican Friar Paul Christiani' (Heb.), *Hagut ivrit ba'amerikah*, 3 (1974), 61–73.

—— 'Religious Tolerance in Medieval Biblical Commentary' (Heb.), in id., *Studies and Sources* [Mehkarim umekorot], i. 203–13.

—— *Studies and Sources* [Mehkarim umekorot], 2 vols. (Jerusalem, 1967).

—— 'The Talmud on Trial', *Jewish Quarterly Review*, NS 47 (1956–7), 58–76, 145–69.

ROSSI, AZARIAH DE, *Writings* [Kitvei azaryah min ha'adumim], ed. Robert [Reuven] Bonfil (Jerusalem, 1991).

—— *Meor einayim* (Vilna, 1866); Eng. trans.: *The Light of the Eyes*, trans. and ed. Joanna Weinberg (New Haven, Conn., 2001).

ROTH, CECIL, 'Historiography', in *Encyclopaedia Judaica* (Jerusalem, 1971), vol. viii, cols. 551–67.

ROTH, NORMAN, 'Forgery and Abrogation of the Torah: A Theme in Muslim and Christian Polemic in Spain', *Proceedings of the American Academy for Jewish Research*, 54 (1987), 203–36.

—— *Jews, Visigoths and Muslims in Medieval Spain: Cooperation and Conflict* (Leiden, 1994).

—— 'The "Theft of Philosophy" by the Greeks from the Jews', *Classical Folio*, 32 (1978), 52–67.

RUBIN, ZEEV, *The Christianization of Europe* [Hitnatsrutah shel eiropah] (Tel Aviv, 1991).

SA'ADIAH GAON, *Perush al daniyel*, in *Mikra'ot gedolot* (Tel Aviv, 1959).

—— *Sefer hanivhar be'emunot uvedeot*, ed. Joseph Kapah (Jerusalem, 1973).

SABINE, GEORGE H., *A History of Political Theory*, 4th rev. edn., ed. Thomas Landon Thorson (Hinsdale, Ill., 1973).

SAÍNZ DE LA MAZA, CARLOS, 'El converso y judío Alfonso de Valladolid y su Libro del Zelo de Dios', in *Las tres culturas en la Corona de Castilla y los sefardíes: Actas de las Jornadas Sefardíes, Castillo de la Mora, noviembre 1989, y del Seminario de las Tres Culturas, León, Palencia, Salamanca y Valladolid, febrero de 1990* (Salamanca, 1990), 71–85.

SALLUST, *The War with Catiline*, trans. John C. Rolfe (London, 1965).

SALVADOR MARTÍNEZ, H., *Alfonso X, the Learned: A Biography*, trans. Odile Cisneros, Studies in the History of Christian Traditions, 146 (Leiden, 2010).

SAMBARI, JOSEPH B. ISAAC, *Sefer divrei yosef lerabi yosef ben yitshak sambari: elef ume'ah shenot toladah yehudit betsel ha'islam*, ed. Shimon Shtober (Jerusalem, 1994).

SÁNCHEZ-ALBORNOZ, CLAUDIO, *La España musulmana según los autores islamitas y cristianos medievales* (Buenos Aires, 1960).

SÁNCHEZ DE ARÉVALO, RODRIGO, *Suma de la política*, ed. Mario Penna, Biblioteca de autores españoles, 116 (1959), 249–309.

SAPERSTEIN, MARC, 'Christians and Jews: Some Positive Images', *Harvard Theological Review*, 79 (1986), 236–46.

—— *Decoding the Rabbis: A Thirteenth-Century Commentary on the Aggadah* (Cambridge, 1980).

—— *Jewish Preaching, 1200–1800: An Anthology* (New Haven, Conn., 1989).

—— 'Stories in Jewish Sermons (the 15th–16th Centuries)', in *Proceedings of the Ninth World Congress of Jewish Studies* (Jerusalem, 1986), 101–8.

SAQUERO SUÁREZ-SOMONTE, PILAR, and TOMÁS GONZÁLEZ ROLÁN, 'Las cuestiones sobre los dioses de los gentiles del Tostado: Un documento importante sobre la presencia de G. Boccaccio en la literature medieval española', *Cuadernos de filologia clásica*, 19 (1985), 85–114.

SAX, GEOFFREY (dir.), *The Disputation* [film] (Electric Rainbow Production, 1986).

SCHÄFER, PETER, MICHAEL MEERSON, and YAACOV DEUTSCH (eds.), *Toledot Yeshu ('The Life Story of Jesus') Revisited: A Princeton Conference*, Texts and Studies in Ancient Judaism, 143 (Tübingen, 2011).

SCHEVILL, RUDOLPH, *Ovid and the Renaissance in Spain* (Hildesheim, 1971).

SCHLICHTING, GÜNTER, *Ein jüdiches Leben Jesu, Die verschollene Toledot-Jeschu-Fassung Tam ū-mūʾād: Einleitung, Text, Übersetzung, Kommentar, Motivsynopse, Bibliographie* (Tübingen, 1982).

SCHMITT, JEAN-CLAUDE, 'La parola addomesticata: San Domenico, il gatto et le donne di Fanjeaux', *Quaderni Storici*, 41 (1979), 416–39.

—— 'Recueils franciscains d'"Exempla" et perfectionnement des techniques intellectuelles du XIIIe au XVe siècle', *Bibliothèque de l'École des Chartes*, 135 (1977), 5–21.

SCHOLEM, GERSHOM, 'Abraham ben Alexander (Axelrad) of Cologne', in *Encyclopaedia Judaica* (Jerusalem, 1971), vol. ii, col. 134.

—— *The Origin of the Kabbalah and Sefer hababir: Lectures by Prof. G. Scholem in 1962* [Reshit hakabalah vesefer hababir: hartsaotav shel profesor g. shalom bishenat 1962] (Jerusalem, 1986).

—— *Explications and Implications: Writings on Jewish Heritage and Renaissance* [Devarim bego], 2 vols. (Tel Aviv, 1982).

SCHRECKENBERG, HEINZ, *Die Flavius-Josephus-Tradition in Antike und Mittelalter* (Leiden, 1972).

—— *Rezeptionsgeschichte und textkritische Untersuchungen zu Flavius Josephus* (Leiden, 1977).

SCHWARTZ, DOV, 'The Controversy about Astral Magic in Fourteenth-Century Provence' (Heb.), *Zion*, 58 (1993), 141–74.

—— *The Messiah in Medieval Jewish Thought* [Haraʾayon hameshiḥi bahagut hayehudit biyemei-habeinayim] (Ramat Gan, 1997).

—— 'Philosophical Commentary on the Bible and the Aggadah as a Factor of History and Culture' (Heb.), *Maḥanayim*, 7 (1994), 158–65.

SCHWOEBEL, ROBERT, *The Shadow of the Crescent: The Renaissance Image of the Turk (1453–1517)* (Nieuwkoop, 1967).

Sefer hayashar, ed. Joseph Dan (Jerusalem, 1986).

Sefer bitekufot umoladot, in Abraham [Albert] E. Harkavy (ed.), *Both New and Old: Sources and Studies in Jewish History and Literature* [Ḥadashim gam yeshanim: mekorot umeḥkarim betoledot yisraʾel uvesifruto] (Jerusalem, 1970), 256–60.

Sefer yosipon, ed. Hayim Hominer (Jerusalem, 1956); ed. David Flusser, vol. i [text] (Jerusalem, 1979).

Sefer zerubavel, in Yehuda Even Shmuel (ed.), *Midrashim of Salvation: Jewish Apocalyptic from the End of the Babylonian Talmud to the Beginning of the Sixth Millennium* [Midreshei geʾulah: pirkei haʾapokalipsah hayehudit meḥatimat hatalmud habavli veʾad reshit haʾelef hashishi] (Tel Aviv, 1943), 55–88.

SERMONETA, JOSEPH B., 'Engaging in the Liberal Arts in Jewish Society in Fourteenth-Century Italy' (Heb.), in *City and Community: The Twelfth Conference on the Study of History* [Haʾir vehakehilah: hakenes hasheneim-asar leʾiyun behistoryah] (Jerusalem, 1968), 249–68.

SERRANO, LUCIANO, *Los conversos Don Pablo de Santa María y Don Alfonso de Cartagena* (Madrid, 1942).

SEZNEC, JEAN, *The Survival of the Pagan Gods: The Mythological Tradition and Its Place in Renaissance Humanism and Art* (Princeton, NJ, 1961).

SHAHAR, SHULAMIT, 'The Idea of Chosenness in Heretical Movements in the Middle Ages' (Heb.), in Shmuel Almog and Michael Heyd (eds.), *The Idea of Chosenness in Israel and the Nations: A Collection of Articles* [Ra'ayon habeḥirah beyisra'el uve'amim: kovets ma'amarim] (Jerusalem, 1991), 179–90.

SHAMIR, YEHUDA, 'On the Meaning of an Excerpt from Abraham Galante's Commentary on Lamentations, *Kinat setarim*' (Heb.), in Issacher Ben-Ami (ed.), *The Legacy of Spanish and Eastern Jews: Studies* [Moreshet yehudei sefarad vehamizraḥ: meḥkarim] (Jerusalem, 1982), 225–34.

—— *Rabbi Moses Ha-Kohen of Tordesillas and His Book 'Ezer Ha-Emunah': A Chapter in the History of the Judeo-Christian Controversy* (Leiden, 1975).

SHATZMAN, ISRAEL, *History of the Roman Republic* [Toledot harepublikah haromit] (Jerusalem, 1990).

SHATZMILLER, JOSEPH, 'The Albigensian Heresy in the Eyes of Contemporary Jews' (Heb.), in Menahem Ben-Sasson, Robert [Reuven] Bonfil, and Joseph Hacker (eds.), *Culture and Society in Medieval Jewish History: Studies Dedicated to the Memory of Haim Hillel Ben-Sasson* [Tarbut veḥevrah betoledot yisra'el biyemei-habeinayim: kovets ma'amarim lezikhro shel ḥayim hilel ben-sason] (Jerusalem, 1989), 333–52.

—— 'Étudiants juifs à la faculté de médecine de Montpellier, dernier quart du XIVe siècle', *Jewish History*, 6 (1992), 243–53.

—— 'Paulus Christiani: Un aspect de son activité anti-juive', in Gérard Nahon and Charles Touati (eds.), *Homage à George Vajda* (Louvain, 1980), 203–17.

—— 'Politics and the Myth of Origins: The Case of the Medieval Jews', in Gilbert Dahan (ed.), *Les Juifs au regard de l'histoire: Mélanges en l'honneur de Bernard Blumenkranz* (Paris, 1985), 49–61.

—— 'Provençal Chronography in the Lost Work of Shem Tov Shanzolo' (Heb.), *Proceedings of the American Academy for Jewish Research*, 52 (1985), Heb. section, 43–61.

—— 'Solomon ibn Verga and the Expulsion of English Jewry' (Heb.), in Aharon Mirsky, Avraham Grossman, and Yosef Kaplan (eds.), *Exile and Diaspora: Studies in the History of the Jewish People Presented to Professor Haim Beinart on the Occasion of his Seventieth Birthday* [Galut aḥar golah: meḥkarim betoledot am yisra'el mugashim leprofesor ḥayim beinart limelot lo shivim shanah] (Jerusalem, 1985), 349–55.

SHEPARD, SANFORD, *Lost Lexicon: Secret Meanings in the Vocabulary of Spanish Literature during the Inquisition* (Miami, Fla., 1982).

SHINE, SYLVIA, 'Jerusalem in Christian Spirituality' (Heb.), in Joshua Prawer and Haggai Ben-Shammai (eds.), *Jerusalem: The Crusader and Ayyubid Period, 1099–1250* [Sefer yerushalayim: hatekufah hatsalbanit veha'ayubit 1099–1250] (Jerusalem, 1991), 213–63.

SHIRMAN, HAIM, *Hebrew Poetry in Spain and Provence* [Hashirah ha'ivrit bisefarad uveprovans], 2nd edn., 2 vols (Jerusalem, 1961).

SHIRMAN, HAIM, *The History of Hebrew Poetry in Christian Spain and Southern France* [Toledot hashirah ha'ivrit bisefarad hanotserit uviderom tsarfat], ed. Ezra Fleischer (Jerusalem, 1997).

SHOHAT, AZRIEL, 'Rabbi Abraham Zacut in the Yeshiva of Rabbi Isaac Shulal in Jerusalem' (Heb.), *Zion*, 13–14 (1948–9), 43–6.

SHOPKOW, LEAH, *History and Community: Norman Historical Writing in the Eleventh and Twelfth Centuries* (Washington DC, 1997).

Sifrei on Deuteronomy [*Sifrei al sefer devarim*], ed. Eliezer A. [Louis] Finkelstein (New York, 1969).

SILVER, ABBA HILLEL, *A History of Messianic Speculation in Israel* (New York, 1927).

SIMONSOHN, SHLOMO, *The Apostolic See and the Jews*, 8 vols. (Toronto, 1991).

—— 'The Jews of Christian Europe according to *Seder eliyahu zuta*' (Heb.), in Attilio Milano, Daniel Carpi, and Alexander Rofé (eds.), *Arye Leone Carpi Memorial Volume: A Collection of Studies on the History of Italian Jewry* [Sefer zikaron le'aryeh le'oneh karpi: kovets mehkarim letoledot hayehudim be'italyah] (Jerusalem, 1967), 54–71.

—— '*Seder eliyahu zuta*: "Chronicles" and "Stories of Spain"' (Heb.), in Elijah ben Elkanah Capsali, *Seder eliyahu zuta: toledot ha'otomanim uvenetsiah vekorot am yisra'el bemamlekhot turkiyah, sefarad uvenetsiah*, ed. Aryeh Shmuelevitz, Shlomo Simonsohn, and Meir Benayahu (Jerusalem, 1976–83), iii. 73–82.

SIRAT, COLETTE, 'Les Différentes Versions du Liwyat Hen de Levi ben Abraham', *Revue des Études Juives*, 122 (1963), 167–77.

—— 'The Political Ideas of Nissim ben Moses of Marseilles' (Heb.), *Jerusalem Studies in Jewish Thought*, 9 (Shlomo Pines Festschrift [Sefer hayovel lishelomoh pines], 2) (1990), 53–76.

SLOUSCHZ, NAHUM, 'Forced Conversions in Maimonides' Time' (Heb.), in Yehudah L. Hakohen Fishman (ed.), *Memorial to Rabbi A. Y. Hakohen Kook* [Azkarah lenishmat harav a. y. kook], vol. iv (Jerusalem, 1937), 100–23.

SOLOMON B. MOSES B. YEKUTIEL, *Edut hashem ne'emanah*, in Judah M. Rosenthal, *Studies and Sources* [Mehkarim umekorot], vol. i (Jerusalem, 1967), 373–430.

SOUTHERN, RICHARD WILLIAM, 'Aspects of the European Tradition of Historical Writing, 3: History as Prophecy', *Transactions of the Royal Historical Society*, 22 (1972), 159–80.

SPEIGEL, NATHAN, 'Plotinus' Thought' (Heb.), in *Plotinus' Enneads* [Ene'adot me'et plotinus], trans. Nathan Speigel, vol. i (Jerusalem, 1978), 11–167.

SPERBER, DANIEL, 'Chief Magdiel: Diocletian' (Heb.), in Aharon Oppenheimer, Isaiah Gafni, and Menahem Stern (eds.), *Jews and Judaism during the Second Temple, Mishnaic, and Talmudic Periods: Studies in Honour of Shmuel Safrai* [Yehudim veyahadut biyemei bayit sheni, hamishnah, vehatalmud: mehkarim likhevodo shel shemu'el safrai] (Jerusalem, 1993), 243–5.

STARR, JOSHUA, *Romania: The Jewries of the Levant after the Fourth Crusade* (Paris, 1949).

STEARNS, JUSTIN, 'Two Passages in Ibn al-Khatib's Account of the Kings of Christian Iberia', *Al-Qantara*, 25 (2004), 157–82.

STEIN, SIEGFRIED, *Jewish–Christian Disputations in Thirteenth-Century Narbonne: An Inaugural Lecture Delivered at University College London, 22 October 1964* (London, 1969).

STERN, MENAHEM, 'Josephus's Historical Method' (Heb.), in Isaiah Gafni, Moshe David Herr, and Moshe Amit (eds.), *Studies in the History of the Jews in the Second Temple Period* [Meḥkarim betoledot yisra'el biyemei habayit hasheni] (Jerusalem, 1991), 408–13.

—— 'Josephus's *Jewish War* and the Roman Empire' (Heb.), in Uriel Rappaport (ed.), *Josephus: Historian of Palestine in the Hellenistic and Roman Period* [Yosef ben matityahu: historyon shel erets yisra'el batekufah hahelenistit veharomit] (Jerusalem, 1983), 237–45.

STITSKIN, LEON D., *Judaism as a Philosophy: The Philosophy of Abraham bar Hiyya* (New York, 1960).

STOUFF, LOUIS, *Arles à la fin du Moyen-Âge* (Aix-en-Provence, 1986).

STOW, KENNETH R., *The '1007 Anonymous' and Papal Sovereignty: Jewish Perceptions of the Papacy and Papal Policy in the Middle Ages* (Cincinnati, Ohio, 1984).

—— 'The Attitude of the Jews to the Papacy and the Papal Doctrine of Protection of the Jews, 1063–1147' (Heb.), *Studies in the History of the Jews and the Land of Israel* [Meḥkarim betoledot am-yisra'el ve'erets-yisra'el], 5 (1980), 175–90.

—— 'Jacob of Venice and the Jewish Settlement in Venice in the Thirteenth Century', in Nahum M. Waldman (ed.), *Community and Culture: Essays in Jewish Studies in Honor of the Ninetieth Anniversary of Graetz College* (Philadelphia, Pa., 1987), 221–32.

STRAYER, JOSEPH R., *The Albigensian Crusades* (Ann Arbor, Mich., 1992).

SUÁREZ FERNÁNDEZ, LUIS, 'Castilla (1350–1406)', in Luis Suárez Fernández and Juan Reglá Campistol (eds.), *España cristiana: Crisis de la reconquista, luchas civiles*, Historia de España, 14 (Madrid, 1976), 3–378.

SUETONIUS, *Lives of the Caesars*, trans. Catharine Edwards (Oxford, 2000).

Sumario de los reyes de España, por el Despensero Mayor de la Reina Doña Leonor muger del Rey Don Juan il Primero de Castilla con las alteraciones y adiciones que posteriormente le hizo un anonimo, ed. Eugenio de Llaguno Amirola (Madrid, 1781).

SZITTYA, PENN R., *The Antifraternal Tradition in Medieval Literature* (Princeton, NJ, 1986).

SZPIECH, RYAN, *Conversion and Narrative: Reading and Religious Authority in Medieval Polemic* (Philadelphia, Pa., 2013).

—— 'From Testimonia to Testimony: Thirteenth-Century Anti-Jewish Polemic and the *Mostrador de justicia* of Abner of Burgos / Alfonso of Valladolid' (Ph.D. thesis, Yale University, 2006).

—— 'Scrutinizing History: Polemic and Exegesis in Pablo de Santa María's *Siete edades del mundo*', *Medieval Encounters*, 16 (2010), 96–142.

—— 'Translation, Transcription, and Transliteration in the Polemics of Raymond Martini, O.P. (d. after 1284)', in Charles D. Wright and Karen Fresco (eds.), *Translating the Middle Ages* (Aldershot, 2012), 171–87.

TALMAGE, (FRANK) EPHRAIM, 'A Hebrew Polemical Treatise: Anti-Cathar and Anti-Orthodox', *Harvard Theological Review*, 60 (1967), 323–48.

—— 'Keep Your Sons from Scripture: The Bible in Medieval Jewish Scholarship and Spirituality', in Clemens Thoma and Michael Wyschogrod (eds.), *Understanding Scripture: Explorations of Jewish and Christian Traditions of Interpretation* (New York, 1987), 91–2.

Targum, in *Mikra'ot gedolot* (Tel Aviv, 1959).

TATE, ROBERT B., 'El cronista real castellano durante el siglo XV', in *Homenaje a Pedro Sainz Rodríguez*, vol. iii: *Estudios históricos* (Madrid, 1986), 659–68.

—— 'Mythology in Spanish Historiography of the Middle Ages and the Renaissance', *Hispanic Review*, 22 (1954), 1–18.

THOMAS OF CELANO, 'Vita prima Santi Francisci', *Analecta Franciscana*, 10 (1926–41), 1–117.

TIERNEY, BRIAN, *Foundations of the Conciliar Theory: The Contribution of the Medieval Canonists from Gratian to the Great Schism* (Cambridge, 1955).

TISHBY, ISAIAH, *Wisdom of the Zohar* [Mishnat hazohar] (Jerusalem, 1982); Eng. trans.: 3 vols., trans. David Goldstein (Oxford: 1989).

TOLAN, JOHN VICTOR, *Petrus Alfonsi and His Medieval Readers* (Gainesville, Fla., 1993).

Toledot yeshu (*Das Leben Jesu nach jüdischen Quellen*, ed. Samuel Krauss (Berlin, 1902)).

'Travels in the Land of Israel by an Anonymous Sage' (Heb.), in Judah D. Eisenstein (ed.), *A Treasury of Journeys* [Otsar masaot] (Tel Aviv, 1969), 130–9.

TURNER, VICTOR, *Dramas, Fields and Metaphors* (Ithaca, NY, 1974).

URBACH, EPHRAIM E., 'Eastern Jewish Literature: An Introduction' (Heb.), *Pe'amim*, 26 (1986), 4–8.

VAJDA, GEORGES, 'Les Idées théologiques et philosophiques d'Abraham bar Hiyya', *Archives d'histoire doctrinale et littéraire du Moyen Âge*, 15 (1946), 191–223.

VALDEÓN BARUQUE, JULIO, *El chivo expiatorio: Judíos, revueltos y vida cotidiana en la Edad Media* (Valladolid, 2000).

VALLA, LORENZO, *De falso credita et ementita Constantini donatione*, Monumenta Germaniae historica: Quellen zur Geistesgeschichte des Mittelalters, 10, ed. Wolfram Setz (Weimar, 1976).

VAN ENGEN, JOHN, 'Dominic and the Brothers: *Vitae* as Life-Forming *Exempla* in the Order of Preachers', in Kent Emery and Joseph Wawrykow (eds.), *Christ among the Medieval Dominicans* (Notre Dame, Ind., 1998), 7–25.

VAN HERWAARDEN, JAN, 'The Origins of the Cult of St James of Compostela', *Journal of Medieval History*, 4 (1980), 1–35.

VANSINA, JAN, *Oral Tradition as History* (Madison, Wis., 1985).

VASARI, GIORGIO, *The Lives of the Painters, Sculptors and Architects*, 4 vols., trans. Allen B. Hinds (London, 1966).

VELTRI, GIUSEPPE, 'The Humanist Sense of History and the Jewish Idea of Tradition: Azaria de' Rossi's Critique of Philo Alexandrinus', *Jewish Studies Quarterly*, 2 (1995), 372–93.

VEYNE, PAUL, *Did the Greeks Believe in Their Myths? An Essay on the Constitutive Imagination* (Chicago, 1988).

VICENS VIVES, JAIME, *Historia crítica de Fernando II de Aragón* (Zaragoza, 1962).

VIDER, NAFTALI, 'The Burned Book of Judah ibn Shabbetai' (Heb.), *Metsudah*, 2 (1944), 122–31.

VIELLIARD, JEANNE, *Le Guide du pèlerin de Saint Jacques de Compostelle* (Mâcon, 1978).

Vikuaḥ haradak, in *Sefer haberit and David Kimhi's Disputations with Christianity* [Sefer haberit uvikuḥei radak im hanatsrut], ed. [Frank] Ephraim Talmage (Jerusalem, 1974), 83–96.

VINCENT DE BEAUVAIS, *The Mirror of History* (*Speculum historiale* (Douai, 1624)).

VIRGIL, *Aeneid*, trans. Allen Mandelbaum (Berkeley, Calif., 1982).

VON DOLLINGER, JOHANN JOSEPH IGNAZ, *Fables Respecting the Popes of the Middle Ages* (London, 1871).

VOSE, ROBIN, *Dominicans, Muslims and Jews in the Medieval Crown of Aragon* (Cambridge, 2009).

WEBER, NICHOLAS A., 'Nicholas III, Pope (Giovanni Gaetani Orsini)', in *Catholic Encyclopedia* (New York, 1907–12), xi. 56–7.

WEICH-SHAHAK, SUSANA, *Romancero sefardí de Marruecos: Antología de tradición oral* (Madrid, 1997).

WEINRYB, BERNARD D., 'The Beginnings of East-European Jewry in Legend and Historiography', in Meir Ben Horin, Bernard D. Weinryb, and Solomon Zeitlin (eds.), *Studies and Essays in Honor of Abraham A. Neuman* (Leiden, 1962), Eng. section, 445–502.

WEISKE, BRIGITTE, *Gesta Romanorum*, vol. i: *Untersuchungen zu Konzeption und Überlieferung* (Tübingen, 1992).

WEISS, ROBERTO, *The Renaissance Discovery of Classical Antiquity* (Oxford, 1969).

WELTER, JEAN-THIÉBAUT, *L'Exemplum dans la littérature religieuse et didactique du Moyen Âge* (Geneva, 1973).

WHITTICK, ARNOLD, *Symbols, Signs, and Their Meaning* (London, 1960).

WILKEN, ROBERT LOUIS, *John Chrysostom and the Jews: Rhetoric and Reality in the Late 4th Century* (Berkeley, Calif., 1983).

WINKELMANN, FRIEDHELM, 'Charakter und Bedeutung der Kirchengeschichte des Gelasios von Kaisareia', *Byzantinische Forschungen*, 1 (1966), 346–85.

XIMENA JURADO, MARTÍN (ed.), *Catálogo de los Obispos de las Iglesias Catedrales de Jaén y Anales eclesiásticos de este Obispado: Estudio preliminar e índices José Rodríguez Molina y María José Osorio Pérez* (Granada, 1991).

YASSIF, ELI, *The Hebrew Folktale: Its History, Genres and Significance* [Sipur ha'am ha'ivri: toledotav, sugav, umashma'uto] (Jerusalem, 1994).

—— '*Penai* and *ruaḥ reḥavah*: Theory and Practice in the Formation of the Hebrew Story in the Late Middle Ages' (Heb.), *Kiryat sefer*, 62 (1988–9), 887–905.

YEHIEL OF PARIS, *Vikuaḥ rabenu yeḥi'el mipariz miba'alei hatosafot im mumar eḥad lifnei ludvig hateshi'i melekh tsarfat vehahegmonim bepariz bashanah harishonah la'elef hashishi*, ed. Reuben Margaliot (Lwów, 1928).

Yemot hamashiaḥ, in Yehuda Even Shmuel (ed.), *Midrashim of Salvation: Jewish Apocalyptic from the End of the Babylonian Talmud to the Beginning of the Sixth Millennium* [Midreshei ge'ulah: pirkei ha'apokalipsah hayehudit meḥatimat hatalmud habavli ve'ad reshit ha'elef hashishi] (Tel Aviv, 1943), 90–8.

YERAHMIEL B. SOLOMON, *Sefer hazikhronot hu divrei hayamim liyeraḥmi'el*, ed. Eli Yassif (Tel Aviv, 2001).

YERUSHALMI, YOSEF HAYIM, 'Clio and the Jews: Reflections on Jewish Historiography in the Sixteenth Century', *Proceedings of the American Academy for Jewish Research*, 46–7 (jubilee issue) (1978–9), 607–38.

—— 'The Inquisition and the Jews of France in the Time of Bernard Gui', *Harvard Theological Review*, 63 (1970), 317–76.

—— *The Lisbon Massacre of 1506 and the Royal Image in the Shevet Yehudah* (Cincinnati, Ohio, 1976).

—— *Zakhor: Jewish History and Jewish Memory* (Seattle, 1982).

YUVAL, ISRAEL JACOB, 'History without Wrath and Bias' (Heb.), *Zion*, 59 (1994), 351–414.

—— 'Towards 1240: Jewish Hopes, Christian Fears' (Heb.), in *Proceedings of the Eleventh World Congress on Jewish Studies* [Divrei hakongres ha'olami ha'aḥad-asar lemada'ei hayahadut], vol. ii/1 (Jerusalem, 1994), 113–20.

—— *Two Nations in Your Womb: Perceptions of Jews and Christians in Late Antiquity and the Middle Ages*, trans. Barbara Harshav and Jonathan Chipman (Berkeley, Calif., 2006).

—— 'Vengeance and Damnation, Blood and Defamation: From Jewish Martyrdom to Blood Libels (Heb.)', *Zion*, 58 (1993), 33–90.

ZACUT, ABRAHAM B. SAMUEL, *Mishpat*, in Malachi Beit-Arié and Moshe Idel, 'An Article on the End of Days and Astrology by R. Abraham Zacut [National Library of Israel MS Heb. 8° 3935]' (Heb.), *Kiryat sefer*, 54 (1979), 174–94.

—— *Sefer yuḥasin*, ed. Tsevi [Herschell] Filipowski, introd. A. H. Freiman (Frankfurt am Main, 1905).

ZERAHIAH B. SHE'ALTIEL HEN, *Igeret*, in 'A Letter of Raphael Kirchheim' (Heb.), *Otsar neḥmad*, 2 (1857), 117–24.

ZFATMAN, SARAH, *Between Ashkenaz and Sefarad: On the History of the Jewish Story in the Middle Ages* [Bein ashkenaz lisefarad: letoledot hasipur hayehudi biyemei-habeinayim] (Jerusalem, 1993).

ZIER, MARK, 'Nicholas of Lyra on the Book of Daniel', in Philip Krey and Lesley Smith (eds.), *Nicholas of Lyra: The Senses of Scripture* (Leiden, 2000), 173–93.

ZINBERG, ISRAEL, *History of Jewish Literature* [Toledot sifrut yisra'el], 3 vols., trans. and ed. Solomon Z. Ariel, David Canani, and Baruch Karou (Tel Aviv, 1955–8).

ZOMEÑO RODRÍGUEZ, AMALIA, 'Abdallāh ibn Buluqqin: "Kitāb al-tibyān 'an al-ḥāditha al-kā'ina bi-dawlat Banī Zīrī fī Gharnāṭa"', in David Thomas (ed.), *Christian–Muslim Relations: A Bibliographical History* (2014), available at <http://referenceworks.brillonline.com/entries/christian-muslim-relations/kitab-al-tibyan-an-al-haditha-al-kaina-bi-dawlat-bani-ziri-fi-gharnata-COM_23328> (accessed 3 May 2014).

ZONTA, MAURO, 'Latin Scholastic Influences on Late Medieval Hebrew Physics: The State of the Art', in Gad Freudenthal (ed.), *Science in Medieval Cultures* (Cambridge, 2011), 207–16.

ZUNZ, YOM TOV LIPMANN (LEOPOLD), *Haderashot beyisra'el*, ed. Chanoch Albeck, trans. Moshe E. Jacques (Jerusalem, 1974).

Index